Business Communication

Business Communication

DEBORAH C. ANDREWS
University of Delaware

WILLIAM D. ANDREWS
Westbrook College

Macmillan Publishing Company
New York

Collier Macmillan Publishers
London

Copyright © 1988, Macmillan Publishing Company,
a division of Macmillan, Inc.

PRINTED IN THE UNITED STATES OF AMERICA

Macmillan Publishing Company
866 Third Avenue, New York, New York 10022

Collier Macmillan Canada, Inc.

Library of Congress Cataloging-in-Publication Data

Andrews, Deborah C.
  Business communication.

  Bibliography: p.
  Includes index.
    1. Communication in management.   2. Business writing.
I. Andrews, William D. (William David), 1945–
II. Title.
HF5718.A743   1987   808′.06665   87-5526
ISBN 0-02-303510-2

Printing: 5 6 7   Year: 0 1 2 3

ISBN 0-02-303510-2

Preface

This book provides the tools for succeeding in business through effective communication. By *succeed* we mean

- Meeting the goals of the organization.
- Meeting the goals of the people you work with.
- Meeting your personal goals.

By *effective communication* we simply mean writing and reading, talking and listening that work. Strategies for making communication work fill the text. We explain both the why and the how for writing and speaking within a framework of management theory, organizational behavior, ethics, and research on the writing process.

The scope of *Business Communication* is therefore broad. Throughout the text we weave several key themes:

- Business is *information*-oriented.
- Business is *people*-oriented.
- Business is an *international* enterprise.
- Business practices depend on *problem-solving*.

- Much problem-solving in business, and thus communicating, is carried out in *groups*.
- While business messages depend on words and numbers, readability also requires *visuals* and efficient *document design*.
- Many conventions of language and form shape business communication; particularly important forms are memos, letters, proposals, procedures, and reports.
- Some business communication is routine; some requires a specialized response to the reader or listener. Good communicators select the right form for routine matters and know when nonroutine approaches are necessary.

Each theme is highlighted in an individual chapter or chapters. But the text also underscores the synergy among these themes; discussion of each is woven through all the others. Each chapter is thus both a module of information complete in itself and an exemplification of themes and document forms discussed throughout the book.

We don't give easy answers. Business—and communicating in business—is complex. There are few easy answers. But we do provide a simple structure for explaining the strategies necessary to succeed within that complexity. And we present many models culled from field and classroom to make the discussion concrete. Corporate sources include Du Pont, McDonalds, Hershey Foods, Swissair, Ashton-Tate, Leading Edge, and the Travelers, as well as government agencies, both American and European. Student contributors represent a wide variety of majors, including accounting, finance, psychology, forestry, marketing, management, retailing, fashion merchandising, secretarial science, information systems, personnel, insurance, sports and recreation, and natural resources.

Advice and models are easy to find. Chapters 1, 2, 3, and 23 set the stage. Chapter 1 establishes the themes and discusses how business functions and how communication and management serve business goals. Chapter 2 provides seven short cases to illustrate the concepts. Chapter 3 discusses *writing* to meet communication goals; Chapter 23 discusses *talking and listening* to meet communication goals. Other chapters fill in the details.

Part I focuses on *writing as a decision-making process*. It provides the tools for finding and selecting the right information to write *about*, for assessing the audience and determining the right approach for that audience, for organizing material (we call this *macrocomposing*) and choosing the right words and sentences (we call this *microcomposing*) to make the writing work. (Elements of style are further developed in the Handbook.) We also discuss visual means of presentation—in an entire chapter. Too often, visuals are presented as visual *aids*. Yet in business communication, words are often the *verbal aids* to essentially visual texts. We stress visuals. We also stress the need to see the page itself as a kind of visual and to design documents effectively. Chapters 8 and 10 elaborate on these concerns, particularly the role of computers in developing visuals and whole documents. Chapter 11 discusses group writing, a common form of authorship in organizations. Each chapter isolates certain strategies necessary in *any* business document.

Part II looks at business communication *document by document*, addressing the most common forms: memos, letters, reports, and procedures. Chapter 22 reviews and augments these forms from the perspective of writing *in a corporation*.

Part III parallels Part 1; it traces *oral communication* as a decision-making process. Three chapters analyze the most common situations for talking and listening: phone calls, interviews, meetings (both in person and via teleconferencing), and business presentations. Part IV shows effective communication, oral and written, in the *job search*. Part V (Chapter 28) summarizes the concerns of communication in the *global economy*.

Throughout the text, models of good communication show what success means; integrated case studies and detailed discussions of communication situations show how to get there. We present the diversity of business communication. But our goal is to show the common core beneath that diversity: achieving goals through other people.

Our advice, our models, and our case studies derive from our years in both education and business, particularly as consultants to AT&T Technologies, Battelle-Columbus Laboratories, Hercules, Inc., and RCA. We've drawn on research—our own and others'—and many days in classrooms, conference rooms, and offices to make sure that the advice is sound and practical. We also relied on the experience of our colleagues in the Association for Business Communication. The international emphasis grew as we worked with both American and foreign professionals and executives at multinational corporations here and in England and Europe. We became increasingly aware that American business communication today must be seen in light of the global economy. The combined international and information emphasis is presented visually in the stylized letter "I" that serves as a motif for the text's design. Throughout Europe, the blue-and-white "I" sign alerts one to a source of information.

Several supplemental materials aid both teachers and students in using this text:

Instructor's Resource Manual. This comprehensive manual contains an overview of the business communication course and sample syllabi; an insert on computer-produced graphics and document design; a guide to resources for teachers; a bibliography of sources on international business communication; and a discussion of each chapter including an overview of key concepts, strategies for classroom presentation, commentary on end-of-chapter exercises, and individual discussion of cases in Chapter 2.

Study Guide. Written by Larry R. Andrews of Kent State University, this guide leads the student vigorously through the text. For each chapter of *Business Communication* it includes review points, self-quizzes, further examples and questions for applying the text's concepts, and style exercises. The exercises review spelling, grammar, mechanics, and usage.

Test Bank. Prepared by Edna Jellesed, Lane Community College, this offers 1400 items, both multiple choice and essay questions geared to each chapter in the text.

Acetate Transparencies. Fifty 2-color transparencies bring key items from the text to the screen. They are all referenced in the instructor's resource manual.

Microtest. A computerized test generator is available for both IBM PCs and Apple computers.

This book, like much of the writing the book discusses, was a collaborative effort. We'd like especially to thank the following: Joyce A. McKeller, the F. P. Corporation; James A. Edris, now Director of Investor Relations, Hershey Foods Corporation; Robert Kelton, Foundation Computer Systems, Inc.; Ortrun Pohler, Institut Straumann AG; Fred Orensky, CoreStates Financial Corporation; Jean-Pierre Sottas, Union de Banques Suisses; Larry Andrews, Kent State University; William R. Brown, Philadelphia College of Textiles and Science; Marie E. Flatley, San Diego State University; John J. Brugaletta, California State University, Fullerton; Jone Rymer, Wayne State University; Fay Beth Gray, Arkansas State University; Kevin J. Harty, La Salle University; Edna Jellesed, Lane Community College; Barbara Jewell, Pierce College; Alice J. MacDonald, University of Akron; Natalie R. Seigle, Providence College; Chris Shafer, West Virginia University; the Department of Linguistics at the University of Delaware; and at Macmillan—Eben Ludlow, Vicky Horbovetz, Pat Cabeza, and Alma Orenstein. D.C. Andrews owes a special thanks to Zack Bowen, former chair, Department of English, the University of Delaware, whose leadership made work not only possible but fun, and to the Unidel Foundation which supported her research in international business communication.

In the end, the major collaborators were our students. This book is theirs.

Deborah C. Andrews
William D. Andrews

Brief
Contents

ix

PART **II** ☐ The Forms of Written Communication

PART **III** □ The Process and Forms of Communicating Orally

PART **IV** □ The Job Search

PART **V** □ *The International Dimension*

Detailed Contents

PART **I** ☐ *The Process of Writing*

8   *Composing with Visuals*   117

14 *Letters That Inform*

15 *Letters That Persuade: Good News, Mixed News, Bad News*

19 Business Reports: Structure and Style   352

20 Business Reports: Ancillary Elements of the Formal Report   377

PART **III** □ *The Process and Forms of Communicating Orally*

Business Communication

Introduction

The Challenges of Business Communication

3

Successful communication is good for business and good for you.

That's a sweeping statement, easy to make but hard to prove. Before you read and use this textbook, however, we want to tell you why we think the statement is true and why understanding it will make you not only an effective user of this book but an effective business communicator.

We need two working definitions, one of *communication* and one of *business*:

- Communication is the transfer of information to achieve a goal.
- A business is an organization, that is, a collection of persons, structures, and processes bound together to achieve one or more goals.

We'll look at these terms and their implications for a student of business communication.

A Communication Model

Figure 1–1 is a highly simplified model of communication. In it, the sender (S), desiring an outcome, encodes a message in a medium and transfers it to a receiver (R) to induce action or understanding. The receiver returns a message (feedback) to the sender in some medium, and the sender checks this feedback against the intended outcome to see if the goal has been achieved. The medium may be oral or written, words or numbers, text or pictures: a telephone call, a memo, a table of numbers, a graph. This model illustrates a single communication act. But communication is not static. It is a dynamic activity, a set of interconnected loops with messages moving back and forth in various media between sender and receiver.

A simple situation can illustrate. Suppose you are sitting in a draft in your classroom because the professor opened the window. To induce action (to get the professor to close the window) you raise your hand and ask the professor to close the window. The medium of your message is oral. The professor receives the message and acts or doesn't act on it—that is, does or does not supply the outcome you aimed for. If the outcome is achieved, then the communication loop is closed: You got what you wanted.

It's possible to imagine other ways in which this communication might occur. You might pass a note to the professor (same message, different medium). You might write a complaint to the dean of students (same message, different medium, different receiver). You might squirm, glance angrily at the open window, pull your coat over your

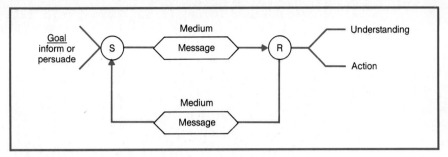

FIGURE 1–1. A simplified model of communication.

ears, don gloves, stamp your feet—that is, use body language to convey your point (same message, nonverbal medium).

It is also possible, of course, for you to decide not to communicate at all but to get up and close the window yourself. You take action directly rather than attempting to transfer information to another to cause him or her to take the action. If, however, you elect communication over direct action, you can select from many options in messages and media. Each varies with and depends on your desired goal. The *receiver* also has many options in action or understanding and in feedback. Thus a seemingly simple, commonplace situation is really quite complex. Presenting it in a visual model is somewhat deceptive, but it is useful as long as you remember the range of possibilities available in messages, media, receivers, and feedback.

The key point underlying this example is that communication is *goal-oriented*. It is an act meant to elicit a response in another—either direct action by the receiver or the acquisition of understanding. Communication is not just the transfer of information, but *purposeful* transfer.

Purposefulness, or goal orientation, is also the key characteristic of the organization, the business in which communication occurs. We'll repeat the definition of an organization given before: a collection of persons, structures, and processes bound together to achieve one or more goals. It isn't necessary here to elaborate on this definition or to discuss organizational theory. It is important, though, to recognize the wide range of organizations in modern society and to understand that in this book, our discussion of "business communication" is applicable to all organizations. We use the terms *business* and *organization* interchangeably, for convenience. "Business communication" goes on in Fortune 500 companies, small software firms, churches, colleges, government agencies, sports teams, fraternities, and so on.

The distinguishing feature of these organizations is that they are goal-oriented. The goals obviously vary, from saving souls in the case of a church to increasing return to investors in the case of a business enterprise. But having a goal is the common thread. Because communication is goal-oriented, it should be obvious that in business communication, goals are of the utmost importance. Let's now explore this view by looking at the functions that communication plays in organizations.

Successful Communication Is Good for Business

We said at the beginning of this chapter that successful communication is good for business and good for you. Having defined the two key terms in that statement, we can now answer the question of why successful communication is good for business. In the next section, we answer why it is good for you.

Communication serves three broad purposes in organizations: definition, control, and maintenance. At the highest level of importance, an organization has to define itself and articulate its goals. It has to say what it's all about and what it tries to do. This is definition. The organization then has to *do* what it defines as its goal or mission. The activities aimed at achieving goals have to be planned and monitored. This is control. While goal-oriented activities occur, the organization has to maintain itself, has to keep going as an organization. This is maintenance. Let's now look at each of these functions to see how communication serves them.

Definition

It's standard advice in management education that a company has to know its business. It has to say in a clear and precise way what it does.

A company that prospered by selling metal safes to banks found that when the explosive growth in branch banking ended, the firm's sales began to fall rapidly, and this threatened its very existence as an organization. Recognizing that they were not in the "safe business" but in the "bank support business," the company shifted to the production of electronic teller machines, a growing market. The company's survival depended on a sharp definition of its business, and this definition, of course, required communication at the very highest level.

The process of definition in this case began on an informal level, with officers of the firm talking among themselves about markets, products, and opportunities for growth in a new banking environment. The discussion spread out to the sales force, whose members were asked to survey their customers about what products banks would need in the future. Such discussions eventually led to memos and proposals, formal written documents that officers and the board of directors debated and finally approved. Then the newly sharpened definition of the company had to be communicated widely, first throughout the organization itself, to all employees on whom success depended, and then to the customers, the financial institutions, the news media, and the various publics with which the firm dealt. Throughout this process, words and pictures and numbers had to be put together to create the right definition of what the company was and what business it was in.

In this case, definition saved the company. And communication—at first, oral and informal, later written and formal, internal and external—supported the critical definition function.

Control

Once an organization has defined itself and has communicated that definition both inside and outside, the work of meeting the goal begins. For the former safe manufacturer, new business operations began. Electronic teller machines had to be designed, built, sold, distributed, and maintained. Communication again played a key role. Designs were proposed. Manufacturing processes were developed to build the machines. Advertising literature was developed showing specifications and prices. Orders were booked and processed so the machines could be shipped and installed. Invoices were sent, payments recorded, bills and wages paid. At each point in these activities, people communicated, orally and in writing, with other people inside and outside the organization to produce results.

Communication provides the means of keeping track of all this purposeful activity so the right work is done by the right people at the right time. This management function is called *control*, and successful communication is central to control. Facilitating the ongoing activities of the firm to help it achieve its goal is thus the second key purpose of communication in organizations.

As a college student, you encounter this aspect of organizational communication frequently. When you register for a course, you write a number on a form that is eventually processed by the registrar to produce a bill, to put your name on a class roster, and to generate a grade card that your instructor completes at the end of the term. That card, in turn, leads to an entry on your transcript, and when all the right entries have been made (and the bills paid, of course), the college tells you and your employer that you have graduated. Thus, at a very simple level, the college's business—graduating educated persons—is accomplished through this communication flow supporting the control function.

Maintenance

In addition to defining its business and carrying out that business, all organizations also have to maintain themselves. They hire people and pay them a salary; they open the doors in the morning and close them at night; they buy typewriters and microcomputers and paper; they clean the washrooms and polish the floors. Some of these activities are routine and unexciting, and they often seem distant from the activities, like manufacturing and selling, that are obviously at the heart of the firm's goal-oriented functions. But these maintenance functions are crucial to helping the organization achieve its goals.

Communication supports the maintenance function. To hire a new person, you have to write a job description, place an ad, review applications, interview prospective employees, start a personnel file, and make sure that the new employee has a desk if needed, and that a check will be produced for her or him at the end of the week. These activities require communication, oral and written, formal and informal, internal and external. The purpose of such communication is to maintain the organization so it can do its work and meet its goals.

Communication promotes success in every area of an organization's life, from defining goals through the purchase of supplies to keep the organization going. Organizations can't exist without a purposeful flow of information. And it's important to understand that the need for good communication skills pervades organizations. All employees must be good communicators. Obviously, some will always be better than others, and some will have specialized needs and skills that make them better than others at certain forms of communications. Advertising specialists, for example, have more highly honed skills in using various media to develop and promote an image of a company's product than does a financial analyst, whose skills are in distilling from a vast body of numbers a clear picture of the firm's financial position. But regardless of the organizational slot one occupies, good communication skills are crucial for the long-term health as well as the daily functioning of business organizations. That's why we said at the beginning of this chapter that successful communication is good for business.

Successful Communication Is Good for You

We also said that successful communication is good for you, the employee or future employee of a business. Why? Successful communication helps you

- Promote job success.
- Achieve personal satisfaction.
- Meet ethical and social obligations.

Job Success

Job success depends on many factors, from your specialized skills and knowledge to simple luck. Over and over in surveys and personal statements, however, business leaders point to good communication skills as being among the two or three most important characteristics needed for success. Being able to write and speak clearly and effectively complements one's technical abilities and reflects understanding of people, the two dimensions of management most often cited as keys to organizational and individual success. The evidence is overwhelming that good communicators do succeed in business.

Personal Satisfaction

Personal satisfaction derives in part from vocational success but extends beyond promotions, raises, and pats on the back for a job well done. Growth and mastery are required, and these are measured against one's individual standards as much as those of the company. Being able to summarize a complex legal situation in a single-page memo or to produce an imaginative visual that captures the interconnection between market share and volume growth provides immediate pleasure and reward that extend beyond job success. It just feels good to do well. Writing a clear report or delivering a powerful speech gives you a feeling of mastery that reinforces your sense of achievement and promotes personal satisfaction.

Ethical and Social Obligations

Ethical and social obligations are clearly not easy to define. What *I* may regard as such an obligation may be to *you* only an irrelevance. But to different degrees, most of us feel such obligations, and good communication provides a way of satisfying them. Communication depends on trust, on the assumption of the honesty, integrity, and fair dealing that must accompany relations with other people. Displaying those traits—and thus exhibiting trust—in communication fulfills, in part, the obligation one has to others. In a sense, honest communication affirms membership in the human race. It says that you respect others and want them to respect you. The Quakers have a saying with broad nonsectarian applications, especially in communication: In all your dealings, leave the other people at least as well off as you found them. If in everyday speech, office memos, corporate advertising campaigns, and the preparation of annual reports, to name just a few instances of business communication, you behave in a manner that conforms with this statement, then you have communicated well.

The Challenges of Business Communication

For the reasons we have discussed, successful communication has historically been good for business and good for employees. But what of tomorrow? What role will communication play in the organizations of tomorrow and in the careers of their employees—college students like you who will shortly bring your skills to these organizations? Everything we can see on the horizon suggests that communication will play an even more critical role in business in the future than it has in the past or does today. This is true because of the ways in which business is changing. To understand the challenges of business communication, we must understand the changes business is experiencing. Three broad changes are leading to direct and indirect consequences for the future role of communication:

- Business is increasingly *information*-oriented, and information is, in turn, increasingly affected by *technology* in storage, retrieval, transmission, and manipulation.
- Business is increasingly *people*-oriented.
- Business is increasingly *international*.

Information and Technology

It's hard to read a newspaper or magazine without seeing a headline or story on the "information age" in which we live. Social scientists say that the Industrial Revolution that changed economic life in the nineteenth century has its modern counterpart in the Information Age. Whereas the Industrial Revolution introduced technology to manufacturing and created new forms of economic organization and consequent adjustments in social and political life, in the Information Age the information itself and the ways in which it is created, stored, transmitted, and interpreted are producing fundamental shifts in the economy and throughout society.

Information is exploding. There is simply more of it. One indicator of this growth is that the number of books published yearly in the

United States *tripled* in just twenty years, from fifteen million in 1960 to forty-five million in 1980. The growth in periodicals and separately published documents has been similarly dramatic. In addition, technological innovations—telecommunications and computerization, especially—are creating new ways to store and move the information around to users. Because there is more of it and because it can be handled in new ways, information assumes a greater and more critical role in the way people live and work.

Although all of business and industry is affected by the information explosion, the service sector is especially information-oriented. And it's significant that in the United States and most of the Western world, the service sector, compared to the manufacturing, is the largest, fastest growing, most dynamic, and most influential. (A simple distinction: In manufacturing, some*thing* is produced, whereas the "product" of the service sector is intangible.) In 1985, about three fourths of the U.S. gross national product was produced *outside* the "industrial" sector. Some typical service industries are government agencies, education, banking, finance, insurance, marriage counseling, and public relations. Just think of how important information is to each of these. In the absence of a concrete product, service companies are really information brokers, creating and transmitting information for the benefit of their customers. Indeed, in many cases, the "product" of a service firm is simply information itself.

The growth in information and its increasing business importance are directly related to *technological change* in how the information is handled. Computers, especially, have revolutionized information storage and transmission, and the process has been intensified by related developments in telecommunications, which make possible the linking of computers with each other and with other forms of electronic communication.

At a simple level, information technology is changing the nature of business communication by making possible the immediate transfer of information on-line as a substitute for written forms. Instead of drafting a memo in longhand, passing it to a typist for production, proofing the copy, making duplicates for the files, and sending along the final version to the audience, you can now enter your memo directly into a computer network, push a button, and have the information awaiting the audience's use instantly, across the hall or at a remote site in another country. This method of transferring business information differs markedly from the paper memo method. It is obviously faster and cheaper, two characteristics that make it quite appealing to business organizations. It is also more immediate, creating a relationship between sender and receiver that is closer to the one that prevails in oral than in written communication. Consider, for example, the opportunity for feedback—that is, for the receiver to respond to the sender with nearly immediate questions and comments that, in turn, elicit additional communication from the original sender.

The use of computers in writing is discussed in detail in Chapter 10. But word processing is only one illustration of the impact of information technology on business communication. The use of new technologies in the storage and retrieval of information is changing the nature of libraries and is making the job of finding and using information both faster and more complex. Chapter 5 discusses information use in this context.

Without question, the continuation of the information age will change how organizations collect, maintain, and use information—and how they communicate.

People in Communication

Despite the impact of technology, it goes without saying that business communication is a people-related function. There is every evidence that greater attention will be paid to people within organizations in the future; and as a consequence, the "people" part of management, and hence of communication, will increase.

Part of the reason lies in the shift toward the service sector of the economy that we briefly discussed earlier. In services, people play a much greater role than they do in manufacturing. But even in production-oriented businesses, the last decade has seen a greater emphasis on people. The popularity of books and articles on Japanese management, or "Theory Z" management, reflects the growing awareness that in the United States, at least, insufficient attention has been paid to people in business enterprises. This sharpened awareness has led to the creation of "human resource management" functions and positions within most companies and many nonprofit institutions. Making people a vital part of the management process, soliciting and following workers' suggestions, forming "quality circles" to involve workers in decisions, and adopting flextime working schedules to accommodate off-the-job commitments—all reflect this concern for people.

All the signs suggest that management education and theory will stress even further the need to put people skills high on the list of criteria used for the selection and promotion of employees. Because communication is perhaps the highest people skill, it's clear that the emphasis on good oral and written communication abilities will grow in American corporations.

Closely related to the *skills* of dealing with people are *ethical questions* about dealing with employees and with the public. Skills alone are inadequate. One must also have a keen sense of the moral dimension of the actions and decisions that emerge in communication situations. Some of these are dealt with in Chapter 11, where we discuss group writing projects, and in Chapters 23 and 24, which discuss oral communication. Underlying those discussions is the belief that honesty in communication is not simply the best but the only acceptable practice. Words can be manipulated to manipulate people. Persuasion, after all, is aimed at, in a nonpejorative sense, manipulation, the effort to convince someone of the rightness of what you say or write. The words you use and the information you transmit must be true.

Although truth may be a relative concept, and one person's truth may be another's lie, the honest effort to base communication on accurate information and to use clear and direct language is a prerequisite to credibility. Lies are eventually discovered, and liars are seldom believed. Sometimes, of course, the desire to avoid hurting a person leads to the use of half truths and of obscuring rather than illuminating language. Fired CEOs are said to leave their posts "to pursue personal business interests." Totally incompetent employees are told that they should seek employment elsewhere that better suits their interests and skills. Unqualified applicants for jobs receive letters that say that the choice was made difficult by the splendid credentials they possess and that their applications will be kept in the active file in case a suitable opening occurs in the future. Are these lies? Selective truths? However one labels them, they are obviously used not to hurt but to avoid hurt, to soak out some of the pain that often accompanies personnel decisions. Good intentions, of course, do not excuse the deliberate resort to falsehood, but the moral imperative to treat others as you yourself would want to be treated governs one's careful use of language and information that may not pass the test of pure truth. Obviously these are knotty ethical issues, and the effective communicator must weigh them and be persuaded that the information and words he or she uses are honest and accomplish the aim of treating people fairly, decently, and humanely—as we all wish to be treated.

International Dimensions

No one who shops for a car, a camera, or a calculator can miss the fact that business is an international enterprise. Imports pose severe problems for business in the United States, and the trade deficit is a subject of continuing political and economic concern. "Buy America" bumper stickers are common, and it's not unusual to find labels that proclaim the native origin of everything from sweaters to apples.

Americans traveling to Europe for the first time are often surprised to find that they can buy their favorite soft drinks, snack foods, and running shoes in Munich as easily as in Omaha. International trade is simply that: Goods move with great freedom across national borders, and it's highly unlikely that protectionist campaigns will stop the trend. Observers of business contend that we are in the middle of a major shift in trade practices that promises cultural readjustments parallel to those required by developments of the Information Age. The United States, for example, is seen as moving toward being a "service" nation that provides research and development, marketing, distribution, and financial services and leaves production to developing countries. The textile manufacturer of the future, it is said, for example, will be a broker who, instead of knitting sweaters in South Carolina, will sit at a computer terminal and direct the distribution of yarns and finished goods to and from producing nations in the Far East.

Obviously the continuation of such shifts in the world economy will produce further dislocations in American society, but the trend seems clear. And it has major implications for business communication. Chapter 28 discusses these at length. Worldwide linkups through satellites provide computers with the ability to transfer information instantly across the globe. Buyers and salespersons take long trips to distant cities. Computer engineers in Japan speak—and program in—English. Deals are made in the Middle East during ceremonial meals that leave Westerners frustrated and occasionally dyspeptic. These are all aspects of communication in the global economy.

At the most basic level, business communicators accommodate to such new challenges through the acquisition of languages other than their own. Ads for jobs frequently specify fluency in another language, and management training for promising young executives often involves language study. Familiarity with other cultures as well as languages is also an increasingly common requirement for employment and promotion in the global economy. Knowing that waiters in Vienna always allow twenty minutes after being asked for the bill before presenting it helps one to avoid unpleasantness. Sitting erect in a meeting with Japanese buyers rather than slumping and crossing the legs may help clinch the sale. The complex history of tribal integration in Nigeria is useful background for the marketing manager contemplating an advertising campaign for a new Western product. Sensitivity to the culture as well as knowledge of the language makes one a better communicator and hence a better businessperson in the global economy.

Your Future in Business Communication

The Information Age, the growing awareness of people in management, and the increasingly international dimension of business all interconnect to make the challenges of business, and thus of business communication, sometimes frustrating but always exciting. The business communicator of tomorrow will certainly have to meet these three challenges:

• Appreciating the information explosion and mastering the technology of information use to maximize the value of information in managing organizations effectively and efficiently.

• Understanding the human element in business communication and behaving ethically toward people in all communication activities inside and outside the organization.

• Perceiving the global scope of business enterprise and dealing effectively with multinational issues in business communication.

If you approached this textbook thinking that good business communication meant just proper spelling and solid paragraph development, we think you will be pleasantly surprised to discover these challenges. We also think you can meet them.

Cases for Business Communicators

At work in any organization, people experience communication "problems" every day. Some are vast: how to communicate to the world what happened when a nuclear reactor came close to meltdown. Some are tiny: how to communicate to your boss that you would like to leave the office early on Friday.

This chapter presents seven cases concerning communication "problems." They capture situations that arise in work settings and that require solutions. The cases illustrate concretely the large issues and themes previewed in Chapter 1 and provide you an opportunity to experience some "real-life" problems.

As you work through these cases, remember that few problems are simple: While one issue may dominate, almost every case illustrates the interconnection of issues in business communication. At the end of each case, we raise specific questions, but these are intended only to get you started in analyzing the issues and identifying the solutions. As you discuss the cases in class, you'll see that many viewpoints emerge and that apparently simple situations can be quite complex. (For more advice on handling cases, see Chapter 18.)

 ## Case 1. *Bill Golden Meets the Surly Guard*

On his first day at work as a manager, Bill Golden was stopped by the guard at the company parking lot and asked to show his identification card and parking pass. Then he was directed to a space at the back of the lot, even though there were numerous empty spaces nearer the entrance to the office. The same thing happened the next day, and Bill became angry when he saw two secretaries from his division being directed to spots closer to the front. When he was again sent to the back spot on the third day, Bill became furious and wrote a memo to the director of administration, whose responsibilities included parking and security. Bill complained about the guard's "surly" treatment and asked that the guard be ordered to assign him a space at least as good as those given to the secretaries.

The director of administration brought Bill's memo back to him and kindly explained that the guard in question had been with the company for years, knew the secretaries well because they were also longtime employees,

and was really a good guy once you got to know him. The director suggested that Bill spend a few minutes each morning chatting with the guard and asking about his family, of whom he was especially proud. In the meantime, the director said, he wanted Bill to hang onto the memo and consider whether he wanted to resend it later.

After a few weeks, Bill developed a friendly relationship with the guard and began to get better parking assignments. One foggy morning, he left his headlights on, and the guard phoned Bill at his desk to tell him. That day Bill tore up his original memo and delivered the scraps to the director of administration.

Questions for Discussion

1. Should Bill Golden have written the memo? Why or why not?
2. What were the long-term advantages of the "personal approach" to solving the problem? How do they compare to the short-term ad-

vantages of writing the memo to try to get a quicker response? Is there a middle ground between the two approaches?

3. What were the ethical and managerial responsibilities of the director of administration in helping Bill Golden understand this situation?

Case 2. Sharon Hines Prepares a Report

Sharon Hines was told by her supervisor in the marketing department to prepare a report on the sales of ArtSweet, a new artificial sweetener developed by the company and test-marketed in five midwestern cities. She spent a week gathering data from sales reports and ended up with a computer printout showing sales by the week over a three-month period for fifty-seven stores in the five cities. For each of these, she calculated the rates of increase week-to-week and then prepared a large table comparing increases, in raw numbers and percentages, for each store. She prepared another table comparing sales by type of store in each city, and another aggregating sales figures by city.

When she finished, Hines had five two-page tables, five charts, and a thirty-six page printout. Pleased with her work, she handed the report to her supervisor. It took him two days to go through the data and pick out the three details he wanted for the report he had to make to his vice-president.

Questions for Discussion

1. Did Sharon Hines misunderstand her assignment? Did her supervisor misassign it?

2. If you were the supervisor, would you return the report to Hines? If so, what would you tell her?

3. Could Hines have done anything at the outset to get a better sense of her assignment? What?

Case 3. Sloan College Looks for a Woman

Everett Lamar, Dean of Sloan College, had to fill the position of director of the academic computer center when the current director resigned. Although it is a coeducational college, Sloan had few women in administrative positions, a situation Lamar wanted to correct. The minimum requirements for the job were set as five years of experience in college computing and a master's degree in a computer-related area. In the position notice, Lamar tried to signal his desire to hire a woman by using "she or he" in references to the director and by including this statement: "Applications from women and minorities are especially invited."

From the applications he received, Lamar selected three finalists, two men and a woman. Each met the minimum standards, but one of the men, Robert Antonucci, also had a Ph.D. in information science. Lamar knew that the faculty members on the search committee would favor the person with the doctorate, but he wanted to hire the woman, Janet Brock. The search committee evaluated Brock and Antonucci as both acceptable but ranked Brock second based on credentials.

Lamar was unsure what to tell the search committee after he decided to offer the position to Brock. He also wondered if he should explain the reason for the decision to

Antonucci, as he was afraid that a simple rejection might alienate a person who could be a candidate for a future faculty position in computer science that the college anticipated.

Questions for Discussion

1. What should Lamar tell Antonucci? If he decides to explain, should he write a letter or call?

2. What are Lamar's ethical obligations in communicating his reasons to the search committee?

3. Did Lamar meet his ethical obligations to potential candidates in the phrasing of welcome to women and minorities in the position notice? Should he have written something different?

 ## Case 4.   *Lisa Dobbins Anticipates a Change*

Lisa Dobbins prided herself on being well organized and efficient. She hated to get behind in her work. When her company decided to implement a new flextime plan that would allow the word-processing operators in her department to schedule their hours to fit personal needs, she immediately called a staff meeting to describe the plan, even though it was not scheduled to take effect for four months. She wanted all her employees to understand the new system and to prepare for it.

During the week after her staff meeting, eight persons in her group started coming in earlier and leaving earlier, and three stopped taking lunch hours so they could go home earlier. She had to remind them that the flextime schedule was not yet officially in place. The week before the schedule was to start, she made some remarks to some workers about getting their schedules to her in writing. They said they hadn't realized the new schedules had to be submitted to Dobbins for approval. She curtly reminded them that she had discussed this requirement at the staff meeting nearly four months before. When individuals came to her to ask for more information, she realized that she would have to set up another meeting. She was annoyed because, as she said, she would "have to go over it all again."

Questions for Discussion

1. Did Lisa Dobbins jump the gun in announcing the flextime plan so far in advance? Why or why not?

2. Should she have issued a written statement at the beginning? If so, what information should she have included in it?

3. If she schedules another meeting, how should she begin it? Should she try to explain why she has called another meeting on the same topic?

 ## Case 5.   *John Riley Writes a Memo*

John Riley supervised the assembly room of a television-manufacturing plant. He oversaw the mounting of the sets in cabinets and the installation of the fittings—knobs, handles, and labels. He noticed that out of every dozen or so sets that came into his facility, one had screw holes on the bottom that were slightly misaligned enough so that someone had to jiggle the set to match up with the cabinet holes for final mounting. This process took extra time and thus reduced the productivity of his group. He also feared that the rough handling of the sets required for the alignment would cause damage and result in rejection by the quality control department, to which the sets were shipped when they left his assembly room.

Riley decided to call the engineering design department, which he knew had final authority over the design of the sets. A junior engineer to whom he spoke there told him to write a memo about the problem to the senior design engineer. He did so, but two months later he still had no response. Riley discussed the problem at lunch with a fellow supervisor in the chassis room, from which the sets came directly to the assembly room. This person was surprised that Riley had even bothered to contact engineering design at all. He said that Riley should just have mentioned the problem to him directly, and he would have followed up on it right in the chassis room. Engineering design, he said, never liked to deal with production people. Even if they got involved it would take months of study before they would agree to a design change, whereas he, as supervisor of the chassis room, could modify procedures on his own to correct the problem.

Questions for Discussion

1. Whom should Riley have contacted when he first spotted the problem? Should he have communicated orally or in writing?
2. Should the junior engineer in engineering design have told Riley to write the memo? Why or why not?
3. Should Riley have waited two months for a response to his memo? What alternatives did he have?

Case 6. Dan Lanier Works in Another Culture

Dan Lanier was assigned as a sales manager to the Mexico City office of Advanced Data Products (ADP), a distributor of word-processing and electronic-mail systems headquartered in Tulsa, Oklahoma. Before his new assignment, Lanier had worked for ADP for four years as a sales rep in Massachusetts and Saint Louis. He had joined the company immediately after graduation from the University of Utah, where he was a marketing major. Growing up in the West, he had learned a bit of Spanish informally and had taken conversational Spanish in high school.

In Mexico City, Lanier supervised four sales reps, all Mexican nationals. One, Jose Ortega, had been with ADP for five years and had asked to be considered for the sales manager's position that went to Lanier. Maria Villas, office manager and supervisor of three clerical workers at the Mexico City office, had been with ADP for three years.

Lanier's first act when he arrived was to change office procedures. To promote career growth and to meet ADP's affirmative action goals, he put Villas in charge of coordinating all sales reps' schedules and maintaining centralized records on sales calls, inquiries, and sales. He also asked her to serve as his informal tutor in Spanish, to help him reacquaint himself with the language and learn specialized Spanish business terms.

Ortega was outraged when he was told of the new procedures for scheduling and coordinating the sales reps. He told the other three that he would "never work for a woman." He also made a point of belittling Lanier's use of Spanish, saying that if Lanier wanted to run the Mexico City office, he ought to have mastered the language first.

The situation came to a head when Lanier issued his first memo in Spanish to the staff. It was grammatically correct but stiff and unnatural. Ortega posted a copy by the water cooler and added this comment at the bottom: "For Spanish lessons, see Ms. Villas."

Questions for Discussion

1. Should Lanier respond to Ortega's action? If so, how?

2. Is Ortega right that Lanier should have come to his job with a better understanding of Spanish? Was it ADP's or his responsibility to see that he could use the native language of the country in which the office was located?

3. Is Ortega's feeling about "working for a woman" a result of cultural conditioning? Or sexism? Or anger about not getting the manager's job? Should Lanier have taken any of these possible views into account before changing procedures in the office?

4. Should Lanier have written a memo in Spanish, or should he have assumed that the staff could read English? Should multinational companies like ADP establish one language (English, for example) to be used for all corporate documents in its offices worldwide? Or should documents be written in the dominant language of the office's location?

Case 7.   *Peggy Lane Rounds Up the Facts*

Peggy Lane was the supervisor of nursing at a large university hospital. She reported to the director of patient care, Linda Garvey. Following a series of complaints from patients about the inattentiveness of the night-duty nursing staff, Garvey asked Lane to check into the situation and specifically to find out if night-duty nurses were different from day-duty nurses in any measurable way (age, education, experience, performance ratings, and so on) that might account for the higher number of patient complaints against the night staff.

Lane did a quick but thorough study of personnel records and discovered no real differences between the two groups. When she phoned Garvey to report this, Garvey said she wanted the information in writing. Lane wrote a one-page memo summarizing the results of her investigation. She included a simple table that listed four characteristics for each of the two groups. A quick glance at the table, Lane thought, would convince anyone that there was no real difference between the day and evening nursing staffs and that therefore the number of patient complaints had to be explained by other factors.

After Garvey received the memo, she wrote back to Lane to request that a "full-scale report, with substantiating data," be submitted as quickly as possible.

Questions for Discussion

1. Why might Linda Garvey prefer a large report to the one-page memo? What purposes might it serve?

2. Who is responsible for Peggy Lane's having to do the job again in a different way? How might the assignment have been otherwise given and received?

3. How could Lane have avoided the problem of a report that didn't work?

PART 1

The Process
of Writing

Writing to Meet Communication Goals

It's 8 A.M. By noon, you need to finish a memo summarizing a recent visit to the company installation in Moab, Utah, where you reviewed security procedures and found some problems. Your supervisor requested the memo. He'll send it on to Moab, so you need to think about how the security chief there will respond. This was your first on-site inspection, and you want to sound confident, trustworthy, and in control. Moreover, you like to travel and hope to be sent to other plants, particularly one in Austria. You know your supervisor will read this memo for its information, of course, but also to get a fix on how good *you* are.

This chapter begins a series of chapters that survey the process for writing such a memo—and *any* document you compose on the job. The chapter is divided into two parts. First, it elaborates on the elements of the communication model (Figure 1–1) implicit in the memo on Moab: your goals, you as the writer, the readers, the message, and the medium. Second, it provides advice on managing the *process* of writing to put the model into action.

Subsequent chapters detail essential strategies in the process:

- Understanding, finding, and documenting business information (Chapters 4 and 5).
- Macrocomposing: organizing and paragraphing (Chapter 6).
- Microcomposing: creating an effective and efficient style (Chapter 7).
- Composing with visuals (Chapter 8).
- Revising (Chapter 9).
- Writing with a computer (Chapter 10).
- Managing group projects (Chapter 11).

Goals

Writing on the job differs from writing for a class. In college, you write to produce the paper, which is an end in itself. On the job, the document is a *means* to some goal for you and for the organization. In analyzing the goal or goals, think of four levels:

1. The organizational goal.
2. The operational goal.
3. The information goal.
4. The communication goal.

First, assess the organizational need that your writing must meet. Chapter 1 discussed three broad needs: to define, to control, and to maintain. (Chapter 22 surveys documents that meet each of these corporate needs.)

Second, within that broad need, narrow your goal. State it in terms of actions and quantities. That is, make the goal *operational*. Translate an organizational goal of "improving productivity" into measurable units:

• Produce twenty-five more widgets a week with 20 percent less scrap and no additional hiring.

Here's how Pierre Jules Boulanger, then chief executive officer of Citroen, made operational his company's goal to design a "people's car," the 2CV, introduced in 1948:

> design a car that can carry two farmers in wooden shoes and 50 kilos of potatoes at a top speed of 60 kph, and travel 100 kilometers on three liters of gas.[1]

Third, define the goal in terms of *information:* What facts, observations, interpretations, and opinions are needed? Chapters 4 and 5 detail this goal.

Fourth, determine the project's *communication* goal. Throughout this book we'll emphasize three options:

1. To record.
2. To inform.
3. To persuade.

Sometimes your writing aims to *record*. During a project you record observations to preserve them, perhaps mainly for yourself. Sometimes you share this record with others who can advise on its accuracy and validity. Don't trust your memory to hold all that you see and think. Here's the goal statement from such a *documentary* report:

> This field report records my observations of security procedures and equipment and summarizes my conversations with personnel in security at Moab during my visits on March 12, March 16, and March 18.

Second, you can write to *inform* a reader about your work and to aid the reader in his or her work. Often you take documentary writing and shape it to a need that you share with the reader. In the terms of

[1] As quoted by Thomas K. Smith, "Why a Little Car Won a Big Place in Europe's Heart," *The Wall Street Journal*, 11 July 1984, 1.

the communication model, you aim at *understanding*. Here's a goal statement for an *informative* memo:

> In response to your request, here is an overview of current security procedures at Moab, including an assessment of some problems in equipment and in the deployment of personnel.

Third, you can write to *persuade*. You write to change the reader's mind (and maybe heart) about something, to shift the reader's perspective. To be effective, such a document evidences the writer's careful understanding of both the intellectual and the emotional status of the reader. The document aims at *action*. Here's a *persuasive* goal statement from the visitor to Moab:

> Although some problems in security procedures are evident at the Moab plant, they are not serious and can be easily corrected with the installation of a video camera and a change in the circulation routine of the present guards.

You as the Writer

One side of the communication model is highly personal: You write to get your own thoughts and information together and to enhance your own standing in the organization. You write to meet social and ethical needs. You write to build confidence and trust.

The voice that comes off the page, of course, reflects your writing skills. Moreover, it reflects your attitudes toward the subject of the document and toward the reader. In some ground-breaking work, Douglas McGregor defined two management styles deriving from different assumptions about the motivation of subordinates.[2] A *Theory X* manager assumes that subordinates need discipline, and that they are not self-motivated but depend on the hard-line supervisor to get them going. A *Theory Y* manager, on the other hand, sees management's tasks as creating the conditions that allow workers to serve their own goals best by serving the goals of the organization. Workers, it is assumed in Theory Y, do not inherently dislike work; indeed, they will seek responsibilities and exercise imagination if the conditions are right. The Theory X manager motivates with a stick; the Theory Y manager uses the carrot. (In Chapter 1, we mentioned an extension of these theories to *Theory Z*, collaborative management as practiced principally by the Japanese.) As a way of highlighting the differences between Theory X and Theory Y, here are two memos responding to the same situation: Donna Spellman is continually late for work. The first author leans toward Theory X:

[2]*The Human Side of Enterprise* (New York: McGraw-Hill, 1960), Chapters 3 and 4.

Date: June 12, 19XX
To: Donna Spellman
From: Brian Brown
Subject: Continual Tardiness

You have been late in arriving at the office on each of the following dates during the last month: May 1, 3, 4, 5, 10, 11, 15, 16, 18, 22, 24, 28, and 29. Such behavior cannot be condoned at this company. A duty of every employee is to be prompt. The neglect of this responsibility will ultimately affect your performance evaluation and thus jeopardize your stay here at our Company.

Brown sees the primary goal of his memo as *recording,* for Spellman's personnel record, the details of her lateness. In addition, he *informs* Spellman, more formally than in an oral reprimand, about the ultimate sanction: being fired. She's been given fair warning. Brown's memo is tough. He calls on company policy with images of the "performance evaluation" and "jeopardizing" her stay.

Here's a memo with more Theory Y leanings:

Date: June 12, 19XX
To: Donna
From: Gale Hoverson
Subject: Excessive Tardiness

I'm writing to reiterate the problems caused by your lateness. We have discussed this, but you still seem unaware of the seriousness of the matter.

Please realize that your tardiness causes other employees to become frustrated because they must carry your work load for this time. Moreover, your staff is left unsupervised and therefore does not know what to do on arrival in the morning. Many of them, too, have started coming in late. I'm sure you agree that a section head should set a good example for others to follow. I'll look forward to seeing that good example from you.

Hoverson sees a different purpose for writing: *to persuade* Spellman to mend her ways. Although strong in indicating disapproval of Spellman's behavior, the memo appeals to her sense of responsibility as a supervisor in setting a good model of behavior. It doesn't mention sanctions but focuses on the *positive* aspects of getting the organization's work done.

Both messages are conveyed in the same *form:* a memo. But the voice coming through the page in each is different. Brown writes in what we call the *business voice*, a style characterized by abstraction and some old-fashioned word choice, as you'll see in Chapter 7. Hoverson writes in a more personal style, using "I," contractions, and fewer abstractions and appeals to the company in general.

The *way* you say things often conveys almost as much information as the content of the document. Sometimes it conveys more. Your style should be a matter of strategy, not accident. Particularly where the situation is complex or politically sensitive, allow yourself the opportunity for revision to find the appropriate voice in which to convey your message. Sometimes you'll want to be forceful; sometimes personal; sometimes, particularly when the news is bad, rather impersonal.[3] Exercise a range of approaches, but make sure that the range is still tied in to *you.* Don't just imitate some document that has been hanging around the office. Chapter 7 suggests options in style for you to choose from.

One caution: Be careful with figures of speech. These can signal incompatibilities between writer and reader and may lead to misunderstandings. Some organization people live in corporate stadia. They *quarterback* deals, *end-run* other managers, and play *running games* and *passing games.* Their subordinates are their players, and they are simultaneously coach and star. Those with different perceptions, assumptions, and images may have trouble in reading memos from them and in working with them. Images of battlefields and sports fields, as well as figures of speech from science and technology, work their way through documents and oral presentations as presenters develop analogies both to understand their own materials and to enhance understanding in others. Images are useful. But sometimes they keep out more readers than they admit, particularly in documents aimed at international audiences. (One translator of American documents for European readers says his first step is always to change all the football images to soccer ones.) Screen figures of speech carefully.

In addition to writing as an *individual,* you'll have many occasions on the job to write as a member of a group. Such *collaborative* writing is discussed in detail in Chapter 11.

Readers

Your own or your group's goals in writing can usually be achieved only *through* the reader or readers. The goal must be shared. Incom-

---

[3] For an excellent article on business style, see John S. Fielden, "What Do You Mean You Don't Like My Style?" *Harvard Business Review,* 60 (May–June 1982), 128–138.

patibilities between you and the reader must be overcome or neutralized. Here's C. Northcote Parkinson, author of *Parkinson's Law,* on the subject:

> To succeed in the art of communication we have to make a big effort and it is initially an effort of imagination. We have to put ourselves in the position of the people we seek to influence, which is for most of us the most difficult task of all.[4]

That task is difficult enough when you write to one reader whom you know well. The task is compounded when you write to many readers—a common situation on the job—and when some or all of the readers are *unknown* to you. You may find some comfort in the organizational chart, which dictates reporting lines. Given a certain topic, like a monthly progress report, you may be told that every project member, by virtue of being a member, will receive a copy. Sometimes, however, the choice is less clear. Uncertain about the politics of reporting, writers sometimes send memos to everyone they can think of. But such a shotgun approach brings its own problems. It compounds the writer's task in achieving clarity in anything other than a simple message. It increases the temptation toward blandness as a way of mollifying everyone. It decreases the likelihood that any one reader will feel responsible for reading the memo and for action. Everyone leaves it to someone else on the distribution list.

Whenever possible, target your document to the *one* reader who has leverage in the system to achieve the document's goal. Figure 3–1 provides questions to aid you in profiling that reader and his or her relationship to you.

When your document must address *multiple* readers, many of whom may be unknown to you, think of the general *categories* or *levels* of readers. Here is one classification developed by Thomas Pearsall:

> *Is he a layman?* Then perhaps all he wants to do is read and enjoy your paper and file away a few interesting facts to add to his awareness of the world around him.
>
> *Is he an executive?* He has a profit motive. He may use your paper to make stock-buying decisions or to explore new markets for his company.
>
> *Is he an expert in the subject?* Then he wants new information to add to the large store he already has. Your information may stimulate him to further research or to design a new piece of equipment, or it may help him do a familiar job better.

[4]"Parkinson's Law of the Vacuum (or, Hoover for President)," *Forbes,* 12 May 1980, 137.

1. Why did you choose this reader (or why did this reader ask you to write)?

2. What is the reader's relationship to you in the organization?

3. What does the reader expect from you? How does the reader view you?

4. Is your credibility already established with the reader or do you need to develop credibility?

5. What does the reader already know about the topic? about the specific project?

6. What interest does the reader hold in the topic and project?

7. What other documents discuss this topic? How does your document fit into that context?

8. What opinions has the reader expressed, in other documents or in conversation, about the topic and project? Is the reader open to change?

9. How much detail does the reader need to understand and act on the document?

10. Can you foresee any misunderstandings that the document might evoke or any mistakes the reader might make in acting on your document?

11. Will your document change in any way the reader's role or standing in the organization?

12. What do the reader's behavior, education, and personality indicate about his or her reading of the document, for example, dress and body movements, general public conduct, choice of office (and perhaps home) decoration, hobbies, schools attended, family life, and daily routine?

13. What groups does the reader belong to, both informal and formal, within and outside the organization? Do you belong to some of these, too?

14. Who are the reader's heroes, particularly outside the organization?

FIGURE 3–1. You and your reader: A profile.

Is he a technician? He wants information that will help him understand and maintain the equipment the engineer or scientist has given him to work with.

Is he an operator of equipment? Then he wants clear, unequivocal instructions, step by step, in how to get the most out of the equipment he operates.[5]

The reader's level of understanding determines the terms you use, the amount of detail and explanation needed, the appropriate forms of visuals, the appropriate statistical presentation—and much more, as subsequent chapters show.

In addressing multiple readers, clarify for yourself not only the *individual* readers, but their *connection* in reading. A document aimed at many readers may reach all at the same time. Or the readers may read in sequence as your document moves along an approval route. Sometimes these readers' needs and interests conflict. Indeed, much of the difficulty of writing on the job derives from attempts to mediate among several readers. Chapters 18, 19, and 20, on the business report, address this problem more closely. But let us mention briefly here one scheme for considering multiple readership proposed by J. C. Mathes and Dwight Stevenson.[6] They note three priority levels: *primary readers,* who have requested the document and whose needs are most important; *immediate readers* within the organization, who will approve the document and route it to the primary reader; and *secondary readers,* who do not have decision-making power but will be affected by the implications of the document.

The trip report concerning the visit to Moab has a *primary* reader (the supervisor) and a *secondary* reader (the security chief at Moab), but not *immediate* readers. Here's an example with all three: The president of a bank, concerned because an excessive number of customers are closing their accounts, asks the head of the customer relations department to report on the causes of the closeouts. The head assigns the report to his assistant, who turns the task over to you. You write the report. The *primary reader* you address is the president. But along the way, you must meet the needs of the *immediate* readers—the assistant and the head—who, in effect, become your coauthors as the report moves through their hands. The president may pass the report along to the supervisor of personnel, who may provide copies to the tellers because they are, in part, responsible for the problem. The supervisor and the tellers are *secondary* readers.

Your message, of course, will not work, no matter how well it's

---

[5] From *Audience Analysis for Technical Writing* (Beverly Hills, Calif.: Glencoe, 1969). Used by permission.
[6] *Designing Technical Reports* (Indianapolis: Bobbs-Merrill, 1976), 9–23.

written, if it addresses the wrong reader or readers, in the wrong sequence. Inform yourself about who performs what roles in the organization and address the person or persons who can best deal with what you have to say. If you are unclear about who the primary reader will be, one authority advises, "Go for the person who's got the money."

The Message

When they *don't* think about readers, writers are often tempted to tell everything they know, which may be more or less than what's required. Instead, base your message on the readers. Tell readers only what they need, not less than that, and particularly not more. The manuals that document computer systems are a case in point. Many readers find them frustrating because the manuals include a level of detail that makes it impossible to use the system. Think how someone will apply what you have to say. Gauge the readers' familiarity with the topic and with the context for your report. Can you assume a knowledge of accounting practices in general so that you need to examine the distinctions only of *funds* accounting? Can the readers read a balance sheet? Whenever you're in doubt, tuck in more extensive explanations somewhere—for example, in a glossary or appendix—where an uninformed reader may find it but the informed reader won't be bothered by it. A reader can always skip what she or he knows. It's harder to fill in a gap if the text isn't there.

In assessing information, remember that much of what you write on the job is part of a series of documents (and conversations and meetings) on the topic. Although you might find it stifling to read the whole file on a project, you should be aware of at least the most pertinent literature and make sure that your own document acknowledges it and fits the politics and the information of that documentary context.

One reason for reading the files is to get a fix on the players—to see who comes up on what sides of any argument. Particularly if your goal is persuasion, you need to enter the discussion prepared to defuse any opposition your reader may present. Readers read a lot into and out of a text. Control the message as best you can to get the work done.

The Medium

The message is conveyed through a *medium*. You have many options. Broadly, of course, you can choose to write or choose to speak in response to a communication need. Chapter 23 discusses some of the rationale for deciding whether you need to compose a text on paper or electronically or whether you need to *talk* with someone. Then decide: Words, visuals, or numbers? What *form* of presentation? A brief memo? A letter? A report? What *style* within the form?

A major constraint on your medium of communication, of course, is the reader's ability to read you. Measuring that ability is difficult, but you should make at least some attempt to do so. Most *readability measures* are based on the assumption that short words are easier to read than long ones, and that short sentences are easier to read than long ones. So various readability scales predict ease of understanding against those measures. Several, like the Flesch Reading Ease Scale, G. R. Klare's formula, and Robert Gunning's Fog Index, are available as software for checking writing (see Chapter 10). You may be required to meet these standards in documents, particularly those for the military. Moreover, several states have mandated that such contracts as rental agreements, insurance policies, and bank statements meet measures of "plain English" to match consumer readability. But largely because these standards apply only to words and sentences and not to the document as a whole and are based on some outdated assumptions, they are flawed and should be used with caution. Current research emphasizes the need to test the document as a whole with a sample of potential users.[7]

Managing the Writing Process

Putting the communication model into action to *write* is a management process parallel to the management of any other activity in an organization. Don't just assume the writing will somehow get done. The result of much of your work on the job will be a document—a memo or letter report, for example. But that document has roots deep in your own thinking, in the organization's goals and your role in achieving those goals, in the technology of the document's transfer, in the information base of the subject you are writing about, and in the reader or readers who need that document to do their work. Approach the writing, then, in increments:

- Assess the available resources and secure the needed ones.
- Divide the project into discrete tasks, each with a deadline.
- Establish a control system to monitor progress.

[7] For an excellent analysis of readability standards and the improved alternative of user-testing, see Janice C. Redish and Jack Selzer, "The Place of Readability Formulas in Technical Communication," *Technical Communication*, 32 (Fourth Quarter 1985), 46–52.

- Expect problems and build in loose time to solve them.
- Write.

Assessing Resources

It takes resources to get a job done. If you're going to tune the engine in your car, you know you'll need certain skills, certain materials, certain tools—and a set amount of time. Before you begin, you assess what you need and begin only when you have enough. If it takes three hours to do the job, for example, and you have to use the car in two hours, you'll have to postpone the tune-up. Tuning up a memo or letter or report requires similar resources: time, information, writing tools, and perhaps access to a computer. Make sure you have them.

Dividing the Project into Tasks

Many would-be writers are overwhelmed by writing assignments because the assignment is seen as some mythic whole rather than something to be approached in steps. Every project can be divided into bite-sized chunks. Here, for example, is one writer's schedule for a review of the company's experience with performance evaluations:

Week 1	Interview personnel director
Week 1 and 2	Interview 10 employees and 10 supervisors
Week 2	Review literature on performance evaluations
Week 3	Outline report; check outline with boss
Week 4	Write up literature review; prepare appendixes on interviews
Week 5	Write rest of report and submit draft to boss for evaluation
Week 6	Revise and edit
Week 7	Produce the report through word processing
Week 8	Submit report

Establishing a Control System

A control system provides continuing information about how closely results resemble expectations. Thus an accounting system lets managers know, for example, how actual receivables stack up against projections. Check your progress against your schedule to avoid slippage. Here is how a student team writing a case study analysis in a management class chose to monitor its activities:

- One student assigned to the "steering" role to note and correct for slippages.
- One student assigned to the "gatekeeping" role as final editor to monitor the quality of information and presentation in the document.
- One student assigned as document preparer with a mandatory check on a draft at the university's writing center.
- A Gantt chart of the team's schedule, created at the first team meeting, circulated to each team member.
- A meeting scheduled every two weeks with an agenda circulated earlier.

Expecting Problems

Promise only what you can deliver. Build in enough slack time in a project to cover the likely occurrence that some important data you need will be delayed or the word-processing system will be down. Even if all goes well, the worst that can happen is that your project will be early—never a problem.

Writing

With the preliminaries covered, begin to draft your message.

Warm Up

Stretch a bit before a major writing task as you would before a run. If you have to produce a report, warm up by jotting a note. If you slump in the middle of writing, shift to another, easier writing job. When that's done, you can return to the bigger project with your pace and rhythm restored.

Play to Your Strengths

Begin to write at a point in the document that you know well. That's often a discussion section or a tabulation of results—the most specific material. You may come to the introduction only at the end of a writing session or two. No problem. Think of the report as existing in discrete (though, of course, connected) segments.

Play to your strengths, too, in the time and place for writing and the method of composition you use. Lots of people who hate to write only reinforce writing's drudgery by writing when they are most tired and bored. They schedule the good hours of the day for what they enjoy. Instead, schedule some good hours (the early morning if you're a morning person) for writing. If you need quiet for writing, don't try to write in the cafeteria at noon. If typing is hard for you, make a draft in longhand, or dictate into a tape recorder if you think you're better at speaking out your ideas than at committing them to paper. Writing can be difficult enough without bucking your own personality in the process.

Don't think of writing as open-ended ("I'll be here *forever*"). Set a limit in time or in number of pages. But quit writing only when you're ahead, when you know what your next line or section will be.

If you think in terms of *segments*, you'll be able to write in small units that don't require long stretches of time. Most business days are filled with interruptions. Try to segment your writing so that you can work in pieces.

Be Ready to Change

Perseverance is a wonderful trait, but it can be overdone. If the yellow pad doesn't seem to come up with prose you like, try typing into a terminal. Maybe at this one time, you need some noise to write by even though you usually like quiet. If your outline isn't working, abandon it. Your sentences themselves, spinning out before you, may lead you in an uncharted but potentially profitable direction. Go with it for a while. Be willing to adjust your style of writing a bit if something isn't working.

Keep Writing

Then, just write. Forget about grammar for now. Don't cross the page as you would a mine field about to blow with every error. Relax. You'll have time later to fix any problems in expression.

Think of the process as a game to be won. It has its rules and routines, but they are less obstacles to overcome than directions to follow. It has its moments of frustration and despair, but they can be turned into exhilaration as you break through a conceptual snag or reinterpret a piece of evidence to fit the puzzle. The process of communicating is the process of discovery: sorting through the statistics to find the trend or forcing some vague notion into the precision of words. If you approach the process positively, anticipating the pleasures and emphasizing the accomplishments, you will work with greater speed, less waste in time and energy, and better results, than if you view it all as punishment. Revision will eliminate any false starts, inconsistencies, or dangling modifiers. It will make you look good and make the reading comfortable for the reader—just what you want.

Exercises

1. As a class exercise in goal setting, take a topic and generate as many goal statements as you can at each level for some specific application. For example, take the topic of "personnel motivation." Define an organizational situation: a small, family-owned deli, "The Family Deli." The manager-owner employs seven people, all part-time, all either high school or college students (including her son). The employees are pretty lax: They don't clean up as they should; they fail to order the necessary supplies; they don't prepare the salads, lunch meats, and so on as they should during low customer times; and they talk on the phone while customers wait to be served.

(a) *Organizational goal:* to motivate employees toward better performance.

(b) *Operational goal:* lots of possibilities, depending on how you analyze the workers' problems. Here are some:

- To have each worker leave a clean store, with sandwich preparations completed, at the end of each shift.
- To establish worker identification with the deli through a program of training in sandwich preparation and the wearing of identifying T-shirts.

(c) *Information goal:*

To find techniques in the literature for motivating part-time workers.
To determine worker attitudes through interviews and a meeting.
To elicit customer suggestions through a survey.

(d) *Communication goal:* to write a memo *persuading* workers to, for example, prepare sandwich components during slack time on their shift.

2. Review the questions in Figure 3–1. Then, in response to one or more questions, write a one-paragraph profile of someone who reads your writing, for example, a supervisor or a professor. Here is one student's paragraph describing her supervisor on a summer job:

> On my first day of work, Mr. Larsen gave me a lecture on perfection and precise spelling. His gestures, comments, and surroundings reinforced that lecture all summer. He glided down the halls with his head high, always showing that he had everything under control. Moreover, he always shook his head with disapproval when an employee wearing "dungarees" passed by. A well-pressed suit, collared shirt, and matching tie—this was his only attire. His office was as clean as a hospital. His chair was never left out when he was gone. No file drawers were ever left open. And only one file at a time was on his desk. Yet, most impressive was the folder on the top right corner of his desk that contained an alphabetical listing of all topics in his files and the number of the drawer that held each of these topics.

3. Choose a topic for a report you are required to write in a business communication (or any other) class. *Limit* that topic and select an approach to writing based on a consideration of *who* would like to read about that topic. Try different strategies for different readers. For example:

Topic: "Corporate Fitness Programs"

Your Supervisor. Assume you are on the staff of a human resources department in a large corporation. Your supervisor is interested in corporate fitness programs, but he doesn't know much about them. He asks you to prepare a statement concerning fitness programs at other companies similar in size and staff to yours. Your goal is to *inform* the supervisor.

Vice-president for Human Resources. You're still in the human resources department, but assume that your supervisor asks you to recommend a program for the staff. Your recommendation will be read by the supervisor as the *immediate* audience. But the *primary* audience is the vice-president for human resources. The *secondary* audiences will include, for example, the personnel department, which will hire any new staff you recommend. In addition, purchasing would have to approve any expenditures for equipment; the physical plant staff would have to act on any recommended renovations. Will any other audiences be affected? How would you assess company needs? How would you gather the information about equipment and services? What strategies would you need to *persuade* the vice-president? (See Chapter 18.)

Human Resources Directors at Several Companies. Assume that you are a self-employed fitness consultant to corporations. Write a sales letter (see Chapter 16) marketing your services to a particular company.

Think of other situations for writing about fitness. Who would read about the topic? What different kinds of information—and what different purposes—would shape your writing?

4. Assume that you are a supervisor of several clerks in a bank's operation center. One clerk in your group continually parks his car in a space reserved for the vice-president for operations. The vice-president complains to your supervisor, who complains to you, with the warning, "Get that car out of the VP's space!" You talk to the clerk; the car returns. Now, write a memo to the clerk. Perhaps the entire class can write memos. Then, compare your strategies for dealing with the clerk. Assess any differences in management style as they reflect, perhaps, Theory X or Theory Y. See Chapter 12 for advice on the memo form.

5. For a week or two, analyze all the mail you receive in terms of the three general goals of writing: *to record, to inform,* and *to persuade.* What is the purpose of each letter? How does the letter make its purpose known? What *strategies* are used to accomplish the purpose? Note, too, your role as *reader* of each letter. Is the letter addressed *only* to you? Or are you a member of some *set* of readers of the letter? If so, why were you chosen to receive the letter?

6. Here's how Loren Kline, the soccer coach at the University of Delaware, explained a problem with the team's play:

> The players were tight. They were trying too hard or just trying to make the perfect play all the time instead of just relaxing and making the easy play.

By analogy, can you apply such a diagnosis to what happens as writers write?

7. Fill out the following questionnaire concerning your composing process— the way you write.[8] Fill out the questionnaire again *after* you finish your business communication course. Any changes?

---

[8]Questionnaire is based in part on Linda Flower, *Problem-Solving Strategies for Writing,* 2nd ed. (San Diego: Harcourt Brace Jovanovich, 1985), 39–40.

1. How often do you write (once a week, at the end of a project, every day in a lab notebook)?
2. How do you feel about writing? (circle one)
   Enjoy it   Neutral   Dislike it
3. What forms of documents do you write (essays, term papers, lab reports, case analyses, marketing surveys, questionnaires)?
4. What do you do between the time someone asks you to write something and the time you actually start to write? What do you worry about?
5. Describe any rituals you perform as you sit down to write. (One person we know, for example, must wear a particular green baseball cap to write; others clean their desks or make sure they have adequate coffee.)
6. How do you decide what information to put where? Do you outline before you write?
7. If you use a computer for your writing, do you write out a draft longhand first and then type it in, or do you compose directly at the keyboard?
8. Once you get going on a draft, when do you start looking back to revise?
   (a) After every sentence?
   (b) After every paragraph?
   (c) Not until you have written for a specific period or filled the screen?
   (d) That depends (describe your approach to looking backward).
9. What cues do you look for in the text that tell you what to revise?
10. How long do you write in any one writing session? If you write for different amounts of time on different projects, describe what determines when you start and stop and how you get going again.
11. Comment briefly on what you consider the strengths and weaknesses of the way you write (your process of composing) and of what you write (your style).

Understanding Business Information

4

Business organizations and nonprofit institutions daily produce, file, process, shuffle, and try somehow to stay on top of a wealth of information: sales projections, audit data, personnel policies, judicial decisions, stock quotations, figures on the gross national product, purchase orders. Indeed, the vast amount of information that large organizations have to deal with causes information overload, a vexing problem.

But the value of information in business can hardly be overstated. Walter B. Wriston, the former chief executive officer of Citicorp, observed that "information about money has become almost as important as money itself."[1] Coming from a banker, that is a striking statement of the importance of information. Because business communication is the purposeful transfer of information, it's not surprising that information itself is called the raw material of communication. This image, although perhaps accurate, is oversimplified, implying that information gets turned into communication in the way milk gets turned into ice cream or cotton into yarn. The processing of information is a bit more complicated—and a bit more interesting.

The purpose of this chapter is to help you understand information. We'll first look at the role of information in business communication. Next we'll classify information and provide a tool to help you assess it. Third, we'll examine the internal characteristics of information so you can judge the quality of the information you have. Finally, we'll discuss patterns of information use and present guidelines for interpreting or explaining information in the documents and talks that you prepare.

The Role of Information in Business Communication

Information's role in business communication varies, depending on the purpose of the document or talk. As we have observed, there are three broad purposes for writing in organizations: to record, to inform, or to persuade. Sometimes these overlap. If you are writing a memo "for the record" or an informative letter, information is, of course, dominant but can really be said to play a *passive* role. Let's say you are asked to get bids on a new television set for your club and present a report to the finance committee at next Monday's meeting. Your report is certainly centered on information; indeed, that's really all it is. But the information plays a passive role; it's just there. Of course, you try

---

[1]"Publishers Go Electronic: An Industry Races to Relearn the Information Business," *Business Week*, 11 June 1984, 85.

to present it clearly, concisely, simply, and attractively, perhaps in a nice table that aids understanding. But you are really just conveying the information and letting it do its job.

On the other hand, in communication that aims at persuasion, information plays an *active* role: It helps you convince someone of something. If your original club assignment had been to recommend which new television set to buy, you would be making a persuasive report. You would gather the information just as you did for the informative report, but then you would use it as a tool in persuasion. This doesn't mean that you manipulate the information in any devious way, only that you structure and shape it to fit the purpose at hand. We'll see some examples of these different uses of information throughout this chapter.

To summarize, the role that information plays in business communication depends on whether you are communicating principally to record or inform, or principally to persuade. If recording or informing is your goal, information will be passive—that is, presented for its own sake. If persuading is your goal, information will be active—that is, used to advance an argument or support a recommendation.

Classification: The Info Grid

Regardless of the specific goal of your document or talk, and hence of the role the information plays in it, you must understand information in a broad sense. What is information? One way to classify it is according to its source; this approach is taken in Chapter 5. Here we want to look at a classification scheme for information that we call the *info grid*. The scheme helps to put information into perspective according to its internal characteristics rather than its sources.

With respect to its internal characteristics, information can be divided into four types:

- *Fact:* undisputed or accepted knowledge.
- *Observation:* record of sensory perceptions.
- *Interpretation:* explanation of an event or characteristic.
- *Opinion:* statement of preference or viewpoint.

These four types of information differ according to the extent to which they are "accepted"—facts being the most widely accepted and opinions being the least widely accepted. For example, if we say that water freezes at 32 degrees Fahrenheit, we are stating something that is widely accepted. Indeed, this is a fact by definition, a universally agreed-to position (assuming, of course, the use of the Fahrenheit scale). If we say that we prefer snow to rain, this is a statement of personal preference and applies only to us; others have different views.

These examples are quite straightforward. What about the statement "It rained in Seattle yesterday"? Obviously this is an observation, the record of a sensation. If you were in Seattle yesterday and got wet, then you observed that it was raining. When the National Weather Service records the weather in Seattle as rain, then the observation really turns into a fact because it achieves a kind of official status. It is written down, recorded in retrievable form, and set above debate. But note that the "fact" is based on an observation. Now let us look at this statement: "It rained in Seattle yesterday because a cold front passed over a warm front." We call this an interpretation because it explains a phenomenon. Is it a fact? Meteorologists hold that the collision of warm and cold air masses produces rain. But there are other interpretations. Primitive peoples believed that rain came in response to supplications to the gods, and even today rainmakers perform ritual dances to bring relief to drought-stricken areas. Who is to say that one interpretation is better than another?

As you can see, we are getting into tricky territory here because if we push logic to its limits, we might argue that all facts, observations, and interpretations are merely opinions. If we go too far in this direction, we begin to call into question a lot of views that people have a great stake in keeping settled. It just doesn't make sense to debate every "fact," because we need to have broad agreement on many matters simply to get along in life. In sports, it's a settled point that the official is always right. If the homeplate umpire calls the pitch a strike, that becomes a fact. To debate it endlessly would mean that the game would never proceed. If the batter or the crowd has a different opinion, they are welcome to it, but the game must go on.

To understand the nature of information and the differences among facts, observations, interpretations, and opinions, we can construct a grid (see Figure 4–1). The horizontal axis runs from "Disputable" to "Accepted." The vertical axis runs from "Recorded" at the bottom to "Unstated" at the top. On this info grid, we can place all types of information. Items in the upper left corner are the least accepted—or the most susceptible to disagreement. This is the general area of opinion. Items at the bottom right are the most widely accepted. This is the area of fact. Pieces of information can be located at an infinite number of points on this grid, and that possibility should remind us that the difference among facts, observations, interpretations, and opinions is not fixed for all time.

Let's see how the info grid can help us assess the nature of information that is used every day in business. Suppose that you are asked

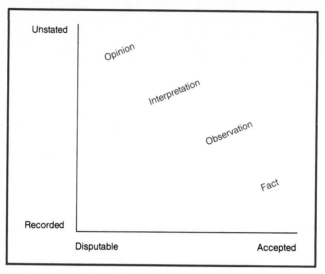

FIGURE 4–1. The info grid.

to send your supervisor a memo reporting on the progress you are making on your assignment to develop a new benefits package for assembly-line workers in the Houston plant. In preparation for writing the memo, you gather the following information:

1. The average benefits package for similar employees in the Houston labor market, according to the Texas Department of Labor Statistics, amounts to 42 percent of their base salary.

2. According to the personnel office, the benefits package in place at your company's Houston plant costs an amount equal to 48 percent of base salary.

3. A survey you conducted of workers in the Houston plant reveals that 66 percent are "satisfied" or "very satisfied" with the current benefits plan.

4. The general manager of the Houston plant wrote in a memo to you that he regards the existing package as "unnecessarily costly" and "not appreciated by the workers themselves."

5. Several people in the personnel office in Houston told you that they fear that imposing a new benefits package that reduces contributions from the employer could lead to pressure for unionization among workers.

Here you have five pieces of information. Before you pull them together for your memo, you need to assess them, to determine the use-

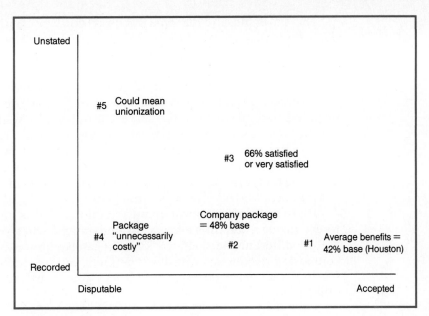

FIGURE 4–2. The info grid applied.

fulness of what you have available to work with in composing your memo. Here's where the info grid can help (see Figure 4–2).

It's pretty easy to see that the first two items on the list are facts as we have defined them: information that is agreed on. It is possible, however, to imagine disputes that could arise over them. For example, the question of what constitutes "similar" workers might be raised to call into doubt the data from the Texas Bureau of Labor Statistics. Exactly what benefits are included in calculating the company's contribution ratio might also be questioned to discredit the 48 percent figure that was given by the personnel office. But as in baseball, at some point you have to agree on what is accepted as a fact—or at least on who gets to make the final call that will be considered official.

If we look at the fourth and fifth pieces of information, we would probably agree that these are not facts but either interpretations or opinions. They belong on the left of the info grid. They are subject to disagreement depending on who looks at them. This doesn't mean that they are useless, only that they are not recorded facts of wide acceptability, as the first two are. We simply need to classify them as separate from facts so we can use the information with maximum effectiveness. Notice also that the fourth item, a memo, is placed at the "Recorded" end of the vertical axis, whereas the fifth is closer to the "Unstated" end because it's not in writing.

The third piece of information is trickier to classify according to our scheme. In one way, the level of satisfaction among current workers might be called opinion because the responses to the survey are obviously expressions of personal viewpoints. However, the statement that 66 percent of those surveyed considered themselves "satisfied" or "very satisfied" can be regarded as a fact—that is, presumably, an undisputed conclusion from the survey. If the results were accurately reported, then it's a fact that the satisfaction level, according to this particular survey of those particular workers at that particular time, was 66 percent. We might want to call this piece of information an observation rather than a fact because it is the record of a perception. It belongs near the middle of the info grid.

There's nothing magical about the info grid. It is a tool you can use to get inside your information, to understand what you have, and to see the differences among the kinds of information available to you in composing documents or talks. The more you understand about information, the more effectively you can use it to communicate with others.

The Quality of Information: Internal Characteristics

In the final analysis, the effectiveness of information depends on the use you make of it in communication. We'll shortly discuss that aspect of information. But as we have just seen, its effectiveness depends also on how well you understand it. We have tried to show the differences among facts, observations, interpretations, and opinions. Another characteristic of information you need to assess is, to put it very simply, the *quality* of the information.

Quality is a difficult concept, but it's a practical one. People often ask, "How good is your information?" They want to know its quality. There are many ways to measure quality in information. Here are five commonsense tests that information you use in communication should meet. Information should be

- Accurate, or correct.
- Timely.
- Relevant.
- Reliable.
- Sensible.

Information should always be *accurate,* or *correct.* If you are presenting data on sales at five branch stores over a two-month period, make sure that the numbers are correct—that is, that you have verified that they were properly gathered, that you have checked them against the original sources where possible, that you have performed the arithmetic correctly, and so on. And of course, don't forget to check the numbers in your memo against the numbers on the printout from which you worked; copying accurately is part of meeting the test of accuracy. Similarly, if you are quoting someone, you can't prove the accuracy of what the person said, but you can be certain that you are quoting that person correctly. Whatever the information you use, make sure that it is accurate. People can still disagree with you, but give them correct information to disagree with.

Information should be *timely.* The debt owed by less developed countries to U.S. banks should be reported from the latest available figures, not from the ones you happened to run across in an old newspaper. If you want to value the assets of a company, find out today's receivables, not last month's. If you are quoting the views of an economist on the relationship between the federal deficit and interest rates, be sure you are quoting her most recent writings or speeches. What she said last August may not be what she believes today. Always aim for the most recently available information, unless, of course, historical comparisons are required. The more up-to-date the information you cite, the more willing your audience will be to believe it.

Information should always be *relevant* to the question at hand. Relevance is, of course, relative. In examining the investment attractiveness of a new software company, for example, you may not consider its stock-option plan for executives relevant, but that information may indeed be quite relevant to determining the nature of the firm's commitment to its personnel, the future liabilities it may incur, and the prudence of the management. You have to gauge relevance according to the issues you are addressing and the point you want to make. Citing the views of an astrologist on the movement of the stock market illustrates an extreme of irrelevance that few serious persons would be guilty of. On the other hand, if the astrologist's record is better than your broker's, you might want to reconsider. In general, though, relevance is fairly easy to determine.

Like relevance, *reliability* is a test that you have to apply with care. The simple question to ask is "Can I rely on this information?" Answering this question means evaluating the source. The daily *Wall Street Journal* is a reliable source of information on new debt offerings, stock prices (from yesterday, of course), and management changes at large corporations. Your hometown newspaper gives greater detail about the problems of your local utility in bringing its newest nuclear reactor on-line. But a phone call from a friend hinting that a merger may occur soon between two oil companies clearly doesn't meet the test of reliability. Whenever possible, use standard, recognized sources of information, preferably printed ones (see Chapter 5). When you are quoting unpublished sources, reliability is harder to measure, but if you always aim for the highest level of dependability, you will seldom go wrong. At the very least, you can always flag a dubious source or piece of information by indicating that it comes from "usually reliable sources" (if it does) or is "speculative" (if it is). The golden rule of being honest with your reader applies here as it does everywhere in communication.

Finally, the best test of information is its *sensibleness*. If you are quoting a source that says the world will end next week, you should certainly be aware that many people will regard that prediction as silly. If your computer printout shows that sales of frisbees increased 500 percent in the Cherry Hill store every day for five days, you should be alerted to the possibility of error. Maybe sales did exhibit that pattern for some logical reason, for example, because the International Frisbee Contest was held in southern New Jersey that week. But information that looks odd to you may, in fact, *be* odd—and it will certainly look that way to others, which will reflect poorly on you and perhaps undermine the goal of your memo or report. Be wary about major changes in data over time that don't have obvious explanations. Reread quotations carefully if a surprising statement appears: "The President said yesterday he doubted that his wife would support his campaign." Be on the lookout for the startling or the bizarre. Sometimes truth is startling or bizarre, but you are skating on thin ice if you report information that just doesn't make sense.

Information that is accurate, timely, relevant, reliable, and sensible is, of course, not perfect. Your tests for these qualities may lead you to different conclusions from those that someone else would reach. These are subjective matters. As we will see in the next section, the final test of information is its particular usefulness in a given document or presentation. But before you get to that stage, you have to be sure that the internal characteristics of the information meet your standards. In short, you have to understand the nature of the information itself if you are going to use it with maximum effectiveness in communicating with others.

Patterns of Information Use

Since in communication information is not an end in itself, we are interested in more than its internal characteristics. We have to be concerned with how the information is used in communicating. The "how" varies with the goal you have in producing a particular document or talk. You first have to identify your goal and then develop a strategy for deploying the information to help you reach the goal.

Suppose you are tracking stocks with the aim of potential investment. You jot down pertinent data each day; that is, you *record*. The only constraint on the form of the record is that the information must be accessible. Now suppose that you are a broker whose client asks for a list of ten stocks in the retail industry that have a price–earnings ratio under 10, a yield of at least 6 percent, and a price under $35. You might prepare a simple list with the stock names in the left column and the pertinent information in three columns to the right of the names. The client can then run down the list and find what he or she wants. Your goal here is to *inform*.

If you are asked not just to inform the client but to make a recommendation on a stock to purchase—that is, if your goal is to *persuade*—you might present the same simple table but also include a paragraph or two in which you advance reasons why one or several issues are more desirable than others. Or you might include data, within the text of a letter rather than in a table, on the one or several stocks you recommend.

In these instances, the same information assumes different form depending on the goal: recording, informing, or persuading. If you are writing to record, the criterion for information use is ease of access. The presentation of information is determined by the characteristics of the information itself. Writing to record often calls for tables and other visual forms of presentation that make the information most accessible. You want the information to *be there*.

Writing to inform requires added attention to the reader's needs. You are recording for an audience. Again, visual forms of presentation are desirable. You also need to pay attention to potential problems in accessibility caused by special features of the information. Uncommon or ambiguous terms may require explanation. Grouping of data for ease of understanding may be appropriate. For example, if you are recording survey results, you would list all responses, whereas if you are summarizing the results to inform someone of conclusions, you might concentrate on the number and percentage of, say, the negative responses, regardless of the scale of negativeness. Information used in communicating to inform remains, as in recording, generally passive.

If the communication goal is persuasion, the criterion for information use is support of the point or recommendation being made. The presentation of information is governed by consideration of the writer's specific goal and perception of what the reader needs to be shown to accept the argument being made. In these circumstances, information plays an *active* role. It is not just there; it is there in a way that advances the writer's intention and helps to persuade the reader to adopt the writer's point of view and suggested action. Easy access and understanding are, of course, essential, but arrangement of the information is also determined by the outcome that the writer or speaker desires.

To support arguments in persuasive writing, you line up facts toward an interpretation of *what* should be done and *why*. Facts, as we have seen, are undisputed or agreed-to statements in numerical or verbal form: dates, numbers, names, and so on. Interpretations are explanations of the facts and the relationships that may exist among the facts. For example, it may be a fact that sales of Product Y increased 18 percent in June over May, and it may be another fact that advertising expenditures for the product increased 10 percent in June over May. Saying that there is a direct causal link between the two facts—that the increase in sales resulted from the increase in ad spending—is an interpretation, an explanation of the relationship between two facts. Because most business problems concern *why* rather than just *what*, when you prepare documents or talks you will frequently find yourself interpreting information. We'll look in this section at some of the common patterns of interpretation and a few of the problems that can occur in trying to interpret facts. We'll start with a case study.

 ## Case Study: An Effort to Control Drunk Driving

In September 1981, a new law in the state of Maine imposed penalties on drivers who operated their vehicles under the influence of alcohol. The OUI law (for "operating under the influence") was designed to reduce the fatalities on Maine highways that apparently resulted from driving while drinking. Here are some facts on this issue:

• In the three years before the law went into effect, there had been 260 fatalities in Maine involving trucks and cars, and 65 percent of these had been determined to be related to alcohol use.
• In 1982, the first full year under the new law, there were 167 fatalities, 50 percent of them linked to alcohol.
• In 1983, there were 227 fatalities, 57 percent of them related to alcohol.

• In 1978, drivers arrested for drinking had an average blood alcohol level of 0.15 percent; in 1983 the level was 0.19 percent.

Auto safety officials in Maine had to report these facts to the public and to state agencies. They were also called on to explain or interpret the facts to evaluate the effect of the new OUI law on the problem of alcohol-related auto fatalities. It seemed easy to conclude that in its first year, the new law had reduced fatalities: Deaths had dropped from 260 to 167, and the proportion of these attributed to drunk driving had declined from 65 percent to 50 percent. This explanation was widely accepted. After all, the point of the new law was to reduce deaths caused by drunk driving, and it seemed to have worked.

But in the second year of the law, 1983,

fatalities increased from 167 to 227, and the percentage identified as alcohol-related rose from 50 to 57. This increase was disturbing because it suggested that the impact of the new law had been short-lived. One official advanced the explanation that intensive publicity in the first year of implementation had increased the effect of the law itself, whereas the publicity had declined later and people had apparently resumed their old habits, no longer as conscious of the legal implications as they had been when the law first went into effect. On the basis of this interpretation, officials called for more publicity and new ways of dramatizing the consequences of drinking while driving (well-publicized road blocks, for example, were suggested, not so much to catch more drunks but to reinforce in the public's mind the toughness of the law).

Another safety official came forward with a further interpretation, based on the data on the change in blood alcohol level. He concluded that the increase in blood alcohol level in persons arrested for drunk driving between 1978 and 1983 had resulted from a differential impact of the new law. Social drinkers, he said, had been deterred by the toughness of the OUI statute, but serious drinkers had not been deterred. As a result, he said, the law had had the effect of keeping social drinkers off the highway but had not impeded heavy drinkers. Thus, his explanation of the information led to a different conclusion: Instead of a broad campaign to publicize the OUI law, he recommended that the police specifically target heavy drinkers, and that the courts impose tougher sentences on them. Why go after everyone, he asked, when the real problem came from a small group who had not been deterred by the new law?

This case reflects some interesting points about the use of information to support recommendations. We see two quite different arguments resulting from the same set of information, each believable in its own right. The information and the way it was used caused the differences in conclusions. Our goal here isn't to determine which interpretation was "right" or "wrong," but only to show that evidence is subject to multiple interpretations and that care must be exercised to ensure the most credible and persuasive use of it.

Guidelines for Interpreting Information

In addition, then, to ensuring that the information you use meets the tests we have described, you must pay attention to how you are interpreting evidence to support a recommendation. Here are four basic guidelines:

- Make sure that specific details adequately support your generalizations.
- Test cause-and-effect relationships carefully.

- Avoid oversimplification and exaggeration.
- Use all available information, not just those parts that appear to support your argument best.

We can apply these guidelines to the Maine OUI case to show their general value in interpretation. Generalizing about the difference between social drinkers and problem drinkers based on a single set of data about average blood alcohol levels from two different years is risky. The difference (0.15 percent versus 0.19 percent) is rather small to begin with. And averages themselves are often deceptive. Rather than a simple average, one ought to have a full distribution, showing the range of levels. A few instances at the extremes can easily distort averages.

Cause-and-effect relationships are always extremely tricky. In our OUI case, both recommendations are based on assumptions about causality that may be faulty. The first assumes that the decline in fatalities related to drinking that came in the first year under the new law had resulted from massive publicity about the law. This may or may not have been so. To test this assumption, one would have to gather much more information, for example, on awareness of the new law, on the public's specific source of information about it, and on individual decisions to drive or not under different circumstances. The second recommendation—relating to the difference between social and heavy drinkers—assumes that those who drink more are more willing to risk punishment, perhaps because they are unable to control their behavior. But this assumption that moderate drinkers are more cautious may or may not be true. Again, one would have to gather different evidence to support that claim. The test of a causal conclusion is whether there is another, equally plausible explanation for an event. In this case, it is possible to argue that the decline in auto fatalities in the first year of the new law resulted not from the law but from some other source: a general decline in driving that year brought on by frequent snow in the winter, or an increase in gasoline prices, or a decline in summer tourism, or a general decline in the economy that caused fewer people to drive to work, for example. You have to test all the possible explanations before settling on a single explanation of an event.

Although it is often said that the simplest explanations are the best, the danger of oversimplifying is apparent in this case. Attributing a complex phenomenon to a single cause (the new law) probably oversimplifies the case. Most changes in behavior result from more than one cause. Reducing the complex to the simple risks misinterpretation and exaggeration of results.

Each of these recommendations, as we have seen, was based on little evidence. In addition, each ignored some of the evidence that was available. Partial use of evidence is always dangerous. The second recommendation, for example, was built on the changes in blood alcohol level and generally ignored the changes in fatalities and the percentages of them that were attributable to alcohol. It is always tempting to seize on those data that support what you want to say, but excluding other relevant information undermines the strength of the conclusion you want your audience to accept. Although it is hard to build explanations that recognize every available bit of information, leaving aside some information exposes you to the charge of being biased—or simply sloppy. You should develop conclusions that are supported by as much of the available information as possible. If some pieces don't fit, you should at least admit that and thus let your readers or hearers know that you are aware of other evidence that may be less supportive of your claim.

To summarize, when you interpret information to advance a recommendation or proposal, do so with a full understanding of the need to generalize carefully and on the widest base of data; attribute causation carefully and be aware of the assumptions you are making; avoid oversimplifying or exaggerating; and don't ignore available evidence in order to concentrate on some small piece that conveniently supports your view.

Of course, complete proof is never possible. Remember that in litigation, "probable cause" and "preponderance of evidence" are common standards. But simply recognizing the complexity of interpretation will prepare you to explain evidence carefully and to make the logical links that are necessary to persuade an audience, whether your topic is as complex as how to reduce alcohol-related fatalities or as simple as which desk to buy for a new office.

Exercises

1. A survey on alcoholism included this question: "Have you ever been closely associated with someone who was an alcoholic—either a family member, or a close friend, or someone you worked closely with?" The results varied dramatically according to the region of the United States in which the respondents lived. Following are the percentages of "yes" answers by region:

West, 71
Midwest, 62
South, 56
East, 41

Here are some "conclusions" that different people drew from the results: (a) Westerners are more likely than easterners to have alcohol problems; (b) Westerners are more likely than easterners to discuss personal problems; (c) It's safer to drive in the South than in the West. Place these sentences on the info grid. Discuss the implications of this placement. How could you use the "conclusions"? Discuss the technique (and the potential dangers) of drawing inferences from survey data.

2. Study the data in the following table:

Country	1984 Health expenditure in $ per capita	Life expectancy at birth	Deaths from heart disease per 100,000
United States	1,500	75	435
West Germany	900	73	584
Japan	500	77	266
Great Britain	400	74	579

Where do these data belong on the info grid? Can you infer that there is a direct relationship between health-care expenditures and life expectancy? Deaths from heart disease? Is there an *in*direct relationship? Any relationship at all? Use the data and any conclusions you can reasonably draw from them to make an argument in favor of (a) reduced and (b) increased health-care expenditures.

3. The average cost of purchasing an existing 2,000-square-foot home with three bedrooms, two baths, and a two-car garage was calculated for the following cities in July 1983 and January 1984:

City increase/decrease	July 1983	January 1984	Percentage
Reno, Nevada Increase	$100,000	$115,000	15
Houston, Texas Decrease	105,000	95,000	10
Columbus, Ohio Decrease	93,000	89,000	4.3
Raleigh, North Carolina Increase	78,000	85,000	9

On the basis of this information, a student wrote a report indicating that housing costs are directly linked to the health of the local economy. She noted that Houston's oil boom had broken during the six-month time period, and thus housing costs had been reduced. Does this seem like a valid inference? Are there other possible explanations? The student had difficulty interpreting the data for Columbus because its economy had seemed to remain healthy. A friend who lived in Columbus advanced this explanation: Less affluent buyers had begun to enter the market and thus more homes in the lower brackets were selling in January 1984. Specifically, she pointed out that before July 1983, many people had been moved into Columbus from the New York area by American Electric Power Co., which had relocated its headquarters from New York City to Columbus. These people had owned relatively high-priced property in the New York area and so were able to buy Columbus houses in the higher price ranges. By January, additional workers were moving in from the company's Canton, Ohio, offices. Because prices in Canton were lower than prices in New York, this new wave of people were buying lower-priced houses in Columbus. Does this explanation help account for the apparent conflict in the interpretations? Are there other possible explanations? In addition to the basic information presented, would you advise the student to gather more details before making any inferences? What might she look for?

Finding and Documenting Business Information

5

The information used in business communication, as we saw in the last chapter, is richly complex. Understanding its complexity is a prerequisite to using it effectively to produce the letters, memos, reports, and talks common in business. After you understand the nature of information, you learn to find the specific information that your document or presentation requires. Finding information and then documenting its use—two closely related activities—are the subjects of this chapter.

The Search for Information

The search for information begins precisely when any search begins: when you know what you are looking for. What do you need to know? When you answer that question, your search is under way. Without a clear objective, however, the search will almost certainly dead-end. To shape your search, you should have a clear goal in mind. Fill in the blanks:

I need _____ so I can _____.

Let's look at three statements students made to launch their search for information:

1. I need a book on accounting.
2. I need an article on Japanese management.
3. I need a newspaper story on auto sales.

Note two qualities of these statements. First, they fill in only one of the two blanks, omitting the purpose ("so I can . . ."). Second, they specify the object of the search not as information but as a *source* of information: a book, an article, or a newspaper story. Let's modify them:

1. I need to know how to write a Sources and Uses of Funds statement.
2. I need to know the basic elements of Japanese management so I can write a paper contrasting it with American practice.
3. I need a list of auto sales by manufacturers so I can write a memo that compares the sales of American-made and imported cars by month for 1986.

You can see that the three revised statements are not just more precise but are specifically directed toward information rather than source and are related to the intended use of the information in a communication. This distinction points to the most important rule of setting up an information search: Know exactly what *information* is required and why. If you phrase your objective in terms of a source, you have already directed the search in a way that may prove unproductive or wasteful. Perhaps the best information on Japanese management isn't in an article but a book. Perhaps auto sales data by month for an entire year can't be found in a single newspaper story but must be looked up in a reference source. You must also indicate clearly to yourself the reason for the information: to write a memo, a paper, whatever. Knowing that can help you discover the best source of the best information rather than limiting you to something that may not answer your questions.

Once you know what you are looking for, you need to establish a process that will aid you in finding it. This means essentially relating the need to the source that can furnish it and then identifying the steps needed to get at the source. Here's a sample process, based on the second example above:

Need:

I need to know the basic elements of Japanese management so I can write a paper contrasting it to American practice.

Sources:

• Books on Japanese management.

• Articles on Japanese management in professional and scholarly journals on management.

• Newspaper and magazine articles on Japanese management and how it works.

• Views of American management professors and American businesspeople about Japanese management and how it contrasts with American management.

Steps:

• Check library catalog for books.

• Check indexes to periodical literature in library to find good articles.

• Interview professor of management and president of a local company.

Of course, this is a simplified scheme, but it does illustrate the basic procedure you should follow: (1) identify the needed information; (2) identify the likely sources; and (3) identify the steps you have to take to locate and use the sources that will supply what you need. The more complex the task, the more care you have to use in identifying the steps here. For example, if you are writing a dissertation on the subject, you need much more information than if you are writing a three-paragraph story for your school newspaper. And if more information and sources are involved, you need to develop the steps of the process of searching more fully and with attention to the time you will need to carry out the search. You may have to block out the work into units and assign weeks or months to each, being sure to allow enough time for each and connecting them in the right order. It would be best to survey the published literature before you interview a professor or businessperson, as you want to come to such an interview well armed and in control of the basic information, which you shouldn't rely on an expert to provide.

Like any intellectual task, searching for information requires you to know your goal and to have a reasonable plan for achieving it. Avoid the temptation to head to the library for some casual browsing. Although browsing is always fun and can yield uniquely valuable information if luck is with you, it's better to rely not on luck, but on your own powers of analysis and planning.

Sources of Information

As we saw in Chapter 4, information can be classified into various types and can be assessed for internal characteristics and methods of explanation. We can also classify the *sources* of information. Basically, there are four sources of business information: (1) personal observation or experiment, (2) interview, (3) survey, and (4) literature. The type of information that will be produced varies with the source. We can relate these four basic sources to the types of information described in the info grid in Chapter 4.

Let's now look at each of the four sources to examine its strengths and weaknesses and to find out how to use it to get the information needed to solve a communication problem. (*See* **Table** on p. 62).

Personal Observation and Experiment

If you want to know how long it takes to assemble individual components into a stereo system, the easiest way to find out is to time yourself as you assemble the system. In doing so, you have performed an experiment. Many problems in business require information that comes from such experiments or direct observations: What is the total of ac-

Sources of Information	Can Yield	Type of Information
Personal observation and experiment		Observation
Interview		Opinion Interpretation Fact Observation
Survey		Opinion Under certain conditions, also fact, observation, and interpretation
Literature		Opinion Interpretation Observation Fact

counts receivable this month? What is the average length of time a customer must wait in line at the checkout counter? How large should the new desk be to accommodate a microcomputer? How long does it take to walk from the desk to the men's room? Each of these questions can be answered with information that comes from direct observation.

An obvious problem with such information is that it is subject to dispute. The time it takes me to assemble a stereo system may differ from the time it takes you, depending on our experience and dexterity. You can measure the size of the new desk, but what standard should you use? You may want a desk that just accommodates the new computer, whereas the person who will sit at the desk may want one a foot longer to accommodate a telephone and an ashtray. It may take you five minutes to walk to the men's room from your desk, but your boss may make the trip in just two minutes.

Thus the information that results from experiments or observations must always be presented with explicit recognition of the source: "Such-and-such an experiment yielded such-and-such a result"; or "Under the following specific conditions, the following results were observed." Making clear the origins of the information will alert the reader or hearer to the potential problems that accompany experimental data and will allow you to interpret the information to meet your communication goal without worrying endlessly over its acceptance.

Interview

The purpose of an interview is to gather facts, observations, interpretations, and opinions from a single individual, usually an expert on a particular topic or a specialized part of a topic. Which of the types of information you gather (facts or opinions, for example) depends, of course, on what you want and should not be left up to the interviewee. If you're after facts, don't settle for the person's opinions. The interview should be used only to gather information that is not readily available in another form. Don't interview an expert as a substitute for doing basic research in the library. Go to an expert to supplement general information or to provide specialized views or facts that cannot be found in published works.

It should be noted here that we are discussing interviews as a source of information, not as ends in themselves. Doing a profile of the company's oldest retiree or youngest vice-president or most athletically proficient accountant requires an interview, but the purpose of such interviews is to flesh out the character of the individual rather than merely to provide information. Some of what is said here may be relevant to that approach, but "doing an interview" for the company or school newspaper is really a different topic.

Guidelines for the Interview

Here are seven guidelines for maximizing the effectiveness of interviews as a source of information for business writing or speaking.

1. Select the interviewee carefully. Picking at random the name of a management professor to interview for your paper on Japanese management style probably won't produce satisfactory results. Have a reason for selecting the person because he or she will probably ask. If possible, you should interview someone who is not only recognized as an expert in the subject you are studying but is also known to be both helpful and available. It helps if he or she is a reasonable person who will answer your questions carefully and concisely and send you on your way, rather than a fanatic who will try to convert you to some viewpoint or a lonely soul who will tie you up for the day looking at old photographs. Finding out as much as you can about the prospective interviewee before requesting a meeting will help you avoid unpleasantness or wasted time.

2. Arrange the interview in advance and at the interviewee's convenience. Don't ask the CEO of a Fortune 500 company for an interview on Friday at 4:15 because you will be in town and free then, and don't corner your professor after class and demand an immediate meeting so you can gather information for the term paper that's due tomorrow. Always write or phone to request an interview (with an explanation of your request, of course) as far in advance as possible, and offer a number of possible days and times to suit the person's schedule. It is best to interview only persons you know, but that is rarely possible. The next best thing is to have an intermediary, someone who knows both you and the interviewee. But in the absence of such good fortune, you just have to call or write—perhaps both if you want to be sure of getting on a busy person's calendar.

3. Prepare for the interview. As we said, an interview should be relied on not to supply basic information that is otherwise available, but to supplement that information with the specialized viewpoints or knowledge of the expert. This means that you should be thoroughly versed in the basics of the topic before the meeting. Interview the expert only when you have made yourself as expert as possible so that you have something intelligent and important to ask.

4. Have a plan for the interview, including specific questions. Don't go into an interview with a vague sense of what you want—"some information" on Topic X, for example. Jot down questions in a logical order and make every effort to proceed through your list. Don't be rude, pushy, or impatient, but politely try to keep the interview focused on specific questions and move it along toward the goal you have set. Sometimes the interviewee's asides or apparently irrelevant comments will turn out to be gold mines, but you should not count on that. The person being interviewed will respect you for having specific questions and a clear sense of direction.

5. Make a record of the interview. Take notes or record the interview on tape, being sure, of course, to secure the person's permission in advance in either case. Don't rely on memory to get the "drift" of the conversation, and don't think that the most important points will automatically stick with you. Of course, simply jotting down answers or even recording the whole meeting won't guarantee that you will understand all that was said or that you will emphasize the right portions; but it does mean that you will have something to look over or to listen to afterward to jog your memory or confirm what you thought was said.

6. Thank the interviewee orally and in writing. Common sense dictates that you thank the person at the time, and it should be equally obvious that every interview requires a written acknowledgment. Even if the person was cranky and useless, a prompt note of thanks is absolutely required.

7. Finally—and above all—treat the interviewee with the utmost respect before, during, and after the interview. Don't badger, fawn, or show your own feelings. Don't get into a debate, even though that's what the interviewee may really want. Don't expect too much (and, of course, don't settle too quickly for too little). Remember that the person who grants you an interview is giving you a gift: his or her time, skills, and knowledge.

Survey

While the interview elicits specialized knowledge from an individual, the survey gathers collective viewpoints from groups of persons. It thus provides opinions. Under certain circumstances, however, the survey can also yield information that may be classified as facts, observations, and interpretations. For example, demographic data gathered in a survey may be thought of as factual (within the conditions of surveys that we will discuss shortly): age, marital status, educational level, income, home ownership, and so on. If you have asked respondents about their views of how certain events are connected, you might say that you have gathered interpretations. For example, a question asking for a respondent's level of agreement with the statement "High deficits cause high interest rates" would yield interpretations—or, more precisely, opinions about interpretations. Because, as we saw in the last chapter, these distinctions get tricky, it is best, as a practical course, to think of surveys as providing collective opinions.

The value of surveys in doing this is generally described in terms of two qualities: validity and reliability. The term *validity* refers to the degree to which a survey yields the information that you want. A survey is said to be valid if it measures what it sets out to measure. For example, if a survey asks people to indicate which of three products they are most aware of based on TV advertising, it would be invalid to claim that the product that people are most aware of is the one they will actually buy. Their awareness may not be directly related to their decision to purchase. Validity is a question of the internal characteristics of the survey, that is, what it measures.

Reliability has to do with the predictive power of the survey. A survey is said to be reliable if its results can be replicated to a reasonable degree among a different group of respondents. If 54 percent of your respondents say they prefer sugarless soft drinks, the results can be considered reliable only if a similar response is obtained among other groups. If your first group included only dieters, you might suppose that the results will not be replicated among a group of people who are not dieters. Hence the survey would not be considered reliable for a broad range of the population, although it would be reliable within the given group if three versions of the survey administered to three groups of dieters produced the same results. Reliability, then, is a function of the persons surveyed rather than of the internal characteristics of the survey instrument.

Surveys are complex and are properly the subject of treatment by social scientists and statisticians. We cannot cover all aspects of survey research here, but within the two broad categories of validity (the internal characteristics of the instrument) and reliability (the characteristics of the group surveyed), we can provide some rough guidelines for using surveys to gain the information needed to solve a business problem.

Guidelines for Developing the Questionnaire

1. Limit the number of questions you ask. If you construct a questionnaire that asks everything you want to know, chances are that your respondents won't cooperate, or if they do, they will get bogged down and begin to answer too quickly. Select questions carefully to balance your need to get answers against your respondents' tolerance for being involved. Some very useful questionnaires ask only one or two questions, and often those answers are all that is really needed.

2. Phrase questions clearly to avoid ambiguity, tricks, or automatic responses. A respondent might readily be confused by a question like this: "If the presidential election were held today, and if your income were 20% higher than it is now, and if a third-party candidate were running, would you consider voting for a Democrat?" A question to which a respondent might feel obligated to answer one way is also useless: "Should executives be ethical?" Construct questions that are simple yet elicit useful information.

3. Aim for responses that can be readily tabulated to yield meaningful information. The simplest questions require yes or no answers, but sometimes you need to gauge degrees rather than poles. That's why scales of response are generally used in surveys. For example, you may want to know whether persons who have used a product like it. Instead of giving a yes-no choice, offer a range of possible responses that will better capture the reality of consumer attitudes. A five-part scale is typical: "agree strongly," "agree somewhat," "neutral," "disagree somewhat," "disagree strongly." Although you may also want to make room for comments, try to pin down responses to specifics that can be measured. An open-ended questionnaire is useful if you want people to speculate and make free associations, but it presents enormous difficulties in tabulation. Whenever possible, construct response categories that can be easily converted to numbers.

Guidelines for Selecting the Population

Before providing specific guidelines, it is necessary to discuss briefly the concept of sampling. Surveys gather representative opinions, and if the group surveyed is well selected, it is then possible, within certain constraints, to make generalizations about the larger populations that those groups represent. Of course, if there are thirty people in your class, you can, in fact, ask each of them to respond to certain questions and then say that this is what the class thinks. You have surveyed the entire population of that class. But if you want to find out what the entire school of fifteen hundred people think, you probably cannot survey them all. You have to choose a smaller group: a sample. That sample should be representative in characteristics of the population and large enough in total number to allow you to make generalizations about the population it represents. Our guidelines, then, relate to sample size and sample composition:

1. Select the largest practical sample. *Practical* is the operative term here. A practical sample size for a survey you are doing to write a paper for your marketing course will be smaller than the sample that Proctor & Gamble can use to test a new product. Although sample *composition* is more important than sample *size* in determining a survey's reliability, a good rule of thumb is that the minimum size of a sample is fifty, simply because descriptive statistics for smaller sizes lack meaning.

2. Use random sampling techniques to select the sample. A random sample is not a haphazardly selected one, but one in which the probability of inclusion of all the elements of the population is known. Although there are many variations of random sampling technique, the three most common are simple, stratified, and systematic.

(a) *Simple random sampling* gives every element of the population from which the sample is drawn the same chance of being selected. Drawing names from a hat is a common simple random sampling technique since every name in the hat has an equal chance of being pulled.

(b) *Stratified random sampling* puts all elements of the population into relevant categories and then uses simple random sampling to identify the sample. The result is that the gross characteristics of the sample reflect the gross characteristics of the population. For example, if the population is 60 percent female, you would separate men from women and randomly sample each group so that the total sample was 60 percent female.

(c) *Systematic random sampling* requires you to select the sample in a systematic or fixed way—for example, every fifth name from a list. Again, this approach ensures that every element of the population will have a known probability of appearing in the sample.

Sampling technique is a specialized branch of knowledge, with its own texts, experts, debates, and issues. If you use surveys as the source of information for business communication, you must become familiar with sampling technique so that the information you use is acceptable to those to whom you are communicating. Our discussion here should be considered merely an overview.

One other issue in using surveys that you should weigh is the mechanical process by which the questionnaires are administered. You can conduct a survey by phone, in person, or by mail. Each approach has advantages and disadvantages, and the choice depends on convenience, time, and cost. The most direct method is obviously to administer the survey in person, but this method is often not practical. Again, you should become familiar with the specialized knowledge in this field if you expect to rely on surveys for identifying information to be used in documents or talks.

Literature

Probably the most familiar source of business information is literature. We don't mean poetry or fiction, of course, but publications. For our purpose here, the term *literature* refers to documents that are external to the firm. Plenty of information is published internally in a variety of forms, but we will concentrate on public literature. We can classify this public literature into two types: primary material and secondary material or indexes. The latter are access tools that provide entrance to the former. Because the primary material actually supplies the information, we'll start with a brief description of various types of primary published materials and then took at the indexes that help you access the primary materials. In a search, of course, the indexes are the first items you use.

Primary materials include periodicals, books, and reports. Periodicals are also called serials. They are commonly called magazines and newspapers, but the terms *periodicals* and *serials* are more inclusive and also suggest the key feature of these items: They are published on a regular basis—daily, weekly, monthly, or whatever. We can further divide periodicals into the popular and the professional. Popular magazines and newspapers are meant for a wide audience of lay readers; professional journals are for specialists. Many so-called popular business periodicals do, however, carry quite specialized information, but it is broader and written for a nonspecialist audience. Table 5–1 lists a number of popular business sources. *The Wall Street Journal*, for example, is a business newspaper of wide circulation that is read by many people for its excellent political and social coverage, but it is a particularly useful source of detailed economic and financial news: daily stock and bond reports, news about executive changes, and company information of all sorts.

TABLE 5–1. Some Common Business Periodicals

Popular	Professional
The Wall Street Journal	*Harvard Business Review*
The New York Times	*Journal of Business*
Business Week	*Journal of Accountancy*
Barron's	*Journal of Marketing*
Fortune	*Journal of Marketing Research*
Forbes	*Journal of Finance*
	Administrative Science Quarterly
	Management Science
	Personnel Journal
	Personnel
	Academy of Management Journal
	Journal of the Academy of Marketing Science
	The Accounting Review
	Accountancy

Books differ from periodicals in being published once (although, of course, they may be reissued in revised editions). Books are obviously less timely than periodicals, but they are usually more definitive. Studies of specialized topics, general works on subjects like marketing practices and management techniques, and reference volumes (dictionaries, encyclopedias, and factbooks) are all books that may provide information about business topics.

Reports fall somewhere between periodicals and books in their publication characteristics and definitiveness. Reports are issued by government agencies, foundations, universities, and professional societies. They are generally quite specialized, dealing with a limited topic. Census reports, for example, are rich sources of demographic data that marketing specialists must be familiar with. The reports of accounting societies set standards for the field. Reports on wages, unemployment, and exports and imports, as well as other government documents, are often valuable for business topics.

Getting at the information you need in periodicals, books, and reports requires a knowledge of indexes. Be aware that indexes are secondary materials—that is, not the source of information but guides for finding the information. Table 5–2 lists some common indexes.

The New York Times Index, for example, indexes that newspaper. If you wanted to find information about leveraged buyouts, you would consult that entry in the index and from it get the titles and dates of articles in the *Times* on the subject. You would *not* get listings of what appeared in other publications, only those in the *Times*. The *Business Periodicals Index* is probably the best general guide to materials on business topics appearing in a great many popular and specialized pe-

TABLE 5–2. Indexes to Business Information

Indexes to Specific Periodicals	Indexes to Multiple Periodicals
The Wall Street Journal Index	*Business Periodicals Index*
The New York Times Index	*Readers' Guide to Periodical Literature*
Barron's Index (Published with	*Public Affairs Information Service Bulletin*
The Wall Street Journal Index)	*Insurance Index*
	Accounting Articles
	Accountants' Index
	Personnel Management Abstracts

riodicals. The *Readers' Guide to Periodical Literature* is broader than the *Business Periodicals Index* and would be useful for topics of more general interest relating to business—for example, the growth in two-income families and the effect of this phenomenon on marketing might be treated more broadly, with attention to its social dimensions, in periodicals other than those surveyed in the *Business Periodicals Index*. Here the *Readers' Guide* would be a helpful complement. The more specialized indexes to professional journals help you to access scholarly articles. Examples of these indexes are also given in Table 5–2.

Probably the most familiar "index" is the catalog of the college or public library. Every student is familiar with this tool, and it is indeed a great one. But recognize that the catalog merely indexes the literature held in that particular library. If you look up "Footwear—imports" in your college catalog, you will probably find books and government reports on that topic, and if you are using a large research library, you can have confidence that you are getting a good sample of the available literature. But the catalog is limited to the books and other separately published items that that library holds. There is bound to be more information, and perhaps better and more timely information, available in other sources. Don't stop with the library catalog.

You should be aware that many of these indexes are published electronically and are available in computerized search services. Table 5–3 lists some common reference services accessible through computers. Most college libraries provide such services, sometimes for a fee. They scan large data bases according to search words that you provide and print out references (author, title, and place and date of publication) that you then secure directly through the library. They also often give short summaries, called abstracts, that let you know whether the article or report in question covers the topic you are researching. Computerized data bases speed the literature search, but they really offer nothing generically different from what you can find in published indexes.

The enormous quantity and range of literature on business topics

TABLE 5–3. Some Computerized Search Services for Business Information

Data Bases (Available Through On-line Vendors)
ABI/Inform
Management Contents

On-line Vendors (Which Search Data Bases)
DIALOG
Dow Jones & Co.
BRS
Dunsprint
CompuServe
A. C. Nielsen
SDC Search Service

make a complete survey out of the question here. You should simply be aware of the types of publications available and then develop a more specialized familiarity as you research particular topics.

Documenting Information

Information derived from interviews, surveys, and literature should be considered an asset that you are using to reach a particular communication goal in writing a report or giving an oral presentation. It is valuable. It supports your argument; it convinces people that you are right and that you have "done your homework." You must therefore be careful to document the information you use. There are three broad reasons to document information: to credit the source, to support the claim you are making, and to allow your readers or hearers to check the information and make use of it themselves.

When information is proprietary—that is, when it comes from and really belongs to someone else—honesty requires documentation. For example, if *Business Week* hired reporters and paid their expenses to get a story, the information in the story is theirs, and if you use it, you must give proper credit. Failure to do so puts you in violation of the law and makes you subject to legal penalties. Failure to document may also subject you to academic penalties; plagiarism, the use of someone else's material as if it were yours, is a serious offense in colleges.

Self-protection is thus one good reason to document. Strengthening your argument is another. Quoting *Business Week* or a government report adds credibility to your case by showing people that it is based on more than your own ideas or efforts. Documentation also allows your audience to follow up on what you've said, to dig more deeply into a topic by referring to the sources you've cited. So it's good practice to document fully when you use information that you didn't develop on your own. We'll now briefly describe two methods of documentation commonly used in reports. Then we'll look at the special problems that the need for documentation causes when you are using information in an oral presentation.

Documenting Written Communications

In a report or a memo that you prepare for a class or on the job, you can credit sources through either notes or references. Notes—called *footnotes* if they are placed at the foot of a page or simply *notes* if they appear at the very end of the whole document—list the sources of your information. If you are documenting a published source, you include the author (if given), the title of the work, and the relevant publishing information. For an article, the publishing information includes the title of the article, the periodical in which it appears, the date, and the page references. For a book, the publishing information includes the book's title, the place and date of publication, the publisher's name, and the page references. Various styles are used. Table 5–4 shows several sample notes in a simple style. The style you use may vary according to corporate policy or a professor's requirements. The operating principles are always the same: Supply full information, and be consistent throughout a single document.

Notes are keyed to the text by numbers that appear after the cited material, usually in superscript—above the line. A reader wishing to know your source then looks at the corresponding note. The numbers run consecutively through the document, and each citation is given its own number, even though the material may come from the same source.

References are used quite differently. In the reference system, all sources receive a number. The sources, listed at the end of the piece, are arranged alphabetically by author, or chronologically by date of publication, or by order of appearance in the text. If there are six sources, they are numbered 1 through 6. References to them in the text are by that number, often also with a page reference following the source number. These numbers are put in parentheses (sometimes in superscripts, but that method of numbering may be too easily confused with the note system) after the citation. In this system, it is thus possible that the first reference number you find will not be 1, as it must be in the note system. Numbers are keyed to the order of the reference list, not to the order of citation in the text. Numbered references are most

TABLE 5–4. Notes and References

Sample Notes

Book	[1]Thomas J. Peters and Robert H. Waterman, Jr., *In Search of Excellence: Lessons from America's Best-Run Companies* (New York: Harper & Row. 1982), p. 81.
Article	[2]Bryan Burrough, "Collapse of an Old-Boy Oil Network Places Tesoro in Vulnerable Position for Takeover," *The Wall Street Journal*, 12 June 1984, p. 37.
Report	[3]U.S. Department of Education, *The Nation Responds: Recent Efforts to Improve Education*, Washington, D.C., 1984, pp. 8–12.

Sample References (in Alphabetical Arrangement)

1. Burrough, Bryan. "Collapse of an Old-Boy Oil Network Places Tesoro in Vulnerable Position for Takeover," *The Wall Street Journal*, 12 June 1984, 1. [*note:* In the text, the source is cited by number, with page numbers following. Example: (1,6). This means page 6 of reference 1.]

2. Peters, Thomas and Robert H. Waterman, Jr. *In Search of Excellence: Lessons from America's Best-Run Companies*. New York: Harper & Row. 1982.

3. U.S. Department of Education. *The Nation Responds: Recent Efforts to Improve Education*. Washington, D.C., 1984.

common, but sometimes the author's name is used instead of a number. Thus you might find "Continued high inflation will cause political pressure on the Federal Reserve to contain the money supply (Arkwright, 23)." Arkwright is the author whose work is referred to. The full citation is given in the list of sources at the end of the document. The point in question is made in page 23 of Arkwright's article.

Whether you use notes or references, the kind of publication information that you give is generally standard if you are citing published material. Documenting interviews or the results of surveys is somewhat less standardized. If you are quoting something said to you in an interview, you can use a note like this: "James Hartley, interview with the author, 23 January 1984." Or if a section of your paper is based on your interview, you can state that in the text ("In an interview on 23 January 1984, James Hartley made several observations on this subject") or in a note referring to the whole section and appearing at the end of that section. Information from a survey should be treated similarly, with a clear indication in the text itself or a note that covers the relevant section—for example, "These data were developed in an interview of thirty-five college students conducted in January of 1984 at Chico State College." If your report is based largely on a survey, some part of the report should be devoted to a discussion of the survey itself—how and when it was conducted, the statistical assumptions made, and so on. From then on in the report, you may omit specific documentation as long as the source is clear.

Students often wonder when to document and tend to swing to one of two extremes: providing no specific documentation at all or putting footnotes on every sentence. Common sense should help you to find the balance between these two extremes. As a general rule, you *must* document direct quotations. You *must* also document proprietary information—that is, specific information (for example, statistics) developed by someone else. And you should generally document all information that is not common knowledge. It's common knowledge that the pound sterling is the official currency of the United Kingdom (you don't need to tack a note on that), but it is not common knowledge that the relationship between the pound and the Japanese yen may fluctuate in indirect proportion to the fate of British cricket teams. If indeed someone makes that argument, you need to document it because few people would regard that as common knowledge.

Documenting Oral Presentations

Notes and references are easy in written communication, but what do you do if you are giving a talk? Many talks are based on information derived from other sources and hence also need documentation. In a speech, if you are quoting someone, you should clearly indicate the source (by name if that is appropriate) and show through a use of your hands or voice where the quotation begins and ends. Similarly, with information that is not directly quoted but that is the result of someone else's work, indicate in the speech that you are now using data you found in such-and-such a report or article or book. Documentation in a talk is oral, but be ready to back it up in writing. You should have available a list of your sources keyed to your text so you can hand it to anyone in the audience who expresses an interest or challenges a point. Some speakers like to hand out a sheet of references before or after their talk. This practice not only ensures conformity with fairness and the law but also strengthens the points you are making and enhances your credibility as a knowledgeable person who has done her or his homework.

Exercises

1. Using only the card catalog of your college library, note the number and type of sources you locate on the following topics:

(a) Productivity in the U.S. auto industry.

(b) Capital investment in the United States by foreign governments and private investors.

(c) ERISA.

(d) Operations research.

(e) Theory X and Theory Y management.

(f) Computer manufacturing in West Germany.

Is each topic listed in the catalog as it is here? Or did you have to do some sorting and shifting to find the entries?

2. Look up the same topics as in Exercise 1 in the most recent year's edition of *Business Periodicals Index*. What differences in the number and type of sources do you find? Which approach yields the "best" information? Why?

3. Which of the following topics should you look up in (a) the card catalog, (b) the *Business Periodicals Index*, or (c) *The New York Times Index*? Why?

	a	b	c
"Employment at will"			
U.S. trade deficits			
J. M. Keynes			
Westinghouse			
Inventory control			
Griggs v. *Duke Power*			
Apple, Inc.			
Cotton production in China			
U.S. Steel			

4. Construct a simple survey to determine the attitude of new students toward your college's social life. List the questions you would ask. Identify the sample and explain how you chose it. What should you do to assess validity and reliability? Explain what information you will gain from the survey and how you might use it to make a report.

5. Prepare a reading list of what you consider the five most useful published items you can find on one of the following topics:

(a) Quality circles.

(b) Nonprofit accounting.

(c) Zero-based budgeting.

(d) Investing in municipal bonds.

How did you identify these items. That is, what sources did you use to locate them? What standards did you use to determine usefulness?

6. Identify the most important scholarly and professional journals in your field (for example, accounting, marketing, or retailing). Examine the documentation system used in each. (Some may even have a special note telling contrib-

utors how to document material, and others may refer contributors to a specific style manual.) Is one system common to all the major journals in your field? Which seems more popular, the note or the reference system?

7. Organize each of the following groups of information into note form and then reference form.

    (a) "How to Increase Your Insurance Protection" was published by Harry Higgins in the April 7, 1985, issue of *Invest* magazine on pages 18 through 27.

    (b) Barry Lehman's book *Money and Banking* gives the information on page 281. The book was published in 1980 by Harvard University Press in Cambridge.

    (c) In the *Journal of Retailing*, Susan Kane and Dennis Black published "Inventory Control for the Specialty Shop." The information is on page 8. The article was published in volume 12 in the spring of 1984.

    (d) The article "Consumer Price Index Found Wanting" is on the front page of the *Denver Post* of July 4, 1986.

    (e) Stanford Greenberg gave this information on page 92 of *Human Resource Management*. The book was published in 1987 by Harper & Row in New York.

    (f) Professor Claudia Dawkins gave these data in an interview on October 9, 1984.

8. A survey of 100 students at Montgomery County Community College revealed that 60 were aware of their advisers. Of these, 50 percent felt their advisers did a "good" or "excellent" job of providing academic information. There are 4,200 students at the college. The 100 respondents to the survey were interviewed as they came out of the registrar's office during the drop-add period. Answer the following questions:

    (a) Is it *valid* to conclude that "60 percent of the students at the college know their advisers"? Why or why not?

    (b) Is it *valid* to conclude that "half of the students at the college think their advisers do a 'good' or 'excellent' job of providing academic information"? Why or why not?

    (c) How could you test the *reliability* of the survey results?

    (d) Comment on the size and selection of the sample.

    (e) Suggest additional kinds of information that you might want to gather (by survey or other means) to complement the data from this survey in the preparation of a report to the dean of students on academic advising.

Macrocomposing

As the last two chapters have shown, a professional in business is an *information broker*. Writing up the information finishes the investigation—or finishes one phase of the investigation.

Everyone, of course, has his or her own routine for writing. When you write you're required to do many things: Think about your information and your goal for writing, plan your approach, draft a text from the plan, reword things if they don't sound right, and think about how the reader will respond to your writing. Different writers spend different amounts of time—at different points in the writing—on each of these tasks. Rarely does anyone move straight ahead. Writers tend to circle back, now drafting, now looking for more information. Different writing assignments on the job also demand somewhat different routines. You may write a brief memo quickly, pulling information from your memory. A formal report may require months of information gathering, several preliminary plans and drafts, and several reviews by other readers before it works.

Whatever your individual process, however, ultimately you must incorporate four strategies for writing in organizations. One we call *macrocomposing*, that is, isolating the big picture of your document and structuring information to make that picture clear to the reader. That's the subject of this chapter. Chapter 7 deals with another strategy: *microcomposing*, that is, selecting the right words and composing effective sentences. Chapter 8 deals with the third strategy: *composing with visuals*. Chapter 9 discusses the fourth: *revising*.

The Goal: Writing That Works

Figure 6–1 shows the text of an announcement distributed to commuters on a suburban train line. The goal is to get the riders to understand the delays necessitated by track work.

Imagine the reader: late coming home in the evenings, stranded in a hot train sitting on the tracks miles from a station. The Southeastern Pennsylvania Transit Authority (SEPTA) wrote the announcement to explain the delays once, rather than having conductors explain them individually many times. The announcement takes up one page; certainly no longer explanation is desirable. SEPTA could have included lots of details, such as maps of the network and drawings of faulty cable but decided not to for this audience. Another report, for an oversight group, would indeed include engineering specifications.

The announcement has two goals: to explain the cause of the delays (overtly stated in Sentence 1 and illustrated in that paragraph and the next two) and to apologize (the last paragraph). The author chose to

Continuing Media—West Chester delays
caused by defective signal cable

The continuing delays on outbound trains on the Media—West Chester Regional Rail Line are being caused by deteriorated signal cables running from 49th Street Station to Media Station. Sections of the 30,000 feet of signal cable are in poor condition and must be replaced. This has caused SEPTA to instruct train crews to approach two inbound and two outbound signals at reduced speeds, then to stop before proceeding at restricted speed.

While delays on inbound trains have generally been minimal, outbound service is operating 10 to 15 minutes late due to the location of the inoperative signals. Those signals have forced slow train operation over long sections of the outbound railroad between 49th Street and Media.

Because of its present condition, a completely new and modern signal system is under design for the line. However, that system will not be in place until 1986 at the earliest. In the meantime, SEPTA personnel are replacing sections of the defective cable as quickly as possible and restoring the signals to normal or near normal operation. Service delays will continue until all of the cable replacements are made.

We sincerely apologize for the inconvenience this problem has caused. Nevertheless, we hope you understand that the slower service is necessary for a safe operation.

FIGURE 6–1. An announcement that works (*Source:* Notice distributed by SEPTA—the Southeastern Pennsylvania Transportation Authority, 10/84-2379-154. Used by permission).

explain *before* the apology, assuming that the explanation would win the reader to SEPTA's side and strengthen the weight of the apology. The author could have *started* with Paragraph 4, but that start might have seemed weak and uninformative. In structure, the announcement moves from effect (the continuing delays) to cause (deteriorated signal cables).[1] The whole announcement simply traces the chain of causes.

[1] For a discussion of cause-and-effect reasoning, see Chapter 4.

The Big Picture

Readers found the SEPTA statement simple to understand and convincing. Your writing in an organization should also ease the reader's understanding and produce conviction. When you have a lot of information to organize, that information itself may obscure the main point for a while. You have to sift through the facts to find connections. You need, as one writer puts it, to "break the code." To do so, try brainstorming:

1. Take out small, individual slips of paper or one large sheet—or open a file on a computer.

2. Jot down words that characterize your information. This list can be called your *data dump*. Figure 6–2 shows such a dump of topics concerning personnel problems at a deli. Don't put the words in any order. Let your associations skip from word to word. Don't censor anything, even if it seems a bit farfetched.

3. Live with the sheet for a while. Scratch in new items as they occur to you. Never erase.

4. Reread the list every now and then, and let your subconscious find connections.

5. Sort the items. Try different principles for selecting items that go together. Underline in a particular color all items that seem to belong in one group, or circle them and connect them with a line, or run through the computer file of notes in search of key words. (Some software will do this automatically, retrieving all items that include key words.) Figure 6–3 shows the data dump sorted. In sorting, think of different purposes to be served by your information for different readers.

6. Write down a general term that characterizes each of the groupings and make sure that the items you thought belong together really do. Account for any items straggling outside a category.

Brainstorming is a powerful technique for sorting information. The central principle, of course, is *classification*, that is, distributing items into groups. Build smaller groups into larger ones. The biggest is the big picture.

Organization

After you've shaped the groups, arrange them in support of your goal for writing. You may have to eliminate some information that isn't relevant to your purpose and develop other information to fill gaps.

part-time workers—little motivation

young manager

should we be open 24 hours?

college town crowd and workers at industrial plant

few sales in midnight—6 a.m. range

try to increase sales?

customer survey results—they think employees are sloppy, inconsiderate, and inattentive

employee survey: no incentives to work hard
  no sense of loyalty to the deli

shift schedules

any time everyone could meet?

training

low inventories of needed supplies

customer greeting: "What are you out of today?"

record of sales over two weeks
    breakout into sandwich types, groceries
    breakout by amount of sales per time period
    breakout of number of customers

night-shift person asleep most of the shift

faulty equipment, especially the fryer

even when we have potatoes, we can't get the fryer to work

peak hours of sales: during the week, 7:30–9; 11–2; 5:30–8
    weekends: 9–2, 5–midnight on Saturday; 11–3, 5–10 on Sunday

preparation tasks: clean grill and fryer, sanitize slicer, cut steaks, stock and clean store

motivation: monetary vs. nonmonetary

store identification: T-shirts for workers, hats

establish rules for employees

list equipment on sheet-have each shift report on the status of the equipment and supplies

MBO possible? employees set own performance standards, reviews in person with the manager

awards program? stars? happy faces? silly? have customers give them?

standard ways to increase productivity: automate or change store design

sense of belonging and teamwork and accomplishment needed to keep employees from just working for themselves.

compare the Taber Rd store with the Nelson St. one?

info about the Deli: location, annual revenues, # of employees, overview of the menu

FIGURE 6–2. Data dump of information—The Family Deli.

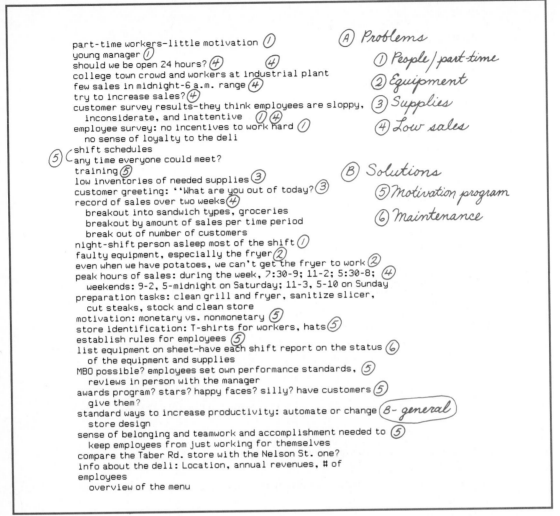

FIGURE 6–3. Data dump classified. Look for *key terms* by which you can *group* information and select an emphasis for the reader. Here, the writer has grouped information to isolate *problems* at the deli and some possible *solutions*.

Outlining

To discover and establish the best order for presentation, draw up an outline. If your assignment for writing stipulates an order, fit your information to that scheme. If not, then build an outline from your data dump. Use the traditional form if you're comfortable with it:

I.
  A.
  B.
    1.
    2.

Many people in business resist linear outlines. At least for the first cut at their material, they use *nonlinear* plans. For example, they may sketch the branching of items from a key word or statistic, as in Figure 6–4, which shows the implications of the term *nonmonetary motivation.* Be careful to balance the branches; one very long branch may indicate insufficient development of other topics. Originally the author began her branching from the term *motivation,* with two branches: monetary and nonmonetary. But the "monetary" one stopped dead at the second level because the deli had little money for an increase in wages or incentive programs. Therefore she concentrated on the other side: nonmentary. Or you may want to line up material in rows and columns. Such a device helps not only to order what you already have, but also, like any structuring device, to predict what's needed. Empty spaces indicate a need for more information (Figure 6–5). If you like flowcharts, use one to sequence the arrival of information in your document as you would sequence the arrival of equipment on a construction site (see Chapter 8).

    Figure 6–6 shows an outline form that reinforces the need to subordinate evidence to a main point. One writer has programmed this form to appear on his screen whenever he begins to organize a docu-

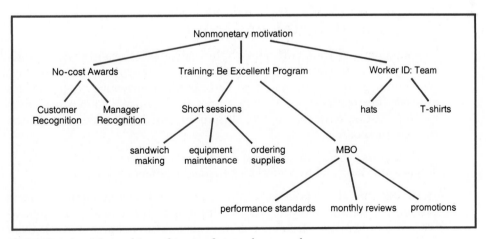

FIGURE 6–4. A branching of topics from a key word.

Deli location	yearly sales	market segment	inventory	workers
Taber Rd.	$100 k	50% students 20% factory 10% small business 20% other	supplies: $X equipment: $Y	FT: 1 manager PT: 10 college students
Nelson St.	$150 k	50% neighborhood 20% factory 20% students 10% other	supplies: $A equipment: $B	FT: 1 manager 1 other PT: 4 college students, 3 high school students

FIGURE 6–5. A tabular comparison of two delis.

ment. But you don't need a computer; simply outline the columns on a large sheet of paper and fill in your information in pencil:

1. Place a one-sentence summary of the big picture—your *control statement*—right at the top. The summary will serve as a constant target and a corrective to wandering thoughts.

2. Distribute your information. Start, if you'd like, with the appendix and work backward. Exploit opportunities to siphon details into visuals (noted as "grph" for "graph" on the chart). Check the balance of emphasis and the amount of discussion devoted to each topic. Work in any direction; the result will be a pattern of presentation from left to right, top to bottom.

3. Think globally. You can see the whole of the document on one screen (or printed out on one side of one sheet of paper) and thus check on the flow and turns in your discussion. Make sure, for example, that anything suggested in the introduction is developed later.

Direct and Indirect Order

As you construct your outline—whatever form you use—think not only about your information but about your best approach to the reader. When your goal is to inform, and you assume that your reader is eager to learn the results of your work to get on with his or her work, then be direct. Start with the control statement that summarizes the results and the purpose:

> *Control statement:* This memo suggests some practices to motivate our part-time help and to control supplies and equipment at the deli.

Assuming that the reader is familiar with the deli's problems—and is looking for solutions—you address the suggestions head on. If, however, you sense that the reader is unaware of the problems—or is even deliberately trying to ignore them—then you might proceed indirectly.

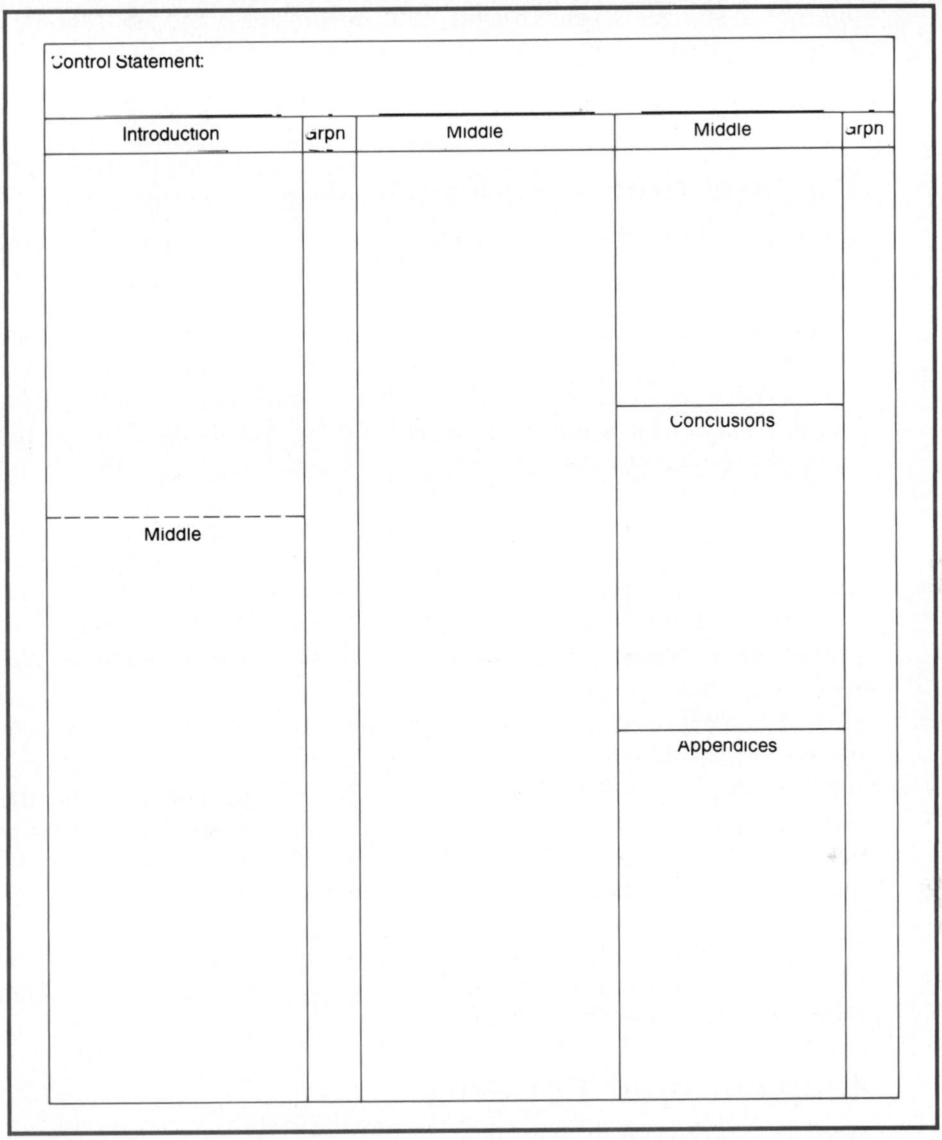

Control Statement:

Introduction	Grpn	Middle	Middle	Grpn

Middle

Conclusions

Appendices

FIGURE 6–6. A large-sheet outline (courtesy of Earl Grim. Based on a concept developed by Dolores Landreman).

Build your case first. Lead the reader through your analysis of the problem. Establish or confirm the reader's confidence in you. Persuade the reader to agree. A bald statement of the solutions might threaten or anger the reader and might keep the reader from reading. Bring in the control statement near the end of the document—although, of course, as the *writer* you should know that statement *before* you write. Chapters 13–20 provide detailed advice on direct and indirect ordering in letters and reports. Most of the time, for most documents, be direct.

Introduction–Middle–Ending

The outline form shown in Figure 6–6 reinforces another important concern in ordering information: *All* documents of whatever length, whether direct or indirect in their approach to the reader, have three segments: an introduction, a middle, and an ending. In a memo, the introduction and the ending may consist of one sentence each. In a report, those segments may consist of two or three pages, and the middle may extend for a hundred pages or more. Yet the *function* of the segments remains the same:

- *Introduction:* In a *direct* document, the introduction overtly states the results of the investigation, the writer's purpose, and the plan of the document to prepare the reader for reading. In an *indirect* document, the introduction begins to build the case, often with a narrative of the problem, a statement of authorization, and/or a setting of the context.
- The *middle* provides the proof, arranged in segments clearly connected to the big picture.
- The *ending* finishes the discussion. A *direct* document ends on the last main topic promised or recapitulates the big picture. In an *indirect* document, the ending states the big picture, often in terms of a recommendation, a call to action, or a final sales pitch.

The beginning and the ending of the document receive the greatest attention from the reader, so make sure that your main point is clear there—not buried in the middle.

Conventional Patterns

Within the segments of a document—particularly in the middle, which often presents the greatest organizational challenge—arrange your material in a conventional pattern. You have several choices. Here are the most common in business writing:

- Cause and effect (often, problem and solution).
- Classification and analysis.
- Comparison and contrast.
- Narrative.

Cause and Effect

Figure 6–1 on the delayed train, for example, moves from *effect* to *cause*. You might structure a memo on the deli from *problem* to *solution:*

- Problems in supplies.
- Problems in equipment.
- Problems in worker motivation.
- Inventory practices recommended to prevent shortages.
- Practices recommended to maintain equipment.
- Recommended motivational program.

Classification and Analysis

Instead of moving from problem to solution, you may *classify* your information. For example, sort customers at the deli into different groups to arrive at a picture of your market:

- Students.
- Workers at a nearby factory.
- Workers from small businesses in the area.

You might also present an *analysis* of your sales over a two-week period to determine, for example, the peak sales periods or the major products sold.

Comparison and Contrast

You may be able to understand and explain one set of information best if you see it and present it in comparison with another. Ask, "How is X like Y"? For example, in announcing the United Way campaign in a large organization in 1986, the campaign leaders chose to compare the United Way with Halley's comet which appeared in that year. The memo began with a paragraph on the comet:

> The year 1986 is a special one because Halley's comet will pass close enough to earth for many of us to see it. Unlike "falling stars" or meteorites which blaze across the night sky and burn out, Halley's continues. Although it is always present in our star system and has a definite orbit, it is visible to us on earth only once every 75 years.

The memo then continued:

> Halley's comet and the United Way have much in common. The United Way, through its member agencies, is always present in our community. The assistance the United Way provides, though not always visible, provides service to one of every three people in our county. . . .

The last paragraph tied the analogy together:

> To see Halley's comet may be the chance of a lifetime, but your contribution to the United Way is a chance to help the people of our community every day.[2]

The memo was developed *by analogy*, that is, by a special form of comparison. Just make sure that the two items resemble each other more than they differ.

One salesperson for citrus fruit began a sales letter this way:

> Citrus fruits vary as much as people, so their size, color, rind thickness, etc., are not uniform.

People and fruit, however, didn't really have enough in common. A few sentences later, the author abandoned the comparison. But reasoning by analogy *can* work well. Look for similarities, for example, between a retailing problem where you work and some problem you've read about in a management class. Apply the textbook analysis to the new conditions. Or look within your material for similar items. For example, you could *compare* the Taber Road store with the Nelson Street store. Analyze your information first according to some criteria: yearly sales, market segment, inventory, or workers. Then frame your comparison (as a linear form of Figure 6–5):

Taber Road
    Yearly sales
    Market segment
    Inventory
    Workers
Nelson Street
    Yearly sales
    Market segment
    Inventory
    Workers

Or:

Yearly sales
    Taber Road
    Nelson St.
And so on

For another form of comparison, assume that your boss has asked you to come up with ways to increase productivity at the Taber Road deli.

---

[2]Written by Paula Dayton for the 1986 United Way Publicity Committee, E. I. Du Pont, Chambers Works. Used by permission.

She's mentioned that a change in the design of the store seems a likely solution. You know that design changes can aid in enhancing retailing productivity, as can automation, but you think the *real* problem is the attitudes of the part-time help. Develop your comparison of the alternative solutions, then, *by order of elimination:*

- Problem: low productivity
- Criteria for solution
- Solution 1: Design changes
- Solution 2: Automation
- Solution 3: Worker motivation programs

Present each solution in terms of such criteria as cost, amount of time needed to implement, and ease of implementation. Make sure that you apply the same criteria to *each* solution.

Narrative

A *narrative* is a tracing of events over time. Write a narrative of the events, in chronological order, that led to the current problems in the store. Or record, task-by-task as you performed these tasks, your efforts to solve the problem. A narrative, however, presents each event at the same level of importance. It doesn't emphasize. Often, one of the other patterns is more efficient.

These conventional patterns are simple. Look for them within the complexity of your information. Then line up that information to make the pattern show. Chapter 19 provides detailed examples of the patterns in action in reports.

Cues to Readers

When you have found a good structure for your information, your macrolevel work is almost done. *Almost.* You still need to make that structure obvious to the reader. You need to make the page *look* inviting and easy to read. A page of solid text is often uninviting. Balance white space and text. Highlight important points with underlining or boldface type (but don't overuse either one). Look for information that can be put into list form. Incorporate visuals to highlight the discussion and to vary the method of presentation. Indeed, think of the whole page—and the whole document—as a visual. What the page *looks* like sends as much of a message as what the page *says* in words and numbers. Figures 8–3 and 8–4 (in Chapter 8), for example, show two notices: One is inviting in design, and the other is just solid text. Several features of document design are discussed in Part II of the text. Here, let's focus on three devices for cuing readers: parallelism, headings, and paragraphing.

Parallelism

One important cue is *parallelism*, the expression of like ideas in like form. That repetition of form works at many levels. For example, all documents in a series should look alike: same cover design, same main segments, and same page layout. Within a document, the segments should be parallel. If, for example, you are discussing six characteristics of a *manual* filing and posting system in contrast with an *electronic* one, then the discussion of electronic data processing should follow those same six characteristics, in the same order. Check for parallelism in your outline as a way of troubleshooting imbalances in development. Comparable visuals should also be parallel in scale and design. Be particularly careful with lists, either within sentences or consisting of several sentences. Use bullets or numbers to itemize the list and to make them stand out on the page. Select an appropriate *enumerator* term to govern the logic of the list, and make sure that each item is indeed part of the same class and is put in the same form as the first item. Good parallelism builds momentum, underlines elements in a comparison or series, and aids the reader in skimming a text or visuals.

Headings

Another important cue to the structure of a text is *headings*. Headings break up the page, direct the reader to topics and turns in your presentation, and aid the reader in remembering your main points. Most business documents use them. Headings provide markers for *segments* in a text in the way that commas, for example, group and separate phrases and clauses within a sentence. Headings are generally derived directly from your outline. They come in two kinds: descriptive and informative. Descriptive headings are general labels for the parts of routine documents, for example, "Introduction," "Conclusion," and "Recommendations." Informative headings are specialized. They derive from the subject matter of the document itself, for example, "Trends," "Colors," "Widths," "Colorado Avalanche Warning Program," "The Seward Highway Example in Alaska." Although you will use some descriptive headings, prefer informative ones, particularly in the middle of long documents. Two cautions: First, although you will frequently use the heading "Introduction," *never* head the middle section of your report "Middle" or "Body." Those are terms used to *talk about* that segment, not to be used in the document itself. Second, avoid broad headings like "The Facts" or "The Selection." Tie down the idea.

Headings also indicate the *levels* of discussion. They show what fits within what. The *title* is a heading for the whole document. Then you may include *first-order headings* that define major segments. Major headings for routine reports are usually preestablished. Use them. Your company may also have a specific scheme for headings in nonroutine reports. If so, follow it. Figure 10–1 in Chapter 10 shows different typefaces for headings. Here's a common way to indicate the levels:

0 ORDER HEADING

(Chapter title—centered, bold, underlined, capped)

FIRST-ORDER HEADING

(Major head in chapter—centered, bold, capped)

Second-Order Heading

(Heading within major segment—centered, underlined/upper and lower case)

Third-Order Heading

(Heading within subsegment—at left margin, underlined, upper and lower case)

Fourth-Order Heading

(Heading within subsubsegment—indented, underlined, upper and lower case)

Fifth-Order Heading. The heading is run in at the beginning of the paragraph of text.

Headings should not exceed one line of type; usually a few words will do. All the headings at the same level should be parallel. Subheads should also be logical components of the main heading. If the main heading is "Steps," for example, then make sure each subhead is indeed a step. Try to minimize the number of heading levels. It's often confusing for a reader to have to delve down very many layers into the subsubsubsegments of your discussion. In revising, look for ways to enrich the headings and to reduce the number of levels if you find you're into fourth- and fifth-order headings.

Headings in sales letters and other persuasive documents often bear the sales messages in full sentences:

THE SYSTEM IS DESIGNED FOR **YOU**
MIS Makes Accounting Easy

Where headings are simple terms, however, generally avoid *the* before the heading.

Paragraphing

A third cue—and probably the major cue to the reader about how to read your discussion—is *paragraphing*. When you divide your text into paragraphs, you provide signals about components of the discussion and you help to pace the reading. In dividing the whole discussion into components, however, you must also make sure that the components *connect*, that is, that the whole is coherent. You don't want the reader to fall between the cracks.

Marking Components

The three major segments of a discussion, as we've seen, are the introduction, the middle, and the ending. In a short document, one paragraph—or less—may be devoted to each function. A brief memo may contain one paragraph that is both introduction and middle and may close with a one-sentence paragraph like "I look forward to hearing your comments on this matter." Longer documents will have more clearly articulated major segments. Moreover, each segment itself will be divided into component paragraphs. Each paragraph discusses some core of information that can be identified as separate from other cores. The paragraphs must connect externally as components of an entire discussion; sentences within each paragraph must also connect. That connection is fostered by certain signalling devices whose use is shown in the model paragraphs that follow:

- Pronouns that stand for earlier nouns.
- Summarizing and predicting terms *(These delays, Those signals, these issues, Both parties)*.
- Repetition of key terms.
- Signal words or phrases:
    To add: *in addition, moreover, also, first, second.*
    To contrast: *but, on the other hand, however.*
    To sum up: *finally, in conclusion, as a result.*

To cite: *for example, as an illustration, for instance.*
To change scale: *more broadly, in detail.*

Within a segment or a whole document, paragraphs perform introductory, supporting, ending and transitional functions.

An *introductory* paragraph provides the context and briefs the reader about what's to come:

Predicting
Term
Adding Terms

> This report on the preferences of workers over 55 years old in planning for retirement is divided into <u>two</u> parts. **First,** the report details the results of our survey of a sample of 150 employees. **Second,** the report suggests some implications of that survey for corporate retirement policy.

Once the framework is established, then *supporting paragraphs* provide the back-up details wrapped around core subpoints, each point given a paragraph. Often, the first sentence of the paragraph is the link that connects what was given in the paragraph above with the new material to be developed in the paragraph to come. Note how this first sentence, for example, cues the reader:

Adding Term

> <u>Another advantage</u> of locating in Ireland is the access that location provides to the countries of the European Economic Community.

The adding term "another advantage" reminds the reader that at least one advantage has already been presented and that a pattern of discussion of advantages will be maintained in the new paragraph. The rest of the sentence predicts the evidence to come: facts or opinions about why Ireland would provide good access to the EEC. Indeed, this paragraph could be a framework for several subsequent paragraphs, each detailing market or other data for one EEC country.

Unless you have some reason for indirection, build an opening sentence that the rest of the paragraph can either restrict or expand on. Here's a paragraph that restricts the theme in the first sentence:

Repetition
Repetition

Pronoun
Adding Term
Repetition
Contrast

> Many executives are <u>skillful</u> at avoiding <u>conflict</u> with coworkers. But that very <u>skill</u> may cause organizational problems. When <u>different</u> people hold <u>conflicting</u> opinions about something, those <u>differences</u> can inhibit action, of course. But **they** may also be the source of innovation. *Moreover,* smoothing over <u>conflict</u> may only postpone inevitable difficulties. The real skill, then, is not in avoiding <u>conflicts,</u> **but** in managing conflicts to advance the goals of the organization.

Here's another paragraph that expands on the opening sentence (note, by the way, how the word "also" in the opener cues you to this paragraph's position in the middle of a discussion):

Adding Term
Repetition

Pronoun

Contrasting
Phrase

Pronoun/
Contrasting
Phrase

Americans and Europeans <u>also</u> differ in how they assess someone's credentials. **Americans** are apt to judge people by their accomplishments. In response to a question like "Tell me about yourself," *they* list primarily their education and work experience. "I went to college at . . . ," "I worked for . . . ," "I am a [doctor, lawyer, Indian chief]," are typical responses. **On the other hand,** Europeans are often judged by, and judge others by, their family connections and their professional associates. When asked about themselves, *they* tend to respond *more indirectly* with information that connects *them* to people: "My mother, Frau Doktor Wilmanns of Munich, has had an important influence on me."

This paragraph balances its evidence on the contrast between Americans and Europeans concerning one topic: credentials. (Note, by the way, the consistent use of plurals to maintain a coherent point of view.) Some paragraphs enumerate the evidence; they move through equal items in some category, for example, alternative fund-raising methods, advantages of a computer system, or a series of steps in a process. After the subject is announced, each following sentence has the same shape (see Chapter 7 for more on sentence shape) into which new information is inserted. That parallel shape reminds the reader that the points of information match, and that each is equal in weight to the other. Here's a paragraph that develops by enumeration:

Repetition

Pronouns

The university is a big organization that performs many roles in addition to teaching and research. <u>As an</u> entertainer, **it** stages dramatic events, musical events, and athletic events. <u>As a</u> restaurateur, **it** feeds 55 thousand students and faculty every day. <u>As a</u> hotel keeper, **it** houses 30 thousand students in many varieties of accommodations. <u>As a</u> security force, **it** maintains order and discipline among all the constituents. And <u>as a</u> transportation department, **it** maintains the roads, the parking lots, and the garages.

Once you have established a pattern, stick to it. Don't for the sake of some foolish variety, or by accident, send the reader mixed signals about how to read.

Ending paragraphs finish off the discussion—either the whole document or one segment of the document. Here's the ending paragraph of a letter to stockholders that built to a positive conclusion after an opener and middle that gave bad news:

| Contrasting
Term
Repetition
Summing
up Term | <u>In spite</u> of slippage in the product development program, new products coming on stream are expected to contribute significantly to **sales and profits. Revenues** from new products, combined with ongoing sales of existing products, *thus* lead us to reasonable prospects of improved results in the third quarter. |

In long reports, you may need to show how segments connect to other segments. For this purpose you use *transitional* paragraphs. These add no new information; they just remind the reader about the territory already covered in the discussion and preview the next segment.

| Summing
up Phrase
Summary and
Prediction | Having examined <u>three problem areas</u> in our operation—inventory control, waiter service, and bookkeeping—let's turn to a description of the **solution** for all of these: a Management Information System. |

Pacing the Reading

Transitional paragraphs allow the reader some breathing space. They are usually short—welcome relief if the rest of the discussion has exhausted the reader. Readers read at different rates. Some are highly motivated and willing to work. Some need to be cajoled. As you write, consider the reader's capacity for paying attention. Use short paragraphs for difficult information and less motivated readers, longer ones for easy material and the motivated. Break up a series of long paragraphs with a short one for emphasis. Never allow a whole page without a paragraph break. On the other hand, avoid a page of one-sentence, and thus undeveloped, paragraphs.

Many business documents are *flat;* item of information follows item of information without shape. There is no sense of levels, no changes in terrain, no changes in pace and emphasis. There is no obvious introduction, middle, and ending. The reader doesn't know what's important. The reader also has trouble *finding* what's needed because it's buried someplace where he or she is never told to look for it. Good writing displays information in meaningful levels with meaningful connections. It works for the reader.

Exercises

1. In the library (or at home or at a telephone company office), find the yellow pages from telephone directories for at least two different areas: an urban and a rural directory or perhaps two cities. Then examine the entries under one category, for example, "Accountants—Public." Generate as many data as you can from the listings. For example, count the total number of listings in the category in each directory; note any similarities in entries (listings for national

firms, for example); count the number of boldface and display entries as opposed to plain ones; count private practices as opposed to group practices; assess (by telephone exchange or address) the geographic spread of the offices. Then play with different ways to write up a comparison. Develop a control statement *for the record* that summarizes the material as broadly as possible, and sketch an outline (linear or nonlinear) for incorporating the material in a report. If other students have also completed this assignment, note how your analysis differs from theirs.

2. Journalists often use another term for what we have called a *control statement*. They call it a *lead*, an apt term because the sentence "leads into" the story. Here are some lead sentences. Write two or three paragraphs to support these leads. Compare your paragraphs with those of other writers in the class:

- Management, simply stated, is choosing the right people for the job and letting them do it.
- Here's what to do if your car won't start.
- You can manipulate statistics to prove anything you want to prove.
- Follow the old preacher's advice to write a good report: First you tell them what you're going to tell them; then you tell them; then you tell them what you told them.

3. Note the *pattern of development* of your paragraphs in Exercise 2. Did you use cause and effect? Or classification and analysis? Or comparison and contrast? Or narrative? Or another pattern?

4. Here are some *control statements.* Are they effective? What bias do you think each writer shows? What information would you, as a reader, expect in the document that develops each statement? What pattern of presentation would convey the information most effectively?

- I think the Taber Road store is in trouble.
- As a Bay Area Transit rider, you are entitled to know what the financial condition of your transit system is and why we are forced to propose major fare increases and some reductions in service within the next three months.
- Here's the information on the goals, staffing, and costs of corporate fitness programs that you asked for in our staff meeting last month.
- Let me review for you some of the events of the last several months that have caused our current budget crisis.

5. Here is a data dump of information about a trip you might have taken to attend a training session at a company site in Portland, Oregon. Assume that you scribbled these notes on the plane home. *Test* different control statements and structures for the information. You may, of course, omit some information. Consider what belongs in an appendix. Perhaps arrange your outline as a *group* project. Assess what each group member considers important:

seminar was fifth in a series of such seminars

seminars are given at the request of an individual company site

they may be given on site or in Portland

seminars last 2½ days

Portland seminar was Dec. 2, 3, 4

see list of other locations requesting seminars and tentative
    schedule

see list of all attendees

purpose of seminars

see brochure describing seminar, "Quality Control: Now or Never"

name and biographical information on seminar leader

each seminar includes ½ day lecture; 1 ½ day fieldwork;
    ½ day review; ½ day feedback

outline of topics covered

lots of international information, particularly Japanese model

sees quality control as a management and ongoing function, not
    something tacked on at the end of production; continuous
    rather than batch or sample testing

copies of student evaluation sheets

I stayed at the Four Poster—OK food, lousy room, too noisy; NOT
    recommended

my recommendations about the seminar

my conclusions: I learned a lot, good applicability to our unit

seminar cost: $500 (plus expenses)

copies of handouts and vugraphs

6. As a group project, organize the following topics concerning parking at your college or university. Add topics if you'd like. *Choose* a reader: the head of the student government, if you're writing from a student perspective, or the head of the safety division, or the student newspaper editor. Then select a *purpose:* perhaps to *inform* about the current parking situation, perhaps to *persuade* someone to reform parking regulations. Select a *form:* a letter or memo, perhaps a proposal (see Chapter 17). Develop an outline—linear or nonlinear—and key words that can become headings:

- Total number of cars on campus
- Total number of spaces in campus lots
- Security in the lots: lights, vandalism, theft
- Percentage of day and night students, residents and commuters
- Turnover of spaces in an average day
- Fees for parking
- Distinctions in parking stickers: certain lots designated for faculty, others for staff, others for students
- Aesthetics of lots: eyesores? trees to hide?
- Convenience of parking near buildings versus aesthetics of ring parking lots and a treed central campus
- Costs of a parking garage; relative land values on and near campus
- Relationships with home owners near campus on streets where students park

7. For your next outlining task, try a *visual* means to represent the big picture of your report and its main segments. Use an analogy if you like, for example, your report as a car. Or use one of the nonlinear forms presented in this chapter. Experiment with different ways of seeing the structure in your material.

Microcomposing

This chapter concerns microcomposing. It looks at strategies for selecting words to convey your message. It also looks at ways to assemble the words in sentences that express information accurately and precisely, that are clear to the reader, and that meet your own and the organization's goals.

Words

Words, like numbers, are symbols, things that stand for other things. What the word stands for or symbolizes is its *referent*.

Concrete and Abstract Words

When the referent for a word is something detectable by the five senses, then the word is *concrete*. Other words are *abstract*, in varying degrees. Figure 7–1 shows a narrowing from the abstract term *facility* to precise phrases: "100 cars," "3-story parking garage." Abstract terms can have different meanings for different readers. A movement down

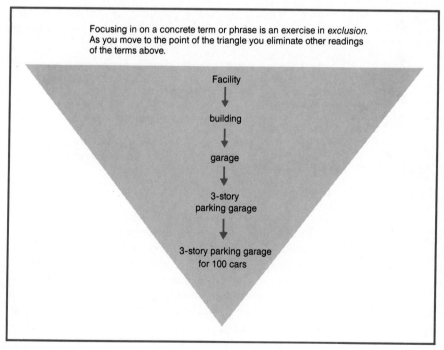

Focusing in on a concrete term or phrase is an exercise in *exclusion*. As you move to the point of the triangle you eliminate other readings of the terms above.

Facility
↓
building
↓
garage
↓
3-story
parking garage
↓
3-story parking garage
for 100 cars

FIGURE 7–1. Focusing meaning from the abstract to the concrete.

to the concrete term excludes possible misreadings and focuses on creating the same referent in the writer's mind and on the reader's mind. To prevent misreadings, be concrete.

Denotation and Connotation

Words have two different kinds of meanings: *denotations* and *connotations*. The denotation is the meaning or meanings stipulated in the dictionary, the literal meaning. Connotations are the associated attitudes and images that your words evoke in the reader's mind. Words, like electrons, have charges. Sometimes, quite deliberately, you'll use a positive-sounding word to cover a negative referent, as in saying someone "passed away" rather than "died." These positive words, called *euphemisms*, often aid an author in dealing with material he or she finds uncomfortable. Americans in particular, for example, tend to use euphemisms for bodily functions and the places where they occur. Throughout the United Kingdom and in Europe, one can find large signs in major cities directing people to "toilets." In America, we prefer terms like "comfort facilities" and "rest areas." Corporate personnel officers are often uncomfortable referring baldly to firings. Instead, they use euphemisms like "derecruit" or "placed on special assignment." The army never retreats; it "engages in retrograde motion." Here are some other differently charged words for the same referents:

Negative	Neutral	Positive
huckstering	selling	marketing
broken down	doesn't work	temporarily inoperative
kicked the bucket	died	passed on
skinny	thin	svelte

Sexist Language

The charges on words, too, reflect certain gender biases. Although English common nouns do not regularly show gender as in, say, French (*la lune, le congrès, la pomme*), certain nouns do bear a masculine bias: governor, poet, major, chairman, spokesman, businessman, to name just a very few. Note the feminine form of the first three: *governess, poetess, majorette*. In the feminine, the noun has quite a different meaning and shows diminished importance. The woman's movement has focused increasing attention on how some nouns embed derogatory attitudes toward women. Moreover, documents have traditionally used the masculine pronouns (*he, him, his*) exclusively to stand for all persons. Such usage seems to perpetuate a sense that only men are important.

Such biases—*sexism*—are, of course, complex, reflecting deeply rooted cultural attitudes. These biases are more than a matter of language. But they are, in part, a matter of language. Concerned writers are scrutinizing their words for sexism. They sometimes incorporate both *she* and *he* more-or-less randomly in a text to substitute for nouns; or they use a combined form *she/he* or *s/he;* or they use *you* or the gender-free plural *they* (being careful, of course, to watch out for a lack of agreement with the noun that the pronoun stands for). The best solution is not to call attention to one's pronouns, but to eliminate them where possible:

> *Inappropriate:* The average man's decisions are based on his self-interest.
> *More appropriate:* The average person's decisions are based on self-interest.

Changing or eliminating masculine pronouns is fairly straightforward. Avoiding nouns that carry connotations derogatory to women is somewhat more difficult. The context is critical. Sometimes it's a matter of parallelism: You refer to the *men* and the *girls* at the office—even if they are the same age. *Men* should match *women; boy* matches *girl.* Sometimes it's simply a matter of changing an ending: *chairperson* (or, better, *chair*), *spokesperson.* Sometimes it's a problem in modification: the use of *female doctor* or a *male nurse* when the simple nouns—*doctor* and *nurse*—should work for both cases. As with all the words you use, test them against your intent and the reader's perceptions.

Levels of Usage

Another way to look at words is to examine *levels of usage.* You use *colloquial language—slang*—in some contexts, like conversations and letters to friends. Other contexts, like reports, usually demand more *formal* word choice. One document should maintain a consistent level of formality. Any inconsistency may draw the reader's attention away from the message. Note the inconsistencies in the following examples:

> Meanwhile a plethora of gadgets, gizmos, and doohickeys will bring incredible new functionality to their buyers—if they know which are useful, which not worth the cost.

> Had Bell not gotten the shivers during the antitrust trial, had technology not beckoned so alluringly, had deregulatory fervor not gripped the nation's lawmakers, AT&T might have stood fast, stonewalling any break with tradition.

As an entity it is a fabulous, giant transcontinental computer, with over 10,000 internal switching nodes, each composed of millions of components, 200 million input/output ports, billions of internal circuit miles, and a bevy of 1 million keepers. As a switching device it rivals the human brain for complexity. The nation's telecommunications system is the best in the world. Why monkey with it?[1]

Jargon

One special level of usage is jargon. Each discipline or professional group develops its own code words and patterns of expression (its own jargon) within the general language (English, for example) of its culture. Indeed, some linguists and historians of science maintain that the text—that is, the language that colleagues use—*defines* the discipline. Inside the group, jargon provides a shorthand for quick communication and identifies group members. Computer experts speak in *bits* and *bytes;* marketing experts *segment* and *target;* statisticians *regress linearly.* New words enter the language, or old words take on new meanings, to match new professional ways of seeing and manipulating reality. Sometimes words simply shift their part of speech in jargon (*access,* for example, becomes a verb).

Jargon aids in reassuring a speaker or writer that some situation fits within norms and is part of a pattern. The familiar jargon reaffirms a sense of control and builds confidence. Once you have defined a set of difficulties as a "cash flow problem," you are on the way to solving it. Indeed, much business and technical language grew up to define hardware or circumstances; the reuse of such terms makes you comfortable in the company of old friends.

Jargon was originally a neutral term referring to this specialized language. However, it has taken on negative connotations, particularly when it is used by specialists in inappropriate contexts or is adopted by persons in other fields. The government variety is called *gobbledygook.* Other forms go by similarly pejorative names: *officialese, markettalk, computerese, gibberish, legalese, bureaucratese.* The term *jargon* earned these connotations in part because of its uses to confuse and deceive. George Bernard Shaw called professions, and their language, "conspiracies against the laity."

Sometimes business talk deliberately traps the uninitiated.[2] A company that calls itself "people-oriented" means, according to one cor-

---

[1]Advertising Supplement, "Business Communications: Challenges for the '80s," *Fortune,* 4 April 1983, 40.

[2]The examples in this paragraph were presented by Mary Bralove in "Taking the Boss at His Word May Turn Out to Be a Big Mistake at a Lot of Companies," *The Wall Street Journal,* 4 June 1982, 29.

porate recruiter, "Our salaries aren't high, but we give out turkeys at Christmas." Or one that calls itself a "close-knit team" or says it runs a "lean staff" is really saying it doesn't have enough people for the work. "A very creative shop," especially in the advertising business, means one that pays little but allows employees to wear whatever they want.

Such understatement and overstatement may be fairly innocent, a code that you get used to. Or it may deceive and cheat. Indeed, language has a way of not "leaving the other at least as well off," the modest measure of ethical behavior discussed in Chapter 1.

The Business Voice

Let's call the form of jargon common in business the *business voice*. One authority, William R. Brown, sees this as the language of function and functionaries.[3] He contrasts it to direct speech, which he sees as the language of power and leadership. Where does the business voice come from? Here are four sources:

- Laziness.
- Self-display.
- Reduction.
- Groupthink.

Laziness

Much of what you write in business resembles something you or someone else has written before. Many documents are thus leftovers, warmed up for a new context. Faced with a writing task, authors often copy a form. Sometimes that's necessary and efficient, but often, the copying just substitutes for thinking. Copying is particularly troublesome in letter writing, as you'll see in Chapter 13. The following opening of a letter is written in archaic business language:

> We wish to take this opportunity to advise you that, pursuant to a mutually agreed upon activity, your mortgage loan has been transferred for servicing from the L&B Mortgage Company to the FBM Mortgage Company. With regard to this matter, please be assured that this transfer of servicing is solely a business transaction based on the data and knowledge obtained in an extensive study to accommodate

[3]"Jargon and the Teaching of Organizational Communication," paper presented at the American Business Communication Association Eastern Regional Meeting, Philadelphia, 22 April 1983.

the servicing of all residential mortgage loans by one company and does not, in any way, reflect any dissatisfaction on anyone's part with your mortgage loan. Effective as of the date of this transfer, your mortgage payments should be forwarded directly to FBM.

The letter might have begun simply:

To consolidate and thus improve our service of residential loans through one company, we have transferred your mortgage loan from L&B Mortgage Company to FBM Mortgage Company. This transfer is simply administrative. Your loan remains in force exactly as you contracted for it, but beginning on April 1, please send your payments to FBM.

Whenever you're tempted to slip into leftover language or feel like writing such clichés as "first and foremost," "last but not least," "a step in the right direction," or "a chip off the old block," *think again.*

Self-display

Second, people sometimes use jargon to sound important and to intimidate. They may use several terms where one would do; they prefer abstract terms and plural nouns. Here's a college men's athletic director trying to prove to the administration that he's not just a jock:

We recognize certain emerging facts of life in our United States. Our society is becoming less structured and it is also becoming a more leisurely society. If man fails to acquire during his youth those habits, skills, appreciations, and knowledges essential to successful participation in some vigorous lifetime sports or suitable activities, then there is a high probability that man will be confronted with excessive idleness. We feel that an overly passive existence for mature adults will not only be physically harmful but, from the standpoint of mental health, deleterious.

Here's an example from a design publication:

The reemergence from clandestinity and the dropping of inhibitions reintroduce the free display of a "totemic material" resistant to any zeroing of codes; whilst the commerce with historical repertories sends trauma and the shock of the new into the groove of an uninterrupted disciplinary continuity.

Such self-display, however, may merely cause a serious reader not to take the author seriously.

Reduction

Being able to apply a term to a problem helps in solving it. That's a positive use of jargon. But on the negative side, the business voice may be used as a way to *hide* a problem, to prevent its solution by covering reality in a coating of language. The control is illusory. The abstractions are only falsely reassuring. One career consultant advises, when the boss says "don't worry," don't take these words at face value: "Management deals with change with studied casualness. The bigger things are the more people try to speak of them casually."[4]

Examine some annual reports of companies that you know are in trouble and see how the writers encased bad news in neutral language designed to reduce the impact of the loss.

Groupthink

Another source of the business voice is what we may call *groupthink*, the need to write in groups or as a spokesperson for an organization. Here's the economist John Kenneth Galbraith on the subject (his comments, from an "About Men" column, use the masculine pronoun):

> What [the aspiring corporate leader] says is required by the rules and ethics of organization to be both predictable and dull. He does not speak for himself; he speaks for the firm. Good policy is not what he wants but what the organization believes it needs. In the normal case, his speech will be written and vetted by his fellow organization men. In the process, it will drop to the lowest common denominator of novelty. Lindbergh, as has too often been told, could never have flown the Atlantic with a committee. It is equally certain that General Motors could never have written Shakespeare or even a column by Art Buchwald. Executive expression is ignored because, by the nature of organization, it must be at an exceptionally tedious level of organization stereotype and caution.[5]

 *Case Study: The Business Voice*

Here is a statement in the business voice that introduces a company's quarterly report at the end of a bad quarter. The language attempts to reduce the readers' anxiety and to assure them that the situation is under control.

In September, the Consumer Products Division created the Profit Team, whose mission was to develop a revised Strategic Plan for the Division. In pursuing its work, the Profit Team en-

gaged more than a hundred people throughout the division, forming teams to assess the competitive environment, the markets in which we compete, our mills, our products, our management process—virtually every aspect of our business from both an external and an internal viewpoint.

The work of these many people led to revisions in our basic strategy, and to the conclusion that changes were required in the way we run the

[4]Bralove, 29.
[5]"About Men: Corporate Man," *The New York Times Magazine*, 22 January 1984, 39.

business if we are to significantly improve our competitive position. The resulting plan, as you will recall, contained three principal thrusts:

1. Dramatically reduce our inherent costs so that they are lower than a large portion of industry capacity.

2. Improve earnings from segment value-adding activities by striving for brand leadership in Consumer and full-line leadership in Commercial.

3. Achieve competitive advantage by rigorously pursuing excellence—being the best in everything we do.

In focusing on these thrusts, we indicated that what was happening and would continue to happen in CPD was unprecedented, but in our estimation, it was achievable because, first and foremost, execution of our plan was dependent on people and organizational issues. To be specific, we said:

1. We must achieve business focus.

2. We must align our functional activities with the plan.

3. We must change the way in which we manage the business.

Note the business voice:

1. *Laziness.* One can't say for sure that the writers were lazy. But much of the language is leftovers, like "virtually every aspect of our business from both an external and internal viewpoint," "first and foremost," "being the best in everything we do."

2. *Self-display.* The text is pompous. It creates big names (with capital letters): "the Profit Team," "Strategic Plan for the Division." It talks abstractly about "mission," "thrust," "engaging more than a hundred people," "significantly improving our competitive position," and "achieving a competitive advantage by rigorously pursuing excellence." It all sounds positive.

3. *Reduction.* But it's covering negative

results. The goal here is to reassure. At first reading, the language seems forceful. There are two numbered lists of steps—surely an indication of action. But look for the reality beneath the words. Here's what the words boil down to:

In September the division created a profit team to revise the division's strategic plan. The team looked at our competition, markets, mills, products, and management process. The team noted the need for some changes and revised the plan to emphasize three goals:

1. Reduce our costs so that they're lower than our competition's.

2. Improve earnings: strive for brand leadership in Consumer and full-line leadership in Commercial

3. Pursue excellence in everything.

So far, the text, if dull and predictable, is readable. But with the paragraph beginning "In focusing . . ." the statement moves away from anything concrete. It's dealing with negative information: why the September plan didn't work. It makes no sense: How can "what was happening" be "achievable"? The term *unprecedented* is a euphemism. That the plan depends on people and organizational issues is a given—not something new, as it's presented. The three last items are hardly specific; they're exceedingly general: "business focus"? "align functional activities with the plan"? Item 3 is the dead giveaway. Obviously, the company must change—that's what Items 1 and 2 are about. The question is *how*. There is no answer.

4. *Groupthink.* This statement represents the work of one chief writer and many reviewers. It uses *we* to represent itself and the company. There's little sense of individual integrity here. The text is simply corporate language.

Overcoming the Business Voice

Specialized language helps you communicate efficiently within a profession or organization, control circumstances or assure others that you are in control, and plot constructive responses. Once words are attached to a patient's condition, for example, at least some of the patient's fear is removed.

But sometimes the business voice prevents or delays proper action. A frustrated sailor in a ship that was taking on water replied to the captain, who was discussing navigation strategies, "Don't talk about navigation. BAIL." At times, we need to discuss navigation. At times, we need to bail.

Those who know their specialty best are the ones best able to express it at many levels: in shorthand jargon to colleagues and in a range of simpler expressions to others. They can change voices and styles to accommodate different information and different readers—while still maintaining their own integrity.

In an excellent study of American prose style, Walker Gibson defined three categories of style: tough talk, sweet talk, and stuffy talk.[6] Tough talk is centered in the "I," the speaker. It doesn't bother to give the reader background or overviews; it just begins and tells the tale, usually in crisp, concrete words and short sentences. Sweet talk is "you" talk. It is the language of advertisements and sales pitches in general. It deliberately sets out to cajole and engage the reader, often with chatty images and anecdotes. Its voice is friendly and familiar. It refers to people by name. It would shake your hand if it could. Figure 7–2, for example, is the text of an advertisement for a savings bank that wants to project an image of close personal attention to customers. This advertisement addresses *you* directly: "If *you* want *your* business to grow." The language is *colloquial*, without technical terms. Note the contractions. Note the use of the name of the banker—"Bill Betty"—to show that the bank is made up of people and is not just an impersonal organization. Note, too, all the puns on fish and fishing, beginning with the headline, "little fish," "hooked up."

Stuffy talk is "it" talk. Gibson sees this as the language of corporate America and the government. The prose in the business-voice case study is stuffy. So is the athletic director's. Stuffy talk suffocates its topic and doesn't give the reader any breathing room, either. Here's how Gibson defined stuffy talk:

Anyone who has worked on a committee preparing a document to be signed by all fellowwriters knows some of the difficulties. Disagreements of opinion and emphasis can produce a voice that is hardly a

[6]*Tough, Sweet, and Stuffy: An Essay on Modern American Prose Styles* (Bloomington: Indiana University Press, 1966).

Phil Di Febo wasn't content to be a little fish, so he hooked up with us.

When Phil Di Febo cast about for the capital he needed to open Feby's Fishery, he found out that we were as eager as he was to break new ground. He and Bill Betty of our Commercial Lending team worked out a package of financing for construction, working capital and equipment that helped Feby's grow from a small fish market to a whale of a business on Lancaster Pike.

If you want your business to grow, you need a bank that's as eager to be a big fish as you are. For any type of commercial financing, call our Commercial Lending Department today at 571-7103. Get the attention you deserve and the prompt action you'd expect from a team that's out to catch your business.

Wilmington Savings Fund Society/FSB
Equal Opportunity Lender
© WSFS 1984

FIGURE 7–2. An advertisement in "you" talk (reprint courtesy of Wilmington Savings Fund Society, FSB, Wilmington, Delaware).

voice at all. Constant qualification makes for weakness. The various writers, all too aware of their audience as real people, may try to anticipate hopelessly conflicting prejudices and objections. Everybody has a point he wants included, but what is worse, no one feels any personal responsibility for the tone of the whole. Nobody cares, really. Contrast the situation of the single writer alone at his desk, who can establish a single speaking voice and an ideal assumed reader to listen to it. Yet a great deal of modern prose is written, or at any rate rewritten, not at a lonely desk but around a table where everybody talks at once. The loss of personality almost inevitable under such circumstances should cause us anguish whenever, as so often happens, we have to read or write the prose of organization life. When we speak of official prose as stuffy, we are referring, I think, directly to this loss of personality.[7]

C. Northcote Parkinson noted a similar problem:

Come now to the importance of style, which is the imprint of character upon what we do and say. Any effective announcement or message conveys a sense of personality. While precise and terse, it goes beyond precision and brevity. It comes from a known character, not from a faceless management. It never includes long words and involved constructions. Short words are best, each one a hammer blow and not a handful of cotton wool.[8]

Capturing a voice for the "prose of organization life" and overcoming groupthink is a worthy pursuit. Rules are of little help here, although you should at least write grammatically. Within generally accepted grammatical principles, however, you have room to move around.

The usual advice for correcting the excesses of jargon emphasizes the need for clarity and brevity: short words, short sentences, no made-up words, and few abstractions. Be precise. Prefer plain English to specialized terms wherever possible. Most of the time, such advice works. Sometimes, however, you need long words, long sentences, abstractions, and specialized terms. The test is whether the text works for the reader.

For many reasons, lots of readers are comfortable with jargon and prefer it to simple, direct prose. Often, those readers are in management; clever writers who report to them learn quickly to ape favorite phrases. Ultimately, however, loose writing takes more time to read and fosters less precision in action. Its days are numbered.

You'll want to stay on top of the jargon that circulates in your office and in your profession and to use it to your advantage when the reader looks for a favorite phrase. But develop your own voice around it. Your main goal is to achieve fresh expression as opposed to the tired, leftover talk that comes from the business voice.

[7] Gibson, 91.

[8] "Parkinson's Law of the Vacuum (or, Hoover for President)," *Forbes*, 12 May 1980, 138.

Case Study: The United Way

One routine corporate assignment that often evokes the business voice is the annual appeal for the United Way. Faced with the task of writing such a memo, many people simply dig into their files, find the memo from the year before, change some topical references, and send it along. The language is often stuffy:

The United Way campaign at our organization will be conducted October 24–November 7.

Please give generously to continue the spirit of people helping people, people from all walks of life combining their efforts for the common good to enhance the quality of life in our community.

And so the memo goes, on and on. But hear the fresh voice in Figure 7–3.

Date: October 4, 19XX

To: Department

From: E. A. Nickerson

Before you put this annual United Way appeal in the back of your desk drawer, think again.

If you give, your money will go to help care for the aged, through Geriatric Services of Delaware, or care for the children of working parents, through the Newark Day Nursery, or help with vocational training for teenagers and others, through Opportunity Center, Inc. It will help care for the retarded and the chronically ill. It will help with work to combat crime and delinquency and to shelter battered children. *If* you give.

As you know, the economy is in trouble. If you agree with the President that private charity, not governmental action, is the way to help society—then give to the United Way. If you disagree with the President and think government should do the whole job, you also know that government is *not* doing the whole job and is not likely to do the whole job for years to come. So give to the United Way.

Please.

Take your check or cash to Linda Russell in Room 202 as soon as possible.

FIGURE 7–3. Nickerson's memo (used by permission of Edward A. Nickerson, Director of the University of Delaware's Journalism Program).

This memo works because it is *concrete*. It addresses the reader directly in the first sentence—and throughout. It notes specific agencies and purposes for the money. It discusses the economy. The author is not afraid of short sentences—even one-word: "please." You sense a person behind the prose.

Sentences

The United Way case memo also works because its sentences are well shaped. Let's look at how Nickerson composed his sentences.

Sentence Patterns

First, Nickerson used different patterns for combining ideas in sentences:

- Chronology.
- Series of items.
- Balance.
- Antithesis.
- Cause.

Chronology

> Before you put this annual United Way appeal in the back of your desk drawer, think again.

One of the easiest ways to recall action in writing is through chronology, that is, connections along a time line. You retrace a story. You talk about before and after.

Series of Items

> If you give, your money will go to help care for the aged, through Geriatric Services of Delaware, or care for the children of working parents, through the Newark Day Nursery, or help with vocational training for teenagers and others, through Opportunity Center, Inc. It will help care for the retarded and the chronically ill. It will help with work to combat crime and delinquency and to shelter battered children.

These sentences build a series of examples. Lots of sentences in business break out into lists of items: a list of company products, a list of the components of a system, a list of people and their managerial responsibilities. The items may be placed side by side in the sentence or may be enumerated on separate lines. The chief constraint on the pattern is *parallelism*. Each item in the list must belong to some common class of items, indicated by an enumerator term, either expressed or implied ("Services provided by the United Way" is the unexpressed enumerator for the list in the quotation), and each item must be expressed in the same grammatical form.

Balance

> If you agree with the President that private charity, not governmental action, is the way to help society—then give to the United Way.

If . . . then is a form of balance. You shape the sentence to reveal the balance. The principle of parallelism still applies to the expression of the two parts. Sometimes you balance two sentences against each other, as in the next sentence of the memo:

> If you disagree with the President and think government should do the whole job, you also know that government is *not* doing the whole job and is not likely to do the whole job for years to come. So give to the United Way

Antithesis

The sentences on agreeing and disagreeing with the President offer a contrast; they are connected by antithesis. Sometimes key words underscore the contrast, such as *on the one hand . . . on the other hand, although, but, yet,* or *however.*

Cause

The entire memo deals with cause and effect. In the second paragraph, the *cause* is your giving; the *effect* is care for the aged, for children, and the like. In the second paragraph, the author argues persuasively that whether you agree or disagree with the president (cause), the effect should be a donation. Often, you will need to use sentences that pull together causes and their effects.

Sentence Branching

In addition to these patterns for adding words together in a sentence, you can think about where you might place modifiers for emphasis. Think about how the sentence *branches* into subordinate elements. Sentences that complete the main clause first and then deploy modifiers branch right. Sentences that interrupt the main subject and verb with qualifiers branch in the middle (mid-branching). Those that build up to the main subject and verb branch left.

The most common pattern in English is the right-branching sentence:

> She gave to the United Way because she found Mr. Nickerson's memo persuasive and felt that her own needs as well as those of the community would be well served by her gift.

This form is also probably the easiest for readers to understand because they know the main thought before they learn about the modifiers that qualify it. When all the modifiers come first, the readers have to hold them *before* knowing what to do with them, and they may forget and have to reread the sentence. But piling up modifiers first does build suspense:

> Because she found Mr. Nickerson's memo persuasive and felt that her own needs as well as those of the community would be well served by her gift, she gave to the United Way.

Drafts of technical and business papers are often filled with mid-branching sentences, because, after naming the topic, the author interrupts the thought for some interesting sidelights before getting to the verb. Readers may have trouble, though, remembering the subject by the time the verb appears, and many mid-branching sentences are therefore best transformed in revision.

Here, for example, are two right-branching sentences:

> The market mounted a vigorous rally last Friday reaching 19½ points, despite all the gloom of a budget deficit, higher interest rates, increasing tensions internationally, and banking problems.

> Management must recognize certain constraints: that research cannot stay in the lab forever, that there are overall economic timetables to be met, and that a transfer plan is necessary.

Let's change these to the mid-branching form to show how much you have to remember before you get to the verb:

> The market, despite all the gloom of a budget deficit, higher interest rates, increasing tensions internationally, and banking problems, mounted a vigorous rally last Friday reaching 19½ points.

> Certain constraints—that research cannot stay in the lab forever, that there are overall economic timetables to be met, and that a transfer plan is necessary—must be recognized by management.

Note the suspense that is built when the sentence follows a left-branching form.

> Despite all the gloom of a budget deficit, higher interest rates, increasing tensions internationally, and banking problems, the market mounted a vigorous rally last Friday reaching 19½ points.

That research cannot stay in the lab forever, that there are overall economic timetables to be met, and that a transfer plan is necessary: these constraints must be recognized by management.

Choose the form of sentence that matches your emphasis and your audience's reading sophistication. For straightforward information—that is, most of the time—you'll probably choose sentences that branch right. The others tax the reader a bit more—something you should do only with caution. But you may want just that emphasis:

Before you put this annual United Way appeal in the back of your desk drawer, think again.

Your Style

In this chapter, you have learned some strategies for microcomposing: using words and sentences. From the general language and the general patterns of sentences, select what sounds like you, what expresses your information accurately and precisely, and what meets the reader's needs.

Exercises

1. The Committee on Public Doublespeak of the National Council of Teachers of English publishes a *Quarterly Review of Doublespeak*. Since 1974, the committee has also presented yearly "Doublespeak" awards: "The award is an ironic 'tribute' to American public figures who have perpetrated language that is grossly unfactual, deceptive, evasive, euphemistic, confusing, or self-contradictory." The U.S. State Department, for example, has won the award for redefining the word *kill* as "unlawful or arbitrary deprivation of life." The National Transportation Safety Board has also been nominated for calling an airplane crash "controlled flight into terrain" and the Pentagon for renaming peace as "permanent prehostility," combat as "violence processing," and civilian casualties in nuclear war as "collateral damage." Other terms cited: running a *negative deficit* in a not-for-profit program; *therapeutic misadventure* instead of *malpractice;* and *vertical transportation corps* for elevator operators. Read some issues of the *Review* in your library. Then scan the newspapers and business publications to nominate statements (and staters) for the award.

2. According to *Writer's Digest* (November 1982), the Department of Commerce's word processors are programmed to flash a warning whenever anyone uses one of forty-three forbidden words or phrases, including *viable, maximize, effectuate,* and *final outcome.* As a class or group exercise, develop a list of leftover phrases, clichés, and euphemisms to avoid in your own business writing.

3. Here is the first paragraph of a memo to the "Enforcement Section Staff" from the "Attorney Inspector" concerning "Interoffice Procedure with Reference to Assignments and Docket Control." It is written in legalese. What are some of the elements of jargon you see here? Can you translate the memo into English?

> With regard to the matter above referred, as of even date herewith, the hereinafter reflected and contained detailation and/or formal sequence of events shall be hereby and hereafter immediately implemented and followed both to the extent practicable and to the extent that the same is not currently being so implemented. Initially, all persons within the Section will immediately inventory those matters on which they are either working, have been working, or have any materials pertaining thereunto in their possession and submit a copy of the same to me no latter than 12 noon, November 20, 1989. Thereupon, and also prior thereto, each such person shall *personally* inspect the index files to ascertain which matters contained and reflected in said inventory have complaint or case numbers and those for which no number has yet been assigned.

4. Examine several corporate annual reports to determine the style of each company. Look in particular at the levels of language used as a key to understanding the intended readers. Are there many technical terms? What's the relative emphasis on statistical presentation and verbal presentation? Is the language concrete or abstract? Are positive words used to cover negative referents (for example, the use of "negative profitability picture" instead of *loss*)? Is the language highly formal? Or does the company affect a more casual approach?

5. Computers have produced many changes in society, including changes in language. Make a list of some terminology from computer development that has entered daily talk (for example, "I'd like to have your *input* on the proposed change"; "I'm *programmed* for success"; and "One more party and my system will *crash*"). Other terms, too, have entered business jargon: "core dump" (to tell everything), "off-load" a task on someone, and, of course, "interface."

6. Examine several publications of your university or organization to test for sexist language. Is the masculine pronoun *he* used exclusively to stand for nouns? Do any statements carry connotations derogatory to women? Does the document make any overt attempts to avoid sexism by including, for example, photographs that show both men and women in the classroom or on the job?

7. The voice that comes through in the following paragraph (from a progress report about a group's performance in analyzing a case study in a business class) waffles between stuffy and informal. Using your knowledge of paragraph structure (see Chapter 6) and of expression, try to diagnose the problems in the paragraph and make some suggestions for improvement:

> In any type of project where an individual is involved with a cluster of six diverse people, they will encounter many positive and negative attributes.

The performance of our group on our initial project was very good; however, the quality of the group members, together with the necessary dedication, will lead to an improved case analysis the next time around. The members of our group are all friendly and work well together. We all interact and communicate well together. This is vital to a group's performance. Once we started working as a unit, we started rolling. A second aspect of our performance that added to our final outcome was the preparedness of the group members. We all were psyched about the project and did our homework. In each meeting, we voiced our opinions and elicited the most important and relevant facts. The fact that all the members were well prepared for interaction enhanced our total group output. We also kept an eye on the clock at meetings. We specifically implemented a ninety-minute meeting maximum. In sticking to this schedule, we had to limit the non-case fraternization during group meetings—no grousing and hanging out.

8. Analyze the voice that comes across in the following text of a letter collecting a rent payment that is overdue (for more on collection letters, see Chapter 16):

I know that life as a college student is a hectic life. You always have so many things on your mind that you never have time to remember all of the things that you are supposed to, such as paying your rent.

The past couple of months you have been very diligent in paying your rent on time, but I guess this past month must have been pretty hectic and you had other things on your mind, such as exams, because you forgot to pay your rent.

I truly understand some of the pressure you may have been under and can understand your forgetting to pay your rent, so I'm just writing to remind you about paying it.

I hope that this will be the only reminder I have to send. You have been a good renter and I would hate to loose you as a tenant.

9. To analyze your sentence style, examine a page or two of a draft document you've written. First, with a colored pencil, place a slash mark at the end of each sentence. Is there variety in sentence length? Are your sentences mostly long? Mostly short? Next, note how the sentences branch, that is, your placement of modifiers. Underline modifying elements with your colored pencil and note their location relative to the main clause. Third, note the form of each sentence: chronology, series, balance, antithesis, or cause.

Composing with Visuals

8

117

People in business manage much of their information *visually*. They use visuals like tables and graphs both to *analyze* data and to *present* the results of that analysis to someone else. Visuals are thus essential elements in such business documents as reports, instructions, and literature for customers.

This chapter looks at strategies for composing with visuals—in whatever form of document you are writing. Indeed, you'll often achieve your goal in writing most effectively not by *writing*, in the sense of sentences and paragraphs, but by expressing your information in visual form. This chapter has three parts:

1. Meeting communication goals with visuals.
2. Selecting the appropriate visual form.
3. Composing with visuals: guidelines.

Meeting Communication Goals with Visuals

When someone asks for directions to your home or office, do you write a narrative or draw a map? When someone asks for your schedule next week, do you write a paragraph beginning "First thing Monday morning, I have an appointment with X from the Y company," and then tracing a series of sentences through to Friday at five? Or do you set up a calendar:

	Monday	Tuesday	Wednesday	Thursday	Friday
8					
9					
10					
11					
12					
1					
2					
3					
4					
5					

On the calendar you indicate free times and scheduled times. In which form would it be easier to compare several peoples' calendars to set up a meeting? Which form—a paragraph or a calendar—prompts you to remember each item and not to leave gaps?

Your weekly schedule may be simple stuff, but scheduling activities can become complicated, as can giving directions for finding one's way. For these and a whole range of other situations, visuals are the key to both deriving and presenting information.

Within documents, visuals, like sentences and paragraphs, serve three broad purposes:

1. To record.
2. To inform.
3. To persuade.

To Record

One goal of visuals is to *record* information. The visual provides a framework for establishing and consolidating data. That framework can also ease the prediction of trends and the inclusion of further data. Once drawn, for example, a map can provide you with more information than was necessary to draw it; the drawing itself *creates* information. It establishes relationships and allows comparisons. Likewise, lining up discrete data points on a chart allows you to see the data from a different angle and to understand their implications better than when the data are simply scattered jottings on paper or in your mind.

The chief constraints on drawing such visuals for the record are accuracy and completeness. Indeed, such visuals may be so complete as to be unreadable by anyone but you or a close associate. You may deliberately attempt, for example, to picture a whole year's work on one page. You may play at the terminal with different scenarios, letting a graphics package prompt you to solve the problem that the numbers represent.

Many visuals meant primarily to record find a home simply in your own files. They provide the basis for your own thinking. They may, however, also appear within reports, especially in the appendixes. They appear as well in documents *of record*, like the team standings and statistics that sports fans seek out in the newspaper (Figure 8–1). Abbreviations are used freely, and the information is dense.

To Inform

People do *read* box scores, of course, so they serve more than a merely archival purpose. Often, however, visuals meant to record must be reconfigured to enhance a reader's understanding and ability to come to a decision as well as to achieve the writer's intended emphasis. Usually the reconfiguration amounts to simplifying the presentation in or-

NHL

Wales conference

PATRICK DIVISION	W	L	T	Pts.	GF	GA	Div.	Last 10
FLYERS	34	17	4	72	228	162	13-8-2	3-6-1
N.Y. Islanders	25	23	7	57	189	185	12-8-4	3-4-3
N.Y. Rangers	23	24	8	54	219	216	13-8-3	6-4-0
Washington	22	27	8	52	183	210	9-15-2	4-5-1
Pittsburgh	21	25	8	50	201	195	8-11-4	4-6-0
New Jersey	22	28	5	49	196	246	9-14-1	4-6-0
ADAMS DIVISION								
Hartford	29	21	6	64	188	181	14-8-3	7-3-0
Boston	28	22	5	61	208	179	10-11-2	7-3-0
Montreal	27	24	7	61	190	182	12-10-4	4-6-0
Quebec	23	27	7	53	184	180	10-12-2	6-5-0
Buffalo	18	31	6	42	187	211	8-13-3	5-5-0

Campbell conference

NORRIS DIVISION	W	L	T	Pts.	GF	GA	Div.	Last 10
Detroit	23	24	8	54	176	191	13-10-3	6-4-0
Minnesota	23	24	7	53	209	202	9-10-3	4-4-2
St. Louis	20	24	10	50	182	205	9-7-6	4-4-2
Toronto	22	29	5	49	197	213	11-12-2	3-7-0
Chicago	20	28	8	48	200	227	8-11-3	3-5-2
SMYTHE DIVISION								
Edmonton	37	15	5	79	267	195	13-8-3	6-1-3
Winnipeg	31	20	5	67	200	188	13-7-0	6-3-1
Calgary	30	24	2	62	218	212	10-10-1	5-4-1
Los Angeles	22	27	6	50	223	228	7-12-3	2-6-2
Vancouver	17	33	7	41	187	224	8-14-2	3-6-1

FIGURE 8–1. Standings in the National Hockey League, February 9, 1987 (reprinted with permission of *The Philadelphia Inquirer*).

der to highlight some significant item or trend. Figure 8–2, for example, is a line graph representing the manufacturing capacity growth for the four regional divisions of the F. P. Corporation (in terms of units per day) over two years. Lines are drawn for each on the same grid. This graph puts all the data in one picture. But for a discussion, you might want to break out each line on a separate grid or use another form, such as a pie chart, to show relative growth.

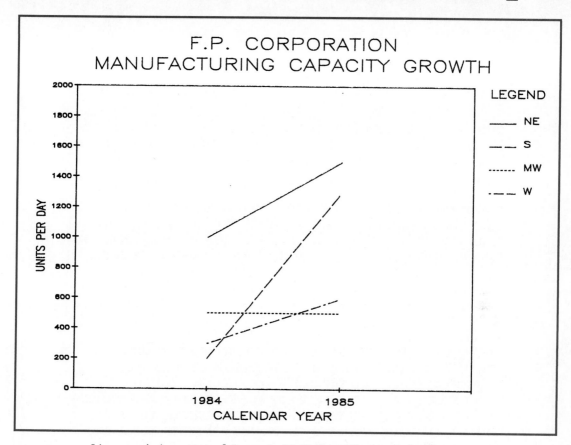

FIGURE 8–2. Line graph (courtesy of Joyce A. McKeller. All visuals for the F. P. Corporation in this chapter were prepared by Ms. McKeller).

To Persuade

Like words, visuals can be effective tools of persuasion. They can help to change a reader's mind or heart. A photograph of a child, thin and crying, helps persuade a reader to contribute to the Save the Children Federation. A line of profits soaring upward in a graph from an annual report persuades the reader to think well of the company—and perhaps to buy more stock. Visuals are important in setting an organization's style, particularly in marketing documents. In Figure 8–3, you see a notice circulated to students concerning a university writing center. The text appears in paragraph form, in the third person ("the student"). It *describes* the center and its services but buries its appeal to students to visit. Printing the text in all capital letters makes it seem

UNIVERSITY WRITING CENTER

THE WRITING CENTER IS OPEN FROM 9:00 A.M. TO 12:00 NOON AND FROM 1:00 TO 5:00 P.M., MONDAY THROUGH FRIDAY, AND FROM 6:00 TO 9:00 P.M., MONDAY THROUGH THURSDAY. IT IS LOCATED IN 015 MEMORIAL HALL. THE PHONE NUMBER IS 451-1168.

THE SERVICES ARE AVAILABLE TO ANY UNIVERSITY STUDENT, PART-TIME OR FULL-TIME, GRADUATE OR UNDERGRADUATE. THE MAIN PURPOSE OF THE CENTER IS TO HELP STUDENTS TO INCREASE THEIR WRITING SKILLS IN AREAS SUCH AS GRAMMAR, SPELLING, PUNCTUATION, DICTION, WRITTEN PRESENTATION, AND ORGANIZATION OF THOUGHTS. IT WORKS WITH STUDENTS ON PAPERS FOR ANY UNIVERSITY COURSE. INSTRUCTION IS OFFERED ON AN INDIVIDUAL BASIS AND IS DESIGNED TO DEAL WITH THE STUDENT'S PARTICULAR WRITING PROBLEMS. ONCE THESE PROBLEMS ARE DIAGNOSED, AN INDIVIDUALIZED, FLEXIBLE WRITING PROGRAM IS DESIGNED FOR THE STUDENT AND IS IMPLEMENTED AROUND THE STUDENT'S ACADEMIC SCHEDULE. APPOINTMENTS ARE DESIRABLE BUT NOT NECESSARY. THE WRITING CENTER'S SERVICES ARE FREE. THE WRITING CENTER WILL NOT WRITE PAPERS FOR STUDENTS, CHECK THE CONTENTS OF PAPERS, EDIT PAPERS, OR PROOFREAD.

FIGURE 8–3. Original notice.

bureaucratic and intimidating. Figure 8–4, however, shows how two students redesigned the announcement to *persuade*. The revised notice stresses benefits. Key terms in the text are broken out in list form. The student is addressed directly in the opening question. The drawing of the hand and the pencil draws attention—and establishes a motif for the center carried through in the bookmark (also in Figure 8–4), reproduced in bright yellow and available in the university bookstore.

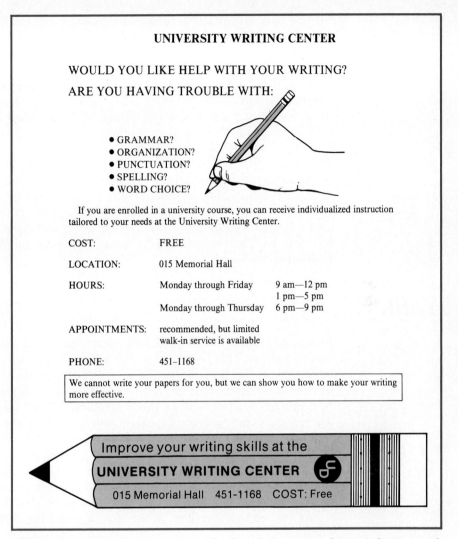

FIGURE 8–4. Redesigned notice and bookmark (courtesy of Kim Schnitzer and Diane Thena).

Selecting the Appropriate Visual Form

Visuals, then, can meet each of the communication goals: to record, to inform, and to persuade. Based on your goal, you select the form that will best develop and present your information. The forms generally fit into two categories: tables and figures. A *table* is any arrangement of related information, words or numbers, in columns and rows. The term *figure* refers to any other visual form: graphs, charts, diagrams, maps, drawings, and photographs.

In general, when your goal is to present complex material to a sophisticated audience, you start with the visuals and decide where you need text to explain. When you're writing for a broad and mixed readership, as in the nonfinancial sections of an annual report, you begin with the text and then decide on what illustrations you need to entice the reader through the text. In a professional report, then, the text often augments the visuals; in a popular one, the visuals augment the text. In revising any document, look for stretches of text that can be condensed into a visual, or for theoretical discussions that need grounding in a drawing or photograph. Let's examine how several different visual forms can help you think about your material and present it to an audience.

Tables

Figure 8–5 shows a form of *table* that's probably familiar to you: a balance sheet. This one is from the annual report of a bank, but balance sheets sum up activities of all sorts of organizations. Statements of earnings, statements of shareholders' equity, statements of change in financial position—all of these are tables. They show precise data. They foster comparisons at many levels, and in their grid arrangement, they remind the investigator of any missing items.

Tables operate on two principles important in prose as well: classification and parallelism. In creating a table you find general headings for categories of information, and you make sure that each item of information fits logically and grammatically into that category.

As you revise a report, a clue to the need for a table is often redundancy:

> During the visit I met with representatives of three companies: IBM, DEC (Digital Equipment Company), and Zenith. Peter Smith, who represents IBM in the metropolitan region, gave me an estimate of $5,000 per unit for the system. He said a yearly maintenance contract with them would run us about $600. The guy from Zenith (his name is Jeffrey Bowman) quoted me $4,500 per unit for a similar system and said the maintenance contract with his company would run us $550. I also talked with Kitsel Outlaw of DEC, who gave an estimate of $4,999 per unit. Her estimate of the maintenance contract per year was $550, the same as the Zenith one.

Delaware Trust Company
BALANCE SHEETS Five Year Financial Review, Continued

	December 31, (in thousands)				
	1984	1983	1982	1981	1980
Assets					
Cash and due from banks	**$ 47,342**	47,552	31,005	27,232	30,341
Money market instruments					
Federal funds sold and security resale agreements	**97,000**	26,100	68,900	56,000	58,969
Interest bearing deposits with banks	**—**	60,006	100,041	55,034	7,000
Total money market instruments	**97,000**	86,106	168,941	111,034	65,969
Investment securities	**209,126**	196,138	149,076	141,348	136,033
Loans					
Commercial	**198,441**	165,971	137,037	119,620	113,395
Mortgage	**101,381**	108,655	118,507	126,105	136,356
Consumer	**207,777**	158,543	95,726	86,248	85,969
Total loans	**507,599**	433,169	351,270	331,973	335,720
Less: Allowance for possible loan losses	**6,272**	4,680	4,122	3,926	3,359
Total net loans	**501,327**	428,489	347,148	328,047	332,361
Premises and equipment	**14,665**	14,218	13,921	12,804	13,198
Accrued income receivable	**8,316**	10,501	8,863	9,622	5,480
Other assets	**5,846**	10,628	1,937	3,418	3,182
Total assets	**$883,622**	793,632	720,891	633,505	586,564
Liabilities					
Transaction accounts					
Demand deposits	**$158,832**	151,573	141,691	136,372	177,872
Interest bearing	**60,202**	51,226	39,314	31,372	8,323
Total transaction accounts	**219,034**	202,799	181,005	167,744	186,195
Savings deposits	**221,428**	200,830	128,345	85,299	102,929
Retail time deposits	**273,542**	250,878	256,940	241,863	191,492
Certificates of deposit—$100,000 and over	**35,196**	27,329	37,641	47,997	43,663
Total deposits	**749,200**	681,836	603,931	542,903	524,279
Security repurchase agreements	**65,765**	43,155	54,827	33,982	12,188
Accrued interest payable	**9,033**	14,292	14,170	12,777	10,300
Other liabilities	**5,651**	5,789	4,215	4,742	4,422
Total liabilities	**829,649**	745,072	677,143	594,404	551,189
Shareholders' equity					
Common stock	**2,006**	2,001	2,000	2,000	2,000
Capital in excess of par value	**25,043**	25,008	25,000	25,000	25,000
Retained earnings	**26,924**	21,551	16,748	12,101	8,375
Total shareholders' equity	**53,973**	48,560	43,748	39,101	35,375
Total liabilities and shareholders' equity	**$883,622**	793,632	720,891	633,505	586,564

FIGURE 8–5. Balance sheet (*Source:* Reprinted from the 1984 Delaware Trust Company Annual Report).

Now see how this information would look in a table:

Company	Representative	Per unit cost (in dollars)	Yearly maintenance contract (in dollars)
DEC	Kitsel Outlaw	4999	550
IBM	Peter Smith	5000	600
Zenith	Jeffrey Bowman	4500	550

Such a short table, an *informal table*, might appear as the extension of a sentence in the text. Informal tables rarely exceed five lines and have no title.

	Neckwear Purchasing Decisions by Income (Percentage of Respondents)			
Purchaser	**Income (in thousands of dollars)**			
	Under 10	**10–19.9**	**20–29.9**	**30 and Over**
Self	35.6	34.1	38.1	43.2
Other	31.2	37.8	33.9	35.2
Don't wear	30.6	24.8	24.4	17.8

FIGURE 8–6. A formal table (courtesy of Jane Bacal).

Use a *formal table* when you have more extensive information to present, as in Figures 8–6 and 8–7, both of which result from surveys. Formal tables are common in reports. They have titles and are often numbered (or lettered) for reference in a series. Conventions for balance sheets are well established and must be followed precisely. For other tables, you'll need to create titles for the whole and for rows (horizontal) and columns (vertical). Place units of measurement in the title, not in each cell. And arrange items in some logical order: alphabetical, geographical, quantitative, or chronological. Because numbers are easier to compare in columns than in rows, they are usually placed in columns. Rows are also limited by the width of the page, whereas columns can be carried over to another page. So place a long string of data in a column. Line up all numbers along the decimal point. Place in the appendix any long tables, which usually aim to *record* rather than *persuade* (hence the term "reference tables").

The Sports Americans Like to Watch

Percentage of respondents who answered the following question, "How interested are you in watching each of the following?"

	Always	Usually	Sometimes	Never
Football	39%	16%	26%	19%
Baseball	28	17	37	18
Basketball	19	14	38	29
Boxing	19	10	29	41
Gymnastics	17	16	40	26
Swimming and diving	14	14	45	26
Ice skating	13	13	35	38
Horse racing	13	9	37	40
Tennis	12	14	38	35
Track and field	12	11	38	37
Skiing	11	13	42	33
Auto racing	10	10	41	39
Marathons	10	9	35	45
Professional wrestling	10	5	22	61
Bowling	9	8	33	49
Golf	8	8	30	53
Surfing	8	6	37	48
Weight lifting	8	6	35	47
Amateur wrestling	8	5	24	61
Boating	7	7	31	54
Soccer	6	6	32	54
Hockey	6	5	35	52
Jai-alai	1	2	12	78
Lacrosse	1	2	11	80

FIGURE 8–7. Another formal table (*Source:* Miller Lite Report on American Attitudes Toward Sports. Miller Brewing Company, 1983. As quoted by George Vecsey, "A Nation of Sports Fans," *The New York Times,* 16 March 1983, B, 11).

the Zoological Society of Philadelphia

Member Benefits

	Invitation to Exclusive Friends Events	Free Tickets To Zoobilee	Preview exhibit openings	Art and Architecture book, First Edition	Special reception with Curators	Invitation to Zoobilee	Invitation to Zoo Trips	Discount on Monorail	Invitation to Member's Day/Evenings	Member's Newsletter	Our Full Color Magazine—Zoo One	Guest Passes	Free Admission		1982
							•	•	•	•	•	•	•	INDIVIDUAL	$20
						•	•	•	•	•	•	•	•	FAMILY	$25
					•	•	•	•	•	•	•	•	CONTRIBUTING	$35	
				•	•	•	•	•	•	•	•	•	SUSTAINING	$100	
		•	•	•	•	•	•	•	•	•	•	•	ASSOCIATE	$500	
	•	•	•	•	•	•	•	•	•	•	•	•	FRIENDS OF THE ZOO	$1000	

FIGURE 8–8. Matrix (used by permission of the Marketing and Development Office of The Zoological Society of Philadelphia).

Matrixes

One version of a table common in business presentations is a *matrix*. The rows are labeled to indicate components or specific items. The columns are labeled to indicate characteristics—in effect, the dependent variables. A notation in the cell at the intersection of the row and the column shows whether that item displays that characteristic. Figure 8–8 is a matrix showing benefits to members of the Philadelphia Zoo. These forms consolidate a good deal of information so that it can be assimilated at one glance.

Graphs

Balance sheets and other tables of financial data are important for the record. But to highlight information in order to inform or persuade the reader, you may plot certain numbers of interest in a graph that shows the changes in one thing over time—trends or rates of change, as in Figure 8–2. The plot shows direction more vividly, although it loses some of the precision of the actual numbers. Many tables can be converted into graphs, but unless data points are noted, graphs cannot be converted into tables. You don't know from Figure 8–2, for example, the exact numbers of the units.

By convention, the independent variable (often a measure of time) falls along the horizontal axis, and the dependent variable is shown on the vertical axis. Label the vertical axis to the left to keep the area

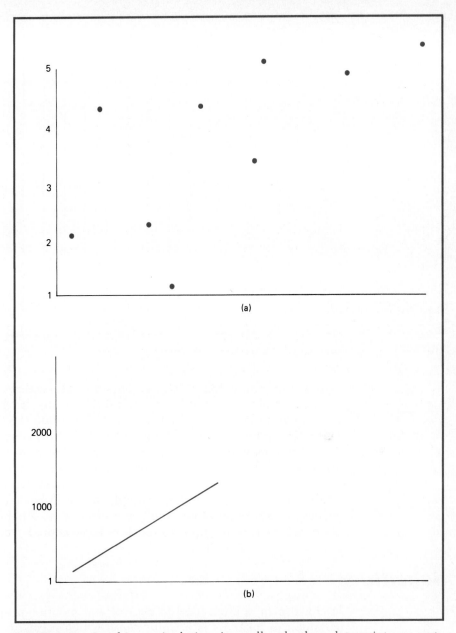

FIGURE 8–9. Graphic manipulation. At small scale, these data points are scattered (a). They fail to line up. But to present a prettier picture—to force the data into a straight line—researchers sometimes just enlarge the scale, which blurs distinctions (b) (*Source:* D. C. Andrews and M. D. Blickle, *Technical Writing: Principles and Forms.* 2nd ed. [New York: Macmillan, 1982], 181. Used by permission.)

TASK IDENTIFICATION		MONTHS FROM START OF PROJECT								
NUMBER OF TASK	BRIEF TITLE	1	2	3	4	5	6	7	8	

FIGURE 8–10. Blank Gantt chart.

within the grid as free of text as possible. Use scales that are easy to read (multiples of 2, 5, 10, and so on). If you display several lines on one graph, provide a key or labels to differentiate the lines (as in Figure 8–2). To emphasize *each* line, you might also consider using a series of figures with parallel axes and scales. In most cases, keep 0 in the scale; if the data do not approach 0, then indicate a suppressed 0 clearly to the reader. It is easy to mislead readers with manipulations of the scales on a graph. For example, a researcher faced with a scattering of data points that won't line up at a reasonable scale can always *make* them line up if the scale is large enough (see Figure 8–9).

Schedules

A chart form is often used to control and monitor projects. The most common in business is a *Gantt chart*, which mixes the elements of a table and a bar chart (Figure 8–10). Another form, often used in the military, is a *PERT* (program evaluation and review technique) chart. A *critical path method* (CPM) diagram indicates a sequence of activities and their simultaneous or sequential relationships around certain decision points (Figure 8–11).

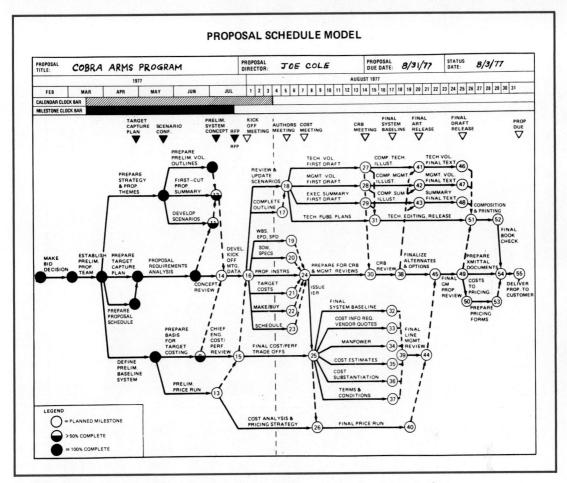

FIGURE 8–11. Critical path method diagram that schedules the writing of a major proposal, by W.A. Waddington, RCA Government Electronic Systems Division (courtesy of RCA).

Organizational Charts

Organizational charts, like the one in Figure 8–12, show the management hierarchy of an organization. They differentiate the levels of some structure. They are often printed in series, with subsequent charts breaking out the structure indicated in one box in a main chart. Figure 8–12, for example, breaks out the structure of the "Helicopter Programs" division, which would be indicated in one box on the first chart representing the entire company. Most organizations denote reporting

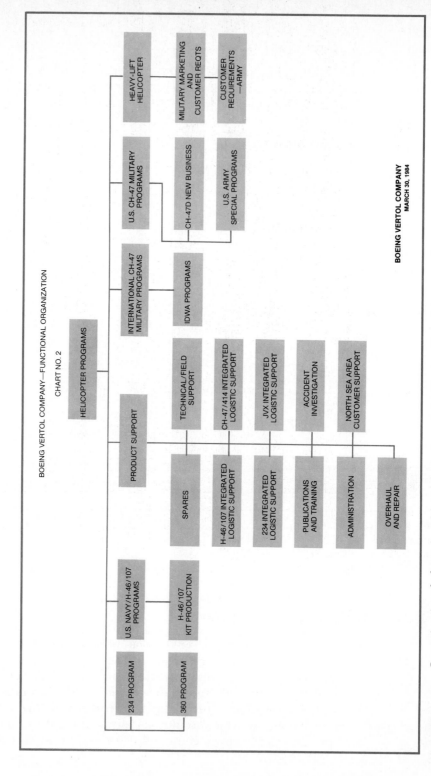

FIGURE 8–12. Organizational chart (used by permission of the Boeing Vertol Company).

lines and responsibilities through an organizational chart. The top manager or administrator is usually on top of the chart. Equal functions read from left to right, subordinate ones from top to bottom. Changes in company structure are envisioned first through "what if" charts. The final revised structure is communicated to the employees in the new chart.

Flowcharts

An organizational chart usually arranges items vertically, from the top of the company or the top of the division down. A flowchart may read from top to bottom or from left to right and shows a sequence of events or steps over time. Symbols, either representational or abstract, are connected by arrows that indicate direction. Figure 8–13 is a flowchart showing improved energy use with electricity from solar conversion.

Another form of such a chart is a *decision tree*, which shows the

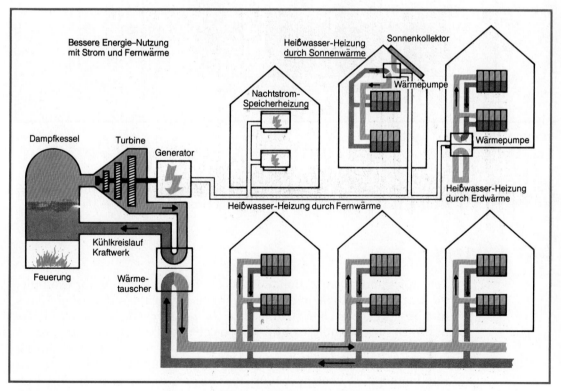

FIGURE 8–13. Flowchart (courtesy of IZE, Frankfurt, West Germany).

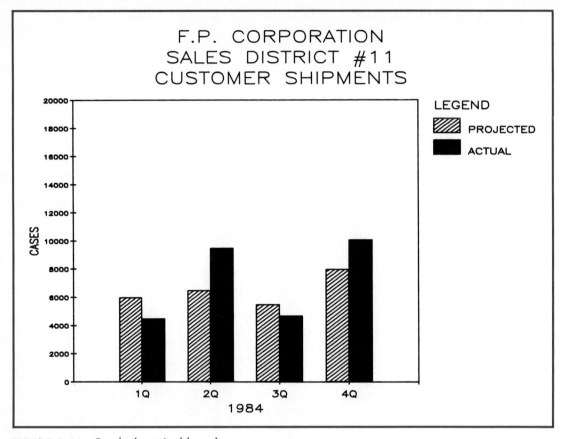

FIGURE 8–14. Stacked vertical bar chart.

branching stages in decision making. It provides a pattern for deciding routine matters or for troubleshooting problems.

Bar Charts

Schedules and organizational charts emphasize *sequence*, for example, the sequence of people in a reporting hierarchy or the sequence of events in a program. Bar charts emphasize *comparison*. The bar chart in Figure 8–14, for example, contrasts projected and actual customer shipments for one sales district of the F. P. Corporation. The juxtaposing of the bars for each quarter (1Q, 2Q, 3Q, 4Q) emphasizes the comparison. Figure 8–15 contrasts household income in two years for the U.S. population over fifty-five years old. The bars dramatize the similarities

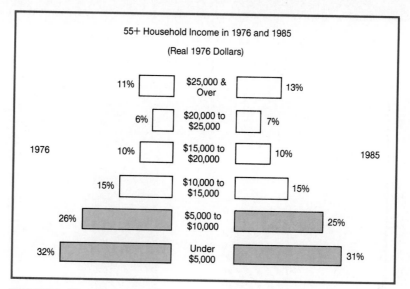

FIGURE 8–15. Horizontal bar chart (*Source:* U.S. Bureau of the Census, *Consumer Income,* Series P-60. Chart reproduced by the Population Resource Center, 622 Third Ave., New York, N.Y. 10017. Used by permission).

in the two years; the percentage figures for each year increase precision for the careful reader.

Bars may be arranged either vertically (as in Figures 8–14 and 8–16) or horizontally (as in Figure 8–15). Two or more units may be juxtaposed in one bar (Figure 8–14), or the bar may be segmented internally (Figure 8–16). Bars should be of the same width and equally spaced. For sales presentations, the bars may be enlivened by being presented in other forms—as Santa Clauses, bags of money, hockey sticks, shareholders, pilots, or planes (see Figure 8–22)—that reinforce the meaning. The cute shape, however, should not distort the information.

Figure 8–16 is based on the same information as that in Figures 8–2 and 8–17. The bar chart emphasizes the regional comparison and probably seems more concrete than the graph.

Pie Charts

On the other hand, the *pie charts* in Figure 8–17 emphasize the *proportion* of total growth. In a persuasive presentation, the Northeastern Division would probably prefer the bar chart because it shows an in-

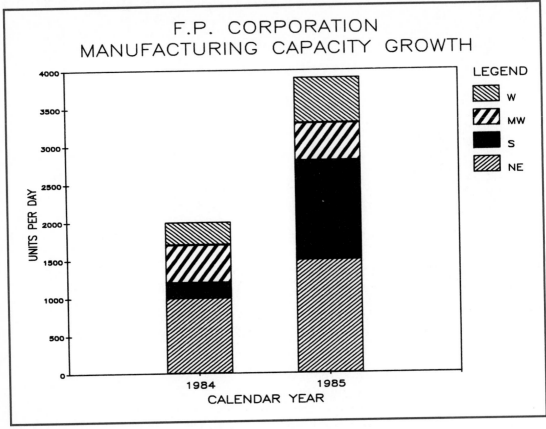

FIGURE 8–16. Segmented vertical bar chart.

crease in *units* produced; the Southern Division would prefer a *pie* chart because that shows how its *percentage* increased (from 10 percent to 33.3 percent). Figure 8–17A graphically displays the Northeast's slip from 50 percent to 38.5 percent. In showing the two pies as the same size, Figure 8–17A ignores, in effect, the total increase; that *increase* is made prominent in Figure 8–17B, for which the computer drew *proportional pies* whose size is calculated to reflect total units a day. Because of the software available for producing them, pie charts are increasingly common in reports. Budget directors use them to explain divisions of the budget. Most college alumni magazines use them to note sources of alumni giving funds. In general, the largest piece appears at the top (or right). If one particular element is to be emphasized, it is often "exploded," or raised from the plane of the pie.

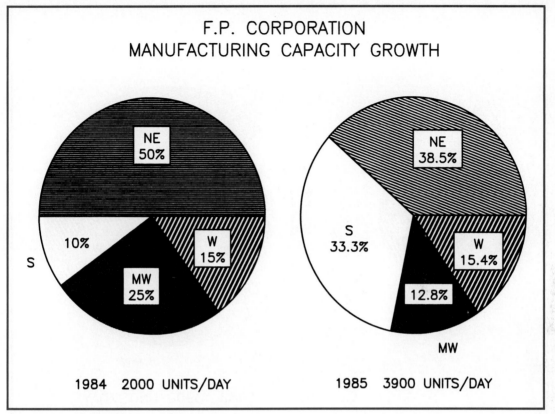

FIGURE 8–17. CHART A Pie charts. In drawing Chart A, the computer ignored differences in total units produced and drew two equal pies; Chart B shows proportional pies drawn to reflect the increase in units.

Pictograms

Pictograms combine the attributes of a diagram and a picture. Figure 8–18 is a pictogram depicting the results of the United Way campaign at The Ohio State University. One visual symbol of the university is its football stadium; to draw interest, the dollar amounts raised in the campaign are superimposed on that image. Customer-oriented literature often uses pictograms to engage the interest of the readers, as in Figure 8–22.

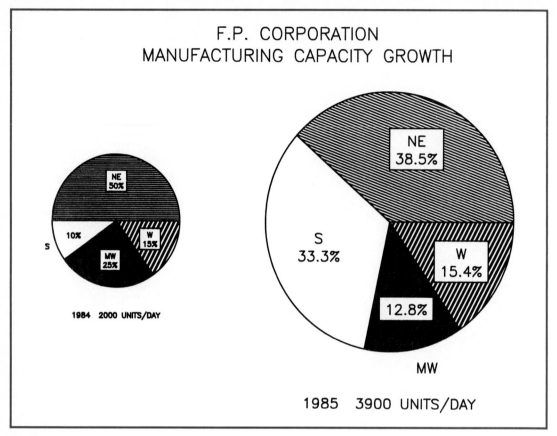

FIGURE 8–17. CHART B.

Maps

Maps represent a territory that you need to know about for some purpose—getting from here to there, for example. Maps show territory at different scales and with different degrees of detail. Figure 8–19, for example, is a large-scale map without much detail. The star indeed locates the state of Delaware; but someone *in* Delaware, or even in the town of *Newark*, where the office is located, would be hard put to find it. Instead, as Figure 8–20 shows, a smaller scale, more detailed map is needed. Computer-generated maps can superimpose, for example, population data on a map of Europe. Mapmaking is a complex art and science. But simply drawn maps may be just right to let a reader envision the spatial relationships you need to describe.

FIGURE 8–18. Pictogram (*Source: On Campus,* December 16, 1982, p. 8. Used by permission, The Ohio State University).

Drawings

A map is one form of *drawing.* Drawings serve several purposes in documents. One purpose is to serve as a *visual metaphor* to explain a concept. Figure 8–21, for example, is a drawing from the user's guide to a data-base management system called Framework. The drawing reinforces the definition of a *frame:*

> A movable and variable container for information. You can place information into a frame, or you can place a frame around information that is already in another frame. Then you can use the frame to manipulate the information inside it.[1]

[1] Bill Harrison, *Framework ®: An Introduction* (Culver City, Calif.: Ashton-Tate Publishing Group, 1984), 4. © Ashton-Tate, 1984. Used by permission.

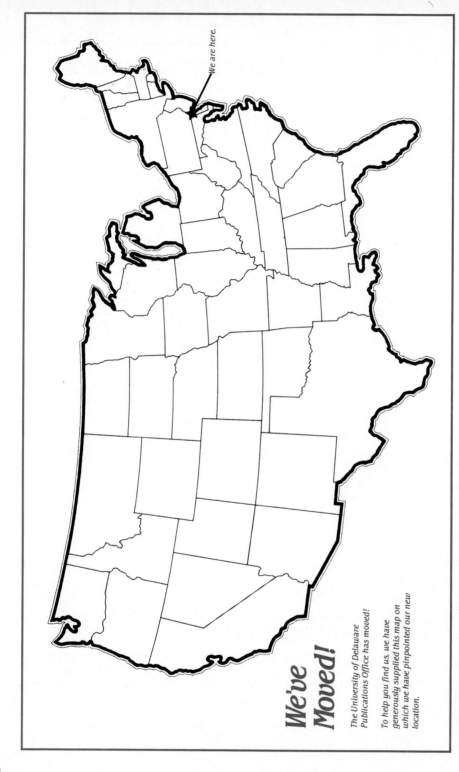

We are here.

We've Moved!

The University of Delaware Publications Office has moved!

To help you find us, we have generously supplied this map on which we have pinpointed our new location.

FIGURE 8–19. Large-scale map showing an office location.

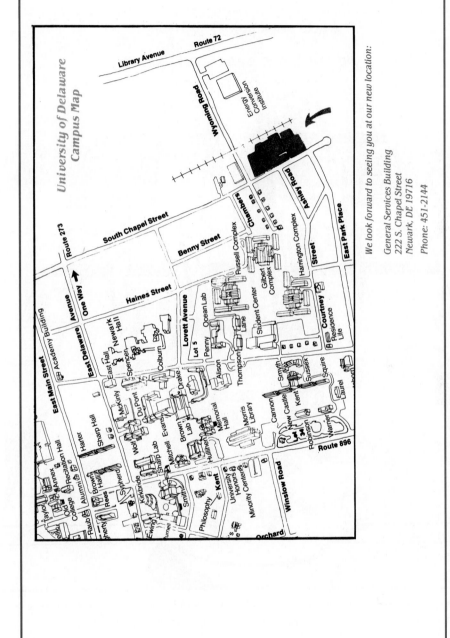

University of Delaware
Campus Map

We look forward to seeing you at our new location:

General Services Building
222 S. Chapel Street
Newark, DE 19716
Phone: 451-2144

FIGURE 8–20. The same spot at smaller scale. Design by Marianne M. Bonsallo. Used by permission.

141

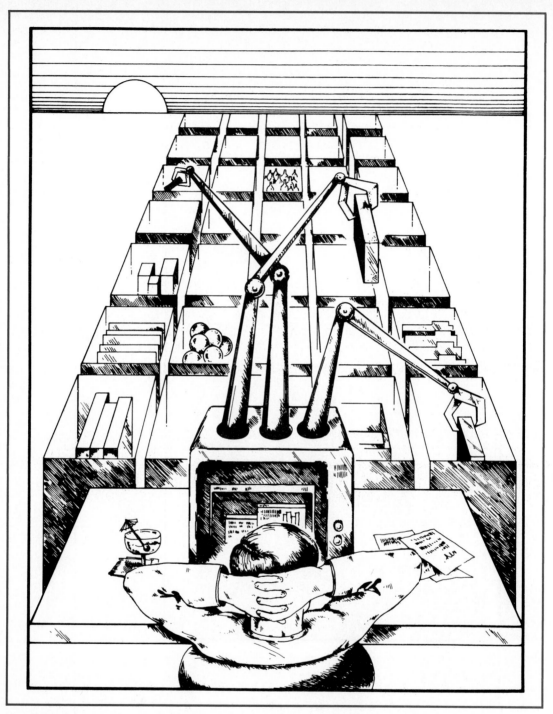

FIGURE 8–21. Drawing that explains the term *frame* (*Source: Framework: An Introduction.* © Ashton-Tate, 1984. Used by permission).

The drawing shows the computer accessing these containers.

Drawings also instruct. Guides for assembling or troubleshooting devices are often best presented visually (see Chapter 21). Even if the reader doesn't know the name for a particular component, he or she can *see* in a drawing what attaches to what. Moreover, in an increasingly multinational culture, drawings overcome language barriers in the explanation of physical systems. Drawings can also show an "exploded" or "cutaway" view, that is, each component pulled apart in relationship to the whole—a way of seeing both the surface and what's beneath it. Drawings may be presented in different scales, sometimes in a series in which you focus in on a point of interest.

Photographs

Like drawings, photographs can show devices, physical spaces, and people. They are often expensive both to produce and to reproduce, but certain communications goals can be achieved only with photographs. Many business documents feature them, particularly annual reports and company magazines, both those that are circulated in-house and those distributed to stockholders and clients (see Chapter 22).

Photographs show vivid detail at the same time that they create dramatic impact. The options for reproducing them are many: in color or black and white, in different sizes, in isolation or in a group of photographs. They confirm the reality of information, systems, and ideas. They are often impressive.

Photographic slides are a major element in many business presentations. Arranged in a series and presented by several computer-controlled projectors on many screens, such photographs can build an emotional high in an audience. Such effects are used frequently in motivational screenings for a sales staff.

But photographs have certain disadvantages. They are expensive to reproduce well. They may also show more detail than one wants: The person or object to be highlighted may be lost in a field of other objects in the photograph.

Composing with Visuals: Guidelines

The *form* of visual you select, then, is determined by your material, your reader, your goal, and your method for producing the visual. For example, here is some information from the U.S. Census Bureau on child care arrangements used by employed mothers:

Another home	40.2%
Child's home	30.6%
Group center	14.8%
At work	9.1%
Other	5.3%

Because this information is stated in percentages, one visual form of presentation is a *pie chart*. For a general audience, a pie would be appropriate (one such pie appeared in *The Wall Street Journal*[2]). The pie gives a nice overview. But if you were a social worker writing a report that recommends stringent supervision of the individuals who care for others' children in their homes, you'd probably want to emphasize that 40.2 percent figure. Thus you might use a *horizontal bar chart*, the longest bar, of course, being that for "Another home." Bars and pies, however, carry connotations of stretching toward the reader, that is, of popularizing information. In a formal report to a company that's considering starting a program of child care at the workplace, a table of percentages might be most appropriate.

Your choice will also reflect the methods available to you for creating the visual. You need only a pen or pencil (perhaps a typewriter) and a piece of paper to create a table. Figures require a bit more creativity. To achieve that creativity, you may work with a graphic artist, or you can buy prepackaged art work in the form of clip-art books. These are commercially available volumes that contain drawings and set phrases ready for photographic reproduction. You just clip what you want and glue it onto a master page. You can also use rub-on letters, Kroy lettering machines, and templates.

But increasingly, you'll turn to computers for graphic creativity. The possibilities are indeed stunning. You simply enter values into a prewritten application, and the software creates pie charts, bar charts, tables—whatever you want. All the charts for the F. P. Corporation in this chapter, for example, were created on a personal computer. Some very sophisticated packages available on personal computers even store maps and drawings that you can call up and modify with a few key strokes. Computers have vastly enhanced the range of visuals that you can create by yourself, at your own desk. You can now do what previously only trained graphic artists could achieve. Such programs have led to "desktop publishing," the creation of finished documents, visuals and text, right from your own terminal (see Chapter 10).

As you gather information, then, wherever possible, develop a *visual* form for its presentation. Sketch a table or figure. Enter your in-

[2] 9 January 1985, 29.

formation into a graphics program and play with different forms. Think about where you can save a stretch of prose by turning the information into a table. Think about the need to comment on the visual in words, or to illustrate words with a diagram or picture. Check on the visual itself and on its integration with the text. Here are eight checkpoints:

1. Simplify.
2. Keep figures in a series consistent.
3. Create informative titles.
4. Document all information.
5. Connect the visual and the text.
6. Consider how the visual will look in final form.
7. Avoid distortion.
8. Design the document.

Simplify

Many of the visuals you prepare to record information are too complicated to express that information well for readers. Because you are familiar with the material, you can interpret a graph that displays eight or nine curves. But a reader coming cold to the discussion might well not be able to untangle the lines. See what can be left out. See if you can select data (without distortion, of course) for an overview chart and supplement that with tables in an appendix or lists in a footnote.

Keep Figures in a Series Consistent

To streamline visuals, develop a series to explain key concepts and information. Break out details from an overview financial presentation, for example. Just remember to keep the series consistent in style, size, scale, color, typeface, and the like. To highlight one item, of course, you can introduce a slight change in format.

Create Informative Titles

Even if you think the content of your graph speaks for itself, your audience may not agree. In a title, you warn the reader about what to expect in the visual, and you provide a way to refer to it. Avoid flat labels:

Organizational Chart

Instead, use the label to interpret the message:

Proposed Reorganization of the Educational Relations Division Under a new Vice-president for Educational Development

Here's the label for a photograph in the annual report of a company that produces temperature control devices for computer rooms. The photo shows researchers wiring a control system:

Research and development are the essential bridge between customer needs and product innovation. Quality control systems have been computerized for maximum efficiency and accuracy. The microprocessor of the Delux System/3 provides complete monitoring and control.[3]

The reader, skimming the report, is drawn to the picture. The label uses that attention to reinforce a message concerning research and development.

Not all labels, of course, should be that long. To condense the label, sometimes information is given in both a title and a subtitle:

Women in Management
The Percentage of Women in Management in Fortune 500 Companies Has Risen Steadily Since 1984.

This title heads a stacked bar chart showing percentages of men and women over five years. Full sentences that show results, not just a topic, enhance the message for the reader.

In addition to a title, all figures and tables in a formal report must be designated by some code as parts of a series. Usually, for figures, this code is a number. Figures may be numbered in sequence from 1 throughout the report or may be numbered by section or chapter (Figure 1–1, 1–2, 2–1, and so on). Tables may be numbered or lettered (Table 1 or Table A). Tables are always labeled at the top, consistent with the headings for rows and columns. Figures may be labeled at either the top or the bottom. Before you produce the report, choose one location and place your labels consistently. Internal labels within figures should read in the same direction. Collect all labels in a "Table of Figures" or "List of Figures" or "List of Tables" at the beginning of the report (see Chapter 20).

Document All Information

You provide a reference note or footnote for borrowed words and ideas in a report. Do the same for visuals. Use one of several systems. The simplest is to write a source line at the bottom of the figure:

Source: The U.S. Census Bureau.

---

[3] *Liebert: 1983 Annual Report,* The Liebert Corporation, 15.

Or use a note tied to your documentation system for the report as a whole (see Chapter 5). The notation belongs at the end of the figure's title. Information within a table or figure that you'd like to put in a note can be marked with an * asterisk, † a dagger, or some other notation; the explanation belongs at the bottom of the table or figure. For figures developed internally in an organization, name the creator and the date so that the reader will know the currency of the figure and the person who might be able to answer questions about it.

Connect the Visual and the Text

It's easiest for the reader if the table or figure and your discussion of it are close together. Gaps between the two reduce the reader's motivation to connect them and reduce the impact you're trying to make with them. One exception: Visuals you'll refer to in several places in the text—a site diagram, for example, for a new shopping mall that your whole report discusses—may be reasonably placed in an appendix (see Chapter 20). You might also consider a foldout form for such a visual, or you might make it somehow detachable, so that the reader can place it next to the text while reading. Every visual must be mentioned in the text, preferably *before* the reader encounters it. Add a page reference for the visual if it is not on the same page as the text.

> Figure 6 (page 14) shows the rise in maintenance costs for the system over a ten-year period. [emphasizes the figure itself]

Or:

> Maintenance costs for the system rose steadily over a ten-year period (Figure 6, p. 14). [emphasizes the content]

Check the report for consistency in data between text and visuals. Sometimes these are prepared at different times, by different people. Someone has to be responsible for making sure that the numbers agree. Of course, check the arithmetic, too, and make sure that columns and pie charts of percentages add up to 100 percent.

Consider How the Visual Will Look in Final Form

Many visuals are reduced before they are placed in a report. Slides are enlarged as they appear on the screen in front of an audience. Allow for reduction and enlargement as you plan presentations.[4]

---

[4]For detailed advice on sizing graphics—and for a good overview of computer graphics—see Betty S. Matkowski, *Steps to Effective Business Graphics.* (San Diego: Hewlett-Packard, 1983)—available from HP Marketing Communications, 16399 W. Bernardo Dr., San Diego, CA 92127.

Avoid Distortion

Like words, visuals can stretch the truth. Sometimes the stretching is accidental. In a statistical presentation, for example, you may include so many figures that the abundance serves as a smokescreen that hides the *one* figure the reader really needs and that reduces the discussion to a trivial level. Sometimes authors deliberately distort information. Photographs can be retouched to eliminate unsightly trash, for example, next to a warehouse. Or labels may deceive: A brochure for a condominium may carry photographs of a "typical" unit that match only one (if any) unit in the group, and certainly not any that a potential buyer could purchase for the stated price. Bars in a chart can be manipulated so that their size appears to contradict the real numbers they represent. Some software houses, eager to get new packages on the market before they are really ready to run, draw pictures of screens showing effects that the software can't really achieve. (Some competitors call this *vaporware*.)

Design the Document

Finally, consider your document *as a whole*. Review not only single visuals but the effect of the visuals as they interact and as they are integrated with the text on a series of pages. Figure 8–22 shows one page of integrated visuals—aimed at a popular audience. Note the balance of the page and the parallelism of the visuals. Coordinate emphasis among the visuals in *your* presentation. Have you devoted visuals to minor points and neglected major ones? Does any information in one visual contradict that in another? Are visuals bunched in one section of the document when they might be spread out to lend interest to the whole text? If two visuals are on the same page, are they balanced? Placing a visual off-center, for example, highlights it, but overdone, such asymmetry may disorient the reader and introduce an unwanted element of eccentricity into the presentation. Make sure that your visuals don't break the margins of the page.

Going Visual

If you are not in the habit of thinking visually, it's time to begin. Many of your readers and listeners will be best persuaded by clear visual presentations, and much business information is best seen and understood in visual forms. Moreover, as Figure 8–22 notes, visuals are indeed at least *one* international language of business. As more and more

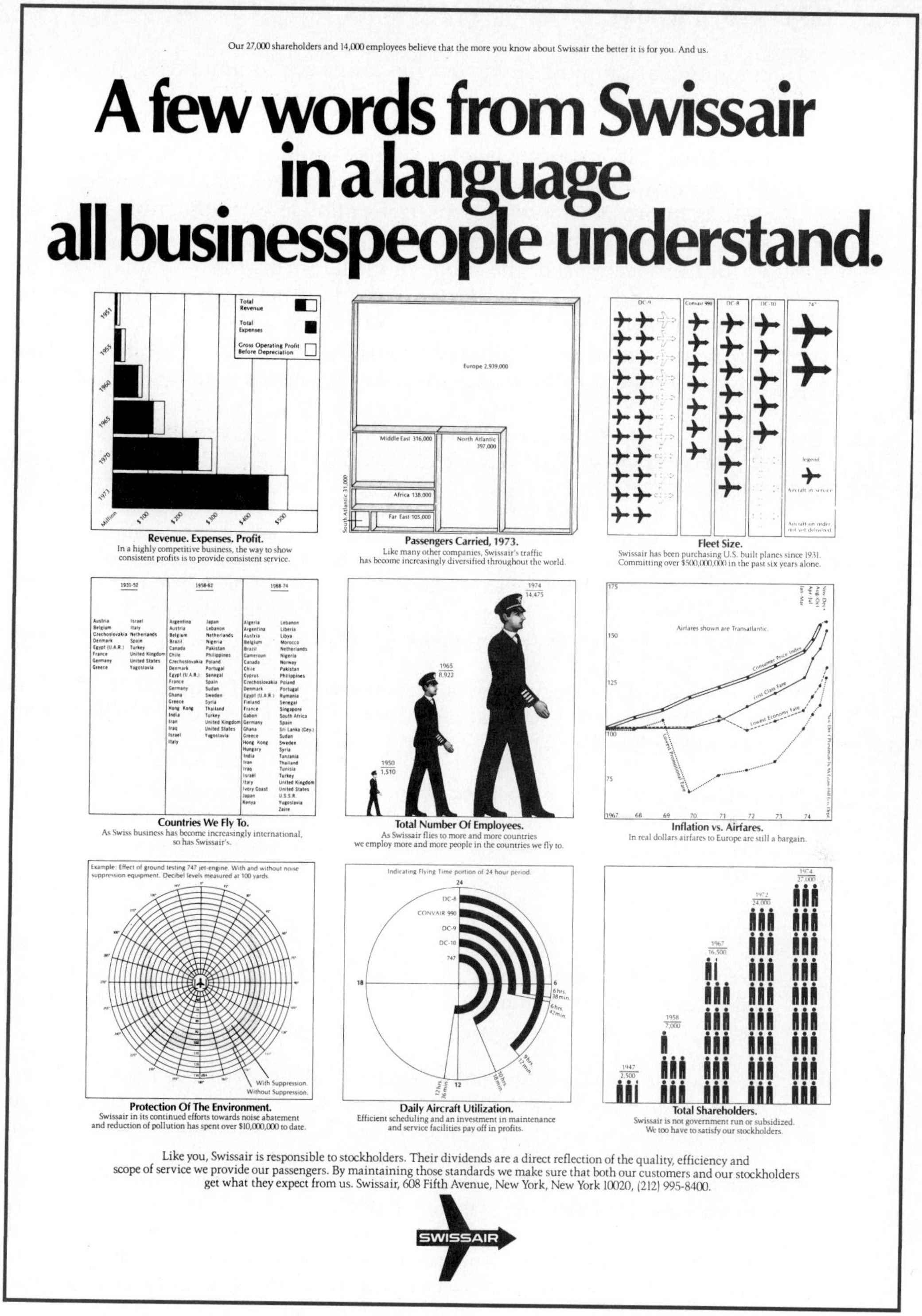

FIGURE 8–22. A well-designed page of visuals (used by permission of Swissair).

communication must serve varying language communities, businesses rely increasingly on visual forms.

Visuals, like words, then, are tools for capturing and conveying information. Like words, visuals can also confuse. They can be misused. Through carelessness or deviousness, an author can lie in pictures as well as in prose. Glossy presentations and clever photographs may deceive more than they inform.

But properly used, the range of visual forms for both analyzing information and presenting it provides an author with expanded strategies for informing and persuading an audience. Here, we've introduced some forms as they fit different contexts. Play with these to see what fits the context for the communication problems you have to solve.

Exercises

1. Collect a sample of corporate annual reports, and examine the visuals. Is the consolidated financial information (all the balance sheets, income statements, and so on) presented in the same form in each? Or are there differences? What accounts for any differences? How are photographs used in the reports? How does the choice of photographs affect the *style* of the reports and reflect the *image* of the corporation in general?

2. Compare this configuration of proportional pies to Figure 8–17A. The creator of Figure 8–17A liked that one better. Do you agree? How do the two figures differ? (see p. 152).

3. Here's a bar chart of cost distribution by region for cases of powder distributed by the three divisions (FRT, A&P, and MFG) of the F. P. Corporation. Is the chart emphatic? Could the information be highlighted better in three separate charts? In what form of document or presentation would such a chart be appropriate? (see p. 153).

4. Here's a pie chart showing F. P.'s regional sales performance for one month. Convert the information into a bar chart. Convert it into a table. Which emphasizes the information more? For what audience would each be best suited? (see p. 154).

5. Examine the visuals in popular business publications, like *Forbes*, *Business Week*, *Fortune*, and *The Wall Street Journal*. What kinds of information do authors tend to include in visual rather than verbal form? Do you think, for any one article, that the visuals are the *basis* of the presentation or were added as interest-getting devices? In other words, which came first, words or pictures? Bring some examples into class and discuss.

6. Label each of the types of visuals presented in Figure 8–22, and discuss how each functions to present a certain kind of information. How is parallelism maintained in the series? What image of Swissair does the ad present?

7. Examine the logos, that is, the graphic symbols, of several companies. You may find these on products as well as on stationery and company-produced brochures. Comment on the *image* of the company that the logo seems to invoke. For example, many people consider the blue IBM logo conservative and understated—and also highly technical and modern.

8. In a full-page advertisement, Mitsubishi Electric showed two items: a piece of pie on a plate and, next to it, chopsticks on a napkin. The picture was meant to reinforce the message, stated briefly in the lower left corner, that a blending of cultures—in this case, Japanese and American—can lead to producing the best products. Bring to class or create other simple visuals that reinforce a sales message.

9. Arrange the information in the following paragraph in a *matrix*. Is anything missing?

> In our survey we examined the hiring practices of four companies. We were chiefly interested in whether they interviewed on campus or not, whether they hired only business students or were interested in talking with other majors, whether they offered starting salaries over $20,000, and whether they had a training program for new hires. Groliers Inc. hires only business students; their starting salaries are over $20,000, and they are interested in talking only with business majors. They interview on campus. Micromessages Ltd. believes that new hires should start with fairly low salaries and work up fast, so they start at under $20,000. They interview on campus for all majors and have a training program. The Kermit Factory, which interviews on campus and pays more than $20,000 in starting salaries, offers training programs and hires only business majors. The last people we talked with were from Bowman Inc., which interviews all majors, and interviews on campus. They offer a training program and start new hires at over $20,000.

10. If you are working on a group project, assign one person to work up visual presentations. That person should be alert in any meetings about the document to chances for exploiting visuals and should prepare the final visuals so that they are consistent with the rest of the text.

11. Obtain copies of *instructions* for assembling or operating equipment intended for a multilanguage readership. Examine the use of visuals to carry the bulk of the instructions. Note particularly international visual symbols for shipping and handling that are contained on the packaging. How easy are the symbols to understand? How much of the instruction can you understand from the visuals alone?

12. Assemble the statistics for the last five seasons of a local baseball, football, or soccer team: rosters, player performances, team performance, gate receipts, schedules, coaches' records, and the like. Then select information and display it to meet the following situations:
Situation 1
Writer: Public relations department of the team
Occasion: newspaper advertisement of team program

Material: schedule for one month
Audience: general
Purpose: to inform fans of the schedule
Situation 2
Writer: Player X's agent
Occasion: contract time
Material: Player X's stats, perhaps some comparative stats, X's salary expressed as a percentage of receipts, and so on.
Audience: the team's general manager
Purpose: to get the most lucrative contract possible

Invent other scenarios as well. Mix in some bad years with the good and determine how to handle that news.

13. Exploit opportunities for using visuals in *your* reports. In particular, you might want to try out some graphics packages that run on computers available at your school or office. All the F. P. Corporation visuals, for example, were produced on a personal computer. Test-drive a graphics package for your next assignment.

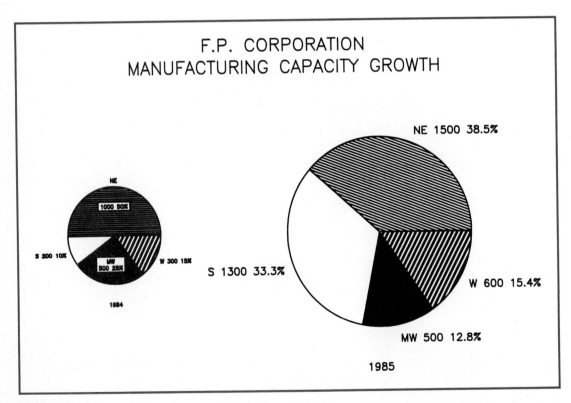

EXERCISE 2.

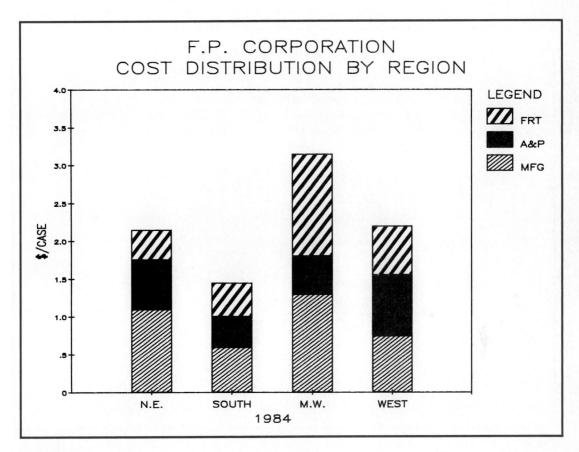

EXERCISE 3.

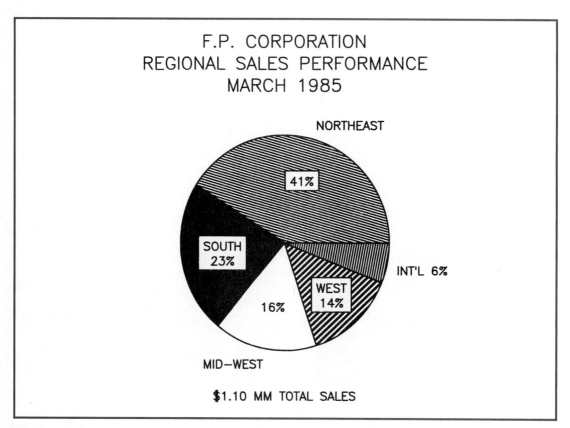

F.P. CORPORATION
REGIONAL SALES PERFORMANCE
MARCH 1985

NORTHEAST

41%

SOUTH
23%

INT'L 6%

WEST
14%

16%

MID—WEST

$1.10 MM TOTAL SALES

EXERCISE 4.

Revising

Revising is quality control, the final step in managing the process of writing. The amount of time necessary for revision varies from project to project and writer to writer, but it's required time. Revision brings into relief concepts and evidence only vaguely approximated in earlier drafts. You work in pieces as you draft; revision makes the product seamless. You also may discover new possibilities as you revise. Revision, then, gives you a chance to look good—to look as if you think only clear thoughts and always write well. This chapter discusses routines for revision. It then presents a three-phase check for ensuring the quality of your prose. Finally, it looks at advice on finishing the document and on reviewing the work of other writers.

Revision Routines

People revise in different ways, some productive and some not. Figure 9–1 provides comments from managers and other professionals in business about how they revise.

As the comments in Figure 9–1 show, individuals vary in their revision routines. Some documents are easy: They seem to write themselves. Some tie the writer in knots. Whatever the document, however, follow these guidelines, whether you spend a few minutes or several days in the process.

Draft with Revising in Mind

Write a draft double- or triple-spaced to allow for insertions of new text. If you know you have trouble writing, resist the temptation to look backward too much as you draft. Remember that you can return to the text and shore things up in revision. If the insertions begin to make the page too messy to read, retype it. A computer, of course, makes drafting and revising physically simple.

Distance Yourself from the Text

After you finish the draft, take a break before revising. Build that break time into any plan for writing. You may have only an hour or so; a day or two is preferable on a long project. Give yourself time to forget and then to come back to the text with new eyes. Try outlining the text from memory on a clean sheet of paper. Can you remember the main points? If not, then they probably won't be clear to a reader of the text. Ask a friend to outline the text for you as a way of gauging the suitability of your organization.

"I'm afraid I'll lose my train of thought if I look anywhere but on the next line as I write, so I glue my hand to what I've written and charge on."

"I usually go back after every paragraph."

"I generally try to follow my outline to the end, using most or all of the information I have. Then, once I've finished, I let the paper sit and take a break (we take a break from each other). Then I come back, reread, and revise."

"I write for a specific amount of time—say, two hours—and look back only for little things when I don't know where I'm going. Then I try to find someone to read what I've written and help me decide what else I need to do."

"I look back every couple of paragraphs to make sure everything is moving coherently. There are some sentences or passages that I may feel need work as I'm writing them. These I mark to look at again when I'm thinking more clearly. After I'm through the draft, I put it aside and come back later."

"I look back all the time. I pause at every word, scratch it out, try to see how I can escape. A sentence may take me fifteen or twenty minutes to write."

"In a first draft, I don't look back until I have covered one of the points in my outline completely. On the next draft, I usually write a paragraph, reread it, revise, and then move to the next paragraph."

"I look back when I think I may be off on a tangent and may have lost my train of thought. I like to see where I've come from so I'll know where I'm going."

"If things are going well, I don't stop. I stop when I'm puzzled, and I revise while I'm waiting for inspiration."

FIGURE 9–1. Managers and other professionals comment on how they revise.

Revise in Increments

Improving a text, like improving corporate performance, requires incremental thinking. "Productivity improvement never is one big home run," noted B. R. Roberts, then chair and chief executive officer of Mead Corporation. "It's achieved by a lot of little base hits."[1] In revising your draft, accumulate base hits. Read through once just for accuracy of information. Read through again looking for main points. Read through another time for organization. Resist the temptation to start fussing word-by-word on Line 1. Note a cumbersome sentence as you're looking at organization, but don't get trapped. Begin your revising with a global search of the text for meaning and structure. Then focus on the local level. Moreover, don't start every revision session on Page 1. Start subsequent sessions somewhere in the middle, or near the end. Otherwise you will always be tired for the final stretch, and the revising there will suffer.

Accept Change

Several writers, both students and professionals, have remarked that revising is an accommodation to waste. You spend a lot of time drafting something, and then you spend a lot of time changing everything you've written. Particularly at a terminal, the time just seems to slip by. You end up after several hours with less than you began with. This process seems wasteful. Such seeming waste, however, is the price you often have to pay for quality. In a large project develop a routine for disposing of drafts. You may make several copies of each draft for review. When the reviews are in, consolidate the comments on one master copy. Keep this copy, perhaps in a three-ring binder for ease of reference. Throw out the other copies. Otherwise, you may find yourself unable to tell which is the corrected version.

Share Your Text

Share your text with a friend, a colleague, or a supervisor who can help you spot weaknesses. Such sharing may be particularly important with politically sensitive documents. Choose someone who can really help, not just someone who will flatter you. The last section of this chapter provides advice on reviewing someone else's text.

---

[1] As quoted by Ralph E. Winter, "Firms' Recent Productivity Drives May Yield Unusually Strong Gains," *The Wall Street Journal*, 14 June 1983, 37.

Read Aloud

Many idiosyncracies of expression, and especially the leftover phrasing of the business voice, become apparent when you read your own work aloud. *Listen* to yourself.

The Three-Phase Check

To ensure quality, think of revising as an *audit* of your text. Three levels of auditing are commonly recognized: Level I (financial, concerned with the actual entries, the details); Level II (economic, which is concerned with efficiency); and Level III (program, which is concerned with effectiveness). By analogy, we can identify three levels of revising:

- Level I—Microrevising: Words and sentences.
- Level II—Macrorevising: Organization, paragraphs, and visuals.
- Level III—Macrorevising: The Big Picture.

Such a three-phase check matches the outcome in a document against your intentions. Begin at Level III and arrive at Level I only when you know that the approach is satisfactory. It's pointless to fine-tune whole sections that may, when you review the text broadly, reveal themselves to be irrelevant.

Level III: The Big Picture

Drafting often leads to complexities. Accidentally written terms spark new thoughts that nudge you toward an important discovery—or drop the text into potholes of details or anecdotes. Through revision, you consolidate and simplify. You focus the big picture. In revising, look at the document *as a whole*. If the document is long, spread out five or six pages beside each other to see how the discussion is advancing without the artificial segmentation of individual sheets. Does it all work together in support of one main point—and is that the right point?

Delete items that raise unnecessary questions. Look for self-serving statements that may backfire. Consider this passage, from a quarterly report of a California company:

> Lack of forest fires in Canada and the United States has also caused losses in our fire-retardant chemical business. We are cognizant of the

impact of these losses on our total business and will take appropriate action to bring about an improvement in this situation.

That appropriate action *could* mean the starting of forest fires—presumably not what the company intends. See that the whole makes sense.

Level II: Organization

Then, make sure that the reader can follow the segments of that whole. Test your organization from the reader's point of view. One easy check: When you think of a new piece of information or idea that you would like to add, do you know right away where it belongs? Uncertainty can suggest that the document is poorly organized—and will cause the reader problems. You may revise organization with four purposes in mind:

1. To meet the document's goal.
2. To simplify.
3. To clarify introduction–middle–ending.
4. To insert cues for the reader.

Restructure to Meet the Goal

Absorbed in your material as you draft, you may need to revise to pull out some main point that the reader would like to see given more emphasis and use it as a peg from which to hang the rest of the information. Here, for example, is the draft of a memo:

> On August 1, I met with David Phillips in Dallas to discuss the new marketing plan. He generally agreed with our approach, particularly with the focus on the college market, but he felt that the techniques were not adequately directed. He also didn't like the "College Kids for Kidder" slogan. He said his son is a college student and hates being called a "kid."
> On August 4 I sent a revised plan to Phillips and to Todd Breckenridge in Toledo and Mark Jennings in Philadelphia. Mark suggested that we target certain selected large universities as a market sample. He also thought we should work with the student chapters of the Public Relations Society of America to sponsor a contest for a market plan. Give the best four in a preliminary competition, say, $1,000 to develop a serious plan and implement one strategy at their school. That would build some grass-roots (ivy-rooted? sorry about the

pun) support. If it were really any good, then we'd use this approach nationwide.

I took the contest idea to our staff meeting in NYC on September 17. (We lost more than a month because of vacations.) They liked it. I'll work on it and have a proposal together by our October 1 deadline.

The framework for this memo is time:

August 1
August 4
September 17
October 1

But that framework deemphasizes the idea of the contest. If your goal is to respond to a supervisor's request for an innovative marketing plan, then restructure:

Big Picture: Student Contest for Marketing Plan

Description
    Work with student public relations group
    Request preliminary proposals, then fund four best
    ($1,000 each) to come up with complete plan
Advantages
    Build grass-roots support
    Etc.
Supporters
    Mark Jennings's comments
    Preliminary approval at September 17 staff meeting in NYC

The restructuring accomplishes several purposes. It provides a central point and a hierarchy of supporting information rather than the flat terrain of the narrative (note, simply, the difference in levels of indention between the time-outline and the marketing plan). The plan provides headings to include in the text as aids to reading. It develops a structure that suggests to you as a writer where you need further information and makes inserting that information easy.

As a simple rule, test every narrative you write for a hidden structure of a main-idea-and-support. Narratives are fine for documentation and for descriptions of processes, but they often need to be transformed into another framework when you want to persuade a reader.

Restructure to Simplify

Here's the outline of a draft manual for officers of a university ski club:

1. Where to take winter ski trips, when to make plans and reservations, and how to make reservations
2. How to start club business in the fall
3. Develop membership drive and dues policy
4. Create publicity for club functions, trips, and activities
5. Maintain proper and accurate financial records

This list waffles. The author considered each of the items a "topic," too broad a category to aid in structuring. The items don't match logically: The first, for example, is much broader than any of the others, and yet it is not used to govern the others. The second suggests a vaguely chronological ordering of tasks (we'd expect, from it, a month-by-month survey of duties). Yet the rest of the items fail to fit a time frame. The third could be part of Item 2 (surely the drive and the policy would be part of the start-up). But it is presented as logically equal to Item 2. In this case, simply checking the headings for parallelism—logically and grammatically—reveals serious rifts in the structure of the discussion.

In revising, the author decided to peg his information to the enumerator term *club functions*. Here's the revised outline:

1. Club records
   Membership
   Financial
   Reporting obligations for Student Activities Council
2. Marketing
   Recruiting
   Advertising for trips
3. Trips
   General
   Planning/relations with travel agents
   Logistics during the trip
   Follow-up
   Trip-by-trip
   Sugarbush
   Elk Mountain
   Moose Mountain
   Wildcat

4. Club meetings
     Schedule
     Topics
     Notices

This new framework has the advantage of simplicity. It uses four main headings, and only one of them (3) has more than a second level of subheading. Sometimes you'll find that a draft has dissolved in sub-headings; you'll need to restructure to achieve no more than three levels.

With the new structure in place, you redraft. How much of the old text should you keep? If the new outline differs radically from the old, then perhaps you'd best not burden yourself with old text. Put that in a folder (or save the file on a disk or in memory) just in case you decide to go back to it, but write anew. If the change is not radical, however, you may want to work between the lines of the old draft. Keep a backup of the old file in case you change your mind.

Restructure to Clarify Introduction–Middle–Ending

Every document has three parts. Readers need these, even if the open-ing and closing are only one sentence each. Check particularly for the introduction. Does it drag, with too much background that delays the readers? Often you can simply cut and summarize the first few para-graphs of a draft. Or does the document really begin in the middle, overwhelming the readers with detail before they receive a framework for assimilating that information? Here, for example, is the first line of a memo from a researcher in a chemical company:

> The color of the substance was brown, almost black, and its composi-tion fell between 10 and 25 on the scale.

The readers may well ask, "What substance? Why is the color impor-tant? What scale?" Save such details for the middle. Step back and briefly describe the context and your reason for writing. If your ap-proach is direct, present the big picture. Make sure, too, that you tie things together at the end, which is always a point of extra attention from your readers.

Check the balance among the three parts. If you presented gener-alizations in the introduction, make sure the details follow in the mid-dle. If no details appear, go back to the field, or the office, or the re-cesses of your mind to find support. If you promised to compare two items, make sure that you've treated both. If you introduced a set of criteria, see that each criterion is discussed. If you announced four topics for analysis, make sure that you have covered four, the same four you announced, and in the same order.

Insert Cues for the Reader

Restructure, if necessary, to accommodate your goal and to simplify the plan. Then insert cues to show the *connections* among items. Where you see connections, the reader may see gaps.

Forecast and review.   Build in generalizations before details and look ahead and backward throughout a long text to keep the reader on track. If such statements aren't already in the text, insert them in revision, when you know what you've done. Insert transitional paragraphs in long reports (see Chapters 6 and 19).

Check headings.   If you haven't used headings at all, consider inserting some (see Chapter 6). If your discussion requires more than three levels of headings, determine whether all are necessary or whether you can simplify your presentation. Check parallelism. Check adherence to the conventions of your company and your readers.

Repeat key terms.   The repetition helps to remind the reader of the importance of the topic. Insert general terms to announce or remind the reader of how discrete items fit together: "these functions," "such investigations," "such students," "these animals."

Level II: Paragraphs

A major cue that keeps readers on track is paragraph design. Review your paragraphs.

Break Up Long Paragraphs

Skim the text to make certain that each finished page of a multipage document will have at least one paragraph indention. If your draft is double-spaced, envision how the text will look when it is reproduced in a final copy that may be presented in smaller type and single-spaced. A one-page memo may require just one paragraph. But if you have several lines of text, consider breaking the discussion into a few short paragraphs, and perhaps numbering each one for ease of reference.

Simplify Paragraph Structure

Here are two segments from the manual for the ski club.

Original

Sugarbush: late winter trip, during break between winter session and spring semester, low price. Price includes five-day pass, condominium lodging. You should expect in excess of 250 people; each year there has been at least a 15 percent increase in number of skiers over the previous year. For 1988, 251 skiers attended this trip. Provide trip ride sign-up and rooming list. Each night, local bars offer specials to university club skiers. Contact the travel agent for a listing of area bars. Each winter bars go out of business, so you should not assume that bars will remain in business from year to year for repeat business. Know that this trip is akin to spring break. Entertainment is first on every one's mind, so *après ski* activities must take a lot of attention.

Reservations and trip dates should be finalized the summer before the ski season. Our agent is Joanne Young of Esprit Tours. She has been handling the ski club's account as long as the club has been in existence. Esprit's office is located in Wilmington. Joanne will probably contact you first by getting your names and phone numbers from the Student Affairs Council. She knows that the club has a certain trip schedule and maintains contact with lodge owners and the mountains year round. All you have to do is give her a positive signal to make reservations. All trips except Sugarbush take one busload of skiers. The size of the bus limits the number of skiers. For Sugarbush, there is no reason that the club should not take as many people as possible. This trip has built itself quite a reputation, not only here on campus but in the Sugarbush Valley, too. The university club is the largest ski club or organization that the valley has ever seen in one week, so the club should allow as many skiers as possible to help create history.

These two paragraphs are unified around one topic: the ski club trip to Sugarbush. But there the unity ends. In revising, the author decided to develop a pattern he could use for descriptions of all trips. To ease the reader's access to the information, he chose to arrange short paragraphs with underlined labels that cued the reader to the content of each paragraph.

Revision

SUGARBUSH

Overview: The trip to Sugarbush (in Warren, Vermont) is the highlight of the winter. Many members join just for this trip. We're also the largest ski club to spend a week at Sugarbush, so we're well known there and we need to keep up our reputation.

Dates: Week between winter session and spring semester.

Cost: Low (about $200)

Number of Skiers: Expect over 251 (the number that went in 1988). Each year the number has increased by 15 percent.

Arrangements: Joanne Young, of Esprit Tours, Wilmington, will contact you in September. She's familiar with the club and its needs. She will organize the buses, condominium lodging, and lift tickets. You need to arrange for sign-up and rooming assignments. You'll also have to arrange for entertainment. *Après ski* is big (like the bars in Lauderdale over spring break). Check for deals at local bars and restaurants. They go out of business regularly, so don't depend on last year's list.

The revision has the advantage of simplicity. The writer has created a framework that can be used to present other trips (and to let him know if he's missing any information). The reader will expect to see each trip presented in the same form and thus will be able to find comparable information—say, on costs—easily.

Level II: Balancing Words and Pictures

As you review your draft, make a list of all figures and tables and check for consistency in numbering and presentation. Make sure all are mentioned in the text and that the information in the text is consistent with that in the visual. In addition, look for opportunities to streamline your presentation by converting text to tables and figures. Use figures for data; use the text to explain. Look for ways to enrich the captions of visuals. Avoid excessive overlap between visuals and text. Chapter 8 discusses in more detail the criteria for choosing methods of visual presentation.

Level I: Words and Sentences

Finally, when you're sure the framework holds, edit line by line. Edit to sharpen your focus and to correct any errors in word choice or sentence construction. Here, let's look at ways to sharpen sentence focus. The Handbook at the end of this book covers common errors in sentences and problems in word choice.

Be Concrete

In revising, remove approximations, especially abstract terms. Sometimes these are signs of the business voice. Pictures and stories hold attention better than strings of abstractions. Boil down abstract statements.

> DRAFT
>
> If man fails to acquire during his youth those habits, skills, appreciations, and knowledges essential to successful participation in some vigorous lifetime sports or suitable activities, then there is a high probability that man will be confronted with excessive idleness.

You recognize the business voice—in this case, the college men's athletic director's voice. He is saying this:

> REVISED
>
> Young people who don't participate in sports grow up to become idle adults.

Here's another draft:

> Engineers and scientific investigators must maintain a strong cooperative interface relationship so that compromise solutions can be made when conflicting requirements exist.

> REVISED
>
> Engineers and scientists must keep in touch to solve conflicts.

Focus on the Main Subject

Many drafts ramble around their topics. In revising, focus clearly on a sentence's real subject, particularly in a series of sentences.

> DRAFT
>
> In the beginning, there were problems concerning our customers' initial reluctance to bank by machine. Customers had been used to dealing with tellers and not machines. Since our ATMs have been in operation for five years, this initial resistance has faded away.

Look how easy revision becomes when the customers take center-stage in each of these sentences:

> REVISED
>
> Initially, our customers were reluctant to bank by machine. They had been used to dealing with tellers. Now that our ATMs have been in operation for five years, however, our customers are less resistant.

Here's another example:

> DRAFT
>
> Although techniques for the continuous monitoring of various stages of yarn processes are available, *knowing* where to direct that

information or what corrective actions to take is still *unknown* to a large extent.

Here, the subject of the sentence (which we've put in italics) is contradicted by a complement in the predicate, *unknown*. That can't be. The author meant this:

REVISED

Although techniques for the continuous monitoring of various stages of yarn processes are available, many companies do not know about them or about what corrective action to take once a problem is spotted.

And another:

DRAFT

The basis for pricing our new products is based on an improved price–performance ratio for the customer only.

Here, the writer started with *basis* as the subject but then focused on pricing. Bring out the subject:

REVISED

The only basis for pricing our new products is an improved price–performance ratio for the customer.

Check Sentence Branching

In revising, correct any inefficiencies in the way sentences *branch*. (See Chapter 7.) Often, a mid-branching sentence needs to be reshaped. Take this sentence, from the director of research at a brokerage firm:

Those that give credence to the January market barometer, that is, whatever way the market goes in January, thus will be its overall direction for the year, the prospects are not promising.

After a couple of readings, you can understand. But the definition of "January market barometer" derails the sentence. If you take it out, the two parts ("Those that give credence . . . the prospects") can't meet. In revision, the writer could split the sentence:

REVISED

According to the January market barometer theory, the market will follow for the year whatever trend is set in January. If this theory is true, then the market prospects for this year are not promising.

Or she could subordinate the phrase "January market barometer" and combine the ideas in a left-branching sentence:

REVISED

If it's true that the market will follow for the year whatever trend is set in January (the *January market barometer theory*), then the market doesn't look promising for this year.

Or a right-branching sentence:

REVISED

The market doesn't look promising for this year if the January market barometer theory is true, that is, if the market follows whatever trend is set in January.

Check Parallelism

Whole segments of the text should be *parallel*. So should all figures in a series. So should all headings. Parallelism is a powerful tool for showing a reader the components of a series and building a rhythm. As you revise, check both the logic and the grammar of any units or lists.

Unbalanced.   Health officials worry about smoking and asthma, and air pollution also concerns them.

Balanced.   Health officials worry about smoking; they also worry about asthma and air pollution.

Unparallel.   The figures were not verified, not accurate, and they weren't very convincing, either.

Parallel.   The figures were neither verified, accurate, nor very convincing.

Unparallel
1. Test.
2. Next, you should revise.
3. Retesting.
4. Then you're ready to roll.

Parallel
1. Test.
2. Revise.
3. Retest.
4. Roll.

Eliminate Unnecessary Words

Clean out words that don't carry their own weight. First, *cut down on expletives* ("there is," "there are," "it is"). We often write these while we wait for inspiration as we draft. Most can go.

DRAFT

There are various advantages to isometric work.

REVISED

Isometric work has various advantages.

Sometimes expletives hide fuzzy thinking, too. In eliminating the expletives, you can also focus the subject:

DRAFT

There are many administrative functions that could be completed by a computer that are not being utilized.

REVISED

The computer could complete many administrative tasks, but its capabilities are not being used.

Note that in revising, the author recognized that she used the term *functions* in two senses in the original: One function concerns what has to be done in the office, and the other concerns the software that could accommodate these tasks. The revision corrects that error, too.

Another:

DRAFT

In regard to bird feeders, there are two major types you can have: the first are the type you can buy, while the second type you can build yourself.

REVISED

Bird feeders come in two types: ready-made and do-it-yourself.

Second, *eliminate stretchers*. Figure 9–2 shows some common ones.

Stretcher	Revised
for the purpose of	to
due to the fact that	because
in the month of June	in June
on the part of	by
in the neighborhood of	about
on a daily basis	daily

FIGURE 9–2. Stretchers and revisions.

Third, *check for unnecessary redundancies*. Figure 9–3 shows some common ones in business letters and reports.

collaborate *together* [Can you collaborate *alone?* Likewise "meet *together*"; "discuss *together*"; "link *together*."]
Athletic sports complex
good benefit
time schedule
simultaneous operation of two runways at the same time
require the need for
a review of past literature [If it is written, it is *past.*]
design plan
advance planning
the necessary number needed
refer back
delete out
prospects for the future
aquatic swim club
the first step in the beginning the project
clam chowder soup
with *au jus* sauce
data information
narrow down
more well rounded [Round is round.]
worthy enough [Likewise "adequate enough."]
perhaps probable
future potential
restore back
crisis situation
temporary ad-hoc team
end result
future projection
empty vacuum

FIGURE 9–3. Redundancies.

A whole sentence may also circle back on itself in redundancy:

REDUNDANT

One of America's fastest growing chains of retailers is growing and needs young managers.

Obviously, if it's "one of the fastest growing," it *is growing*.

REVISED

One of America's fastest growing chains of retailers needs young managers.

REDUNDANT

We received your October 5 letter concerning improper billing, and we are replying in this letter.

Obviously, you *received* the letter if you are *replying* to the letter:

REVISED

In response to your October 5 letter concerning improper billing, we checked our records and found that you are indeed correct.

Fourth, *review negative statements*. Negation adds words. Moreover, readers have a harder time understanding negative statements than positive ones. So instead of saying:

Don't promise what you can't deliver.

Try:

Promise only what you can deliver.

Fifth, *check all passive verbs*. The passive voice requires a helping verb and a prepositional phrase to name an agent and thus always extends the sentence. Active sentences are shorter:

PASSIVE

The meeting was attended by all five supervisors.

ACTIVE

All five supervisors attended the meeting.

MORE ACTIVE

All five supervisors met.

Look for actors who can command the sentence:

PASSIVE

The plan was implemented by the plant manager.

ACTIVE

The plant manager implemented the plan.

Sometimes your goal of brevity, however, is secondary to your goal of presenting information effectively for the reader. You may *need* the passive. You'll need it when the agent is unknown or the action occurs without an agent:

The tree's resistance to disease was gradually worn away.

You may need the passive, too, to reduce the sting of a negative message or to keep from pointing a finger at someone:

> Because the window was left open, the room became damp and the dampness kept the computers from operating.

The passive also allows you to deemphasize the actor when too much repetition of the name would seem pretentious. For example, the board of directors of a company may not want to keep citing itself as the source of action in a letter describing some change in policy. Instead, the text moves to the passive:

> The rights are not being distributed in response to any specific effort to acquire control of the company.

Indeed, many companies prefer that an author remain behind the scenes and avoid references to *I* or *we*. If so, the alternative is often the passive. But constraints on using the first person are decreasing. Finally, you may use the passive to avoid reference to a pronoun that might seem sexist. Whenever possible, however, keep active.

Empower the Verb

As you look for passives, underline *all* the verbs you use in a page of the draft. If you find a preponderance of *is, have, use, do,* or *involves,* revise for power and brevity. Instead of saying "is dependent on," say "depends on"; instead of "come to the decision to," say "decide"; instead of "make telephone contact with," say "call." Avoid "is the thing that is" constructions:

> A strategic plan is a type of plan that is used to set a long-range course for an organization.
> *Instead:* A strategic plan sets a long-range course for an organization.

Vary Sentence Length

Vary sentence length to match units of information and reader interest. Avoid successions of long sentences or short sentences. If you have written three long sentences, make the next one short. Don't fear short sentences. Use them especially to clinch a point. Readers will appreciate this rare commodity in business reports.

Proofread

Check spelling. Check punctuation. Make sure terminology and abbreviations are consistent. For letter-perfect copy, proofread backward, the last word on the document first, and so on. In this process, you avoid the trap of reading along in context. Or have someone read the text aloud as you check another copy. Check pagination. Check the compliance of your format with requirements for the document: line spacing, total number of pages, margins, type of paper, and setup of front matter and back matter. Chapter 20 discusses these elements: table of contents, abstract, executive summary, title and/or title page, appendixes, and bibliography. Don't lose the easy points by omitting some necessary item or by failing to meet a typographic convention, like double spacing.

Finishing

After you have applied the three-phase check, move back to the global level. Skim once more. Finish off with a review of the document's *design*. A welcoming design eases reading. Look at the whole. Then check each page. Advice on design is incorporated in each of the chapters of Part II and in Chapter 26. But in general, review the *whole:*

- Is the size appropriate?
- Is the binding effective?
- Are type style and location of headings appropriate?
- Are section openings clear? [Reread the first sentence of each section.]
- Are visuals clear?
- Have you used special features—for example, sections of text differentiated by different-colored paper?
- Are there section dividers bearing the title of each section?
- Do the graphic devices on the title page and the section dividers reinforce the central theme of the document?

Then look at the *page design* for:

- Adequate margins.
- At least one paragraph break per page.
- Numbers or letters (in proper sequence) to designate items in a list.
- Headings placed for ease of access.
- Perhaps some underlining for emphasis (not overdone).
- Readable typeface.
- Balanced placement of graphs and charts (and titles for each).
- White space around graphs and charts.

At this final stage, consider the text as a whole as a *visual* device. It should look good.

Reviewing Someone Else's Writing

Businesspeople often write in groups. You are both a *writer* and a *reviewer* of someone else's writing. Chapter 11 deals in detail with the management of a group writing project. Let's suggest here, however, some strategies for helping other people to revise their writing while avoiding the ill effects of groupthink. Most of the same strategies that you apply to your own writing work as you review the work of others. But some additional advice may be in order:

1. *Control the impulse to rewrite.* Editing is repair work, not construction. If you rewrite new paragraphs or sections, you're apt to misunderstand the writer's point and therefore change the substance of the passage, and you may introduce a new style or tone that clashes with the original.

2. *Let the writer do his or her own rewriting.* Take time to teach the writer what you want. Once the writer has learned, you will save time when you request other documents.

3. *Be specific in criticism.* Don't just give the document back with a general comment like "I just don't like it" or "It's not what I wanted." Write a summary of your comments on a long report. Use consistent notations. Talk about the *levels* of your review.

4. *Don't nitpick.* The writer has only so much energy for revision. Don't waste that energy by presenting too many minor criticisms. Focus your criticism on main points.

5. *Remember to praise good work and to cite places where the writer handled material particularly well.* Those places will provide the writer's own models for shoring up weaker spots. And being appreciated helps one forge ahead. Everyone needs praise.

Whether you are reviewing someone else's work or your own work from some distance in time, look first and last *at the whole*. Read quickly to find and evaluate the big picture. Then work on the segments that bring the picture alive. Then work on the words and sentences that convey the segments. Then, at the end, read through the whole quickly again. Be confident. Let it go.

Exercises

Revise the following sentences (use the Handbook for specific advice on grammar and punctuation):

1. To develop solutions to the stated objectives, we will solicit ideas from students and faculty.

2. Several of the dimmers are no longer working as well as many of the dimmer switches.

3. Many of the house lights are burned out or are missing, this fact led to an incident of an elderly woman slipping on the stairs because she could not see in the darkness.

4. If it is not feasible for either of these methods because of monetary limits, grants and or donations will be looked into in order to rectify this growing problem.

5. These estimates, which, averaged over two or three semesters, would become very accurate, would enable us to determine our service program earlier in the semester because we would know our spending limit.

6. Because the Ground Round's most important goal is customer satisfaction, it must be sure to give them the proper attention that they need.

7. The incidence of child abuse in this country is rising. There is also a rise in the number of mental problems diagnosed among preschool and elementary-school children—some are a result of child abuse—some are not.

8. Compare the grades of students who were counseled in private schools, with those comparable problems in public schools who have not yet been counseled.

9. For example, the lack of adequate planning before launching into a project might cause efforts to be redone or revised before the project can be successfully completed thereby causing more time and money to be spent than would have been necessary if proper planning took place in the beginning.

10. The system-test work load in terms of staff days required is itemized below. This estimate is contingent on timely completion of the activities, on which the processor testing is dependent, according to the schedules in the processor-testing milestones.

11. The problems that concern most businesspeople are those of communication, activists' lack of misunderstanding of how business operates, the role of profits and profit margins, and what are perceived (among the minority) as the unrealistic, unreasonable, or even hostile attitudes of consumerists.

12. It is extremely important, in delegating, that the manager take whatever steps are necessary to assure complete understanding of the assignment on the part of his subordinates.

13. Much information should be passed on to your staff, but quite often it is not important enough to reproduce a copy for everyone.

14. Even despite the honest efforts of all parties involved to fully understand their objectives, you will probably still experience instances where trial and error will occur.

Revise the following paragraphs:

1. During the summer months at the bank a number of deposit accounts were closed. Since that period of transition, our bank has been continuously losing an alarming amount of customers. The percentage of accounts that are closed each year is 3 percent. This figure is the average for the industry. The rate of closed accounts for our bank is 18 percent.
2. At the end of this past winter term, many students moved back to the dormitories and found they needed to make mid-year room changes. As these changes were attempted to be made, much confusion and inconvenience began to be felt by the students, the resident assistants, the hall director, and many frustrated parents. Piles of students' belongings were left crowding hallways and lounges as students were forced to wait (sometimes as long as two hours) to move into their new rooms.
3. To test my proposal, I will gather and survey the opinions of my coworkers, both buyers and clerks. This will show the consensus of the department. This will be finished within the week. Also, research will be gathered on the cost of the terminals. Because we have the system already, the terminals are the only equipment that is needed. This will be completed by May 2.
4. Mr. Roberts's goals for the company are to constantly improve its research area and reinvest profits back into research. In contrast, management also wants to reinvest, but they need to consider other aspects, such as the stockholders. In addition, Mr. Roberts places value on achieving research goals at the expense of other goals that may benefit the company as a whole. Management considers goals that affect all aspects of the company. Ralph is not aware that it is impractical and possibly even harmful to realize his maximum goals. According to the goal optimization model, managers need to place different emphasis on the many goals in the organization. Therefore, Ocean Electronics should not limit its goals to just research.

Writing with a Computer

I sat down to my trustworthy typewriter and thought to myself, "I should go to the Computer Center and use the computer." Since I was already clad in sweats and situated at my typewriter, I dismissed the idea. As I was typing, I began to feel guilty. I felt as if I was wasting my skills by using a typewriter, that I was beyond the "typewriter" stage. I worked at the paper I was typing and noticed an awkward sentence. There it was, at the top of the page. My fatigue and irritability made me ignore it, and I hated myself for not going to the Computer Center, for if I had, the awkwardness of that sentence could have vanished in a second. I have come to the realization that my writing process has been changed by the computer, and hopefully for the better.

—Diane Thena, a student

If you have access to a computer for word processing at your college, university, or office, then give the system a test drive. It's not that difficult. But because *writing* at a computer is time-consuming and ties up a terminal that other users might need to access more powerful programs, some organizations directly prohibit certain groups (like students and nonsecretarial employees) from writing on the equipment.

Such prohibitions, however, are weakening as the advantages of going on-line become more apparent and the entry cost decreases. Not everyone will find writing at a screen either pleasurable or efficient. And few people will write exclusively on a computer. But for many writers, the computer offers another strong weapon against what are seen as the terrors of prose.

This chapter looks at how a computer can assist you in creating the documents you need to write as a student and on the job. It discusses how a computer can help you *write* a document, *print* the document, and *send* documents through electronic mail.

A Tool for Prose

Word processing, the term most commonly used to describe writing with a computer, covers a variety of kinds of *hardware* (the physical equipment) and *software* (the programs that tell the equipment what to do). Some computers, called *dedicated word processors*, perform only word processing. But microcomputers, the small, sometimes portable machines that serve a single person, can also run word-processing packages designed especially for them by a large number of commercial producers, as can the mainframe systems that handle all the computing needs of a large organization, such as a company or a university.

Letting the System Help

Step one in using a computer to write is learning how to use a computer to write. Your writing will have to wait while you learn. Systems vary in ease of use. Some can be mastered in a few minutes, especially those that run on personal computers and use a mouse (a little hand-held device) to locate items rapidly on the screen and icons to show instructions (like a trash can for text to be deleted). Powerful word processing packages that run on mainframes may take longer to master, in part because some require learning both an editing program and another program that prepares the text for print. As you learn, start with the easy procedures and work toward more difficult ones. Don't try to do everything at once or let yourself be frustrated by the capabilities you are not using or by the writing that, for the moment, you are not producing.

That writing will indeed be eased once you're underway. There are four reasons. First, as you research information, your computer can connect you to on-line data bases (see Chapter 5), including stock reports and news services; you can take notes on the terminal or transfer important information directly to your project file (carefully recording the source, of course). Your word-processing software may also allow you to integrate information you develop in electronic spreadsheets and graphics programs. *Window* programs that split the screen into different pages ease this work.

Second, as you write, you can easily add, delete, and move things around. There's never a mess; the new instantly replaces the old. Knowing how effortless change is may indeed encourage you to plunge into a draft and write rapidly; you'll revise to simplify and consolidate the text once you know how things come out. Moreover, the software can check your spelling, matching your document to electronic dictionaries of hundreds of thousands of words stored in the computer's memory or on disk. Just be careful: If the program recognizes the word it will accept it, even if you use the word in the wrong sense, like a confusion of *affect* and *effect* or a misplacement of *when* for *went*. Don't depend on the computer to proofread. Many programs also include "search and replace" features. If you discover, 100 pages into a document, that you've misspelled a company's name perhaps 25 times, you can tell the program once to substitute the correct for the faulty spelling, and it will find and correct each instance.

Third, sophisticated programs can act as your alter ego and electronic reader with advice on grammar and style. Some contain data bases of certified "good" prose for you to match against your own. They also check for standard errors in word choice, awkward phrasing, and punctuation; they can measure sentence length, types of sentence openers, and percentage of passives. Some can recognize parts of speech and can count almost anything you might want to count in your writing. A few textual analysis programs can measure your prose for readability against either standard measures (like the Kincaid or Flesh readability scales, which count syllables and sentence lengths as a way of determining difficulty for readers) or ones you program yourself.[1] Programs can print out all your headings and all the opening and closing sentences of paragraphs to give you a check on coherence. They can assemble a list of your most frequently used nouns and adjective-noun pairs and search for acronyms. Such programs may remind you about deviations from standard practice and prod you to reform. But because they are arbitrary and usually time-consuming to run, you may find them impractical once you are a seasoned writer.

Fourth, for many documents, the computer can serve as a kind of automatic writer. Much of what you say in standard reports you will have said before, perhaps in a slightly different form, perhaps to a different audience, for a different purpose, on another occasion. But the core remains the same. With traditional typewriter-and-photocopy approaches you may hesitate to change the wording to suit the new occasion. The marginal gain isn't worth the energy. But with the computer's capability for storing and merging blocks of prose you can mix and match texts and tailor documents to particular readers. The computer can also create automatically some elements necessary in reports, like an index, a table of contents, footnotes, and bibliographies (see Chapter 20). And the software can hold standard formats for such documents as memos, résumés, manuals, and letters. You simply insert new information in a general file, and the computer takes care of lining up the information as required.

A few cautions, however. Because of its very ease, and because of a certain hypnotic quality in a computer screen, revision may become pathological. You may find yourself never letting a sentence sit still. You may exhaust your energies on frivolous details and rearrangements to the exclusion of real reexamination. You may also spend energy in computer housekeeping, playing with files and commands rather than text. Such exercise may have two drawbacks. First, your text suffers because your attention is elsewhere. Second, if you're new to a system, you may lose text in entering commands that you don't understand. Many systems provide safeguards against just such accidents (the system may ask you, for example, if you *really want* to delete something), but the possibility of loss is real. Moreover, unless you

---

[1]One pioneer in this field is the Writer's Workbench programs developed by Bell Laboratories, Piscataway, New Jersey. Another is EPISTLE, developed by IBM. See, for example, Lorinda Cherry, "Writing Tools," *IEEE Transactions on Communications* Com-30: 1 (January 1982), 100–110.

specifically program your computer to save all changes, or unless you have access through machine language to the inner workings of your terminal, you will lose any text that you replace with other text. Most of the time such a loss is fine. But it is one of the costs. Our final word on something is not always our best; the other versions, however, are not practically preserved on a terminal. Some writers also complain of eyestrain at the terminal if they use one for more than a few hours at a time. Backs, too, may give out. So assess your time at the terminal early in your adjustment to composing there, and correct for any excesses.

Helping the System

Computers are unforgiving. If you make a mistake, it counts, sometimes with dire results. Even ardent users approach terminals in a somewhat adversarial spirit and with a certain amount of gamesmanship.

Computers are also demanding. You have to reshape your thinking about writing tasks to frame what you need and your instructions to the computer in a code that it can read. In general, computers reward those who work in an orderly manner. They do require some housekeeping—more housekeeping than a pencil or a typewriter requires. Here are some hints for trouble-free operation:

- Save and back up your text.
- Organize files.
- Wean yourself from paper.
- Store your disks carefully.

Save and Back Up Your Text
Writers fear loss. Paper, of course, can get lost. But we probably fear that loss less than the loss of text written in electricity. The power does go off; mainframe systems do crash. But the fear of loss is easily allayed. Just save the text (that is, write it to the disk on a personal computer or into memory on a mainframe) at frequent intervals. At the end of the day or a writing session, back up the whole file. Make a copy of the file on another disk and store that disk and the original disk in different locations. Or copy the file for storage on a mainframe. The really paranoid make three copies: two on disks and one on paper.

Organize Your Files
Name documents with specific and appropriate terms (not just "Report"). Keep a list of which documents are on which disks. In the title,

indicate both the *content* and the *version* of the draft. Version designation is important because, in backing up text, you may store different drafts. You want to make sure you print out and circulate the right one. One horror story in support of this need: Three students, working together on a manual, kept private records of versions of the text and a general record of responsibility for each chapter. One version of a chapter included a coding error that was corrected in the final version. But another student, compiling the whole manual at the end of the term, printed the wrong version. The result was 13,000 pages of paper spun off a high-speed printer bearing only the header on each page—and no text.

Coding blocks of prose for several documents and several users poses even greater problems than creating file names for your own documents. You might use both numbers and letters of the alphabet: Let numbers designate the originating department; use a letter for the type of document (*r* for report, for example); and designate the specific content with another letter or series of letters.

Finally, limit the size of your files. The page limit of a paper file is roughly the amount you can fit into a folder. A computer file is limited by the amount of memory in the system. That may be 8 pages on a small computer, fifty-ish on a floppy disk, or thousands on a mainframe. Different systems treat the storage and recovery of files differently. Usually, however, the amount of time it takes to search through and save a file is directly proportional to its length. Thus you may be discouraged from frequent saving of a file if it's long. Limit your files to 20 to 30 pages, particularly on microcomputers.

Wean Yourself from Paper

At first, either because they don't trust the computer or because they need to see paper to know they've written prose, writers print out frequently. They edit on the page and then transfer the edits to the screen. In effect, they use the computer as a smart typewriter.

But all this printing takes time. Consciously try to accommodate to the screen and print out only near the end of the whole writing project. Be trusting. Keep your text on the disk and reread for revision there. Although screen size is indeed a limit, and it's hard to skim, try noting on a pad of paper the starting page numbers for major sections of your document so that you can move rapidly about the document.

Store Your Disks Carefully

The box that contains the floppy disks for your microcomputer is probably covered with various warnings. Adhere to these. Watch out for coffee, cigarettes, and scratchy pens that may rub out your text. On the other hand, you needn't feel that a computer commits you to a sterile room for writing (except, of course, in a university computer center). You can still sip coffee near a computer and your text will live to tell the tale. Just sip carefully and don't spill on the disk.

Desktop Publishing

With a little care and feeding, word-processing software can greatly aid you in writing and revising. The software can also aid you in seeing a document through to print. Many writers find the opportunities for better-looking documents the most exciting aspect of writing at a computer. Certainly with a mainframe system, and increasingly with personal computers, you have at your finger-tips now the options for polish in printing documents once only available from design studios and print shops. You can create headings, boldface, and italics; you can justify right margins and provide proportional spacing and a variety of pitches; you can type a draft single-spaced and print it out single-, double-, or triple-spaced, and in multiple columns; you can, with many programs, select from a variety of foreign language characters and mathematical notations.

Moreover, all this printing takes relatively little time. Thus you can hold a document in suspension longer before the due date, incubating new ideas and new language until shortly before the deadline. Reports thus gain both in thoroughness of review and in timeliness.

The fastest and cheapest printer is a dot-matrix or line printer. The print resolution is often not high, but the text is at least as readable as that produced by a manual typewriter. Letter-quality printers give better resolution, but they are slower and more costly. The best printing comes from laser and ink-jet systems. Once only available on mainframes, such systems are now available for personal computers and produce publisher-quality texts. Many also offer options for full-page graphics and hundreds of type styles and sizes (Figure 10–1 shows a small sample). Indeed, you can view the document itself as a *graphic* production, incorporating graphics as we discussed in Chapter 8 and displaying the text as a whole in a pleasing design. Such *desktop publishing* is one of the major achievements of the use of computers.

Electronic Mail

While in- and out-boxes have not disappeared from the office scene, office mail increasingly circulates in a form that can't be put in a box. You send and receive messages on a screen. In *electronic mail*, computers—perhaps many of them, spanning short or great distances—are

This sentence is set in Chicago typeface at a 12 point size.
This sentence is set in Chicago typeface at a 12 point size with an italic effect.
This sentence is set in Chicago typeface at a 12 point size with a bold effect.
This sentence is set in Chicago typeface at a 12 point size with an outline effect.
THIS SENTENCE IS SET IN CHICAGO TYPEFACE AT A 12 POINT SIZE WITH ALL SMALL CAPITAL LETTERS.

— — — — — — — — — — — —

This sentence is set in Venice typeface at a 10 point size.

— — — — — — — — — — — —

This sentence is set in London typeface at a 16 point size.

— — — — — — — — — — — —

This sentence is set in Monaco typeface at an 18 point size.

— — — — — — — — — — — —

This sentence is set in Geneva typeface at a 9 point size.

— — — — — — — — — — — —

This sentence is set in Athens typeface at an 18 point size.

— — — — — — — — — — — —

This sentence is set in New York typeface at a 20 point size.
This sentence is set in New York typeface at a 16 point size.
This sentence is set in New York typeface at a 14 point size.
This sentence is set in New York typeface at a 12 point size.
This sentence is set in New York typeface at a 10 point size.
This sentence is set in New York typeface at an 8 point size.

— — — — — — — — — — — —

FIGURE 10–1. A sample of type possibilities available on a personal desktop publishing system (courtesy of R. John Brockmann).

185

linked by telephone. Mail systems may carry individual messages or may link several subscribers through electronic bulletin boards which, like a speedier and bigger version of a board on a wall, collect and disseminate messages throughout one organization or the world on topics of interest to subscribers.

Electronic mail has many advantages. It's fast: Transmission of a message from one terminal to another is almost instant across an organization or even over continents. Such transmission drastically reduces "information float," the time lag in sending and receiving information for major decisions. Electronic mail also usually takes less time than a paper memo or letter to prepare. You write directly on the screen; no typist intervenes. When you're ready to send the message, you can simply call up a distribution list in the computer's memory and with one keystroke dispatch the message to everyone. Electronic mail has an advantage over a phone call, too, in that it *waits* for the person to log onto the system. That capacity for waiting is particularly attractive when you need to share a document with coauthors or approvers. If you draft your work on a mainframe system or on a networked personal computer, the text you write easily becomes a message to send to someone else. No paper need change hands. Someone else just calls up the file you've sent. You can write at midnight when the muse inspires you. Others can read you at their preferred dawn work time, add their corrections and comments, keep it themselves, and copy it back to you. Moreover, because readers know you can incorporate change easily, and they can write easily, they are often more willing to comment on substantive issues and offer suggestions.

But the very ease and speed of electronic mail also present disadvantages. Sometimes people write and send messages too fast in the heat of anger without pausing to reconsider. Indeed, several researchers note the tendency of writers to "flare up" in their electronic messages; such mail, at least at this point, tends to be more terse, informal, and strident than paper mail. Moreover, people may be lulled into sending too many messages to too many people, clogging everyone's mailbox. As one person at a large organization said in despair: "I could spend all day at the terminal just reading my mail, and never get anything done."

Whatever the disadvantages, however, electronic mail systems are powerful and important aids to communication, both within an organization and world-wide, through commercial electronic mail services.

Writing On-line

Writing on a computer has enlarged the possibilities of prose and increased the number of decisions to be made about writers and documents—including even the fundamental decision about what ends up on paper and what remains electronic.

Indeed, some producers advertise that their word-processing software changes everything:

> It's staggering.
>
> It can change the way you work, the way you think, the way you live.
>
> It is more than just an incredible timesaver (although it certainly is that, too). Much, much more.
>
> It's a tool that propels you into creativity, letting you set down an idea, rearrange it, edit it, improve it, decide you liked it better the first time, change Smith to Jones wherever Smith appears, switch paragraphs around, personalize things that ought to be personal, see how what you've written would look with different margins, in all capital letters, or with boldface headings, add or delete names or numbers from lists, file away fleeting ideas and retrieve them whenever you want them, automatically show you a "table of contents" of all your ideas in case you've forgotten them, put a notion on "hold" while you do something else, and prod you into certain secret places that your mind has seldom, if ever before, entered.[2]

Whether word-processing software will propel you into creativity and prod you into secret places is an open question, but probably a computer is not going to turn a poor writer into a great one. It will also not do all your work for you. And as it aids you, it also requires other sorts of work in tending its needs and increased numbers of decisions about the documents you are producing.

In the end, you remain a writer first and a computer user second. It's simply one mode of writing, to be exploited, along with pencils and pens, whenever it serves you. A computer is another tool. It may ease your lot in refining prose. It can certainly enhance the printing of that prose in documents that both clarify the message and please the reader's eye. And at its best, it will foster enjoyment while you work.

Exercises

1. If you have access to a computing facility, check out whatever word-processing programs are available. Are they input- or output-oriented? How easy is each to learn? What special features are available (see Exercise 2)? Test-drive the program or programs.

2. Here is a list of features that writers commonly look for in word-processing programs. If you would like, add your own criteria and specific features within

[2] Excerpt from an advertisement for Leading Edge Word Processing. Reprinted with permission from Leading Edge Software Products, Inc., Needham, Massachusetts.

each category. Then read about several programs in computer-oriented journals or in manufacturers' literature. Construct a *matrix* (see Chapter 8) with the features listed down the left column and the names of the programs at the end of subsequent columns. Fill in the cells to indicate which programs have which features.

- Ease of learning.
- Safety (built-in safeguards against loss of text).
- Documentation (manuals, on-screen explanations and tutorials, reference cards, and keyboard cards).
- Manufacturer's responsiveness and support.
- Editing functions.
- Printing functions.
- Compatibility with graphics and spread-sheet packages.

3. Write a letter of inquiry (see Chapter 14) to a software manufacturer to inquire about its word-processing package.

4. Using the matrix you constructed in Exercise 2, or another matrix, write a memo to persuade someone—your supervisor, your professor, the academic dean at your school—to purchase a particular system. Develop the memo by comparing and contrasting the systems according to the features and criteria you think would meet the needs of your organization.

5. Put some document you have written into a text-analysis program to determine, for example, your average sentence length or your use of specific terms. Perhaps you have access to a system that can measure readability (see Chapter 3). If so, try out your text—and try to vary your word choice to achieve different levels.

6. As you learn to write on a computer, keep a journal on-line to record your struggles and triumphs. Do you write differently at a terminal and in longhand? Does your prose *look* different to you on a screen and on a page? Are you tempted to revise more? Do you tend to write more? End each writing session at the screen with a brief journal entry about *how* you are writing.

Managing Group Projects

11

Computer mail systems and other forms of electronic communication, as we saw in the last chapter, keep people in organizations in touch with each other and allow the nearly instant sharing of information and documents. Such systems are especially useful when you are involved in a group writing project. Even without them, though, you have to approach group writing a bit differently from the individual writing project you are most familiar with as a student.

This chapter discusses the special nature of group writing projects. It also looks at the issue of responsibility in group endeavors. Finally, it suggests specific guidelines for group writing—rules of the road to ensure that the process of composing a document in a group will be as effective as the document that will eventually emerge. The better the process, the better will be the final written outcome.

Group Writing: The Corporate Way

The work of organizations is done in and by groups. This work includes writing, a fact that surprises people who think of writing as a private and lonely act. Of course, sitting down to face the pad of paper or the screen is an individual act and can be lonely, but in an organization, writing is usually a group process. Although one person may, in fact, "write" the text of a report or proposal, many others are involved quite directly. For example:

- A supervisor makes the assignment and ultimately approves the document.
- A colleague gathers data.
- A staff artist prepares the graph.
- An editor oversees production and prepares the final copy.

In large projects—for example, preparing a two-hundred-page proposal for the U.S. Department of Defense—dozens of individuals may be involved directly, and still dozens more indirectly, in collecting information and securing internal approvals for the project.

Even a relatively short and apparently simple document, like a memo asking permission to hire a new computer programmer, may involve several persons, even though one individual—the person initiating the request—actually "writes" the memo. Thus the success of a piece of organizational communication often depends as much on how well the process of writing is managed as on how clear and precise and grammatically correct the document itself is in final form. Indeed, the two are usually directly correlated.

Who's Responsible?

Students sometimes find the corporate emphasis on group projects unsettling. Since first grade, teachers have stressed the importance of doing your own work, of being individually responsible, of not sharing information with classmates. Now someone tells you that in business, most work gets done through groups, and that even writing is, in an organization, a group endeavor.

The chief problem that students perceive in group projects is responsibility. It's obvious that if Mary Jones has a report due Friday, the failure to meet the deadline is Mary's. But what if Mary is a member of a four-person group? Whose fault is it if the deadline passes? Can she blame the others for failing to submit drafts of sections to her on time? Should she?

These are tricky issues of ethics, corporate citizenship, and politics. We can't answer them specifically here; instead, we will establish two basic guidelines on responsibility in group projects:

1. Every member of the group is responsible for the group's actions.

2. The designated leader of the group bears the principal responsibility for its action as long as he or she has the authority to match that responsibility.

These two guidelines may seem slightly contradictory. How can everyone be responsible for everything while one person is more responsible than others? That snare is inherent in organizational life. Each person working in the group must feel personal responsibility not just to complete his or her own portion of the work well and on time, but also to see that the group assignment is met, even if that means assuming extra duties. Membership in the group extends responsibilities. At the same time, each group has a leader, someone who assumes the role by dint of his or her corporate position (because that person is the boss) or by dint of special skills and talents in managing a group communication project. That person has a special responsibility to see that the group's assignment is completed.

However, the added responsibility exists only in proportion to the authority given to accomplish the task. If your position within the corporate hierarchy is such that you can't compel actions from others in your group, then by definition, you shouldn't have to assume increased responsibility for the outcome. That's why it's a poor idea to place a junior person in charge of a writing project that depends for its successful and timely completion on the work of people senior to him or her. As in all aspects of corporate life, in a group writing project authority must match responsibility.

We approached the issue of responsibility here negatively, emphasizing the blame attached when something goes wrong. The issue should also be considered from the opposite perspective: In a group writing project, who gets the credit for a job well done? The answer should be obvious: All members of the group share in the credit. The group leader might be singled out for special praise, but that should be limited to his or her unique contributions and should not detract from the praise earned by the whole group. Credit is shared in proportion to the work done.

Writing Groups

Sometimes writing projects are carried out by groups that already exist in an organization—for example, the staff of the accounting department, the proposal support group, or the marketing division. Sometimes people are brought together from several divisions to form a special group to complete a writing project. Managing the process of group writing differs depending on whether the group already exists or is created especially for the project.

The chief advantage of working with an existing group is that the members are all known to each other and probably have experience in working together on other projects, even on writing projects. The disadvantage is that the pool of talent is fixed: You have to exploit the strengths and overcome the weaknesses of the group as it already exists. The advantage of creating a special group is that you can, within reasonable limits, get what you need. If, for example, the work at hand requires a good many graphs, charts, and views, you can make sure you have a graphics specialist to handle these. On the other hand, creating a group to do a specific project often means that the people haven't worked together before. You may thus be starting at the top of the learning curve and may be forced to spend seemingly unproductive time just forging the team and developing good interactions among the members.

Guidelines for Group Writing

Whether you are managing an existing group or one especially formed to complete a specific writing assignment, the general guidelines applicable to managing your own writing (see Chapter 3) apply. The group must understand the assignment fully, determine the intended outcome, divide the project into discrete tasks and assign deadlines to each, develop a control system, and build in time to solve unexpected problems.

Applying these general guidelines in group writing, though, requires some special twists and modifications. Here are three guidelines that apply specifically to group writing:

1. Make sure that the entire group understands the assignment at the outset.

2. Evaluate the capacities, talents, and special strengths and weaknesses of each member of the group, and make task assignments accordingly.

3. Monitor both group and individual progress to keep everyone focused on the outcome—and the deadline.

Let's look at each guideline in detail:

1. *Make sure the entire group understands the assignment at the outset.* If it is sometimes difficult for an individual writer to grasp completely the full dimensions of an assignment, that difficulty is magnified in a group writing project. Like sports teams, groups must function together to achieve goals, as the result must be more than the total of each individual's performance. But unlike sports teams, writing groups do not operate within fixed rules. The group leader or manager in a writing project must thus be coach and umpire at the same time, inspiring and coaxing the group toward the goal but also developing and enforcing the "rules" as the game proceeds.

The questions that the individual writer must ask and get clear answers to are equally appropriate in a group situation: Who is the audience? What is the purpose? What form should the writing take? How long should it be? When is it due? But now the trick is to make sure that every member of the group understands the questions and can work within the limits that the answers establish. If four members of a five-member group think that the report is being written for the merchandising vice-president and one thinks it's for the sales manager, serious problems can develop. The levels of language, the use of details, the categories of material included, and the forms of presentation will all vary according to the perception of audience. Hence it is critical that from the beginning, everyone in the group know the exact goal.

The best way to promote clear understanding is to bring everyone together at the beginning of the project to discuss it in detail. The group leader must take charge, establishing the parameters of the project precisely and responding clearly to every question. The meeting should be informal and open, so that everyone with questions will get a chance to ask them—and will get a direct, unambiguous answer. Everyone should leave the meeting with a strong grasp of the overall assignment that can be focused in a single statement, for example, "We are writing a fifty-page report due on September 20 on sales of women's accessories in our branch stores in the Newark area to inform the merchandising vice-president of our current operations." No one in the group should misunderstand and think that the purpose of the project is to persuade the reader to drop this line of merchandise, even though that may be the opinion of one member of the team.

Everyone should leave this first meeting with a clear view of the project, but to reinforce it, the group leader should follow up with a written statement like the one just given. At the end of the meeting, it may seem that everyone understands, but if that understanding is not confirmed in writing, you leave open the possibility of later confusion.

At the initial meeting, when the project is clarified, it may also be possible to assign specific tasks. Or it may be necessary to have a separate meeting or even several to make these assignments. At the very least, the first meeting must end with a consensus about the project and a precise statement of it orally and, immediately after, in writing.

2. *Evaluate the capacities, talents, and special strengths and weaknesses of each member of the group, and make task assignments accordingly.* At either a first or a follow-up meeting, the overall project should be divided into discrete tasks to which deadlines are attached. Again the group manager has a special responsibility because he or she must take the lead in segmenting the project, always being flexible and open to suggestions and criticisms. All members of the group should participate in this step, but the group leader has final authority for seeing that the project is completed effectively and on time.

In an individual project, the writer has to identify the separate parts and put deadlines on each. In a group project, it is also necessary to assign individuals to each task. Here is where the manager's people skills are called on. As manager of a group project, you must realistically evaluate each member's abilities and assign tasks to those best equipped to complete them. If you are working with an existing group, you probably already know quite a bit about the members and what they can and cannot do. This knowledge makes it easier to come to a meeting with a preliminary assignment list that can serve as a basis for group discussion and final assignment. If Jaworski is a superb stylist, the group's writer in residence, then you can reasonably assign him to the job of composing the draft. If Hughes is an instinctively good editor who can pull together the drafts of several persons into a seamless whole, then you can give her that job. And so on.

When the group is being specially formed for a project, it may take several meetings—and some private conversations with the individuals and others who have worked with them before—to determine who is best at what. It's worth spending a meeting or two on this, simply talking out the issues and discovering who wants—and is able—to handle what parts of the overall job. Although respecting individual preferences is obviously desirable, once again the group leader is finally responsible and must make the assignments in the way that is most likely to lead to the intended outcome. If both Jones and Marvin may consider themselves whizzes at compiling tables of numbers, and if you need only one person to do this, you will have to choose between them—and keep both happy and productive in the assignments they do receive. Not everyone can play goalie on a hockey team. Several may want to, but someone—the coach—finally has to decide and has to implement the decision in a manner that keeps everyone working together efficiently as a team. Tact and common sense are helpful.

Once the assignments are made, they should be recorded in writing and circulated to everyone in the group so that each understands his or her role, its relationship to the roles of others, and the deadlines that everyone will operate under. For a large project, a scheduling chart is desirable. If the project is small, a less formal approach may be taken. But it is important that everyone know his or her assignment *and* all other assignments. You don't want people to feel they are operating in a vacuum, and you do want them to know who else is doing what so they can informally seek assistance and coordinate their efforts.

If, as is sometimes necessary, several persons have responsibility for the same task, it's important to clarify the boundaries that exist within that task. Say that you assign Levine and Hardy to "writing the draft." Make sure that Levine knows he is responsible for Sections 1 through 4 and Hardy for 5 through 8. Or if one is to write and the other is to edit and rewrite, make sure that is understood. The clearer the division of responsibility, within obvious limits, the more effective will be the result—and the less energy and goodwill lost along the way.

3. *Monitor group and individual progress to keep everyone focused on the outcome—and the deadline.* In group writing a good control system is even more necessary than in an individual project. You can always check with yourself to see how it's going. It may be harder to check with others, who may be located elsewhere in the building, who may keep different hours from yours, or who may not feel obliged to inform you of problems as they occur. Controlling a group project requires a good balance between involvement and delegation. Don't be a mother hen, stopping by someone's office every few hours to ask, "How's it going?" But don't disappear and assume that all's going well unless someone tells you the contrary.

Retaining control of the project and keeping everyone focused are aided by periodic group meetings at which brief and informal progress reports are given (see Chapter 24 for advice on conducting such a meeting). Such meetings keep all members informed about the project and remind them that it is a continuing responsibility. Preparing for such a meeting gives each member the opportunity to consolidate the work to date and to think about how and where it's headed. The process is a form of social control in that it maintains a consistent but gentle level of peer pressure. If necessary, interviews with individuals can be scheduled to follow up in detail on particular issues or to prod those who don't appear to be making good progress. The group meetings should not be used to discuss everyone's work in detail; they should serve the important functions of keeping everyone's attention focused on the group's work and preventing individuals from drifting too far into their own activities as ends in themselves.

Editor or Manager?

The leader of a group doing a writing project is, of course, managing the process. Does that mean he or she is the editor of the document that the process creates? Maybe.

It's an important "maybe," because many people assume that the one who oversees the process is by definition the editor, whereas group managers may feel that editing the final document is the job of a member of the group. The work can go either way, and it's important to straighten out responsibility at the beginning. The key is this: The manager of a group is not necessarily the editor of the group's document but could be if she or he possesses the right skills. A manager is different from an editor.

What makes a good editor is sensitivity to the styles of different people, coupled with a clear sense of what the whole document should be. The good editor, in other words, doesn't bludgeon people's prose to make it all sound the same but does smooth, bend, shape, and fit together individual efforts to make the whole document seem more than a collection of essays. It's a neat trick, and there are no clear rules for guidance. (For general advice on editing, see Chapter 9.)

The important point here is that the skills of an editor are sometimes found in the group manager and sometimes not. If your group has or can find a person to function well as overall editor of the document, and if you don't consider yourself really strong in editing, then by all means assign the editing function to someone else. If you can both edit and manage, do so. But don't confuse the tasks. Editors have verbal skills; managers have people skills. If you have both, fine. If not, make sure you get a good editor in your group—and then respect that person's abilities and accept his or her work.

Exercises

1. You and two other students in your class are assigned to produce a report on student participation in the running of your college or university. It is due in three weeks. Set up a schedule of activities assigned to each of the three of you that will bring the project in on time. Show exactly *who* will do *what* and *when*. Be prepared to explain and justify the assignments and the schedule.

2. Assume that you are assigned to head a team to analyze the success of your company's promotional campaign to introduce a new brand of running shoe. You are to produce a formal report for the marketing vice-president. You can select three people to join you on the team. Briefly describe the qualities, the experiences, and the organizational position of the people you want. Assign specific duties to each.

3. Anne Behnke was a new assistant buyer in the shoe department at a large Kansas City department store. She and her supervisor, the chief buyer, Mary Landers, went to Chicago to preview the new summer lines. When they returned, the merchandising manager to whom Landers reported asked for a detailed memo report on what the two had seen so that the store could prepare a coordinated summer fashion promotion linking clothes and accessories. Landers told Behnke to write a draft of the memo. When it was done, Landers liked the draft so much that she had it typed up under her own name and sent it to the mechandising manager. If you were Behnke, what would you do? Discuss the situation with respect to the ethics of group writing projects.

4. For the staff in his engineering-support department, Byron Black prepared the following table outlining their responsibilities for a large proposal that the group was writing for the U.S. Department of Commerce:

	Writing	Editing	Graphics	Production
George	X	X		
Lisa			X	
Sean			X	
Lou	X			
Byron		X		X
Carolyn				X

Comment on the value of this scheme for assigning responsibilities for the parts of the group project. Is anything missing? Suggest ways to improve the assignments and the table.

5. Harry Lloyd assigned three junior auditors under his supervision to prepare reports on the adequacy of the documentation used by the purchasing department of their company. He asked them to work independently and to submit their reports to him. He told them he would "edit" their reports and produce a draft version of the final report, which he planned to submit to the head of the purchasing office. He told them he would incorporate the "best" of each report in the draft and then ask each of them to comment on the draft before he submitted it. Discuss this approach as a form of group writing. What are its strengths and weaknesses? If you were one of the junior auditors, how would you react to the assignment? If Lloyd asked for your suggestions, what would you tell him to do to improve the process?

PART

1

The Forms of Written Communication

Memos

12

This chapter introduces you to the most common form of written communication in business: the memo. Because it's important to define a term that is widely but differently used in business, we'll first look at *what* memos are. To explain their importance, we'll then look at *why* people in organizations write memos. Finally, we'll discuss some specific guidelines about *how* you can write memos effectively and efficiently to serve various purposes. In each section, sample memos illustrate the comments and advice and give you models to use in writing your own memos.

What? Defining Memos

Even if you've never been on a corporate payroll, you probably know something about memos. They are the lifeblood of organizations—the principal written means by which information is conveyed internally for a variety of organizational needs. Indeed, some people in business and government complain that they send and receive so many memos they fear drowning in them.

The word *memorandum*, of which *memo* is the shortened and most common form, derives from a Latin word for "remembering." It has the same root as for the word *memory*, which provides a good clue to the meaning of the memo. We write memos so that something will be remembered. Memos *record*. Business organizations need to record a lot: the outcome of meetings, the names of persons hired or promoted or fired, the policies that govern corporate behavior, the sales orders that bring revenues to the firm, the accounting data on which managers depend for controlling activities.

But memos are often more dynamic. Like other forms of business communication, memos can *inform* or *persuade*. As we saw in Chapter 3, informative writing shapes recorded information for a reader's need, to induce understanding in him or her. Persuasive writing aims to induce action on the reader's part. Whereas a memo for the record captures basic data, an informative memo organizes and presents the data in the manner most useful for its audience. For example, an informative memo to a supervisor about a staff meeting might record the major conclusions and recommendations, leaving out details and ignoring the chronological order of events characteristic of "minutes" written for the record. Further shaping occurs when the intent is persuasive. The memo develops a case, presenting information in the structure and style most likely to convince the audience to take an intended action.

Memos written to record are usually clearly identifiable; indeed, they are often called "memo for the record." It's harder to keep separate informative and persuasive memos. Often a single memo aims to inform and persuade at the same time. For example, you might write a memo to a subordinate summarizing his record of absences and tardiness. Your purpose might be both to record this information for the employee's and your own use and also to persuade the individual to change his behavior to suit the company's needs. The memo would both inform and persuade.

The three memos presented in Figures 12–1 to 12–3 reflect important qualities of the form. Examine them carefully.

The first memo (Figure 12–1) seems to be one of those forms that

---

SUN-RAY, INC.

INTEROFFICE MEMO
PAYROLL FORM/23A

ATTN: Meyer Comisky
       1st Shift Supervisor
       Manufacturing-4

This notice confirms the hiring of _____John Dreys_____ in your department, effective ____15 September 19xx____. Please verify the following information and return an initialed copy of this memo to the Payroll Office immediately. Note any changes in black ink.

    Wage rate (hourly) _____$7.75____
    Account reference _____4-23C____
    Employee social security number __083-38-5667__
    Personnel Office reference _____09/88/455____

    Confirmed _____
    Date _____

FIGURE 12–1. A fill-in memo.

CENTRAL FLORIDA COMMUNITY HOSPITAL

Interoffice Memo

TO: All Employees, Emergency Services
FROM: Marianne Majesky
         Director, Patient Services
DATE: 17 September 19xx

Effective December 1, 19xx, new procedures will be implemented in the Patient Records Office to ensure that patient admissions from ES to ICU will be handled quickly.

After that date, ES personnel must complete new Form ES-27 for any patient transferred to ICU. A copy of this form should be sent to ICU and to Patient Records.

All ES employees are asked to cooperate with this new procedure. Address any questions to me at ext. 7881.

FIGURE 12–2. A simple memo to inform.

people in organizations frequently complain about having to fill out in triplicate. It *is* a form, but it is called a memo. The memo informs Meyer Comisky, a supervisor in the manufacturing department, that the hiring of John Dreys at a particular salary is confirmed as of a particular date. Further details are supplied (internal accounting, personnel records, and so on). As a recipient of the memo, Comisky must return a signed copy to the Payroll Office so the new employee can be officially entered in the company's payroll and personnel-information system. The main objective of this memo, then, is to *record* so that the recording itself will activate a system and cause good things (like payroll checks) to happen.

The second memo (Figure 12–2) is a bit more complicated. It's more than the fill-in form we just examined, but it, too, is quite short and is also meant to record. The writer is informing employees in the Emergency Services group about a new procedure to be followed in admitting patients to the Intensive Care Unit. Note that she uses abbreviations (ES, ICU) that the audience will readily understand. Although her purpose is mostly to inform (that is, to make sure all appropriate employees know that a new system is in place), it is partially also to persuade—to solicit the compliance of the recipients with the new procedures. So the goal is both recording and persuading.

The third memo (Figure 12–3) is more explicitly persuasive in intent: It is meant not to record information, but to persuade the audience to do something. Joan Leutens, of course, supplies information (name of package, supplier, cost, and so on), but the information is marshaled toward persuading her supervisor to purchase a particular software package. Notice how carefully the memo is oriented toward the specific audience. The first two sentences refer to Mr. Mapes's interest in cost savings. The last paragraph is aimed directly at him again, reiterating the fit between this software and his interest in saving money. Unlike the memo in Figure 12–1, this is not a fill-in form. The writer can't just put words in the blank spaces, but instead, has to plan a strategy for sequencing the information to meet the communications goal. This is a tailored memo, clearly aimed at its recipient and clearly intended to persuade the recipient to make a specific response.

Despite their obvious differences, these three sample memos are all effective in that they are well executed to achieve goals. If we look at what makes them effective, we can identify several key features of the memo form:

1. Each memo is an *internal* document, sent within an organization. Shorthand expressions can thus be used (abbreviations, for example); complex matters can be briefly and generally mentioned (the provision of auditing services to divisions, for example, which would surely have to be explained and expanded on if the audience were outside the organization); and polite expressions and ingratiating phrases can be dropped in favor of directness ("this notice confirms . . ." or "address any question to me at ext. 7881"). These are not messages aimed at customers or others outside the organization. Their shape, style, and content fit their internal audience.

2. Each of the memos is *short*. It is possible, where company style allows or sometimes even encourages it, to have five- or even twenty-page memos. But most people equate the memo with brevity. When he was president of Ford, Robert McNamara had a rule that a good many other chief executive officers (for example, at Proctor & Gamble) have adopted: No memo can be longer than one page. It's a good rule; but even when the rule is not formal corporate policy, the memo is among the briefest of business documents.

3. The brevity of the memos presented here results from their focus

SPRINGDALE VALUE CENTERS, INC.

TO: Marvin Mapes
           Controller
FROM: Joan Leutens
           Staff Accountant
DATE: 15 March 19xx
SUBJECT: Suggested Software Purchase

The cost of providing auditing services to the divisional offices has always been a major concern of yours. When you mentioned at our last staff meeting (3-4-8x) that you wished we could automate some of the functions now performed by staff accountants, I looked into the cost and effectiveness of software that I thought would be available to maintain certain divisional records and perform basic audit functions on the data.

The result of my search is this recommendation that we purchase Act-II, a software package produced by CorpRec, Inc. The package will cost $2,125, and we will have to pay a semiannual maintenance fee of $75, which includes all updates.

Enclosed is a description of Act-II and its capabilities, along with a list of firms currently using it. Herb Burns and I visited one installation (at Letts Manufacturing), and we both think the system will be just what we need.

I'll be happy to discuss this with you at any time, Mr. Mapes. I do think the proposed software will help us meet your goal of reducing the cost of auditing in the divisional office.

Enclosure

cc: Herb Burns

FIGURE 12–3. A memo to persuade.

on a *single topic*. The memo is a focused, limited document. It deals with one topic (and related subtopics, of course). The comprehensive report on the year's activities is not a proper topic for a memo. The results of Division I's third quarter may be. Obviously the topic can be complex and large or simple and small. But one memo should deal with only one topic.

4. Each of the memos is highly *audience-oriented*. Even when the audience is multiple, as in our second example, the language, arrangement, and tone are appropriate to the audience (thus again, the use of abbreviations that are understood within the group). As we saw, Leutens carefully phrased her suggestion to make it consistent with the interests of her boss. Memos should be firmly directed at a known audience.

5. In varying degrees, each of the memos is *conventional*. A heading begins each memo, providing a structured way to indicate audience, writer, subject, and date. The first example is the most conventional because it is really a fill-in form. The second follows the conventions but is structured by the writer without the benefit of blank spaces to be filled in. The third is individual in structure, use of evidence, and language. We have, then, a range of conventions in these sample memos that is characteristic of the whole population of memos: Some are rigidly structured, others are highly open to the control of the writer (to suit purpose and audience), and many sit somewhere between these two extremes.

The degree of conventionality in the format and content of a memo depends mostly on the organization in which the writer works. Many large companies, hospitals, universities, and government agencies have rigid standards. Even when the content of the memo is left to the writer's control, the heading, use of abbreviations, persons to be copied, and so forth are firmly set. If the rules are followed in the company you work for, you may find that writing is made easier as a result. After all, it's simpler to fill in a form than to establish your own pattern of organization and to weigh evidence and language at each step. On the other hand, the open form does allow you to be creative and flexible and to respond more concretely and directly to your audience's needs and your own purpose.

This review of the three sample memos leads us to an expanded definition of a memo:

> *A memo is an internal document that is generally short, focuses on a single topic, is clearly directed to its audience, and to a noticeable degree, follows conventions or formulas in form and content.*

This definition underlies the discussion in the rest of this chapter on why people in organizations write memos and how they can do so with maximum success.

Why? Understanding the Functions of Memos

We've already noted that memos are called the lifeblood of organizations. That label certainly reflects their importance, but it's a metaphor that doesn't directly answer the real question of why people in organizations write memos.

Like all organizational activity, memo writing is purposeful. People write memos to meet certain goals. Memos help to meet both organizational and personal goals. Ideally, of course, the goals of the organization and the goals of the individual employee should be met simultaneously, but in practice there are frequently at least minor conflicts. We'll now briefly review the prime organizational goals that memos serve; then we'll look at individual goals. Finally, we'll try to see how the fit between the two can be made tight—that is, how good memos can serve the company's and the individual's goals at the same time.

Meeting Organizational Goals

Because organizations exist to reach goals, decisions have to be made and actions taken. As we saw in Chapters 4 and 5, decisions are based on information and the intelligent interpretation of that information. The treasurer of a company manages the firm's cash assets to achieve the maximum return consistent with accepted risks. If he has $2 million in cash from receipts that are not immediately needed to run the operations, the treasurer will place that money so that it earns interest until it is required for some other purpose. Leaving it in the checking account doesn't serve the organizational goal of maximizing profit. What can he do?

- Buy stocks?
- Put the money in a money market account at a bank?
- Buy a certificate of deposit?

To make a choice, the treasurer must have information: What are the expected returns? How liquid will the money be in each form of investment? How safe will the principal be? How much will it cost the company to make the investment? Perhaps he knows all the answers based on experience, but let's assume that he needs to get the information from other sources. He might turn to his staff, requesting specific answers. The answers might be oral—in a phone call, for example—but he might want written responses so that he can compare the answers and put together the facts he needs to make a sound decision.

This is the kind of decision (leading to action: invest in this or that stock or CD) that stimulates the production of memos within organizations. Memos supply information on which action-oriented decisions are made. They also document—that is, they establish the formal record of organizational life.

We can summarize the organizational function of memos by saying that their purpose is to provide the right information in the right form at the right time to the right people. Determining what's "right" in each case depends on understanding the goal or goals to be met:

1. The right *information* is the information that is required (whether the assignment is implicit or explicit) to get a job done, to reach the intended goal. Sales data or personnel policies or fund balances may be needed, and the writer of the memo has to provide what is needed in response to a particular assignment.

2. The right *form* is the form that makes the information most readily useful to the person receiving the memo. A simple fill-in-the-blank memo may supply what is needed to activate a payroll entry, or a description of the workings of some auditing software may be needed to persuade someone to purchase it.

3. The right *time* is the time at which the information can be used most effectively to make the decision. The January receivables report will help more in early February than in early March. The interview schedule for a job candidate should be on everyone's desk before the person arrives, not the next day.

4. The right *people* are those who request or routinely need the information. Does it make any sense to send the monthly sales figures to the director of security? Should the vice-president of manufacturing get copies of all memos reporting on the performance of the company's retirement-fund portfolio?

Meeting Personal Goals

We said that memos are written to serve both organizational and individual goals. If the organizational goal is to get the right information in the right form at the right time to the right people (all based on the overall objective of using that information to make decisions leading to action), what individual goals are served? The most obvious individual goal of writing a memo is that it's part of your job. If you are assigned to write a memo summarizing the result of your visit to a potential client, you do it because you're supposed to. But there's another and subtly different individual goal: You do it in the way that reflects best on yourself. Writing memos can thus be said to serve the individual goal of self-promotion, of making you look good.

This statement shouldn't be interpreted to mean that memo writing is a form of showing off. It simply means that a job well done reflects favorably on the person doing it. A good memo serves the writer by demonstrating his or her abilities, knowledge, and capacity to get a job done.

Unfortunately, almost everyone with business experience can recall examples of memos that didn't seem to serve any purpose beyond glorifying the writer, calling attention to what he did or knew or could do. Here's an example:

INTERFAX SERVICES

August 19, 19xx

TO: Doris Ryan
        Employee Benefits Supervisor
FROM: Marcia Henderson
        Retirement Coordinator

The Bay Area Gerontological Society meeting last Thursday was the occasion for presenting this writer with the third annual Gordon Puff Award for contributions to better understanding of the needs of senior citizens. The award recognizes the work done to promote community awareness of the problems and challenges of retirement.

During the presentation many references were made to the preretirement program developed at Interfax and described in several articles in major trade publications. It was very good publicity for Interfax and reflected highly on our entire employee benefits program. Representatives of the local press were in attendance and will probably write a story that will provide further publicity for the company.

This is the sort of openly self-serving memo that is not uncommon in organizations. It appears to perform no function other than promoting the writer. We easily recognize such memos for what they are. However, other kinds of self-promotion through memo writing are also common and a bit more subtle. Consider the following example:

INTEROFFICE CORRESPONDENCE

TO: Production Office/ATTN: Records
FROM: Larry Connors
DATE: March 3, 19xx

Production Report for February

I am happy to report record production figures for the Box Division for February. We completed 62,000 units, compared to 59,500 units in January and 58,700 in February of last year. That represents an increase of 4.2 percent over January and 5.6 percent over the prior-year period.

This dramatic increase was accomplished despite poor weather conditions early in the month that forced us to cancel the evening shift one day and to curtail the day shift another day.

I am proud of the work done by my men. We will continue to work at our highest level to improve production even further in the future.

cc:
J. R. Folsom, VP, Operations
K. McCandless, General Manager
F. W. Fairless, Plant Operations Coordinator
C. H. Bally, Supervisor
W. Rindle, Foreman
T. Post, Foreman
J. P. Burleigh, Foreman

This memo serves an organizational purpose: to report to the production office the monthly production figures of the Box Division. It accomplishes this aim, though the narrative (as opposed to tabular) presentation of the data may be less than efficient. The language of the memo reflects clearly that it has an important secondary function, namely, to glorify its writer. Note that the first word of the memo's text is *I,* and the recurrent use of the first-person pronoun draws the reader's attention more to the writer than to the subject.

Phrases within the document also highlight the accomplishments: "happy to report," "dramatic increase," "proud of the work done by my men," "work at our highest levels," "improve production even further." (One wonders if the writer owns "his" men.) The language is intended to focus attention not on the production numbers, but on the writer himself. One additional sign of this intention is the distribution list, the persons named to receive copies of the memo. It is standard in large companies to have a fixed distribution list for certain routine documents, and many managers require subordinates to "copy" them on any document sent out of the division or section. The seven-member copy or distribution list in this memo, routine or not, reflects the writer's effort to spread his fame far—from foremen to the vice-president for operations. Persons knowledgeable about corporate politics say that you can gauge the political (as opposed to purely functional) nature of an internal document by the length of the distribution list. Exactly who should receive copies of memos is a topic we'll consider in the next section. In general, when you wield a big copy list, at the very least people will guess that you're more interested in impressing your superiors and peers than in getting the work of the company done.

By considering the possible conflict between organizational and individual goals in memo writing, we don't want to imply that you will always or even frequently confront that problem yourself. But you should be aware that quite legitimate personal goals (to be seen as having done a good job, for example) can coexist with organizational goals. As always, the best way to bring credit on yourself is to do a good job. Collecting or discovering the right information and conveying it in the right form at the right time to the right people—in other words, writing a good memo—is one mutually beneficial way to serve the company's and your own goals.

How? Guidelines for Writing Memos

Knowing what memos are and what purposes they serve is, of course, preliminary to what people really want to know about memos: how to write good ones. This section provides advice, centered on seven guidelines:

1. Identify the context.
2. Review your communication options.
3. Determine the structure.
4. Distribute the information.

5. Conform to the conventions.

6. Edit and revise.

7. Evaluate against all goals.

Identify the Context

Why is this memo being written? Who will read it? What can or should he or she or they do after reading it? What do you as the writer want them to do? Answering these questions is a way of fixing the context for a memo. You need to review the subject, the specific purpose, and the audience for the memo.

The *subject* is the topic that the memo is about. For example, if you are writing a trip report in memo form, you must be certain whether the subject is the trip itself (dates and times, routes, meetings attended, people seen, and so on) or a particular event or person or idea encountered on the trip. There's a difference, as the following two memos show:

Memo A

IBEX COMPANY

To:	Charles Fitzgerald
	Director, Hospital Services Division
From:	Wayne Bisbee
Date:	May 5, 19xx
Subject:	Trip Report

The Food Services Association of American Hospitals held its annual meeting at the Conrad Hilton Hotel in Chicago from May 1 to May 4. I attended along with Judy Blake and Howard Hughes. Total expenses for the trip were $3,726 and are accounted for as follows:

Airfare	$ 865
Local transportation	53
Hotel	1,078
Meals	540
Registration	300
Entertainment	890

Full expense documentation has been sent to the business office.

We entertained service managers from three university-based hospitals in Southern California and from American Eldercare, which runs eighteen nursing homes in Florida and Georgia.

Memo B

IBEX COMPANY

To: Charles Fitzgerald
           Director, Hospital Services Division
From: Wayne Bisbee
Date: May 5, 19xx
Subject: Trip Report

At the meeting of the Food Services Association of American Hospitals in Chicago this week, Judy Blake, Howard Hughes, and I met with and entertained representatives of three university-based hospitals in Southern California and from American Eldercare (AE).

AE is a very interesting company. Based in Tampa, it operates eighteen nursing homes in Florida and Georgia. They currently use ARP Services for their Florida units (ten) and FineFood for their Georgia units (eight). They are interested in discussing coverage for the whole operation to simplify billing and contracts. We will follow through quickly to visit AE headquarters and prepare a proposal if that seems indicated. We were told that a competitive proposal submitted by June 1 would be favorably received. Our contact with AE was very positive.

I will, of course, keep you informed.

Although both memos claim, in the subject line, to be trip reports, in fact the subjects differ: The subject of Memo A is the trip itself (dates, place, people, cost), whereas Memo B's subject is the possibility of gaining a contract from the American Eldercare company, whose representatives the writer and his colleagues entertained at the meeting. Knowing the difference between these two subjects—and preferably showing that difference by using precise subject headings instead of vague ones—is important if the memo is to be successful.

The *specific purpose* of a memo is the outcome the writer desires—what she or he wants the memo to accomplish. It should be phrased as one sentence: "The purpose of this memo is . . ." For Memo A, one could write, "The purpose of this memo is to inform Mr. Fitzgerald about the essential details of our trip to the Chicago convention." In other words, the purpose is simply to inform. For Memo B, the sentence might read, "The purpose of this memo is to inform Mr. Fitzgerald about the possibility of getting a contract from American Eldercare as a result of our meeting with their representatives in Chicago." Again, the key word is *inform*. In both cases, the purpose is to pass on information so that the receiver is aware of something. No specific response is required.

However, you should note that the specific purpose is different in the two samples, and the different purposes call for different information, different tone, and different structure. You should also note that in both memos, organizational and individual goals are being simultaneously served. Informing one's boss about an event meets an organizational objective, and putting the writer in a good light (in different ways in each memo) meets an individual one. But these objectives are not in conflict.

The *audience* of a memo is, of course, the person or persons to whom it is sent. In Memos A and B, the audience is identified as one individual, a person obviously known to the writer. There is no copy or distribution list, though trip reports are often sent to multiple audiences, those on the copy list being persons who might benefit from the information conveyed or who typically receive copies of trip reports (the travel department, for example, or all members of the division who need to be kept informed about the contacts being made by travelers).

Most writers find that it's easier to write memos to a single individual than to a group of people because the taste, interest, style, knowledge, and organizational position of members of the audience can affect the choice of words, use of detail, structure, and even length of the document, as we saw in Chapter 3. If your boss understands the niceties of fund accounting, for example, you can simply talk about the plant fund balance without explanation. But if you are writing to three people, two of whom don't know anything about fund accounting, you will need to explain plant fund balance, which might bore the one knowledgeable person in your audience. If the distribution list is routine—people who must receive copies of your memos as a matter of company policy—you can probably pay less attention to the special characteristics of each member of the audience on the assumption that the needs of the primary audience should be met first. Trying to deal simultaneously with specialized and general audiences typically causes grief even for experienced writers. In all cases, you should get the firmest possible grip on your audience by reviewing for yourself just what the primary audience knows, needs, and expects.

Review Your Communication Options

Should you write the memo in the first place? Or just pick up the phone and call the woman in real estate and ask for the information directly? If you have been specifically asked to write a memo, then of course you must—that's your job. But if you have a choice, consider whether an alternative form of communication (probably oral rather than written) would serve the same purpose more effectively and efficiently.

Putting a request or an answer in a written memo makes sense if:

- The information is complex, lengthy, or subject to misunderstanding.
- More than one person should receive the information or the request.
- It's important to document for later use (even legal requirements) that the request was made or the information was supplied.
- Company policies require written documentation.

Here's a simple rule that seems obvious but that requires frequent attention: If there is no good reason to write the memo, don't.

Determine the Structure

Memos take shape from their writer's perceptions of subject, specific purpose, and audience. The skeleton, the overall structure, is determined by the material and by what the writer aims to do and thinks the audience needs and wants.

Like all communications, the memo ordinarily follows a three-part division: introduction, middle, ending. The length and content of each part depend on the subject, purpose, and audience. One clear sentence may properly introduce a memo if the subject is routine or otherwise familiar to the audience, but a long paragraph or even two may be needed to provide background and necessary clarification for those not familiar with the topic of the memo. The body may take the form of a simple table or a sentence or two of explanation of data, but if the subject is complex, much more will be required. The ending may be brief, even abrupt, in a memo requesting information from a subordinate: "Please supply the information requested here by Friday of next week." But a more complex topic or request may necessitate a different approach, as in this example:

Conclusion. The data briefly summarized here lead to several possible conclusions. It is obvious that more resources must be placed behind the marketing effort if we are to gain significant consumer response to the product. This probably means an increase in the ad budget of as much as 50 percent. Likewise, it is obvious that quality control must be improved to ensure better consumer attitudes toward the product. Finally, I believe that a further study of the effectiveness of the advertising campaign currently being run would help us assess our situation and plan for a strengthened program of marketing.

Distribute the Information

The information that a memo conveys cannot be randomly or thoughtlessly distributed within the document. The writer must think about where it belongs, placing it appropriately to achieve the intended outcome and to meet the expectations of the audience. Within the typical three-part division of a communication, the core of information belongs in the body. One would not usually begin or end a memo with the key information, though it is possible to preview or summarize it at the beginning or end. Here are two sample memos written to answer a specific request for information about the attractiveness of the stock of the Ice Chip Company. Notice how differently the basic information is distributed.

Memo A

To: Clarence McGhee
From: Betty Silvers
Date: 17 August 19xx

    This is in response to your request for a report on the attractiveness of Ice Chip Company as an investment prospect. The table below summarizes the basic information you desire:

Bid range	4 to 12
P/E	18
Dividends	.09 quarterly
Current yield	8 percent (current price of $7.5)

    Based on my review of various advisory-service reports and discussions with analysts who follow the stock, it seems that Ice Chip is a well-managed company developing and effectively marketing ice cream sandwiches and related novelties with high margins and excellent prospects for growth in the Sunbelt markets it serves. Its financial position is sound, and it has been favorably recommended for long-term capital appreciation.

    My recommendation is that we take a substantial position in Ice

Chip Company. I will be happy to supply additional information or answer any questions you may have.

Memo B

To: Clarence McGhee
From: Larry Downs
Date: 17 August 19xx

Ice Chip Company is currently paying dividends of $.09 per quarter and yields 8 percent, based on a selling price of $7.50 per share. The P/E is 18, a little high but probably justified by their growth prospects in southern and southwestern cities. The stock has traded in the $4–$12 range over the past six months, which shows that it is a relatively volatile stock, a bit speculative. Management seems good. It looks like a nice investment prospect for us. Please call if you want to know more.

The memos supply the same information, but the distribution of that information in Memo A makes it more accessible to the reader. Memo A follows a clear division into introduction, middle, and conclusion. Memo B throws the information at the reader at the outset, with no context, and with little effort to relate the parts or to separate data from interpretation. The good memo, as this comparison illustrates, not only exhibits a firm structure that helps the reader through it but also distributes information within that structure in a way that highlights key points and keeps recommendations clearly separated from the evidence on which they are based. Good distribution helps the writer to say what he or she wants and helps the reader to learn what he or she wants.

Conform to the Conventions

As we saw at the beginning of this chapter, memos are especially conventional: Most businesses, colleges, hospitals, and government agencies have rules or at least guidelines about how memos should be prepared. These rules generally relate to format, but they may also prescribe style. Two conventions usually covered are the heading and the distribution list:

1. The heading includes the "To," "From," "Date," and "Subject" lines. There are many combinations for these. You simply need to know which combination is required by your employer or sponsor and to follow the rules carefully.

2. The distribution list may be set by corporate policy. For example, some firms require that immediate supervisors be included on the distribution list for all memos, on the assumption that one's boss should always know what one is up to. Sometimes the convention is that all members of a department or unit get copies of all memos sent outside it. These requirements, of course, vary greatly from organization to organization—and from unit to unit within organizations. But there are usually clear enough guidelines to make it possible to know to whom copies must be sent. You can, of course, add to the list if there are substantive (nonpolitical) reasons to do so.

Conventions may also govern a host of lesser points of style. The following are some examples:

Dates.   Military organizations and those who work with them generally write dates this way: 17 September 1973.

Names.   Some organizations use the first or first two initials to designate all employees in memos: W. W. Baxter, or K. Ryan, rather than William Wainwright Baxter and Kathy Ryan.

Position or title.   In some organizations, conventions dictate that the position or title for each person be specified after his or her name: George Blake, Maintenance Supervisor; Maryanne Clark, Head of Records.

Abbreviations.   The government is not alone in making much of abbreviations. Many companies encourage—especially in memos—wide use of abbreviations. If they are common in your organization, by all means use such abbreviations since they make communication simpler and more direct.

Appearance.   Memos simply look different from other documents in most organizations. This is because of conventions that dictate spacing (single or double), placement on the page (large or small margins, and so on), and even typeface (boldface for the "To," "From," "Date," and "Subject" lines, for example, or fill-in forms with these items already printed).

The general rule is that conventions should be followed in every aspect of memo writing to which they apply, from format and appearance to word choice. This is true not just because it's one's duty to follow company rules but because conventions exist to facilitate action. If each time you wrote a memo you had to make a conscious decision about whether to use "To, From, Date, Subject" or "To, From,

Subject, Date," you would waste time and divert yourself from the real job of communicating needed information. You may not like a particular convention (we know people who just can't write "8 August"), but learning and following the conventions established for you can save time and energy and help you to concentrate on the harder tasks. When the easier choices are made for you, you can spend time on the harder ones that writing always involves.

Edit and Revise

Revision, as we saw in Chapter 9, is generally the last step in writing, the final cleaning and polishing before production. Before you hand the final draft of your memo to the typist or enter it into your word processor, you should, of course, subject it to close scrutiny and edit and revise carefully. But we also suggest that the editing stage need not be the very last one in the process of preparing a memo. It's wise to review, edit, and revise the memo at least once before you finally evaluate it against your goals.

Revising a memo should follow the guidelines for revision that apply to all documents. Check to see if the memo has a clear and efficient structure and if the information is distributed properly within that structure. Revision can also occur at the word and sentence level. The specific characteristics of the memo form discussed at the beginning of this chapter should provide hints about what to look for in editing your memo:

1. Because it's an internal document, a memo can use abbreviations, shorthand expressions, and inside phrases known to those who will receive it. It can be abrupt, to the point, more workmanlike, and less ingratiating than a letter to a customer or another person outside the organization. In the editing stage, look for ways to cut formality and to exploit the opportunity for succinctness provided by the internal nature of the memo.

2. Because a memo is short, you have a special reason to use the editing process to prune, cut, and shrink. Try to chop out long and cumbersome expressions ("it is believed to be desirable to," "based on a thorough review of all available evidence, this writer recommends," "owing to the unusually long and difficult process of collecting, analyzing, and verifying the data," and so forth). Make one word do the work of two or three. Shorten sentences and express ideas directly. It's always good to shorten and tighten prose; because of its very nature, a memo must be short—take advantage of that requirement when you revise.

3. The exclusive focus of a memo on a single topic means that in revising you should look for stray comments, points that diverge or

suggest sidetracks. Most writers end up knowing more about their subjects than they can or need to communicate, especially in memo form, where brevity and directness are at a premium. Use the revision process to identify sentences or even paragraphs that don't clearly support the central point of the memo, no matter how interesting the information may be in its own right. Of each sentence ask: Is this really necessary? If not, eliminate it, and then see if the memo hangs together without it. You can always restore a section later if its absence creates a problem in understanding. Subjecting every word and sentence to this kind of scrutiny not only serves the cause of brevity but also helps you to keep the memo focused clearly on its single topic.

4. The strong audience orientation of the memo requires you, as you revise, to measure all aspects of the memo against your perception of the audience's needs: Is this word known to my reader? Will he or she understand that concept without definition? Is this much detail really necessary, or can I condense to a few generalizations? Questions like these must always be asked very specifically about the particular audience (or audiences) for which the memo is intended.

5. Because a memo is conventional, during revision you need to give special attention to whether it adheres to the conventions effectively: Is company format followed? Is the "Subject" line specific and helpful? Does the distribution list include everyone who must receive a copy—and no one else? Company style and format rules and guidelines exist to make communication easier. In memos, they are particularly helpful and should be used as standards to guide revision.

Evaluate Against All Goals

The only reason for writing a memo is to reach some goal. Thus it is reasonable that the last step in the process is to compare the document you've written to the goals you set for yourself to see whether you have achieved them. Of course, the memo's final goal is to accomplish something within the organization, but you can't really evaluate your final draft in that way because you don't know what response it will elicit.

But when you wrote the memo, you should have clearly stated to yourself both the organizational and the individual goals that you designed it to achieve. These are useful and final standards for checking the draft before it is produced and sent out into the system. Let's say you determined that the organizational goal of your memo is to request your supervisor's approval of the purchase of a new printer for your office. You can ask, in reviewing the final draft, whether the specific purpose is absolutely clear, whether the supporting evidence is strong, whether the advantages to the company are made evident, whether the benefits are shown to exceed the cost, and so on. Asking these questions is a way of checking whether the organizational goals of the memo are likely to be met. Such questions help you to focus on the purpose, and that focus gives you a different angle of approach from simply looking for comma faults or misspellings or prolix phrases.

You should also ask clearly if the memo appears to meet the individual goal you set for yourself: Does it present you in a good light—without reaching too far or overstating? Does it show you as an accomplished, capable employee? Does it reflect full credit on you without detracting from anyone else? In short, is the memo an example of your very best? Every memo should be.

Exercises

1. Ask several friends or relatives to define *memo* based on their work experiences. How do their definitions compare with the one given here? Is there a commonly accepted understanding of memos and their functions?

2. Which of the following topics seem to be appropriate for memos? Explain why the others are not and suggest a more appropriate form of communication for each:

(a) A request to your supervisor to purchase new chairs for the reception area of your office.

(b) Your proposed vacation plan, for approval by your boss.

(c) Your company's affirmative action policy and procedures, for review by the top managers.

(d) A change in the reimbursement policy for employees using their own cars on business trips.

(e) A proposed restructuring of the firm to be considered by the board of directors.

(f) Price updates for the toy section of a department store.

(g) Company policy on unsolicited gifts from vendors.

3. Write a brief memo in response to this communication situation: Your department has just been moved to a different floor of the building, but the door locks were not changed and the people in the group that used to occupy your new offices still have keys. You are concerned about security and want the former occupants to turn in their keys. Write to them requesting the keys without offending them.

After you've written the memo, compare it with several written by others in your class and note any differences in tone, structure, and use of conventions. Discuss the differences and identify successful strategies in trying to meet the goal of the communication.

4. Secure a memo from a relatively large corporation (your college is a good choice) and analyze its use of conventions: headings, distribution list, physical appearance, and so on. Note any ways that you think the conventions contrib-

ute to or detract from the overall presentation and the effort to achieve a goal. (You'll have to start by deciding what you think the goal is, that is, what the memo is trying to accomplish.)

5. Here are some typical business situations that call for memos. Write a brief one on each, using appropriate headings and distribution lists:

(a) A new secretary, Anne Weiss, has been hired in your department starting on 12 January at a salary of $14,500 a year. Notify Mr. Griscom, director of payroll services.

(b) You slipped on the ice on the parking lot as you were entering the building. You need to report this accident to the director of buildings and services, to your supervisor, and to the director of personnel (because of possible insurance claims).

(c) You were asked by your supervisor in the marketing department to examine the sales figures for the southwestern region for the past quarter and to compare them with those for the year-earlier period. In the current quarter, sales were $54,898, compared to $53,900 for the same quarter last year.

(d) The three word processors in your office are not under service contracts. Time and parts charges for service for the past year amounted to $824. Service contracts for the three machines would cost $250 a year. Write to Harold Jansky, your supervisor, recommending that the department purchase service contracts for next year for the three word processors.

(e) You traveled to Omaha on company business and have to submit a trip report detailing your expenses: airfare, $345; taxi and parking, $12.50; hotel, $165; meals and entertainment, $87.50. Your supervisor, Mary Lopez, must approve the reimbursement, and Harold Wallace, the assistant controller, has to have the report to write you a reimbursement check.

Letters: Strategies

This chapter sets the context for writing letters, another major form of communication in organizations. You'll see some of the basics here, and in the following chapters you'll find guidelines for writing letters to meet a variety of communication goals. These individual goals fit into the two larger goals of *informing* and *persuading*. Chapter 14 deals with *informative* letters. Chapters 15 and 16 discuss *persuasive* letters. By virtue of being written and sent, of course, all letters *record* information—something to keep in mind when you decide to write a letter, as you shall see. Letters, too, may be written simply to maintain a relationship, like a good handshake every now and then. This chapter talks a bit about such letters.

Before you write a letter, think about whether a phone call might work instead. The call may get you an answer faster. A phone call in response to a letter of complaint ensures personal attention to the complainer; thus some companies routinely make such a call when the complainer is important or particularly angry. A call is also useful in handling sensitive or controversial information that you don't want to commit to paper. And most calls take less time than letter writing. On the other hand, some people prefer letters. A writer has time to work out an argument, to establish a case, and to revise a bit before becoming vulnerable to a reader. The writing provides control. If the person you are trying to contact is hard to find—or talks a lot—the letter may also be faster. Sometimes, as you'll see, your goal in communicating can be accomplished only with a letter.

Then, assess the priority of each letter in your work. Determine the appropriate timing, authorization, and polish. In timing the letter, consider, for example, how long you can wait before writing. All correspondents want immediate replies to their letters, and your credibility is enhanced by promptness. But if you have lots of correspondence, assess each item to determine what you'll do first. Observe the fixed deadlines of financial transactions and filings. Attend to the demands of angry customers and important persons. Second, establish the necessary authority for each letter. Can you write and send the letter individually? Do you need information from others or the approval of others? Particularly with letters that commit your company to some course of action or the delivery date of some product, you'll want to be sure that a supervisor and perhaps a corporate lawyer have approved your statement. Finally, determine the polish necessary to get the job done. Although every letter must, of course, be accurate and grammatically correct, you'll find that some can work as edited drafts while others require fine tuning. You can't give each the same attention. Assess the political value of the letter to figure out how much preparation time it is worth.

One Letter, One Reader

Memos are often public documents. They circulate openly, usually in unsealed envelopes, to one or many readers in a company. Memos also find their way onto the bulletin boards that you walk past or access electronically on a computer. Letters, however, are more private. Indeed, when someone needs to send personal or sensitive information within a company, he or she generally uses a letter. Letters also tend to demand more attention from the reader. For these reasons, at one large brokerage house, so the rumor goes, employees send letters *internally* via Federal Express whenever they have an important or timely message to convey. The interoffice mail, they reason, moves unheralded and too slowly among the many floors of the office.

The You Attitude

A letter is tailored to *one specific reader.* Often the letter is unique to that reader. Sometimes, of course, the letter addresses the reader as part of a set of people, for example, a target population chosen to receive a direct-mail sales message or a statement of policy. But even when the writer sends many similar or identical letters, the *reader* reads as an individual. The reader requires personal attention. That attention has been called the *you attitude.* Figure 13–1 provides some checkpoints for the you attitude.

The Goal

Whatever your goal in writing, you can achieve it only *through* the reader. Make that goal clear and concrete. Decide, broadly, if you mean to *inform* or to *persuade,* and then develop a subgoal and a strategy for presentation that match that need. Chapters 14, 15, and 16 discuss strategies in detail. And don't contradict yourself. One letter from a retirement fund to its subscribers, for example, began by noting that a monthly check was enclosed and ended with the statement that the check would be mailed in a week. The confused reader could not decipher the letter's purpose.

The Reader's Self-interest

State the goal *from the reader's point of view.* Indeed, a major indicator of your potential as a manager is your ability to envision other people's priorities and agendas. On a practical level, count the number of

1. *The goal.* Does the letter make clear what the reader should understand or do?

2. *The reader's self-interest.* Is the letter written from the reader's point of view? Or does it emphasize the writer and his or her needs over those of the reader?

3. *Structure.* Does the letter make efficient use of the reader's time?

4. *Ease of response.* If the letter requires a response, does it make such a response easy?

5. *The reader's code.* Has the writer avoided insiders' jargon and used language that the reader will understand? Does its tone match the reader's expectation concerning his or her relationship with the writer? Has the writer avoided any chance of misunderstanding?

6. *Veiled attacks.* Does the letter contain any veiled attacks against the reader?

FIGURE 13–1. The you attitude.

I references in your letter; more than two or three may make the writer seem self-serving. Especially in a letter of application for a job, be sure to avoid starting every paragraph with *I*. In addressing the reader's self-interest, too, preserve the reader's dignity. That means, for example, that negative letters require particular tact and sometimes a bit of evasion to smooth the relationship. You may, for example, *objectify* the reader:

Positive.   You're hired.

Negative.   We are no longer pursuing your application.

You may also use the passive:

Positive.   I am happy to report that the board has funded your proposal.

Negative.   After a thorough review, it has been decided that your proposal will not be funded.

Use the passive to avoid placing blame:

> The washer had been overloaded, a condition that strained the motor. [Rather than "You overloaded the washer."]

But don't lie. Avoid happy talk for its own sake. Customers expecting straightforward information will not be pleased with a bank, for example, that insists on being cute in its letters.

Structure

Conserve the reader's time by structuring letters efficiently and telling the reader only what he or she needs to know. Work from a plan. In general, keep letters to one page. Only exceed that limit when you have a compelling reason to do so.

Ease of Response

Letters are often written in a series. You write; the reader responds; maybe you write again and the reader responds again. Thus any prior correspondence should be available for reference as you write. Keep a file. Then think ahead. For example, to encourage a reader to return defective merchandise for you to examine, enclose a prepaid mailer or label in your response to a complaint. When you are ordering something, use whatever order form is required and make sure you have filled out every item. In conducting a survey, limit the number of questions and choose questions that can be answered with a few marks on a scale or a yes or no.

Reader's Code

Avoid insiders' language in writing to outsiders. That means, for example, that a financial institution writing to a customer should avoid financial language that the customer may not be expected to understand. Moreover, name items as the reader would. A writer at a textile company began a letter to Running Gear, Inc., an athletic outfitter, as follows:

> As you are aware, the Running Gear, Inc. account is $250,000 in arrears.

But Running Gear, Inc., of course, labels the account with the name of the textile company, not with its own name. Thus the letter should have begun:

> As you know, your account with us is $250,000 in arrears.

In a series of letters, writer and reader come to have certain expectations about each other. Accommodate these expectations in the language and tone of your writing. Look for cues. For example, in a letter to someone you don't know, use the full formal name. If in response you receive a letter signed with a first name, then use that name in future correspondence. Sign your next letter with your first name, too, unless you want to send a specific signal that the reader's friendliness is inappropriate.

Veiled Attacks

1. "Please send us your *correct* social security number."

2. "If shirts are not properly washed, then their useful life is reduced."

3. "Anyone familiar with proper ticketing procedures would not have made the mistake you made."

The *writers* of these statements saw them as merely informative. But the *reader* in each case took offense:

1. Do you think [the reader responded] that I would send you the *wrong* social security number?

2. Are you accusing me of *not* washing the shirt properly and thus causing the seams to come unstitched—a condition I attribute to the faulty manufacture of the shirt?

3. Are you saying that *I* must be responsible for *your* not knowing about ticketing?

Cultivate the habit of reading between the lines of your statements to correct any language that might offend the reader.

Personal Letters in a Business Setting

Although this book emphasizes goal-oriented writing, you may at times write letters that do not aim to get any work done. They aim to create or maintain a relationship on certain key occasions: holidays, promotions and other achievements, retirements, births, marriages, and deaths. Any information in the letter is subordinate to an expression of your feeling for the reader. The you attitude is all; no particular rules apply, short of that one. Be careful to gauge correctly your relationship to the reader. Often, people in a hurry or unsure of their writing skills select commercial cards to convey their feelings on special occasions. That's fine. But a personal note in addition can mean a lot.

Routine Letters

From an organization's perspective, many occasions for writing fit a pattern. One insurance company estimates that 70 percent of its correspondence is routine. Such correspondence includes explanations of new policies and procedures, standard questions concerning account status and replies to common customer inquires, acknowledgments of orders, and the like. To achieve consistency and efficiency in letter writing, companies develop certain *form* letters. The form may be a simple fill-in-the-blank that the writer completes with personal data for the recipient (see Chapter 14). The text is stored in a word-processing system and is easily retrieved and printed for each letter.

Alternatively, the company may provide model paragraphs that the writer can assemble as appropriate. Some companies prepare packets of sample letters to serve as models from which a writer can develop individual responses. Letters addressing complex issues may require the collaboration of several individuals: someone with a technical knowledge of the subject, a public relations person who can ensure accordance with the you attitude, the company's lawyer if the matter has legal implications, and an editor.

Selecting the right form or model is a judgment to be made, of course, *from the reader's point of view.* What's routine to send may also be routine to receive. The reader is satisfied with a form for a straightforward transaction. A careful letter writer, however, must be alert to special circumstances hidden within a routine appearance.

Figure 13–2 is a statement of policy in a form letter geared to the suppliers of a large chemical company. The goal of the letter is to *inform* (or remind—as in the expression "long-standing Du Pont Company policy") suppliers about the company's policy concerning gifts. Paragraph 2 states the policy; Paragraph 3 further clarifies. The letter begins with thanks to "our valued suppliers" and maintains a tone of courtesy and professionalism toward the readers. The letter *protects* the reader who might otherwise feel that gifts were essential. But the letter still allows for small gifts like tins of cookies and boxes of candy.

International Readers

Increasingly, in our global economy, you will write letters abroad. If your command of your reader's language is good, then, of course, use that language. Otherwise, write in English; the reader may well read English or, if not, will have the letter translated. Writing for translation requires strong attention to using words in their *denotative* sense, that is, their direct dictionary meaning. Watch out for asides and local,

EM-6481   REV. 9-82

DUPONT
ESTABLISHED 1802

E. I. du Pont de Nemours & Company
INCORPORATED
Wilmington, Delaware 19898

MATERIALS AND LOGISTICS DEPARTMENT

November 1, 1984

TO ALL VENDORS

GIFTS, FAVORS AND ENTERTAINMENT

As the Holiday Season approaches, it is timely to express
our appreciation to you, our valued suppliers. We wish also
to remind you of a long-standing Du Pont Company policy.

We take pride in the business relationship with our suppliers, but in the interest of proper business relations, our
employees are not permitted to seek or accept for themselves
or others any gifts, favors or entertainment without a legitimate business purpose, nor seek or accept loans (other than
conventional loans at market rates from lending institutions)
from any person or business organization that does or seeks
to do business with, or is a competitor of, the Company.

This policy is not intended to eliminate those entirely
ethical and traditional common courtesies usually associated
with customary business practices such as business lunches,
nor does it preclude the giving of token promotional or advertising items of nominal value.

We believe our policy provides clear guidelines which
are well understood by our employees. We solicit continued
cooperation in observing that policy by your firm and its
representatives.

J. F. KEARNS
SENIOR VICE PRESIDENT -
MATERIALS AND LOGISTICS

FIGURE 13-2.   A form letter stating company policy (courtesy of the Du Pont
Company).

anecdotal information that the reader might not understand, like references to sports or entertainment that the reader may not be familiar with. Learn and observe the conventions of letters in the culture to which you are writing, the proper form for addressing the reader, and the proper way to close the discussion. Chapter 28 discusses international communication in detail.

Legal Considerations in Letter Writing

Letters have several legal implications. First, they provide a paper trail to document a course of action or a decision. If you complain against a company for some error or defect in a product or service, you may receive an immediate adjustment and close the correspondence. But if not, a record of your letters and company responses can become central to court action against the company.

Second, letters often serve as contracts binding the writer to some promise or establishing the terms of a transaction between writer and reader. Employment contracts, for example, are usually in letter form. Sales contracts and commitments for delivery of products also appear as letters, sometimes called *letters of intent*. Letters concerning credit and the collection of debts also commit writer and reader to certain actions and to sanctions when the actions do not occur. The language of such letters is usually set and has been approved by the originating organization's lawyer. As a writer, you should deviate from that language only with further legal advice.

Third, letters may be used to provide evaluations and recommendations for personnel decisions. In such letters, the writer must be careful to avoid libel, that is, malicious and false statements that might injure another's reputation or character. To avoid libel, think ahead. If someone asks you to recommend him or her, agree only if your recommendation can be positive. It's better to demur if you have any reservations. If you are asked by a company for an evaluation of a third party, that request confers a right to provide negative information as part of doing business. Just be accurate and factual; note that the information was requested and ask for confidential treatment of it. Chapter 22 provides detailed guidelines for writing performance reviews.

The term *letter* is also used to cover many official statements, for example, the formal letter from the chief executive officer that opens the company's annual report, the letter from an accounting firm stating that the report's figures were prepared "in accordance with generally accepted accounting principles," and the "fairness" letter that certifies the fair pricing of a company's stock during an acquisition.

The Letterly Voice

Undue emphasis on the legal implications of letter writing leads to problems in the way many letters sound. They display a special variant of the business voice that we can label the *letterly voice*. It's hard to say *why* letter writers revert to archaic language when they write, but the fear of commiting themselves on paper may be one reason. Speaking on behalf of an organization may be another. And some writers assume that letters *must* sound unlike daily writing. Of course, laziness and slipping into old-fashioned forms may play a role, too. Figure 13–3 shows some common phrases—and how to avoid them.

Letterly	*Direct*
Please be advised by this correspondence that . . .	I'm writing to . . .
We wish to advise you that . . .	[Omit; just begin.]
The undersigned	I
Thanking you in advance for your kindness and attention to this matter I remain,	Thank you
Your recent communication relative to . . .	Your letter about . . .
I am in receipt of your letter of recent date	I received your letter
As per your correspondence of X date	Your letter of X
In regard to the matter above referenced	Concerning X
Attached hereto please find	Attached is
Enclosed herewith please find	Enclosed is
Pursuant to your request	In response to your request
As per your request	
Forward your payment to	Send your payment to
Extend an invitation	Invite
Being of service	Serving

FIGURE 13–3.   The letterly voice and the direct voice.

Being professional and "businesslike" does not mean being dull and archaic. Avoid leftover language in your letters.

Conventions

Although the language of the letter should be crisp, engaging, and individual, the *format* of the letter adheres to conventions. Letters *look* like letters, just as memos *look* like memos. Here's a brief review of the major elements of letters today. Electronic technology is changing our concept of a letter. But at least for now, you will be expected to create letters on paper that include these elements. Figures 13–4 to 13–6 illustrate the common formats, with each element labeled. Each format is correct; unless your company has a particular preference, choose the one you like.

Always use good paper—company letterhead, or good-quality bond for personal business letters. Avoid erasable paper because the print tends to smudge. Center the text on the page. Your letter should not look as if it's about to be launched because a small amount of text is perched at the top.

Sender's Address

To let the reader know where the letter is coming from, and where to reply to the letter, you include your own address. Letterhead stationery takes care of this need, sometimes with a logo or other design element that identifies the company of origin. (A mark of some status in a company is to have letterhead that also includes *your* name and title.) If you do not have letterhead, then type your address (not including your name) as the first element.

Date

Always date letters. The date establishes the correspondence as a matter of record and provides a reference point for future correspondence.

Inside Address

It may seem silly to tell the reader his or her name and address. But again, because letters are a matter of record, you include the name of the recipient and his or her title and address, including zip code and mail stop numbers for large corporations. Proofread this element particularly carefully and don't just guess at the company name. Use the full name even if it seems tiresome to type out "E. I. du Pont de Nemours & Company, Incorporated." Don't abbreviate.

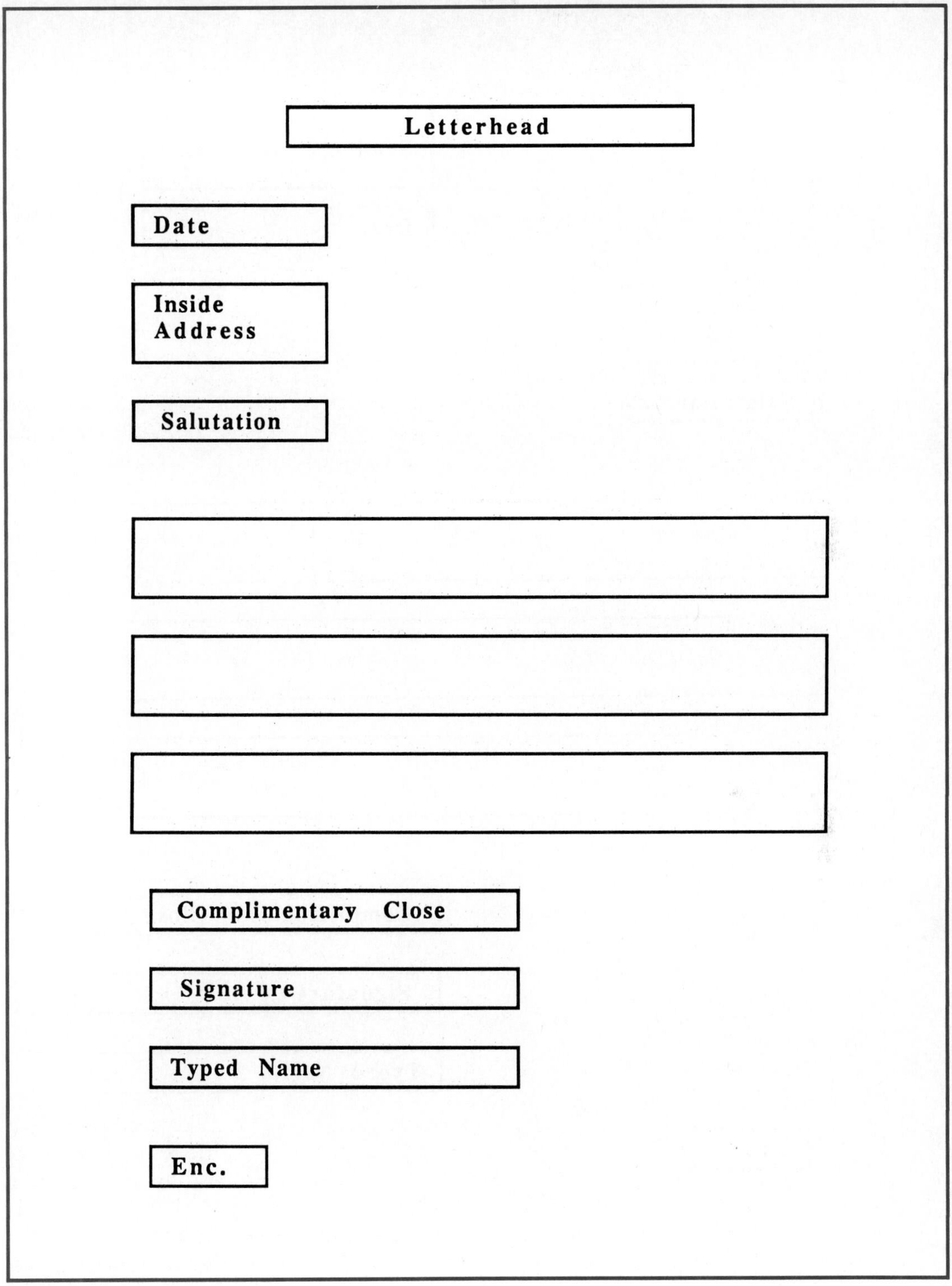

FIGURE 13–4. Block style.

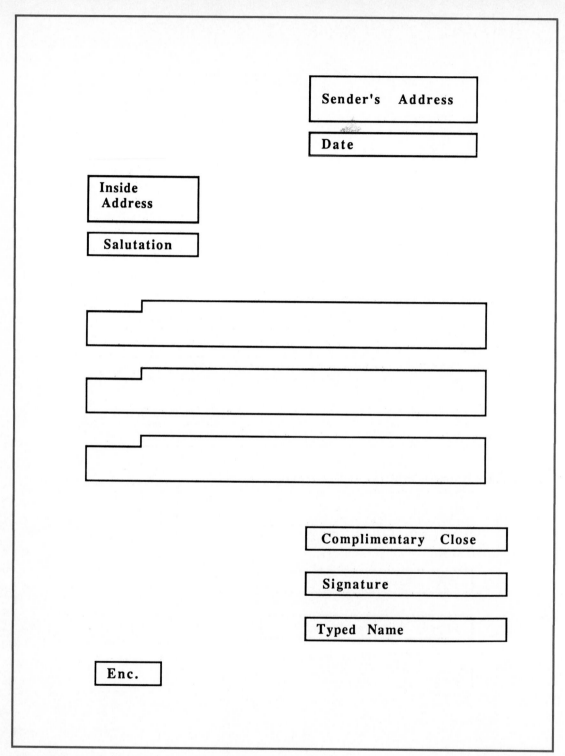

FIGURE 13–5. Modified block style (indented paragraphs).

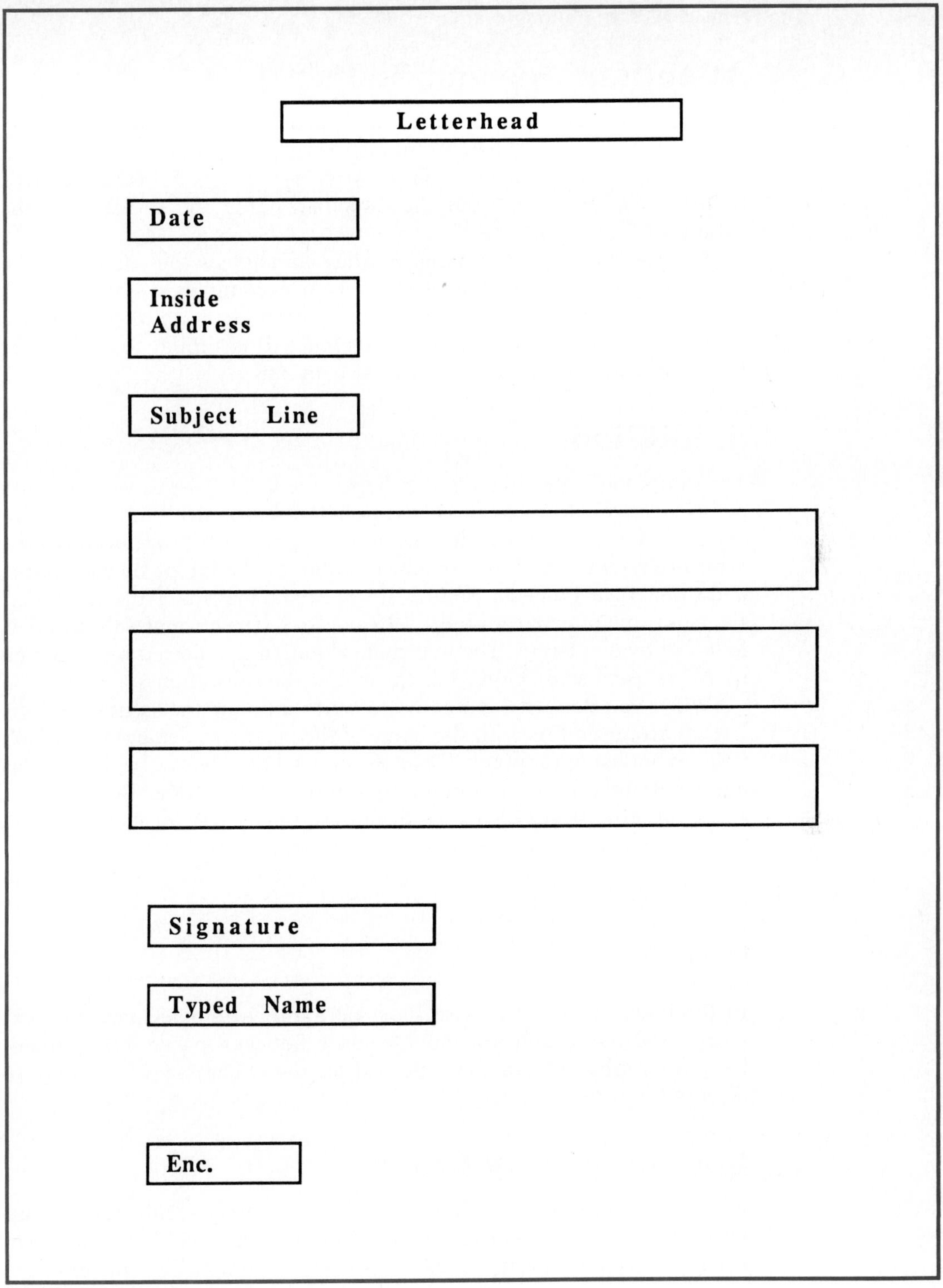

FIGURE 13–6. Simplified style. Note that there is no salutation or complimentary close.

Attention Line and Subject Line

An attention line flags the letter for a particular reader, usually designated by role rather than by name. You might, for example, flag a letter of application to a company "Attention: Personnel Director." It's better, however, to find out the director's name and to use it in the salutation.

A subject line, as the name implies, announces the subject of the letter or may refer to the number of an account or a date of prior correspondence. Such a designation is particularly useful in letter reports and in project-related correspondence. It is similar to the subject line in memos, but it is not nearly as common.

Salutation

The salutation is the greeting that begins the letter. Just as you wouldn't begin a conversation without saying hello, so you need to say hello to start a letter. Commonly, the salutation begins with *Dear* (although it's a bit archaic). If the letter is formal, address the recipient with name and title: "Dear Professor Smith." If you can be informal with the reader, then use an informal address: "Dear Jim." The formal salutation is followed by a colon (:). The informal salutation is followed by a comma (,). *Never* use a semicolon (;) at the end of the salutation.

When you don't have a name to write to, omit the salutation line. Use an attention line with the name of the pertinent department or job title. Avoid using the weak "Dear Sir or Madam." Never begin "Ladies and Gentlemen." Never respond to a blind job ad, "Dear Box 432."

If you are unsure of the gender of the reader—if, for example, you are replying to a letter signed "D. H. Carlisle"—don't take a chance with *Mr.*, a designation that might offend D.H. if she's a she. Instead, use the salutation "Dear D. H. Carlisle."

Text

In the body of the letter, use short paragraphs. Single-space the text within the paragraph and double-space between paragraphs. Indent for paragraphs only in the indented format. Chapters 14, 15 and 16 discuss letter texts in detail.

Complimentary Close

Like the salutation, the complimentary close may seem archaic. But we do need to say good-bye. In fact, American business letters are considered brusque even in the closings that we do use. The conventional closings—"sincerely yours," "yours truly," "sincerely"—differ little in meaning or tone. "Respectfully" implies a certain deference on the part of the writer. "Cordially," "best regards," and "best" are informal. Some organizations have their own standard sign-off or sign their letters appropriately for the season: "Go Fighting Blue Hens!" However, avoid any such closings in formal business letters. If your letter omits a salutation, then omit the complimentary close.

Signature

Type your name several spaces (enough to sign your name) below the complimentary close. A company name may come either above or below your typed name. Although you type your full name, you may sign the letter with your nickname if your relationship with the reader warrants.

Other Notations

Beneath the signature you may include other notations. For example:

Enc(s)	Enclosures. Note the number if more than one: "Encs (3)." Note the title if you'd like: "Enc: ACS Compendium."
Initials	Writer first; secretary second: "DCA:dtd."
Copies	*cc* (or *pc* for photocopy) and then the names of the recipients of copies (after a colon).
P.S.	Don't use, except perhaps in sales letters.
Signed in absence	As a matter of record, let the reader know if the originator of the letter is different from the signer: "Peter Smith for Mary Jones" or "Signed in Mary Jones's absence by Peter Smith."

Subsequent Pages

On rare occasions, you may write a letter of more than one page, particularly in letter reports or contract letters. Head each page after the first one with the recipient's name, the page number, and the date. Use paper that matches the first page, but not letterhead.

Dictation

Many managers dictate letters that will later be transcribed and sent. Dictating is simple if you keep in mind the general strategies for preparing *any* document (see Chapter 6). You may dictate directly to a secretary; more frequently, however, you will use either a personal dictation machine or a company's central dictation system, usually accessed through your telephone. If you are not familiar with the machinery, examine it first, and then *clarify the logistics:*

- Note your name, department, billing code, and the like.
- Specify the layout and the type of stationery to be used.
- Clarify whether this is a draft or a final copy; if a final copy, note the number of copies to be made and the names of the recipients.
- Provide instructions for dealing with any enclosures.
- Establish the priority and deadlines for each letter.

Next, *dictate:*

- Spell out the name of the addressee, along with any other unusual or ambiguous words or punctuation.
- Indicate paragraph breaks ("new paragraph") and special typography, capitalization, and the like.
- Speak in a normal tone; don't shout; don't mumble or speed.
- Take advantage of a stop or pause button if one is available when you need time to think. Take the time.

Finally, when the copy is returned to you:

- *Proofread.* When you sign a letter, you take personal responsibility for the contents, spelling, and the like. Mistakes reflect *you*, not the typist.

Computers and Letter Writing

A survey of 218 business executives by a management consulting firm showed that 10 percent chose dictation for their writing. The vast majority—89 percent—wrote with pad and pencil. Only 1 percent used computers for their correspondence.[1] As more terminals enter the executive suite, it will be interesting to see if those numbers change. Certainly, many people in organizations are now exploiting electronic

---

[1]"Pencils over Computers," *The Wall Street Journal,* 11 September 1984, 1.

technology for letter writing. The technology functions in two ways. First, computers as word processors are speeding up the creation of letters on paper. Direct-mail advertisers are a prime user, as a trip to your mailbox is sure to show. So are the correspondence units in banks, insurance companies, and other financial institutions that handle many transactions with customers. A computer allows for the easy merging of lists of names with blocks of prose to tailor letters to individuals. Second, computers create *electronic mail*. Electronic mail now mainly addresses communication *within* an organization. But gradually it is replacing Telex and paper letters for *external* correspondence as well. Some problems must be overcome, particularly matters of security and authorization. Most transactions still require a valid signature on paper.

But as computer technology becomes more sophisticated and the need for speedy global communication increases, more and more companies will send their letters electronically. The format of the letter will change. Of course, the envelope will be eliminated. A command is entered into the system to route the message. That command looks something like this: *mail louie. UDEL. EDU (Louie. ARPA)*. Each item is a code designating the receiver and the electronic pathway. The address then will appear automatically at the top of the message, along with other computer-generated information concerning the date and time of transmission. Moreover, if current electronic mail is an indicator, the *tone* of letters will become increasingly informal (see Chapter 10). The goal of correspondence will remain the same, however: at a certain date, given certain circumstances, to achieve some understanding or action for yourself or your organization through the reader.

Exercises

1. Interview friends or other people you know who write letters on behalf of organizations. What is their process for composing the letters? How much time do they spend on a letter? If the times vary, why? Do the letters go through an approval route before being mailed?

2. Ask non-American students at your university or ask individuals in a company that does business abroad for examples of letters written in other than an American context. How do they differ from the general American business letter? Do they use different conventions? Different strategies for lining up material?

3. The following letter smacks of the letterly voice. Revise it to sound more engaging to the reader:

Dear Mortgagor(s):

We wish to advise you that your mortgage loan has been transferred from ABC Mortgage Company to XYZ Mortgage Company for servicing.

A new coupon book, beginning with your April 1, 1989, mortgage payment will be mailed to you shortly. Your mortgage payments should be forwarded directly to us at the following address:

> XYZ Mortgage
> One Unity Plaza
> Carrollton, TX 75006

In the event that you are currently enrolled in either a life, disability, or accidental death insurance program, this coverage will be continued with the premium being collected in your monthly payments.

All future escrow analyses and annual statements, regarding transactions to your account, will be mailed from XYZ Mortgage Company effective as of the date of this transfer. It is the policy of XYZ Mortgage Company to include an escrow reserve in your escrow analysis. The escrow reserve amounts to 1/12 of the total annual escrow required for your mortgage. This reserve will be used as a safeguard to offset future increases in real estate taxes and/or insurance premiums. The escrow reserve amount will be listed on your analysis under "Description of bill to be paid from escrow account."

We wish to advise you that this transfer of servicing is solely a business transaction to accommodate the servicing of all residential mortgage loans by one company and does not, in any way, reflect any dissatisfaction on anyone's part with your mortgage loan.

We are looking forward to being of service to you.

If any additional information is needed with reference to this transfer, you may call our Customer Service Department at (214) 361-1234 or you may use our toll free number at (800) 123-4567.

Sincerely,

4. The following letter also incorporates some letterly clichés—and a veiled attack on the reader as well. Revise the letter to emphasize reader benefit:

May we thank you for your letter advising us of a *MATSON* soccer shirt that you feel did not give your son proper service.

All *MATSON* shirts are guaranteed to meet quality standards in workmanship and material. The wear of a shirt often depends on the care given to it by the owner.

However, if you would be kind enough to return your son's *MATSON* soccer shirt to my attention, I will personally inspect and evaluate it. Should it prove to be not up to our quality control requirements, we would be most happy to issue you a new shirt totally free of charge.

Thank you for your cooperation in this matter.

Letters That Inform

14

Many day-to-day business letters are written to *inform* the reader about some transaction. Such letters serve the reader best when they are direct and brief. They are courteous but not fussy. For the most routine situations, form letters are often appropriate. This chapter provides guidelines and models for writing some common informative letters when you expect that the reader will simply use the information to get on with the work at hand. If, however, you sense that the reader may object to the information, or that the information may be emotionally charged, a more persuasive approach may be appropriate, as discussed in Chapters 15 and 16.

Keep informative letters to one page. If you have additional details or facts to send, attach separate sheets. The letter is more likely to be read if the reader can see the beginning and the end of the message at once. In general, use this three-part structure:

Beginning. A short (preferably one or two sentences) first paragraph that states *why* you are writing and provides an overview of the content of the letter.

Middle. Subsequent (short) paragraphs that include any necessary explanation and details. Refer to attachments.

Ending. A courteous closing that states any action required, along with deadlines, and that reaffirms goodwill.

In this and the other chapters about letters, we look at examples of letters from different sources, including several letters written by James A. Edris, Manager, Financial Information, Hershey Foods Corporation.

Figure 14–1 is an informative letter that thanks a contributor to the Animals Depend on People Too (ADOPT) program at the Philadelphia Zoo.

This is a *form* letter sent to each "adoptive parent." Note its approach:

Beginning. The first paragraph encourages reading because it is short, states directly the reason for writing, and provides a warm welcome to the reader.

Middle. Paragraphs 2 and 3 expand on the importance of the gift to make the reader feel good about having given—and to encourage more support. The statement is concrete (down to the crickets and the mealworms). Paragraph 3 moves into the specific reward for giving: the certificate. It asks the reader to keep the certificate for additional stickers. The paragraph suits a zoo need: Certificates are somewhat costly and the zoo doesn't want to keep issuing them. But the zoo's

Dear Friend of the Zoo:

On behalf of the Zoological Society of Philadelphia, it is my pleasure to acknowledge a gift in your name to the Adopt-An-Animal Program, and to welcome you as an ADOPT parent.

The Adopt-An-Animal Program is essential to maintaining the Zoo, as it provides direct support to combat one of our most pressing problems--the rising costs of feeding the more than 1700 animals that comprise our collection. Last year, the Zoo spent nearly a quarter of a million dollars on thousands of pounds of meat, vegetables, crickets, mealworms, hay, and zoocakes to feed the animals. Therefore, the support of our ADOPT Program is extremely important to us. It is through the support of individuals like you and your friends that we can continue to provide the Philadelphia Zoo as the leading cultural institution in the city.

It is very important that you save the enclosed ADOPT certificate, because in the future, if you or someone else renews your adoption, we will send you a sticker for your certificate. This will serve as your record of sponsorship in the ADOPT Program.

I hope you will be able to come to the Zoo in the near future to visit your adopted animal. Thank you for your support.

Sincerely,

L. Scott Schultz
Director of Development

FIGURE 14–1. An informative letter (used by permission, Marketing and Development Office, The Zoological Society of Philadelphia).

need is expressed in *reader* terms: The stickers provide a "record of sponsorship." Moreover, the language of the paragraph, although suitable for adults, also bridges the gap to children readers who may have been given the sponsorship or may have saved for one.

Ending. The last paragraph closes the letter on the best point of connection between writer and reader: "Come to the Zoo." And it does so in personal terms for the reader "to visit *your* adopted animal" (which, in this case, was a fennec fox named "Tom").

For the routine transfer of information, directly structured letters (often form letters like this one from the zoo) are exactly right. Here are guidelines and models for writing several different informative letters.

Placing an Order

A good letter ordering an item or service is *accurate* and *complete*. Here are the guidelines; note how these are carried out in the letter that follows, which is in the simplified format:

Beginning. State the order (in the seller's terms).

Middle. Expand with details.

1. Identify catalog numbers, sizes, colors, material of construction—whatever the seller requires to complete your order. Use lists. Refer to an enclosed order form if necessary.

2. Specify shipment method and deadline.

3. Specify method of payment (enclosed? send bill? bill to credit card?). Calculate subtotals and totals.

Ending. Thank the supplier—or simply end with an indication of payment or shipping.

12 Mc Kinley Dr.
Grosse Point Park, MI 48230
October 18, 19xx

Watson-Jones Incorporated
PO Box 2347
Oakland, CA 94623-0704

Attention: Creative Gifts Department

Please send me the following items advertised in your Fall catalog:

Quantity	Item	Cost($)
5	2-pound selection of The Squire's Cashews	125
3	Hawaiian Macadamia Cakes	30
9	Chilly Cheese Assortments	45
	Total	200

So that I may distribute these to my staff before Christmas, I need to receive them by *December 11*.

Enclosed is a check for $200. I understand that you do not charge shipping on orders over $150, so I have not included an amount for that.

Peter Ramos

Confirming an Order

In *confirming* an order, you may simply send the requested items, with a bill marked to indicate payment made or due. You may also engage in a bit of resale, that is, favorable talk about the items the customer has already purchased. You may encourage further purchases by enclosing a brochure or another order blank. If shipment will be delayed, however, write to confirm the order, and note the problem and the intended resolution, as in the following two letters.

Beginning/Thanks	Thank you for your recent order. We are shipping today the cashew tins and Hawaiian Macadamia Cakes.
Middle/Problem and Resolution	The Chilly Cheese assortments are temporarily out of stock. We will ship them as soon as they are available, certainly no later than November 21.
Ending/Resale	We'll make sure you have *all* the special Creative Gifts you need for the holidays. Thank you for shopping with Watson-Jones. It's our pleasure to serve you.
Beginning/ Problem	We're sorry, but our Day Lily Portfolio is not yet ready for shipment.

Middle/Resolution	We anticipate that the bulbs will be at a proper growth stage about November 1. We will ship them to you on that date.
Ending/Resale	In the meantime, please let us know if we can supply another of your gardening needs. Enclosed is our current catalog, for your perusal. Please note our special sale on Swoes, the ultimate garden tool.

If the customer's order is unclear, you may need to phone or write for clarification. If you no longer carry the product, then write to note whatever equivalent product you do carry or to suggest where the customer may find the product. Don't automatically send a substitute; the customer may want only the thing itself. If you find that you are unable to ship what you had promised, or if a back order continues well beyond a reasonable time, then write a *persuasive* response, as in Chapter 15.

Confirming Receipt

In addition to confirming an order, you may need to confirm receipt— of a payment, a product, a service, or a document. Your confirmation assures the sender that the item is in good hands, as in the following form letter written to these guidelines:

Beginning.   Thank the sender.

Middle.   Expand with details.

1. Specify what was received, on what date, and its disposition.

2. Answer any questions, direct or implied, from the sender (for example, the following letter answers the sender's question about when the payment will appear on her statement).

3. Note problems, if any.

Ending.   Close courteously.

Thank you for your payment of [date] for $[amount], about which you inquired. As the payment arrived after the due date, it will appear on your next statement.

If you have any questions about this procedure, please let us know. We at U.S. International look forward to continuing our service to you.

Requesting Credit

The world of business turns on credit. One reminder of that fact occurred when the People's Republic of China, a country traditionally run on cash transactions, established a "Great Wall Card" credit system for foreign businesspeople who found doing business there in cash excessively burdensome. You may apply to a bank or other organization for credit as either an individual or a business unit. Applying for credit is often a routine matter. Indeed, many companies go out of their way to *encourage* you to establish a credit account through direct-mail appeals and easy application procedures. You may even apply over the phone or with your home computer. A standard application blank is the basis of the process. So when you need to request credit, simply ask about the procedure, as follows (the full text of a letter):

I'd like to open a charge account with Marshall Field's. Could you please send me an application blank and let me know what other information you need?

As an individual or a business unit, you may apply for credit with your first order, as in the following letter in block form written to these guidelines:

Beginning. Place the order as an incentive for credit.

Middle. Expand with details.

1. List the order (perhaps in an attachment).
2. Provide financial information within the letter or in an attachment.

Ending. Suggest what your future business will be with the vendor.

P.C. Bowman and Sons, Carpenters
999 Walnut St.
Newton Highlands, MA 02161
October 15, 19xx

C.B. Diehl
Super Value Hardware
18 Main St.
Winchester, MA 01890

Dear Charlie:

Enclosed is an order for several items. Please fill this on a credit basis. I'll stop by on Tuesday to pick it up.

I've also enclosed our current financial statement. As you can see, our business is growing every day.

On the basis of jobs I've now contracted for, I'll be placing a similar order every month.

Thanks.

P.C. Bowman

Requesting Information

The purpose of many letters, both personal and corporate, is to request information. Target the request. If it is specific and is sent to the right person, you are more likely to receive a usable response. Here are guidelines and two letters.

Beginning. Identify yourself, your need, and your use for the information—*in the reader's terms,* to connect with the reader.

Middle. Expand with details.

1. Ask specific questions. Itemize segments of a complex request. Make it easy to respond.
2. Refer to specific printed material by title or number or other reader-oriented code.

Ending. Close with thanks—and avoid cliches.

Beginning/Reader Connection	I am interested in joining the Carbondale Track Club. My track coach said your club is the best in Illinois. Please send me information concerning rules and regulations for joining.
Middle/Questions	In particular, I am interested in answers to the following questions:

1. What is the minimum vaulting height to join?
2. At what height do you begin to sponsor?
3. To what extent financially do you sponsor?

Ending/Thanks and Reader Benefit	I look forward to your response. I hope I qualify to join your club.

The following letter also requests information. The response appears in Figure 14–2.

12 Garden Court
Houston, TX 77036

January 15, 1986

Mr. K.L. Wolfe, President
Hershey Foods Corporation
100 Mansion Road East
Hershey, PA 17033

Dear Mr. Wolfe:

I recently purchased shares of the common stock of your company for my IRA. My purchase was based on Value Line Investment Survey's high evaluation of your stock.

Please send me a copy of your 1984 annual report and your third quarter report for 1984.

What is the duration of the Milton Hershey Trust? How many shares are outstanding of Class A and Class B, and how much of each does the trust own?

Thank you for your response to my questions.

Sincerely,

David Rittenhouse

Answering a Request

The best way to answer a request is to let the request itself structure your response, as in the following letter from the Carbondale Track Club. Answer each item or explain why you cannot respond. Sometimes you'll need to second-guess an inquirer who may not have directly asked a question that you realize, from your knowledge of the subject, is important to the answer sought. Be sure your information is accurate. If you can't provide the necessary information, say so, or name another source for the reader to contact. If possible, make that contact easy: Supply a phone number or address or, better yet, send along a copy of the request to the other source and ask the source to contact the reader.

Beginning/Thanks	Thank you for your interest in the Carbondale Track Club.
Middle/Answers Question by Question	To answer your questions: 1. The minimum vaulting height is 7'5". 2. We begin to sponsor at 9'. 3. We provide transportation costs to meets for sponsored members of the club, along with uniforms and equipment.
Ending/Personal Note	Enclosed is a brochure about the club. Stop by when you are in town and I'd be happy to talk with you about joining.

Although, as you saw, Mr. Rittenhouse wrote to the president of Hershey Foods, a response came from the manager of financial information, the appropriate source for the information requested. The letter (Figure 14–2) is in modified block form with indented paragraphs.

Some requests can become complex and politically sensitive. Mr. Edris's response to Rittenhouse was simple; but note the response to an account executive at a brokerage house who asked for clarification of Hershey Foods's policy of corporate social responsibility (Figure 14–3). The letter is still organized directly, but it covers two pages of detailed information deemed important for an important reader. (For more information about corporate policy statements, see Chapter 22.)

Inviting

To *invite* someone to do something—to attend a meeting, come to dinner, or join an organization—you may call the person first and confirm in a letter, or you may write as the initial contact. Figure 14–4 is an initial invitation. The following letter confirms a telephone call. Like Edris's letter, it settles in advance the question of who will pay for the lunch ("as a guest of the university"). It also anticipates the reader's question about where to park.

I'm glad you will be able to join other Utah State alumni and friends as a guest of the University at our luncheon concerning planned giving. You'll learn some important insider's tips on ways to insure your financial future while you aid USU as well. Just to confirm:

*[letter continued
on page 260]*

Hershey Foods Corporation
Corporate Administrative Center
P.O. Box 814
Hershey, Pennsylvania 17033-0814
Phone: (717) 534-7500
Telex: 6711079 HERSH UW

January 24, 1986

Mr. David Rittenhouse
12 Garden Court
Houston, TX 77036

Dear Mr. Rittenhouse:

Thank you for your recent letter and for your interest in Hershey Foods
Corporation. We always appreciate receiving comments and inquiries from our
stockholders. Mr. Wolfe has asked me to reply.

Enclosed are the 1984 Annual Report and Third Quarter interim as you
requested. In response to your question regarding the duration of the Milton
Hershey School Trust, it is perpetual.

There are currently 26,235,850 shares of Common Stock and 5,101,262
shares of Class B Common Stock outstanding. Of these, the Milton Hershey
School Trust holds 10,642,831 shares of the Common Stock and 5,051,001 shares
of the Class B Common Stock.

Thank you again for your continued interest in Hershey.

Sincerely yours,

James A Edris

James A. Edris
Manager, Financial Information

JAE/bjr

Enclosures

bcc: R. M. Reese

FIGURE 14–2. Answering a request. The four letters from the Hershey Foods
Corporation in this chapter are reprinted with permission of the Hershey Foods
Corporation. The names and addresses of the recipients, however, are fictitious.

 **Hershey**

Hershey Foods Corporation
Corporate Administrative Center
P.O. Box 814
Hershey, Pennsylvania 17033-0814
Phone: (717) 534-7500
Telex: 6711079 HERSH UW

Mr. J. P. Jones, Account Executive
The Brokerage House   May 8, 1986
Johnson Square
Peoria, IL 61602

Dear Mr. Jones:

    Thank you for your recent letter and for your interest in Hershey
Foods Corporation. In a recent address to the Corporation's
stockholders, our Chairman and CEO, Richard A. Zimmerman, said the
following:

    "Underlying the strength of our existing operations are our basic
    values. These are a caring attitude toward our employees; the
    continuation of superior quality and value of our products and
    services; a history of high standards of conduct and ethics, and a
    results orientation combined with a prudent approach to investment."

    Attached is a statement of our corporate philosophy which is
obviously an amplification of our basic values as well as a statement of
how they are implemented. In addition, you will be interested to note
that Hershey is the sole sponsor of Hershey's National Track and Field
Youth Program which benefits over two million children annually by
introducing them to the positive values of athletic competition
(self-discovery, socialization, friendly competition). The program
begins at the playground level, and while it is open to all children
nationally, its design tends to benefit disadvantaged children to a
greater extent.

    Hershey is also the major sponsor of the Lady Keystone Open, a major
tournament on the Ladies Professional Golf Tour, which benefits many
hospitals in the Central Pennsylvania area. Its division, Friendly Ice
Cream Corporation, supports the Easter Seals Campaign annually and is
involved in a program to promote reading by school students in its market
areas. In addition, the Corporation has been a long-time supporter of the
United Negro College Fund and has a two-for-one matching program for
donations its employees make to institutions of higher learning. The
Corporation plays a role in a variety of ecumenical food banks and
numerous other activities which are community oriented.

FIGURE 14–3. Answering a request for detailed information about corporate
policy.

Mr. J. P. Jones   -2-   May 8, 1986

    Hershey has a long standing commitment to servicing the consumers' needs as expressed through inquiries, complaints and comments. Its division, Hershey Chocolate Company, pioneered nutritional labeling in the United States for chocolate confectionery products and has conducted campaigns to insure that consumers are aware of and knowledgeable about the food products they are eating. The Corporation, through its Science and Technology function, conducts ongoing research to insure that the long-term health effects of all its product ingredients are salutary.

    While Hershey Foods Corporation is a publicly traded company, its majority stockholder is Milton Hershey School. The relationship between Milton Hershey School, a non-profit school located in Hershey, Pennsylvania, for the education and care of children not receiving adequate care from one natural parent, and Hershey Foods Corporation is unique in American corporate history. The School and the Corporation's executive offices and principal chocolate and confectionery manufacturing facilities are located in close proximity to each other in the community of Hershey, which was designed as a model community by Milton S. Hershey, founder of both Hershey Foods and the School. The Hershey Trust, as trustee for Milton Hershey School, has indicated that maintaining its voting control is desirable for the fulfillment and protection of Milton S. Hershey's philanthropic legacy.

    This desire to maintain voting control has a variety of implications for investors. For the purposes of your organization, I should think it would give some level of assurance regarding the continued proper conduct of the Corporation in its business and societal relationships.

    I hope this information will be useful to you and the investors you represent.

                       Sincerely,

                       James A. Edris

                       James A. Edris
                       Manager, Financial Information

JAE/bjr

Enclosures

cc: T. C. Fitzgerald

FIGURE 14–3. *(continued)*

 **Hershey**

Hershey Foods Corporation
Corporate Administrative Center
P.O. Box 814
Hershey, Pennsylvania 17033-0814
Phone: (717) 534-7500
Telex: 6711079 HERSH UW

December 16, 1988

Peter J. Parker
Parker, Smith, and Jones
1111 Peachtree Street, NE
Atlanta, GA 30361

Dear Mr. Parker:

Thomas C. Fitzgerald, Treasurer of Hershey Foods Corporation, and I will be in Atlanta on January 10, 1989, and we would like to invite you to have lunch with us. We thought this would be a good way to get better acquainted and give us a chance to update you on Hershey's progress and prospects.

If any of your colleagues at Parker, Smith, and Jones would like to join us, we'd be delighted. We'll wait to hear from you and perhaps solicit your suggestions regarding a location for the lunch.

Best wishes for a happy holiday season.

Sincerely yours,

James A. Edris
Manager, Financial Information

JAE/bjr

FIGURE 14–4. Inviting.

12 noon to 1:45
Wednesday October 30
The Westin Hotel Utah, Temple Square, Salt Lake City

Park in the hotel lot (access off South Temple Street) and validate your ticket at the registration desk.
See you there!

Certain events require formal printed invitations whose graphic scheme reinforces the organization's image. A design in the invitation may be carried through to the event itself and may be repeated on brochures or other documents available there. Figure 14–5 is an invitation to a fashion show sponsored by the Fashion Group of Philadelphia. Note that it specifies food, drink, attire, and parking, along with the logistics of time, cost, and place. Because the group draws from a local area, the invitation does not need to provide directions to the zoo. An invitation sent to readers from outside one's area should include specific directions to the event's location.

Accepting an Invitation

It's easy to accept an invitation. Just say yes directly and confirm arrangements, as in the following letter:

Beginning/ Acceptance	I'm pleased that you asked me to talk to your marketing class now that I'm out in the "real world" of direct-mail sales. Yes, of course, I'll be there on Wednesday, September 17.
Middle/Review of Details	As you suggested, I'll run through some of the projects we've been working on, particularly the methods we use to develop mailing lists for our group insurance plan. I assume the class period is still fifty minutes; I'll try to talk for less to leave time for questions. Do you still have an overhead chained to the front desk? I'll plan to use one.
Ending/Final Action and Personal Close	I'll plan to meet you at your office about 9:45 so we'll have time to get to class. It'll be funny to be in front of the class instead of taking notes. Thanks again for the opportunity.

Declining an Invitation

When you must decline an invitation, simply say that and perhaps provide a brief explanation. Don't waste the reader's time. If you sense

PARADISE FOUND!

The Fashion Group of Philadelphia
presents a wild evening of fashion innovation
in the fabulous Treehouse
at The Philadelphia Zoo.

Thursday, May 22nd, 1986
6:30 P.M.

Buffet and hors d'oeuvres
Complimentary wine and cash bar

$35 per person

Fashion Show
8:15 P.M.

Proceeds to benefit
The Goldie Paley Design Center
Philadelphia College of Textiles and Science

R.S.V.P. Chris Gentry
Bloomingdale's
660 DeKalb Blvd.
King of Prussia, Pa.
19406

Dress for adventure!
Convenient parking available.

FIGURE 14–5. A printed invitation (courtesy of Southwest Graphics, Barbara Carroll).

that your relationship to the reader requires attention to soften the no, however, you might consider a more persuasive approach. The following is a direct no response:

> Unfortunately, I must say no to your kind invitation to speak with the Toastmasters group about business presentations. On that date I have to give one of those presentations to the Chicago Board and thus cannot join you.
>
> Thank you for thinking of me.

Claiming an Adjustment

When something goes wrong with a product or service, you seek an adjustment from the vendor or provider. You may seek an adjustment on your own behalf or as a spokesperson for your organization. Claims are so common that many organizations have set procedures and forms for making a claim. They may even provide a toll-free number for customers to call with claims. Well run companies take claims seriously. It's more efficient to keep present customers happy than to abandon them and seek new ones. Dissatisfied customers also talk about their dissatisfaction and thus affect new business. On a positive note, customer comments may aid in pinpointing trouble spots in a product or service and may provide tips for marketing. Thus companies often encourage comments by including customer service information in the product packaging.[1]

Before you make a claim, clarify in your own mind what is wrong. Poor or discourteous service? Faulty merchandise? Problems in posting a credit? Fix the details: time, date, and place; merchandise or service purchased; cost (with invoices and receipts); and a brief narrative of the events. Decide what you want the company to do. Then, adhere to whatever form or procedure the company requests. If no procedure is specified, you'll probably start the process with a phone call or a visit to where you bought the item for exchange, repair, or credit. If such a visit is not possible—or you prefer to have a record—-write a claim letter. Here are general guidelines:

Beginning.   Announce the claim.

Middle.   Expand with details.

---

[1]Customer relations departments generally keep logs of complaints and *complainers*. They record the names in part to spot people who may write frequently only, it would seem, as a way of obtaining free coupons for products. Most companies still respond cordially to such people—but omit the coupons.

1. Provide a narrative of the error: For a product, include name, model, serial number, warranty information, where purchased, when, and for how much.

2. Describe your compliance with any requested claims procedure.

3. Refer to any pertinent documents, like sales slips, that you enclose.

4. Describe the requested action: A refund? A repair? A new item?

Ending. End positively: you'll remain a customer if the company corrects the problem.

All this can be done briefly, as in the following letter. The writer considers the situation a straightforward business transaction and doesn't belabor the beginning and ending:

On December 4 I received shipment of the items ordered on October 18. With one exception. Instead of the five tins of cashews ordered, I received only four.

Please send me one more tin of cashews as soon as possible.

The next letter follows the guidelines more explicitly:

I am writing about a problem with a recent order.

On May 15 I received the case of Gobstopper jawbreakers I ordered from you on May 1. Although the package was marked " 1 case: 36 count Gobstopper Jawbreakers," it contained, instead, a combination of jawbreakers and Atomic Fireballs. Moreover, the count was wrong. The case contained a total of 29 packages of candy: 11 fireballs and only 18 Gobstoppers.

In accordance with your guarantee, I am returning the improperly packaged case to you. Please reimburse me for the postage costs and send me a complete case of Gobstoppers.

Thank you. I look forward to some happy chewing.

Responding Positively to a Claim

Most of the time, companies assume that the customer is right and grant the requested adjustment. Moreover, the response provides an opportunity to address a customer directly and to defuse any potential resistance to buying further company products or services. On some occasions, when the customer has elaborated a complaint that is more than a simple claim, the response letter becomes an important sales tool for rebuilding goodwill with the customer and reaffirming the company's reliability, as you'll see in Chapter 15.

Be careful with the *tone* of your response. The following letter goes too far:

> It is with great regret that I am writing this letter to you. Not from regret of any financial loss we may incur as to the outcome of your complaint. Rather, we regret, we *fear*, jeopardizing your valued patronage.
>
> I am sick over the damage you have incurred in your beautiful garden because of our faulty sprinkler system, and I propose to do whatever you suggest to make proper restitution.
>
> Our design engineer as well as our installation foreman feel equally bad, and both admit their error. At this point, anything I say is not enough, except that I am very sorry for all your inconveniences because of our error. I will gladly do whatever you feel is just, including monetary considerations for restoration of your lawn. Of course, this includes installing a new and fault-free system at no charge if you so wish.
>
> I am now at the mercy of your desires.

Such an obsequious letter would probably destroy any confidence the reader might have had in the writer.

As in any response, structure your letter to meet the claim. Moreover, remember that your credibility is questionable when someone issues a claim against you. Use your response to rebuild that credibility. Stress the positive first. Then deal with the particulars of the claim. Use the last line to resell the customer. You need not be elaborate, but you should be courteous. The following are two brief form responses to customers who cited errors in a bank's handling of their account:

> Thank you for notifying us of the correction due your account. Your next monthly statement will include adjustments of $__ and $__ (to refund accrued finance charges).
>
> Please let us know if you have any questions.

> This is in response to your inquiry concerning a credit which was not reflected in your billing statement.

We have now received this credit from the merchant. It will appear on your next statement.

Thank you for contacting us. Please let us know if we can be of further service.

Closing an Account

It's simple to close a checking, savings, or credit account. Just establish the details, as in the following letter:

I am leaving the Houston area and thus closing my checking account, 856-67-6682, as of October 1, 1988.

Please send a check for the account balance to me at the following address:
246 Cherokee Rd.
Pontiac, MI 48053

Thank you.

Confirming Closure of an Account

Like any response, the letter confirming closure of an account reflects the structure of the original letter. In addition, note any action necessary, solicit comments on possible dissatisfaction with the account, and remind the reader that you'd be happy to have his or her business again (if that's true) when the circumstances warrant:

This letter acknowledges your request to close your account. We're sorry to lose this opportunity to serve you.

Please destroy any of our credit cards that you now have. After the balance has been paid, we will close your account.

If we can provide any information to help you change your mind about closing the account, please let us know. We would also be happy to provide credit service once again if you decide to reapply at a future date.

We have been pleased to serve you.

Announcing a Policy or Procedure

Letters are often sent to customers or vendors to announce changes in policy or procedures or as a reminder, at timely intervals, of long-standing policy, as in Figure 13–2 of Chapter 13. Here are guidelines for writing (note how they were carried out in the letter that follows):

Beginning.   State the reason for writing. Announce the policy or procedure *as a reader benefit.*

Middle.   Expand with details:

1. Detail the advantages of the system to overcome any reader resistance to compliance.
2. Show the reader how to comply with the policy or procedure.
3. For a new policy or procedure, note the time frame of the change.

Ending.   Reaffirm your interest in the reader and/or the benefits of the new procedure.

Dear Customer:

To provide you with better check-cashing service through our new electronic checkout system, we are implementing a unique Customer Check-Cashing Courtesy Card System. An application form is enclosed.

Your new card will allow you to cash personal checks in the amount of purchase up to $250. No preapproval will be required. You will also be allowed to purchase merchandise with payroll checks (not to exceed $350) issued by local employers.

Jones Department Stores Inc. will continue to honor your current check-cashing card for ninety days from the date of this letter. To avoid interruption of your current check-cashing privileges, we ask that you complete the Jones Customer Courtesy Card application as soon as possible.

New Courtesy Card applications are processed daily. Therefore, you can expect to pick up your new Courtesy Card approximately two weeks from the date your application is submitted.

We appreciate the opportunity to serve you.

Covering the Enclosure of Something

Many letters are covering letters. That is, their purpose is to alert the reader to an important enclosure. You will write a covering letter to send your résumé to prospective employers (see Chapter 26). You may also write such a letter to transmit a formal proposal or to report to your readers (see Chapters 17 and 20).

Thanking

As you have seen, letters are often part of a series of correspondence between writer and reader. A thank-you note provides an excellent case in point. At one level, such a note is simply a way of maintaining a relationship. Any information in it is subordinate. You thank hosts and speakers. You thank people who have sent you information or products. The letter need not fit a particular format—indeed, it should sound fresh and original. But at another level, the letter often carries real information and suggests future action, as in Figure 14–1.

The letter in Figure 14–6 confirms a necessary action (paying the bill) and invites the reader to visit Hershey.

Moreover, many thank you's are springboards to sales messages, as in the following letter that a veterinarian sends to each client after a first visit—to ensure additional visits.[2] You'll see more obvious sales letters in Chapter 16, but this letter shows how a writer begins to move from an informative purpose to a more persuasive one. Note how the letter is personalized (or, cat-ized); the name of the cat (Rover) is mentioned four times in the text:

Beginning/Reader Connection	Thank you for bringing Rover to us as a new patient. We hope your first visit was pleasant and you found exactly what you wanted in our veterinary service and support.
Middle/Invites Comments, Shows Responsiveness	Please let us know if there was anything we could have done differently or better. We welcome your suggestions.
Services Listed as Benefits/Sales Approach	In choosing Providence Veterinary Hospital, Inc., you have chosen a full-service hospital that can meet all of Rover's needs. Although we hope that he will never be hurt, should you need emergency service you can call on us twenty-four hours a day, seven days a week. We

[2] Courtesy of Peter Herman, V.M.D., Providence Veterinary Hospital.

Hershey Foods Corporation
Corporate Administrative Center
P.O. Box 814
Hershey, Pennsylvania 17033-0814
Phone: (717) 534-7500
Telex: 6711079 HERSH UW

April 16, 1988

Mr. Peter Smith
Executive Vice President/Research
XYZ Inc.
20 5th Avenue
Pittsburgh, PA 15222

Dear Peter:

   Thank you very much for sponsoring Hershey at the Duquesne Club for our
investor relations meeting on April 10. The setting, the food, and the service
were excellent.

   I trust you will have the Club bill us directly for the costs we incurred.
We shall pay the bill promptly.

   Thank you again for helping us make the evening so enjoyable for our
guests. We hope we will be able to count you among that number the next time we
come to Pittsburgh. If you are traveling our direction, please give strong
consideration to touring our plant and having lunch with our C.F.O. We'd
really like to have an opportunity to return the hospitality.

   Again, I appreciate all your help.

                              Sincerely yours,

                              James A. Edris
                              Manager, Financial Information

JAE/bjr

FIGURE 14–6. Thanking.

also provide veterinary medicine, including radiology and a complete diagnostic laboratory, and surgery, including ophthalmology, dentistry, and orthopedics. We'll give the shots he needs to stay healthy and out of the reach of heartworms. We'll bathe him to keep away fleas and other nasty critters. When you go on vacation, he'll find a home here in our kennel.

Ending/Look to Future Business

Thanks again for bringing Rover to us. We look forward to providing continued service to you and Rover in the months and years ahead.

When you deal with people, as when you swing a bat, *follow through*. Attend to the occasions that demand such responses as thank-you letters and answers to requests. *Use* those occasions to maintain good relationships with clients, customers, and sponsors. But always consider the reader's time. Whenever possible, be brief and direct. Don't belabor the letter.

Exercises

1. As Human Resources Manager of Christos, Inc., a large, regional insurance broker, write to Creative Connections (12 W. Temple Ave., Pomona, CA 91768) concerning their gift selections for corporate and customer awards programs. You heard about them from a friend, John Sloan, who manages an agency in Los Angeles. Describe your employees—20 agents (12 men, 8 women) and 55 clerks (50 women, 5 men)—and your customer base, some 1,000 fairly affluent individuals. Ask about the gifts Creative Connections sells and its consulting services for advice on gift giving.

2. Order by mail from Rizzoli Bookstores (31 West 57th St., New York, NY 10019) the catalog from the *Traum und Wirklichkeit* show you saw in Vienna, Austria, in 1985. You've heard that Rizzzoli's has the catalog. You don't know how much it costs, and you'd like an English edition if there is one—and if the English version contains the complete text of the German catalog. Arrange for shipping and payment.

3. In preparing a report for a business communication (or other) class, write to some company or individual for information. Select the right person to give you the information you need. Find the address of the company in a standard business source (see Chapter 5). Use specific questions, in list form, within the letter.

4. As the secretary of a campus organization, write to someone to invite that person to speak to your group. Note *why* you are writing to that individual. Remember the you attitude. Assume that the reader is not familiar with your group; describe it briefly. Provide information on logistics and expenses.

5. Assume that the person you invited to speak to your group (in Exercise 4) accepted your invitation and gave a good talk. Write a thank-you note to him or her.

6. Write a letter closing out your checking account (Number 809-94-51) with the First National Bank of Colorado (3243 E. Fifth Ave., Durango, CO 81301). You've had some problems balancing your account and are thus unsure of the amount remaining in it. In addition, two checks (#3066 for $85 and #3088 for $50), written last year, have failed to clear. Explain to the bank that you'd like it to verify the checks and then to send the balance to you at your new address.

7. Fortunately, you came out of an auto accident unscathed, but your car, a 1982 Scirrocco, did not. You took it to The Body Works auto repair shop, whose estimate for repair was reasonable. You, the shop, and the insurance adjuster all agreed on a price. You paid the bill and picked up the car two weeks later; now, two months later, the paint is peeling and you can see old rust on what was to have been a new part. Write a letter asking the shop to make an appointment with you to redo the work. You're writing rather than calling, by the way, because you want a record of your claim and because you are at school now; the shop is in your hometown, 150 miles away.

8. Assume that you are turning over the responsibilities to someone else for a job you've held. Write a letter to that person both *describing* your duties and providing *advice* about how to best meet the job's demands and get along with your supervisor and fellow workers.

9. You are in charge of calendar sales for a printer. Every year, you send a reminder to your customers to reorder their calendars. Write the text of the form letter.

10. You're in the Accounts Receivable Department of the Goodall Worsted Company. Your company is changing its payment terms from sixty days on all accounts to thirty days. Write a form letter to your customers announcing the change in policy. With the new policy in place, the company hopes to reduce prices across the board.

11. The son or daughter of a friend of your mother is interested in attending your college or university. He or she has not yet decided on a major, participates in baseball and soccer clubs in high school, enjoys music, and likes the outdoors. You've never met this person but have been warned to take the request for information seriously. Describe your school for this high-school reader.

Letters That Persuade: Good News, Mixed News, Bad News

Informative letters, although they must always anticipate the reader's needs, are governed mostly by the logic of the information to be presented. Sometimes, however, your approach to letter writing is better governed by the psychology of the reader. This is particularly true when you are addressing a reader who is upset or when you are delivering a message that the reader does not want to hear—that you would not want to hear if you were the reader. It is also true when you are trying to sell the reader something. For such situations, consider using a *persuasive* strategy. This chapter and the next discuss several letters that are meant to persuade.

Persuasive letters may be longer than simply informative ones and often use an indirect structure. Why? If a first paragraph announces a conclusion, then the reader may stop reading there. That's fine when she or he agrees or when the matter is routine. But if the reader *disagrees* or takes offense, then you have lost the chance to convince with your evidence. To encourage the reader to read and thus come to agreement, you lead the reader to the point *through* the proof. Reading the proof first may encourage understanding and may entice the reader to the same conclusion as yours—and give the reader the sense of having got there on her or his own.

The indirection may be mild—a brief opener before the news. Or the point may be withheld until nearly the end. Often, the strategy encourages you to place good news (something positive in the reader's eyes) before bad news (the negative information or conclusion that the letter must deliver). Just be careful not to deceive or mislead the reader in your indirection.

The general structure, then, is as follows:

Beginning.   The opening connects with the reader: an acknowledgment of a letter received, an expression of a shared frustration, perhaps an apology, perhaps something witty (if also appropriate and tasteful). The beginning should be neutral at the least; positive, if appropriate.

Middle.   The middle builds the buffer. Evidence is given to establish the case as fair and reasonable. At some point in the middle, the decision is given; the more opposition the writer expects, the longer he or she will probably hold off the statement of the decision. But the statement must be unambiguous.

Ending.   The letter closes on as positive a note as is possible, consistent with the message. Some resale may be acceptable. An alternative may be given. The ending should never be cute or Pollyanna-ish, and it should not promise future correspondence or leave the decision open if, indeed, the case is closed.

Courting the Reader

Centuries ago, Aristotle codified three persuasive appeals that remain valid today:

- The appeal to logic (he called this *logos*).
- The appeal to character (he called this *ethos*).
- The appeal to emotions (he called this *pathos*).

Letters that aim to persuade exploit all three appeals, in different degrees, for different readers. In professional correspondence, you're most likely to sway the reader with an appeal to logic. As we'll see, such letters provide explanations: how rolls of plastic wrap break, why a fox needs privacy for breeding, how many people applied for how many places in a program. You convince with evidence rigorously argued.

The good character and the credibility of the person or organization writing the letter establish an *ethical* appeal. The appeal may depend on the status of the letter's source: The source is *authoritative*, that is, an expert, a leader, someone high in the hierarchy. The appeal may also depend on the relationship of the source to the reader. That's why many agencies seeking funds, for example, ask a neighbor to write a brief note personalizing the general appeal for others in the neighborhood. In addition to the source, the ethical appeal depends on the letter's *style*. The voice coming off the page sounds believable. Particularly if you need to *establish* your credibility in a letter, as, for example, in a letter of application for a job, pay close attention to the elements of style. At base, of course, such a letter must contain no errors in grammar or spelling; such errors immediately negate the ethical appeal you need to foster. Moreover, to convince, your voice should sound crisp, professional, and individual. You'll see some guidelines for such letters in Chapter 26.

Finally, you can use an *emotional* appeal that addresses, for example, the reader's sense of fear, or pity, or happiness. The sales letters discussed in Chapter 16 show emotional appeals.

Conveying Good News

When you are telling a reader something that the reader wants to hear, you rarely need to pull in persuasive appeals to encourage reading. A direct message often works. But at times you do need some persuasion. Let's look at two situations for persuasion with good news: responding positively to a customer complaint and recommending someone.

Responding Positively to a Customer Complaint

In Figure 15–1, a letter from Dow Chemical USA, Ms. Collinson uses an indirect strategy to respond to Mr. Williams's complaint about a Dow product. She could have begun the letter:

> Here's a coupon for a free roll of Handi-Wrap. Go buy a replacement for the one that didn't work.

But she thought an explanation would reestablish the company's credibility and persuade Mr. Williams to remain a customer. Parts of the letter derive from standard company paragraphs, but the whole is tailored to Mr. Williams. The letter is in block format. Note the structure:

Beginning.   The letter begins with a thank you for his letter and expression of company concern.

Middle.   The buffer. Paragraph 2 explains what might have caused the problem. It ends with an apology and the main point: We'll replace the faulty roll. The buffer is brief. Following it, Paragraph 3 requests a return of the roll and makes that return easy with a prepaid mailer. The request for return further reinforces Dow's image as a company that cares: They want to know what happened.

Ending.   The letter ends with a restatement of thanks. Note that it avoids the letterly clichés.

Recommending Someone

Although a letter of recommendation does *inform* the reader about a candidate and thus may be direct in approach, usually the recommender wraps that goal within the more important goal of persuading the reader to hire (or promote) the individual. To write a *negative* letter of recommendation is a contradiction in terms. If you are asked by a third party to *evaluate* someone, then your oral report or letter may balance negative and positive information or may even concentrate on the negative. (Chapter 22 discusses personnel evaluations.) But a letter of recommendation is always positive. The chief problem in such letters is that the writer's enthusiasm may not translate into something convincing to a reader. Writing about people often bogs down in abstractions ("dependable," "responsible," "sincere," "honest," "forthright," "kind to animals," "gets along great with people"). The abstractions fail everyone. The writer is shown to be uninsightful, the person the letter is about remains in the shadows, and the reader doesn't get the

DOW CHEMICAL U.S.A.

9550 N. ZIONSVILLE ROAD
POST OFFICE BOX 68511
INDIANAPOLIS, INDIANA 46268

317 · 873-7000
CABLE: DOWPHARM — INDIANAPOLIS

October 11, 198-

J. C. Williams
220 Brighton Rd.
Glassboro NY 19811

Dear Mr. Williams:

Thank you for your letter concerning the Handi-Wrap* brand
plastic film you were unable to use. We are most concerned when
customers have difficulty in using our product and attempt to do
everything we can to correct any problems.

If rolls are wound too tightly or at an angle, if the film is
cut, or if the core is damaged, this could result in the wrap's
coming off in pieces or splitting. We sell many thousands of
rolls of Handi-Wrap each month and it is unusual for a faulty
roll to reach the store shelves in view of the strict quality
assurance program we maintain for this product. We regret you
received such a roll and would like to replace it by enclosing
a complimentary coupon. We hope you will continue to use
Handi-Wrap with satisfaction.

Our quality control personnel would like to examine the roll
of film if you would be so kind as to return the roll and its
packaging to them. A prepaid mailing label is enclosed for your
convenience in returning it.

Thank you for calling this to our attention and allowing us
to answer you personally.

Sincerely,

Nan Collinson

Nan Collinson, Manager
Consumer Communications
Consumer Products Department

Enc. HW cpn and label

*Trademark of the Dow Chemical Company

FIGURE 15-1. A persuasive letter (used by permission, the Dow Chemical
Company).

information that he or she needs to make a decision. Convince with concrete, picturable evidence.

If a form is required for your recommendation, then fill in the form. Otherwise, write a letter. Figure 15–2 is in a simplified form (note the use of the subject line rather than a salutation) and adheres to these guidelines:

Beginning.   State that this is a recommendation and provide the context.

Middle.   Build the case. Note how long and in what capacity you have known the person. Establish criteria for your evaluation, and then measure the person against those criteria. In the following letter, the writer assumes that criteria for the program include a knowledge of technology and an ability to write; she then addresses these issues. If you are unknown to the reader, establish your own credibility as a recommender, as in Paragraph 4. Of course, the careful and graceful writing of the letter itself comments on your credibility and provides an ethical appeal. End with your endorsement (or save that for your ending).

Ending.   Confirm your recommendation if you have not already done so. Offer to respond to questions.

Conveying Mixed News

When you say no to an invitation, or refuse to grant a request, or deny someone a job or a place in an organization, from the reader's perspective you're conveying bad news. Before you write a letter with such a message, consider the reader closely. *From the reader's perspective,* is this simply a routine business transaction? Then be direct with the bad news. But some persuasion is often necessary to make a negative message clear and acceptable to the reader. Figure 15–3 shows a persuasive strategy with *mixed* news, some welcome and some not-so-welcome information about Tom the Fox.

The goal of this letter is to tell Tom's adoptive parents that he has been taken off exhibit. That information is contained, unambiguously, in Paragraph 2. Schultz begins the letter with a buffer reaffirming his appreciation of the reader's support. Then he gives the "bad news," right at the beginning of the second paragraph. That done, he builds toward an explanation and a positive note: pups. The third paragraph

Department of English
Western State University
Pleasant Grove, UT 84062

March 16, 19xx

Mass Media/Science and Engineering Fellows Program
American Association for the Advancement of Science
8th Floor
1333 H St. NW
Washington, D.C. 20005

Re: John Phillips

I am pleased to recommend John Phillips for the Mass Media/Science and Engineering Fellows program.

Mr. Phillips was my student in "Rhetoric for Business and Technical Writers," a course that examines the purposes and structure of writing in different disciplines, particularly in management, science, and engineering. We looked at how professionals communicate with each other and with the public. Mr. Phillips's work in the course was outstanding. Because of his background, first as an electrical engineering major and now in economics, he was comfortable with the technical content of the texts we read. But more than that, he was sensitive to the devices authors use to encapsulate technical information and convey it to various audiences.

Mr. Phillips is also a first-rate writer himself. In several papers concerned with technology and organizational structure in an office environment, he proved his ability to observe well, to select critical information from his readings, and to build a cogent, clear, and engaging discussion.

I am somewhat familiar with your program from discussions I've attended at AAAS meetings and from colleagues who are science journalists. John Phillips seems to me to fit well into the framework and goals you have established for the program. I recommend him highly.

Please call if I can provide any further information for you as you select candidates for the program.

Betinna Rodriquez

Betinna Rodriquez
Associate Professor

FIGURE 15–2. Recommending.

Re: Fennec Fox

Dear Adopt Parent,

Your participation in our Adopt-An-Animal Program here at the Zoo is deeply appreciated. The ADOPT Program brings happiness and satisfaction to thousands of people and organizations who support the care of their favorite Zoo animals. Of course, the program also has an important impact on our ability to operate the Zoo effectively by providing a major source of financial support.

Unfortunately, I have some ''mixed'' news to report to you today. The fennec fox, Tom, which you so generously adopted has been temporarily taken off exhibit. That is the ''bad'' news. The ''good'' news is that the fennec foxes have been taken off exhibit for breeding purposes. Our Animal Management staff feels at this time that the pair of foxes might better produce a pup if they are in more private surroundings. They will be off exhibit for the duration of the summer and hopefully will be back in the rotunda of the Small Mammal House by the fall.

We hope you don't mind this arrangement. Hopefully, we will have them back on exhibit by our ADOPT Parents Recognition Day in October. If, however, you would like your adoption transferred to another animal, we will certainly understand.

Please don't hesitate to call us at the Zoo at 243-1100 (ext. 232). Thank you for your kind and generous assistance.

Sincerely,

Scott Schultz

L. Scott Schultz
Vice President for Marketing
and Development

LSS/mlh

FIGURE 15–3. Conveying mixed news (used by permission, Marketing and Development Office, The Zoological Society of Philadelphia).

provides an alternative (transferring the adoption). The final paragraph (perhaps a bit of a cliché) repeats the thanks.

Here's another letter with mixed news:

Beginning/ Positive Connection to Reader and Builds Mystery	This is a tough letter to write, and you will see why in a minute. First, I have some news to please you. You have been selected to attend the supervisory management program offered by the Management Institute.
Middle/Buffer Explanation	But we have a complication. Five hundred people applied for the program. Each session can accommodate only fifteen. We held to rigid standards for selection—standards I'm pleased to say you met—and compiled a list of 200 qualified applicants. In fairness to these applicants, we have given priority for enrollment on the basis of years with the association. We'd like to serve first those who have been members of the Management Institute longest.
Decision	Thus we cannot grant your request to attend the session on April 11–12.
Alternative	Your two years of membership place you in the group scheduled for sessions 60–70, tentatively, July 18–August 15 of next year. We are currently negotiating with the consultant offering these programs to increase the number of sessions we can schedule. Should the increase go through, we'll make every effort to move you closer to your preferred dates.
Ending/Personal Connection	Thank you again for your interest in our supervisory management program. I'll be in touch with you concerning the schedule for future seminars.
Resale/Another Alternative	In the meantime, I've enclosed a brochure concerning other programs we offer and would be happy to talk with you about ones you would like to attend.

Here's another letter with mixed news about a credit request. Note how the second sentence immediately meets the reader's possible objection, "That's not what I asked for." The second paragraph explains and offers an alternative. The ending uses resale.

We received your request for an increase in your credit line and have raised your limit to $2,000. Although we realize that this is not the amount you requested, we hope it is sufficient to meet your needs.

This decision reflects information obtained from your application and from the ABC Credit Bureau. You may wish to contact the credit bureau directly concerning your credit report.

If you have any questions about this decision, please write to our Credit Department at the above address. Thank you again for choosing a U.S. International Visa card. We appreciate the opportunity to serve you.

Conveying Bad News

Although mixed news may be conveyed either directly or indirectly, most bad news requires indirection. A reader who sees a letter beginning "We regret to inform you that . . ." may well read no further. To persuade the reader to read, find some point of agreement *before* and *after* the denial. Maintain the reader's self-confidence in general while you isolate the one negative point to be conveyed in the letter. Plan on a longer letter for a no response than for a yes response under the same circumstances. The yes letter simply informs. The no letter often must persuade. Let's examine persuasive letters for conveying four kinds of bad news: refusing a claim, refusing an invitation, denying credit, and complaining.

Refusing a Claim

Although most companies agree to adjustments whenever possible, sometimes companies refuse a claim if the failure was clearly caused by the customer or otherwise resulted from conditions not under the company's control. The best of these letters encourage the customer to understand the reason for the rejection and to continue to consider the company reasonable and credible. Figure 15–4 (in block form) adheres to these guidelines:

Beginning.   Show your connection to the reader. Avoid stuffiness or patronizing.

Middle.   Build the buffer:

1. Start with any point of agreement with the reader (for example, that plant hangers are designed to hang plants).

2. Explain *why* the problem occurred. In the explanation, *educate* the reader. Where possible, give the reader an out (as in the last sentence of the second paragraph). Consider using the passive to

The Garden Center

2631 N. High St.
Worthington, OH 43085

August 10, 19xx

Mr. James Bryson
12 Robin Lane
Dade City FL 33525

Dear Mr. Bryson:

We're sorry that our plant hanger caused you so much frustration that you threw it away.

The hanger is, indeed, designed to hang plants. You had every right to expect that it would hang *your* plants handsomely in the window. I brought your description of the problem to our design engineer, who suggested that the handle of your plant holder may have slipped down the hanger because the hanger had been mounted upside down. When mounted, the curve of the hanger should be *above* the small hook on the end that carries the handle of your plant holder. You may logically have thought that the curve holds the handle and thus were frustrated by slippage problems.

Thank you for calling the problem to our attention. I have alerted our packaging department to the difficulty so that they may consider altering our directions for mounting.

I'm afraid, however, that we cannot replace your discarded hanger because it was not indeed defective. We do appreciate your alerting us to a possible problem in our directions; I hope you will accept a $2 gift certificate as an indication of the value we place on serving you. You can't hang a plant on that. But I hope you will apply the certificate to one of the items in our current catalog, which is enclosed. Allow us into your window garden soon.

Sincerely,

Anne D. Smith

Anne D. Smith
Customer Service Representative

Enc. Gift Certificate

FIGURE 15–4. Refusing a claim.

avoid implicating the reader (for example, "had been mounted"). Avoid veiled attacks and "you dummy" attitudes.

3. Enhance your own credibility by showing that you take the reader's complaint seriously (see Paragraph 3).

4. State the no unambiguously (see Paragraph 4).

Ending.   Direct the ending specifically to the reader. Avoid clichés (note the bit of humor in "You can't hang a plant on that"). Engage in resale if appropriate (the gift certificate).

Refusing an Invitation

The following is a persuasive refusal of an invitation. The writer knows the reader well; the approach is thus personal and witty:

Beginning/ Question to Put Writer and Reader on Equal Footing	Why do all the good things always land on the same day?
Middle/Buffer— Agreement	I was pleased to receive your invitation to participate in the HPBA seminar on June 4 and 5. That group is onto something in strategic management, particularly in the emphasis on market and customer orientation. I know you've been trying to push us there for years. And this seminar represents a real confirmation of that effort.
Buffer— Explanation	But June 4 is the date of my quarterly report to Administrative Staff. And June 4 is the date of my divisional performance review. And June 5 is the date of (count them) *six* meetings with representatives of architectural firms proposing new space plans. (Would you believe that Ann scheduled them *all* on *one* day?)
Ending/Refusal and Alternative	So I just can't get away. You know I'd like to. *I* know that this seminar will be a grand success. Please sign me up for the next one—and congratulations on getting us launched into HPBA.

Denying Credit

As the owner of a business or as a spokesperson for a supplier or a financial institution, you may have to write a letter denying credit to someone who has asked for such a privilege. Often, the denial is a routine matter, handled directly with a phone call or a form letter. But at times, your relationship to the applicant will suggest the need for a more persuasive approach. Be particularly careful to be *accurate* in stating the grounds for the denial. Make sure, for example, that you have indeed checked the customer's credit rating, if that's your reason, and have not just assumed it's bad. Avoid any potentially libelous statements about the reader's character. Establish criteria for credit and measure the applicant objectively within them. Don't preach. Don't hide behind such clichés as "it's company policy." Suggest alternatives, like cash payment, partial payment plans, and perhaps discounts for cash transactions. In the end, resell the customer and look to a future approval, if that's realistic. Figure 15–5 responds to a request (see Chapter 14, p. 252). It builds a courteous and effective buffer in Paragraphs 2 and 3, announcing the decision only after a concrete explanation of the criteria and inviting another application when the criteria are met. The last paragraph offers an alternative to credit and resells Bowman on the special supplies available.

Complaining

Most of the time, you'll call or write a direct letter to a company to ask it to correct an error. But sometimes you feel the need to register more than a mere claim; you want to complain. Such a letter often follows earlier direct attempts at correction. The letter, too, may be addressed higher up in the company than earlier claims. You use a persuasive approach to encourage a fair hearing. Appeal to the logic of your case by presenting *evidence*. Appeal to your own good character by writing well and avoiding the sarcasm or flaring up that your anger may inspire. The following letter contains both a logical and an ethical appeal:

Beginning/ Positive Connection to Reader	The convenience of your branch offices and the professionalism of your tellers have made me a satisfied depositor at Columbus State Bank.
Middle/Negative	Thus I was disappointed to learn that my request for an educational loan of $2,500 has been turned down on the basis of an insufficient credit record.
Logical Appeal	I'm sure there must be a mistake, as I hold both a checking account (#11-1232443-33) and a savings account (#45-4567-889) at your bank and supplied you with credit information at the time that I opened these accounts.
Reasonable Request for Action	Please reconsider my loan application in light of this information. The money is essential if I am to continue my studies at the university.

Super Value Hardware
18 Main Street
Winchester, MA 01890

October 26, 19xx

P.C. Bowman and Sons, Carpenters
999 Walnut St.
Newton Highlands, MA 02161

Dear Phil:

Thanks for the order you sent on the 15th. We'll have it ready for you when you stop by on Tuesday.

Like you, many carpenters, painters, and plumbers in the Newton area find all their supplies here—when they need them and at the right prices. Our prices are competitive largely because we buy with cash ourselves from *our* suppliers and take advantage of their discounts while we avoid interest charges. We pass those savings on to you.

So to keep the cash flowing and avoid too much extra bookkeeping, we maintain very few credit accounts. We limit these accounts to local residents whose annual income is at least $30,000. You obviously meet the first criterion. As for the second, you mentioned that your current income is $15,000. What I hear from your customers suggests that figure will be rising. As soon as it does meet the minimum, we'll be glad to reconsider your application.

In the meantime, we hope you'll continue to purchase your supplies here on a cash basis. Let us know, too, if you have special orders for us to fill. We pride ourselves on an ability to find one-of-a-kind hardware items to suit the one-of-a-kind houses and carpenters in our community.

Sincerely,

Charlie

C.B. Diehl

FIGURE 15–5. Denying credit.

Ending/Positive   I am indeed a satisfied depositor and hope to remain so. Please no-
tify me of your decision as soon as possible.

The following letter uses a persuasive approach in returning a defective shirt. It buffers the bad news about the shirt with the customer's assurance of continued business if the error is rectified. It appeals
to Matson as a credible company that would like to keep its credibility. The author establishes her own credibility by her calm tone, by
her narrative (in Paragraph 4) of earlier attempts to correct the problem, and by her fresh, unhackneyed style:

To ease the pain of the end of the soccer season, I recently bought my
son a red long-sleeved Matson soccer shirt with three white strips down
each sleeve, a white neck band, and white cuffs.

He loves the shirt. There is only one problem: the middle stripe on each
sleeve ripped out on the first washing. Only one side of each middle
stripe is now stitched into the shirt.

Clearly, that's not how you intend the shirt to be worn. Torn stripes
make him feel bad and look bad next to the Matson logo on his chest.

I asked the sales clerk at Marshall Field's, where I purchased the shirt,
for an exchange, and they referred me to you. Please send me a new red
long-sleeved soccer shirt (size M 12–14). I'll be happy to send you this
one in exchange, if you would like. Or send me my money back (receipt
copy enclosed: $25).

Thank you. We're avid soccer fans, and thus avid Matson customers, and
we know you'll want to correct this problem.

In your letter, make the complaint clear without alienating the
reader. Everyone makes mistakes. Show your understanding of that
fact, and appeal to the reader's self-interest in correcting the mistake.
Write on the assumption that the reader is honest and fair.

Exercises

1. Revise the two following letters of complaint:

I ordered an electric antenna for a 1972 mustang. The first problem
was, it took six weeks to finally get to my address. I ordered the electric
antenna back in the middle of Febuary. The salesman that I talked to on

the phone told me that your company strived on prompt service and also informed me that I would be receiving my electric antenna in one week. The second problem I encountered was when I opened the item I ordered. It was not the correct model.

I understand that salesman get a large number of phone orders and can make mistakes. I can also understand a few days late, But five weeks late and completely the wrong item ordered. I disagree with your system.

I am sending this item back to your company COD. I also expect a full refund within two weeks due to your large mistake. If I have not received my full refund the Better Business Bureau will hear from me.

Mr. John Jones
Whittier and Smith Securities
xxxxx
xxxxx

Dear Sir:

Exactly what the hell do I have to do to get you to transfer my account to the Boston office?

I've written to you and to Poopsey (or whatever you call the head of your office). Next it will be to the chairman of the board.

2. Revise the following *response* to a complaint. Note the "'letterly voice" here. Develop a more convincing statement. This is, of course, a form letter. What element has been inserted in the form? Does this letter really *respond?*

Thank you for your recent communication relative to your dissatisfaction with a purchase of MICRO potato CHIPS. Your comments have been forwarded to our production specialists for their immediate investigation and whatever corrective action is required to prevent a recurrence.

We sincerely regret the concerns you have expressed but appreciate your bringing this matter to our attention. We continually strive to satisfy all our customers and are disappointed when this goal is not achieved.

In appreciation of your interest, we would like you to have with our compliments a copy of our latest recipe booklet and a refund in the amount of $1.61.

We hope in the future you will continue to be our valued customer and that our products will meet your fullest expectations.

3. You are the personnel director of The Big Company, Inc. Richard Short, the son of a friend, has applied for a sales associate job. He's a likable person, but he has no sales experience (your advertisement specifically stated "five years' experience minimum"). Moreover, you are looking for someone with a strong background in pharmaceuticals (your product); Richard is a sociology major with no technical courses. His letter of application emphasized his strong communication skills. Such skills are certainly important to the job, but they are not enough. Write a letter to Richard Short (address: 120 Clark St., Laramie, WY 82070) that rejects his application.

4. You work for a photographic studio. The studio's policy is firm: No returns on portraits except for *technical* problems. Your own quality control generally screens those out anyway. Steven Smith wants to return his portrait and get his money back. He doesn't think it *looks* like him. There is nothing technically wrong with the prints. Write to Mr. Smith refusing his claim. Or, while noting the "no-returns" policy, offer Mr. Smith a retake of his portrait.

5. You are a broker with Jefferson/Anderson Inc. You have been assigned to manage the portfolio of Amos R. J. Brockmann. Among other suggestions, you advise that he buy into WaterBoard Associates, a manufacturer of sailboards. Purchased at 17 1/2, the stock declines steadily. After a year of ownership, Brockmann, against your judgment, decides to sell at 9. His sell order is accompanied by a letter implying that you recommended Sailboards Inc. only because you *use* their products, not because you understood their position as a business. Brockmann is a solid investor. You want to keep him as a client. Write a letter responding to his criticism.

6. You and some fellow students have become increasingly concerned about the noise level in the library on campus. You are all commuter students and depend on the library as a place to work between classes. You also must do your library research during busy hours; you can't wait for a late-evening lull. Plan a strategy for decreasing the noise level. As part of your plan, decide *who* should receive letters from you about the problem (the director of the library? the dean of students? the student council president? the vice-president in charge of operations?). Then write the letters, tailoring each to the appropriate reader.

7. You are the coach of a soccer team for boys ten to twelve years old. Jeff Sprinter, a twelve-year-old seventh-grader, has attended each tryout and wants to be a goalie. He has extensive (and expensive) goalie clothing, purchased by his father, who has also attended each tryout. By the rules of the league you

compete in, you can carry only sixteen boys on the team. Twenty-two boys tried out. Your policy is that each player must be capable of playing *each* position. That means that all players must be runners. Jeff clearly hates to run and is slow in the field. He also hates the field. He's smart and is a decent goalie, but he's not the *best* goalie (that's Peter Smith) and you don't want to carry a player on the roster whom you can't play. So you cut Jeff. His father is upset. He writes to you and asks for a response *in writing* about why you cut Jeff. Write to Dr. Jeffrey P. Sprinter, 12 The Circle, Randolph Estates, Brattleboro, VT 05301.

Letters That Persuade: Asking a Favor, Collecting Payment, and Selling

16

Being part of an organization requires a lot of give and take. You are asked to take action and you ask others. Often, the writer who requests action of a reader holds out some tangible reward—especially money. But sometimes the reward is less tangible and requires more subtle presentation by the writer. This chapter shows how to apply the principles of persuasion in letters that meet three common goals for organizational give-and-take: asking a favor, collecting payment of a debt, and selling someone something.

Asking a Favor

One mark of professionals is that they are not always directly paid for everything they do. Indeed, this status is codified in the language by which workers are categorized: *exempt* workers are professionals who are *exempt*, (that is, not paid for overtime); hourly staff, or *nonexempts*, are so paid. A lawyer who charges out her billing time to clients down to the 10-minute mark may serve hours without remuneration drawing up plans for an advisory committee to the superintendent and board of a local school district. In asking her to serve, the superintendent asks for a favor.

Inviting

Inviting someone to serve on a committee, join an organization, or give a talk indeed often requires a persuasive approach. Let's look at some strategies.

The following direct letter of invitation gets the information off the writer's chest. But it's written strictly from the *writer's* point of view. The beginning is flat—and probably of little interest to the reader. The logistical details come *before* the reader has any reason for knowing them. They can only bore the reader. Moreover, the invitation itself is phrased in stuffy language ("We would like to extend an invitation") and is not specific. It provides no reason for the reader to feel engaged in reading and accepting the invitation; it's easy for the reader to say no:

Beginning/Flat Announcement

The student chapter of the American Management Association will hold its monthly meeting on Friday, January 6, in 206 Bennett Hall.

Middle/Details Without Relevance

Refreshments will be served at 3:30 and then the meeting will begin at 4. We would like to extend an invitation to you to be the speaker at the meeting.

Offhand Invitation	You could talk about any aspect of management you'd like.
Ending/Cliché	Please let me know your decision as soon as possible.

Contrast that letter with the following one, which builds to the invitation through information about the *reader*. The writer feels that she need not mention the AMA immediately, as the stationery signals that source. Note the suggestion of a topic for the talk that will engage the reader's enthusiasm in the promise of talking about something he enjoys:

Beginning/ Personal Connection	When I asked at our December meeting for suggestions concerning speakers in the new year, your name was at the top of the list.
Middle/Concrete Invitation	Logically enough. Your classes are favorites. Now, we'd like to hear more—particularly about your work on the long-range plan for Panama that you keep hinting at in class. Could you discuss that strategic planning process at our January meeting?
Logistics/Careful Attention to Cookies	The meeting will be held in Bennett 206; refreshments (your favorite Oreos brought in just for the occasion) at 3:30; talk at 4.
Ending/ Encourages Acceptance	I'll stop by during your office hours on Wednesday to learn your response (and to twist your arm, if necessary).

Asking Someone to Respond to a Questionnaire

As you collect data for a project, you often need to ask people to respond to a questionnaire. If the reader is already predisposed to such a response, you may simply write a brief note at the top of the questions. But sometimes responding is not a matter of course; you need to ask a favor. First, be sure that the questionnaire itself has been shaken out, that it is short, unambiguous, physically easy to answer, and easy to return to you. Then, in the covering letter, appeal to whatever connects you and the reader and to the reader's participation in the community of people interested in the topic. Perhaps promise the reward of sending the reader a copy of your report, if that's possible (and do so). The following letter begins with the recognition that the reader is probably asked to fill out many questionnaires; by stating what the reader is probably thinking, the letter defuses the reader's potential displeasure. Then it builds the case for a response by showing why an answer is needed *from this particular respondent* and by promising a benefit—a useful seminar:

Not another questionnaire.

Yes. Why? Over the last several years, the Association for Management and Technology has become increasingly aware of the need to incorporate an international perspective in our programs and seminars. Our members—you—work for multinationals, subscribe to international bulletin boards and electronic mail services, and are increasingly investing abroad. You want to be better informed about the global economy.

We want to provide better information in our programs for you. But we need your help. Thus, the enclosed brief questionnaire.

Responding should take only ten minutes. Take more, if you'd like; we'll be happy to read everything you say.

Your reward? Programs and seminars *you need* to position yourself effectively in the global economy.

Asking for a Letter of Recommendation

While you are a student, and again perhaps after you've been out of college a year or two, you may write to a professor or a supervisor to ask for a letter of recommendation. You know the reader is busy; you want to set yourself up for a strongly positive recommendation (anything less is usually not effective). The following letter is structured indirectly and adheres to these guidelines:

Beginning.   Reestablish your identity in the reader's context.

Middle.   Build the request.

1. Provide the rationale, including a brief work history and the criteria for the job. Refer to any attachments, including a current résumé and perhaps a goal statement.
2. Ask for a recommendation and make sure that the reader knows the necessary logistics: where to send it, to whom, and by what date.

Ending.   Close by reiterating your request—but also allow an out for the reader who may be reluctant. Balance insistence against excessive modesty; don't provide a lazy reader with an excuse, but don't force someone who is lukewarm toward you to write anyway.

In the two years since I took your Organization and Management Behavior course in the fall semester of 19XX, I've had lots of opportunities to put the ideas you taught me into practice, particularly your advice about managing group work and defining and scheduling tasks.

I've been free-lancing for two years on the design of a software system for office management and am now applying to CompuTemps, a large software house in Vancouver. Their position announcement seems perfect for me (see the enclosed).

Could you write me a letter of recommendation? I was pleased that you gave me an "A" on my final report ("A Management Information System for the Datatime Corporation") and in the course. I've enclosed a copy of my current résumé, along with a brief statement of my goal in this position.

Please send the letter to:
Steven P. Smith, Personnel Director
CompuTemps Inc.
100 Fleming St.
Vancouver, B.C.
Canada V5P 3G2

Could you also please write before December 12? I'll understand if your schedule does not permit you to write at this time. But your word would carry a lot of weight with CompuTemps.

Thanks for any assistance you can give me as I try to put what I learned at State into practice.

Collecting Payment

Most of the time, most people pay their bills. When payment is overdue, a creditor sends a reminder about the debt. The first reminder is usually just a note attached to the bill. The second, third, or later reminders may be letters. Often, such letters are direct, as is the following:

This is to remind you of your agreement to pay $23 on May 2. We expect the payment to be in our office no later than five days after this date. A return envelope is enclosed for your convenience.

Please let me know if you have any questions.

But directness is not always the best route. Sometimes you may choose a more persuasive approach. Your letter may aim to overcome reader resistance. Take care not to sound self-serving, and do not attack the reader. The following letter is both self-serving and attacking. Moreover, it is internally contradictory and legally suspect. The reader *did not* renew his subscription; the circulation director (the writer of the letter) did that himself and now accuses the reader of not paying—and thus being a bad debt:

Dear Subscriber:

We have a problem—or perhaps it's just a failure to communicate. Eight weeks ago we entered your *Sports for All* subscription and *extended your credit.* We have sent you weekly issues of *Sports for All* faithfully in that time.

We have also sent you three prior invoices asking for your payment.

So much for our side of the story; now what about you? So far, no payment, no explanation—nothing. That's what I mean about a failure to communicate. It's time you did *your* part.

Return your payment with the invoice in the postage-paid envelope provided. Unless you act quickly, your subscription will be canceled, and your name will be transferred to our bad debt file.

If your payment is already in the mail, you need not worry. But if it isn't, you had better act *today.*

Such a threatening letter is hardly persuasive. It reflects more on the bad character of the writer than that of the reader. Let's look at some more positive—and effective—letters. Collection letters are usually based on different assumptions about the reader's resistance to paying. Often, a series of letters is sent over a few weeks or months to encourage payment. We'll examine four assumptions and letters written with each in mind.

First, you can assume that the reader forgot. Remind the reader with a witty note or some gimmick attached to a second bill, like a pencil for writing a check. Or write a gently persuasive letter. For a good customer, you may send letters over several months based on the first assumption. In part because advertising rates rise with circulation, magazines are often reluctant to let a subscriber go, as you probably have seen. For this reason, many renewal notices are pitched at Assumption 1—and may even offer good terms for renewal, as in Figure 16–1 headed *Memorandum* to make the reader feel like an insider. Contrast this letter with the threatening one you just read. Note the "elitist" appeal to the reader.

MEMORANDUM
from Elizabeth P. Valk
CIRCULATION DIRECTOR

During the past months, we have sent you several reminders about your FORTUNE subscription. And we regret very much that we have had to stop sending you the magazine.

But we can start the biweekly FORTUNE coming to you every two weeks if you let us hear from you.

If we appear determined to have you as a subscriber, our reason is a good one: FORTUNE is not for everyone, and we value highly the readers for whom it is intended.

And precisely because you have been a valued FORTUNE subscriber, we're offering you special low rates.

We hope we can continue to number you among FORTUNE's regular subscribers. All the materials you need for reordering are enclosed. We look forward to serving you.

Elizabeth P. Valk

EPV:1f

THE BIWEEKLY
FORTUNE 541 North Fairbanks Court, Chicago, Illinois 60611

FIGURE 16–1. A gentle reminder (used by permission, Fortune).

The following Assumption 1 letter reflects the interest of the owner of a small dress shop in keeping her customer's business:

Beginning/ Personal Connection to Reader

I'm sure your travel and family commitments have kept you busy over the last several months—pleasantly busy, I hope.

Middle/Buffer Reader Excuse

In the midst of all that, perhaps our monthly bills to you went astray or were otherwise overlooked.

Praise of Customer

You're one of the customers we most enjoy serving here at the Clothes Line. Your credit is always good with us.

Negative News/Gentle Delivery

So could you please help us to clear the charge of $1,005 now owed on your account? We hope to keep serving you and your family for years to come.

Ending/Resale

Please send a check now to confirm our continuing role as your primary source for designer clothing.

Second, you can assume that the reader is withholding payment because of some problem with the bill or with the product. In your letter, solicit the reader's complaint. The following letter addresses that need directly in the opener, then follows with the appeal for payment:

Is something wrong?

We have not yet received the January payment of $105 on your account. If you're withholding payment because of some error or problem, we'd like to hear about it. If you are unsure about the specific amount of the account, we would be happy to explain.

Please send your payment today or give us a call to clear up any problems.

Thanks.

Third, you can assume that the reader is balancing several debts and has put a low priority on the debt to you. Perhaps the reader is short of money and cannot pay. Appeal to the reader's self-interest in preserving a credit rating and to his or her sense of fair-play. Note that this *is* the last minute. Explain the consequences of nonpayment. Suggest a partial payment plan or a bill consolidation loan as a positive alternative to nonpayment and the collection agency. The following Assumption 3 letter appeals to a sense of fair play and is soft in its reference to the collection bureau:

During the past months, we have sent you several reminders about your bill for $54.75, which has been overdue for four months.

As you have not responded to any of our questions concerning a problem with the bill, we can only assume that you have decided not to pay it.

But debts must be paid. Your payment, along with $9 in interest charges as indicated in our credit agreement (copy enclosed), is due *now*. Four months is the agreed-on period for credit before we turn your account over to a collection agency for disposition.

Avoid that step. Ensure that your credit rating will remain sound. Send your payment of $63.75 *today*.

The following Assumption 3 letter suggests a partial payment plan. It also includes the reader's name within the text of the letter, reminding her of the need to maintain her reputation as a person of good character:

We have supplied you with your needed paints, brushes, and other tools over the last several months. Your payment for these supplies, however, is now six months overdue.

As a businessperson yourself, you must realize, Ms. Andrews, that we cannot carry this debt any longer. We also realize that you must collect from your customers to pay us, and that at times you may have to wait for payment.

Thus, although we would prefer a check for the entire amount of your debt ($1,200), we would be willing to work out an alternate plan for payment. Just give me a call.

Fourth, you can assume that the reader has no intention of paying. Your letter may be a direct indication that you are turning over the account to a collection agency or the courts. Many banks have standard forms for such letters, as in the following. Just be careful not to threaten unduly:

When you opened your account with U.S. International, you signed a legally binding contract. The contract provides us with specific remedies should you fail to meet your monthly payments. One such remedy is the legal action we are currently pursuing. We have given you every opportunity to bring your account up to date and are left with no other alternative.

Your account is now being handled by Smith, Jones, and Weir, Attorneys at Law. Refer any questions to them at 614-333-2222.

Selling

From a marketing perspective, *any* letter from a company to a customer or client is a sales occasion. Some letters, however, are explicit sales approaches. You find such letters in your mailbox almost every day. Unless you specialize in direct sales or run your own business, however, you may not have many opportunities to write sales letters. But an understanding of how good ones are written will help you to write any persuasive letter. Thus we end this chapter with a look at letters that *sell*.

The time-tested marketing strategy is *AIDA: Attention, Interest, Desire, Action*. Define your central selling point, then take the customer through each phase.

Attention

You cannot convey your message, of course, unless the reader *reads* the message. Readers resist sales messages. You have to get them to open the envelope and begin. Thus, companies may begin their selling with the envelope. In the spring, for example, when Americans await refund checks from the Internal Revenue Service, some clever sales messages appear in buff envelopes that imitate the shape and graphics of IRS packaging. Official language notifies the postmaster about immediate delivery and conditions of return. A statement urges the purchase of U.S. Savings Bonds. The writer hopes that the reader will open the envelope—and, though disappointed of course, will at least read the sales message.

That message itself must *look* appealing. Often, cartoons or other graphics draw attention. A full-color attachment to the letter, perhaps even of poster size, draws attention. The first line of the letter speaks always in the reader's terms. You may use a headline promising benefits:

YOUR FINANCIAL WORRIES ARE OVER!
No More Lonely Nights
We'd like to give you $50—or more!

Within the text, lead off with a sentence that fits your program for appealing to the reader. Remember the three basic appeals: emotional, ethical, and logical. If you're selling a resort vacation, or a fruit-of-the-month-club plan, or high fashion, your appeal may be primarily *emotional*. If you're selling yourself as, for example, a candidate for a job or an office, or if you're selling your organization, your appeal may be primarily *ethical*, that is, an appeal based on your good character and that of the reader. If you're selling financial services, or an investment package, or a professional journal, then your appeal will be primarily *logical*. Take care to match the appeal to both the product and the audience. Most potential customers of a resort may be interested in vivid pictures of the good life there. But if you're targeting a market segment of convention business, wrap the good-life appeal in at least the appearance of logic, for example, efficient meeting rooms, a quiet retreat from interruptive phone calls, and a worldwide teleconferencing capability. The following are some beginnings that attract attention:

Emotional Appeals

● *Fear:* Do you ever wonder if you're *safe* in your home at night? Do you know how easy it is to intrude through even locked doors?

● *Elitism:* You are one of only a handful of people throughout this country to receive an invitation to join the Investors Club.

● *Bandwagon:* Are you the only person in your neighborhood who hasn't yet experienced the pleasures of home movies and wide television selection with your own videocassette recorder?

● *Guilt:* When was the last time you phoned home?

● *Patriotism:* As a true American, support the fine athletes of your own Olympic team.

● *Nostalgia:* Summer is upon us, and for many of us that means hoisting a pack, lacing up boots, and heading off along some portion of the Appalachian Trail.

● *Pity:* Every year in the Eastern Pacific, American tuna seiners drown twenty thousand dolphins, victims of a fishing process that uses the dolphins to locate the tuna.

Ethical Appeals

● *Authority:* I am writing on behalf of Maestro Riccardo Muti and all of the members of The Philadelphia Orchestra . . .

● *Fair play:* It is now clear that many of the most selfish interest groups, many of the most extreme right-wing ideologues, waited until after their election to turn against social security, to weaken environmental laws, and to destroy the very "safety net" they promised to protect.

• *Common problem of good persons:* A strong opposition to the dangerous and unfair policies of the New Right depends as much on you as it does on your elected officials. We share this problem.

Logical Appeals

• *Rhetorical Question:* Isn't paying for research and then ignoring its results foolish? Yet most businesses do just that when it comes to research bought with their tax dollars.[1]

• *Word Play:* You're on WHYY's gift list. [A reader, expecting an appeal from this public television station, may be disarmed to discover *she*'s on the gift list. See the complete letter in Figure 16–3.]

The following beginning of a letter soliciting contributions to a university's alumni fund combines several appeals: elitism, bandwagon, guilt, patriotic feelings towards the university, and nostalgia. It uses insiders' code (ASPs, ding letters):

Five years ago we were finishing up ASPs . . . counting our offers (and ding letters) . . . weighing the relative merits of a career in investment banking vs. advertising . . . taking refuge from recruiting at happy hours or rugby games . . . wondering what it would be like to go on to a "normal" working environment and end student days.

Interest

Once you have gained the reader's attention, move to the middle of the letter by arousing interest in the product or service itself. Define your central selling point as a benefit to the reader. For example:

• *General statement: Soccer America* covers the college soccer scene across the country.

• *Statement turned to reader:* You will read about the college soccer teams near you in *Soccer America.*

• *General statement: Unique Homes* gives pictures and purchase information about very expensive properties owned by celebrities worldwide.

---

[1] From a circulation promotion letter for "The Innovators Digest," published by The Concepteam, Inc.

- *Statement turned to reader:* Come with **UNIQUE HOMES!** View the private hideaways of America's most famous celebrities! Inspect the palaces of our financial giants! . . . You'll get the facts you need about each property in **UNIQUE HOMES.** You'll get the name, address, and telephone number of the brokers. You'll get the asking price.[2]

Desire

The middle of the letter provides the details, all arranged to support the central selling point and to hook the reader. Avoid both flat lists and exaggeration. Promise only what you can deliver; lies may well end you up in court. The Pet Care Caterers and WHYY letters that follow provide a model for structuring evidence to create desire.

Action

The ending of the letter closes the sale. Many sales strategies emphasize immediate response—and offer rewards for quick action, on the assumption that the longer the potential buyer waits, the less likely the sale.

Combined Approach

Figures 16–2 and 16–3 show two sales letters (both in indented, modified block format) that follow the AIDA approach. Note the understated but clear appeal in the first to elderly customers, considered a good target market for the home delivery of pet care products.

To achieve the desired action, some writers send sales letters in a series. If you choose that approach, make sure that the reader will connect the letters: Use the same design, the same logo, and the same textural voice. The following shows the beginning of a second letter in a sales series:

I wrote to you in May about a simple solution to the mystery of your financial future—BCD supplemental retirement annuities, or, simply, SRAs.

Perhaps a hectic spring schedule kept you from having a chance to read the material I sent you. That's why I wanted to send you a "reminder," hoping that now, with summer here, you might have more time to

---

[2] Used by permission, *Unique Homes* magazine, a Ziff-Davis Publishing Company publication.

PET CARE CATERERS

October 7, 1987

Dear Customer:

We're eager to serve you and your pet!

The top-quality Canine Caterers food products and supplies you have come to rely on will now be delivered to you with even greater savings by Pet Care Caterers, your exclusive home delivery service.

We'd like you to know that the following remain unchanged:

* Regular, dependable, free home delivery
* In-house charge accounts
* Handsome gift certificates for your friends
* Expert, professional nutritional advice

In addition, we would like to introduce you to the following new benefits:

* 5% discount for any pet owner over the age of 65 with a purchase of $25 or more a month
* Acceptance of all manufacturer's authorized coupons for all products that we carry
* 5% discount for the purchase of 100-300 pounds of dry pet food
* 10% discount for the purchase of more than 300 pounds of dry pet food
* Monthly specials

Fill in the enclosed product list for October and call me with your order today. I'll begin delivery immediately and bill you next month. If you need a product that is not on the list, call anyway. The list is too short to cover all the products we carry--and we keep adding products as <u>you</u> suggest them.

We've enjoyed meeting you and your pets and look forward to continuing our service as Pet Care Caterers, your total pet care supplier.

Sincerely

PET CARE CATERERS, INC.

Jon Bailey

Jon Bailey
President

FIGURE 16–2. A sales letter (courtesy of Jon Bailey).

TV 12 **WHYY** 91FM

INDEPENDENCE MALL WEST, 150 NORTH SIXTH STREET, PHILADELPHIA, PENNSYLVANIA 19106, 215-351-1200
FIFTH AND SCOTT STREETS, WILMINGTON, DELAWARE 19805, 302-575-1515

December 19, 1985

Diedre Taber
730 Harvard Avenue
Swarthmore, PA 19081

Dear Ms. Taber:

You're on WHYY's gift list.

Because of the gift you made earlier this year, we have been able to present outstanding programs such as The Nutcracker, River Journeys, The Frugal Gourmet, Christmas Special with Luciano Pavarotti, The Good Neighbors, Wonderworks, and Bleak House on TV 12, and Morning Edition, A Prairie Home Companion, All Things Considered and Fresh Air on 91 FM.

We'd like to give you many more gifts -- special presentations, new series, and favorite programs that may suddenly become available again. The only way we can afford them is through your generosity.

Is WHYY on your gift list?

A special holiday gift from you -- separate from your annual subscription -- will help TV 12 and 91 FM give more outstanding programs back to you, your family, and all the people you love.

Please exchange gifts with the television and radio stations you enjoy so much. Simply return the enclosed form with your special contribution.

All of us at WHYY offer hearty thanks for your loyal, generous, and continuing support.

Sincerely,

Frederick Breitenfeld, Jr.
President

P.S.   Because this may be a particularly good tax year in which to make a substantial gift, a brochure on charitable giving opportunities is enclosed for your benefit.

FIGURE 16-3. A letter soliciting a contribution (used by permission of Mike Quattrone, Director of Television Broadcasting, and Willo Carey, Director of Development, WHYY Inc.).

think about your financial future. And frankly I believe you'll find SRAs can be a valuable part of your financial planning.[3]

The Common Core

Although we have spent four chapters showing how letters *differ,* we'd like to reinforce a note of *similarity* as we close. Every letter has a goal. It is meant to get something done. When letters work, whatever the situations that bred them, they work for the same reasons: They balance the needs of writer, information, and reader. They meet the conventions of form. They sound crisp in an engaging voice that comes through the page. Even in informative letters, but especially, as you have seen, in persuasive ones, pay attention to how you sound. Write as a person writing to another person. That probably seems like pretty pat advice, like always brushing your teeth after meals. But it's simply a matter of getting into the habit. Don't pose. Don't settle for worn-out phrases. Don't copy letters from a book—this book or any other book. *Use* them to help you develop your own strategies. Don't sound like a book. Sound like *you.*

Exercises

1. Here are several opening paragraphs of letters. Each is at best flat. Some actually may create resistance in the reader when the opening should, as we have seen, *defuse* that resistance. Discuss other ways of starting these letters:

   (a) I would like any information you could give me concerning Senator Roth's proposed legislation to create a tax reform.

   (b) Could you please send me copies of the costume and property plots that you devised last spring for Caravel Academy's production of Cole Porter's *Anything Goes?*

   (c) [In a letter to the University registrar] The present process of registering for classes is irritating for both the students and the faculty. With the input of the student body, the registration process may be made simpler, which would serve to benefit the university itself. Please fill in the enclosed questionnaire.

   (d) My name is Mindy Jones.

   (e) I obtained your name from Ann Thompson, career specialist at the Career Planning Office, where I am a student assistant. I am very interested in pursuing a career in counseling, yet I realize that one must define the specialty of counseling one wants to work in.

2. Revise the following letter and questionnaire:

---

[3] Used by permission, Larry D. Hershberger, Vice President, TIAA/CREF.

Attention: Spanish Department Chairperson

As a communications major, I am interested in studying ways to improve communication problems between cultures. a problem that language departments are concerned with every day.

In an effort to help study the problem, I am doing a report on the difficulties that occur between American culture and various other cultures. Will you please give me your opinion on the interactional problems between Spanish culture and American culture.

I have enclosed a questionnaire with some general questions. Any other opinions would be greatly appreciated. Your input would be greatly appreciated. Your input would be a great help and very useful in the study of improving intercultural communication.

Questions

1. What values are most important to the Spanish culture
2. In a Spanish culture, what are the most annoying things that Americans do in a conversation (if any)?
3. What would you say is the general attitude of Americans when in a Spanish culture?
4. Are there any major differences in the communication habits between Spanish and American culture? If so, please explain.
5. What do you feel is most important to remember when in a communication exchange between Americans and the Spanish?
6. Is there anything that you would like to add?

3. Revise the following letter, which forms the center of a campaign to induce high school students to attend the University of Your State.

Dear Graduating Senior:

I am very concerned with the attitude that seniors in X state's high schools have concerning the University of Our State as an educational institute. Many students frown on the thought of attending an in-state university. Why, when the University of Our State has so much to offer?

I am sure that you are aware that you will have to endure many adjustments upon entering college. However, one of the best features that the University of Our State has to offer you, that no other university can, is that it allows you both the experience of growing on your own, away from home, as well as the security of having your family near.

Academically, Our State University is a highly accredited university. The nursing, engineering, physical therapy, and business programs are among the best programs in the area. If you choose to follow a liberal arts study, you will receive a strong academic background that allows for much diversity.

There are a diverse number of social activities that a student may participate in that makes your years in college more enjoyable. Clubs on campus such as religious clubs, hiking and sailing clubs, and student government, just to name a few, meet regularly and invite all students to attend. If a student is interested in athletics, he/she has the option of participating in the interscholastic or intramural programs, which are very organized. Finally, Our State's geographic location adds to its social life. We're not far from many cities, which is not to say that Our Town doesn't have much to offer. There are many shops, night clubs, and theatres here for entertainment.

So, how much will all this cost you? As an in-state student, you will pay half the tuition costs to attend the University of Our State that you would at any other university.

So why go anywhere else. The University of Our State is YOUR university. Apply today!

4. You work for a record shop, I Like It like That, which has a reputation for stocking both classical works and the latest rages in private labels of far-out, avant-garde groups, both American and European. Many customers take advantage of your easy credit terms to buy vast quantities of records. But then they fall behind in their payments. Your boss asks you to write a set of form letters for collecting payment. You'll keep the text on a disk and print out each letter individually. But he wants the text to be short. He also wants to tailor the letters to three groups: the *classics*, that is, people who buy mostly opera and symphonies; the *easy listeners*, who buy Barbra Streisand and Frank Sinatra; and the *punks* (his term), who buy the latest rage. Establish a three-person team to write the letters. Each member might take one audience. Try to achieve a consistent style—remember, it's one record store that's writing. Perhaps two teams could compete to write the best letters. You might also develop a series of letters (based on two or three of the four collection assumptions) for each audience. Be careful not to show bias against any group simply because of its musical preference.

5. You've been employed in an entry-level job for two years after graduation from college. Now you're ready to move on. Write a letter to a former professor asking him or her to write a letter of recommendation for you.

6. You have decided to start a painting company part-time with some friends while you attend school and in the summers. You'll do both exterior and interior painting of residences. Write a sales letter and design a flyer that you'll distribute in your neighborhood soliciting business. Give your company a name. Develop a theme and a major selling point: your rates, your experience, your caring attitude, whatever. Perhaps write the letter as a *group* project and develop follow-up letters as well.

7. You run a small dress shop that caters to an affluent clientele. One of your customers, Mrs. Herbert Barnes, has bought several thousand dollars worth of dresses and accessories over the last ten years. She has always paid her bills promptly. But her payment of $600 has been overdue for two months. Mrs. Barnes is getting a divorce, and her account is in her husband's name. He refuses to pay her bill. She says she doesn't have enough money to pay. Lawyers for each are negotiating financial matters in general. But you think somehow you can appeal to Mrs. Barnes to send you at least a partial payment and to work out credit terms. Her long-term financial prospects seem sound. Write to Mrs. Barnes.

8. As a group project devise a sales strategy for some organization. You might use a real organization that you are familiar with, for example, a campus group. Or you might be working with a public-service agency that would like your assistance in putting together a fund-raising campaign. If you have corporate experience, devise a strategy for a real or imagined product or service. Define your target market population. Develop a series of letters or brochures establishing your central sales point and backing it with evidence. Remember AIDA. Remember the emotional, ethical, and logical appeals. If you have access to a computer graphics package, incorporate both visual and verbal elements.

Bids, Proposals, and Progress Reports

17

Many business documents are, fully or partially, sales documents. We have seen (Chapter 16) that sales letters try to convince potential clients of the advantages of a good or service. In this chapter, we examine two important sales documents, the bid and the proposal, and a third document, the progress report, which is often required following a proposal. We begin with a working definition of bids and proposals and a description of the general mode of bidding and proposing. We then look at specific guidelines and examples and conclude with some tips on writing progress reports.

Bids and Proposals Defined

Although the terms *bid* and *proposal* are sometimes used interchangeably, the two documents differ in ways that influence their preparation. Practice may vary from organization to organization, but these definitions capture the similarities and differences:

A *bid* is an offer to supply an already-available good or service at a specified price.

A *proposal* is an offer to undertake a study leading to the solution of a problem.

Both bids and proposals *offer* something. They are sales documents that aim to persuade a person or an organization to pay a price for having the offerer provide or do something. They differ in their outcomes: The bid aims at a tangible outcome (generally a thing, sometimes a service), whereas the proposal directs itself to the solution of a problem (generally less tangible).

An example will clarify. You might write a bid to sell water-resistant boots to the U.S. Marines. The customer will receive a thing: the boot (many of them). But maybe the Marines think it's time not just to order more boots but to consider Marine footwear needs generally; for example, the desired water resistance, or the appropriate methods and materials of boot construction. You propose to study the question—and to provide the customer with a report that compiles your results and describes your solution.

Bidding and Proposing: The Response Mode

As we saw in Chapter 1, *all* communications can be considered *responses*. Bids and proposals specifically respond to one of two stimuli:

- A request, formal or informal, for a bid or proposal.
- A perceived need that is not explicitly phrased as a request.

A bid or proposal prepared in response to a request is called *solicited*. One that responds to a perceived need not explicitly phrased as a request is called *unsolicited*. This distinction is important because it affects the preparation of bids and proposals in fundamental ways. Some examples will clarify the distinction and illustrate its importance.

If a customer enters your store and asks for the best possible price on fifty desks and chairs to furnish the new offices she is building, you present a bid (oral or written) that responds to that request. In this case, the request is an informal (unwritten) *request for a bid* (RFB). It has been *solicited*. If, on the other hand, you learn that new offices are being furnished and write on your own initiative to the owner, offering to supply desks and chairs at a certain price, your bid is *unsolicited*.

The same terms are used for proposals. If your supervisor tells you to write a memo requesting permission to do an internal examination of the company's sick-leave policy, your proposal (the memo) responds to a *request for proposal* (RFP). The proposal is *solicited*. The supervisor's request may come in a conversation about various matters over coffee. Or it may be handed to you formally in a memo. But if you sense that the company's sick-leave policy can be improved or simply ought to be reviewed, you might, on your own initiative, submit a proposal to review it. That proposal is *unsolicited*.

Bids and proposals, then, are *responses*, communications reacting to either a request or a perceived need. One of the criteria for measuring a bid or proposal, as we'll see, is *responsiveness*. Readers will judge how closely your document responds to the request or problem that fostered it.

Bidding and Proposing: The Problem-Solving Mode

Both bids and proposals are meant to solve a problem or to answer a question. Here are some problems, phrased as questions, to which *proposals* might be addressed:

- What is the best way to reorganize the sales department?
- Will it be cost-effective to supply microcomputers to all middle and upper managers for home use?
- Should all new automobiles sold in Wisconsin be required to exceed federal standards in safety devices?

You could answer each of these questions with a proposal to research the best solution.

A different kind of problem results in a *bid*. Usually, the request for a bid seeks tangible outcomes to be obtained within certain constraints. For example, an RFB might seek:

- A new copier for the accounting department.
- An improved benefits package for all nonunion employees of the company.
- A service contract for maintaining the rotors on the U.S. Navy's helicopter fleet.

Certain constraints might be given: The copier should be able to reduce documents and reproduce color, and it must be available at once at a price of less than $10,000. Your bid must meet these constraints (or explain the disadvantages or even the impossibility of doing so) or risk instant rejection. In the bid, you give a specific price quotation and detailed information on what services or goods will be rendered over what period in what condition for the price.

Both solicited and unsolicited bids and proposals are selling documents, but we should be aware of an important difference. Solicited ones concentrate on selling the *solution* or *answer*. Unsolicited ones sell first the *problem* or *question*, and then the solution or answer. The individual or organization *soliciting* a proposal or bid has recognized that it has a problem: It knows the sales department needs to be reorganized; it has decided it needs a copier. You must understand that need, but you can assume agreement on it. In an unsolicited proposal or bid, however, you must first convince your client that its sales department needs restructuring or that its accounting department needs a copier. Sometimes that's no easy task. And sometimes you need to convince the very person who caused the problem in the first place. In the sections that follow, we look at some strategies for composing both unsolicited and solicited bids and proposals. Let us repeat here, however, that for all their differences, these documents are the same in one essential way: They *respond* to requests or bids. They propose *solutions* to problems or *answers* to questions. The success of a bid or proposal depends on a clear, accurate understanding of the underlying need for action.

 *Preparing Bids: A Case Study*

A case study of an actual bid may help us identify some principles of good bid-writing. Figures 17–1, 17–2, and 17–3 provide the documents in the case.

DENVER COLLEGE OF SCIENCE
1114 Market Street
Denver, CO 80202

Office of the Dean

BIDS REQUESTED

Six (6)IBM-XT microcomputers

     256K memory
     10-meg disk
     320K floppy
     Monochrome monitor

     software:MS-DOS
       BASIC-86
       BASIC-A
       Writer/Speller
       Perfect Calc
       Perfect Filer
       Perfect Link
       Fast Graphs

Two (2) Microline 92A printers

Equivalent substitutes for hardware and software will be considered.

For delivery no later than 15 May 19xx

    Inquiries and bids to: Larson Nader
                      (at above address and phone)

FIGURE 17–1. Request for bid (RFB).

A formal request (Figure 17–1) initiated the bidding process. The RFB, though quite short, contains four essential elements: a precise description of the items required, a formal allowance of equivalent substitutions, specification of the delivery date, and the address and phone of the contact person who will receive bids and answer questions. All this information is conveyed succinctly and unambiguously.

HANSON COMPUTERS

Larson Nader
Office of the Dean
Denver College of Science
1114 Market Street
Denver Colorado 80202

Dear Mr. Nader:

As per your request I submit the following prices on IBM Computer System Units:

1.) - Six (6) IBM-XT Microcomputers — **Discount**
20KB, 128K - 10mb
    List Price: $4995. each — 19%
    Your Price: $4045.95 each

  - For total of 256K for each System you — **Discount**
will need 2/64KB Memory Module Kits
    List Price: ($165. each) $330. — 19%
    Your Price: $267.30

  - Monochrome Moniter for each system: — **Discount**
    List Price: $345 — 19%
    Your Price: $279.45

  - For each Monochrome Moniter you will
need a Moniter and Printer Adapter Cards. — **Discount**
    List Price: $335 — 19%
    Your Price: $271.35

2.) Software Requested
Equivalent or Better Substitute for
Writer/Speller, Perfect Calc, Perfect Filer,
Perfect Link and Fast Graphs would be
Peach Tex 5000, a new software package
which integrates these functions. — **Discount**
    List Price: $250 — 19%
    Your Price: $202

2.) Software Requirements (Continued)
DOS 2.0 plus Basic for IBM — **Discount**
    List Price: $60 — 10%
    Your Price: $54

3.) Two (2) Microline 92A printers — **Discount**
    List Price: $599 — 19%
    Your Price: $485.19

If you should have any questions please feel free to call me at Hanson Computers. We would be very happy to help you. We appreciate the opportunity of submitting this price quotation.

Truly Yours,
Tracy Mulligan

FIGURE 17-2. Losing Bid

JKL PRODUCT CENTER
870 Third Street
Denver, CO 80209

April 18, 19xx

Larson Nader, Dean
Denver College of Science
1114 Market Street
Denver, CO 80202

Dear Mr. Nader:

Thank you for your interest in the JKL Product Center. Enclosed is the quotation you requested for IBM Personal Computers. The quote reflects the educational pricing schedule for educational institutions such as Denver College of Science. I have also enclosed information on the printers that we offer through the JKL Product Center.

If I can be of any further assistance, please feel free to call me at anytime on 768-9711.

Sincerely,

Eileen Holt-Tucker

Eileen Holt-Tucker
Marketing Representative

Enclosures

FIGURE 17–3. Winning bid.

Two responses—two bids—are shown in Figures 17–2 and 17–3. The first is a loser; the second is a winner. Why?

The losing bid (Figure 17–2) has some strengths: It is generally responsive to the RFB, providing price quotations on the items requested. The bid is specific, the numbers are accurate, and the substitution in software is at least mentioned if not fully justified.

But the bid has two serious flaws. One is

Bid

PART#	QUAN	DISC	EACH ($)	TOTAL	DESCRIPTION
5160087	6	20%	4,995.00	23,976.00	PCXT SYSTEM UNIT W/KEYBOARD
1501003	12	20%	165.00	1,584.00	64K MEMORY EXP. KIT (CHIPS)
5151001	6	20%	345.00	1,656.00	MONOCHROME DISPLAY
1504900	6	20‰	335.00	1,608.00	DISPLAY & PRINTER ADAPTER CARD
1525612	2	20%	55.00	88.00	PRINTER CABLE
6329785	2		950.00	1,900.00	Epson FX100 Dot Matrix Printer
6024061	6	20%	60.00	288.00	DOS 2.0 & basic extensions
6024004	6	20%	200.00	960.00	VISICALC 1.2
6871312	6		375.00	2,250.00	Visiword and Visispell
6871322	6		300.00	1,800.00	VISIFILE

SUBTOTAL	$36,110.00
TAX	0.00
TOTAL	$36,110.00

Make sure you get to see all FOUR of our Personal Computers: the PC, XT, Portable PC, and AT. We have a machine for your every need, and can support it with IBM software and IBM service and technical help. Thank you for taking a look at IBM Personal Computers!!

1

FIGURE 17–3. *(continued.)*   **Enclosures.**

that it fails to organize information strategically. What is the total price? This critical question is neglected. One would need a calculator to determine total price because the bid lists the prices only for separate items, not for the package. The recipient of the bid should not have to do the bidder's work. A simple table would address the organizational problem by bringing the relevant data together in an accessible form.

The second flaw is the bid's appearance. A handwritten response is simply unacceptable. At a minimum, a bid (especially one going outside the organization) should be neatly typed. In this case (in which a computer retailer is bidding to supply microcomputers with word-processing capability), it is ironic that the bidder failed to use the very technology she was trying to sell. A handwritten bid reflects either a lack of seriousness or a lack of care. Either is fatal. Indeed, in this instance, the bid was automatically rejected because of its form. If a bidder can't take the time to prepare neat copy, one questions his or her ability to complete the project.

The bid presented in Figure 17–3 is a winner. Like the first, it is responsive to the RFB, presents specific information, and uses accurate numbers. Its one obvious fault is that it fails to explain the substitution of equivalent software. But that weakness is more than offset by its strengths in just those areas where

INFORMATION SHEET: PRINTERS

IBM GRAPHICS PRINTER: $595.00
* 80 CPS
* Impact Dot Matrix
* 9 × 9 Matrix
* Bidirectional
* All points addressable
  —216 dots/inch vertically
  —240dots/inch horizontally
* 18 Character styles
* 4 line lengths (40, 66, 80, 132 characters)
* Pin-feed continuous forms 4″ - 10″ wide
* No sheet feed
* Parallel interface
* 90 day warranty

EPSON MX-100: $769.00

* 100 CPS
* Impact Dot Matrix
* 9 × 9 Matrix
* Bidirectional
* Full Graphics capability
* Line length maximum of 136 characters
* Compressed print mode max 233 characters/line (16.5 cpi)
* Tractor feed continuous forms 4″ - 15.5″ wide
* Forms up to 255 lines can be used
* Friction feed can handle single cut sheets
* Parallel interface
* 90 day warranty

EPSON FX-100: $950.00

* 160 CPS
* Dot Matrix
* 9 × 9 matrix
* Bidirectional

2

* All points addressable
* Line length maximum of 136 characters (10 cpi)
* Compressed print mode maximum 233 characters/line
(16.5 cpi)
* Tractor feed continuous forms 4″ - 15.5″ wide
* Friction feed can handle cut sheet up to 8½ × 12″
* Parallel interface
* 90 day warranty

NEC SPINWRITER 3500: $2,290.00

* 33 CPS
* Bidirectional
* 10 / 12 / 15 cpi & proportional spacing
* 128 Character print element
* Several dozen different "thimble" elements
* Line length at 10 cpi: 136 characters
*   ″   ″ 12 cpi: 163 characters
*   ″   ″ 15 cpi: 203 characters
* Paper width is adjustable up to 16 inches
* Order Cut Sheet Paper Guide, or bidirectional
  tractor feed separately
* Parallel Interface
* 90 day warranty
* NEC Service call 1-617-863-8840
* NEC Technical Support call 1-617-264-8383

IBM COLOR PRINTER: $1,995.00

* 35 - 200 CPS
* Dot Matrix
* Draft: 200 CPS
* Text or Correspondence: 110 CPS
* Near "Letter" Quality: 35 CPS
* Bidirectional
* All points addressable graphics
* Three ROS resident fonts: Helvetica typestyle
* Line length maximum 132 characters

3

* Graphics in three programmable states:
  1. All black
  2. 4 colors: red, green, blue, black
  3. 8 colors: yellow, magenta, cyan, black, orange, green, violet, brown
* Print line maximum 13.5"
* Accepts paper width from 5" to 14.875"
* Line length maximum 132 characters
* Supports single sheet feed or tractor feed
* Parallel interface
* 12 month warranty

COMPACT PRINTER: $175.00

* 50 CPS
* Thermal Printer
* Unidirectional
* 80 characters per line
* All points addressable graphics
* Friction feed continuous or single sheet
* Paper width maximum 8.5 inches
* Serial interface
* Adapter card not required to connect Compact printer to PCjr
* To connect the compact printer to a PC or PC - XT, both the Compact Printer Connector Adapter ($40.00) and the PCjr Parallel Printer Attachment ($99.00) are required

THESE PRICES ARE SUBJECT TO CHANGE WITHOUT NOTICE

4

the first bid fails: organization and appearance.

This is an effectively organized bid. It displays the needed information in a simple table that allows the reader easy access. The table supplies unit price, quantity price, and total. This table allows for comparison shopping; if, for example, another bidder's price on a particular item is lower, purchases can be made from different suppliers to achieve the lowest total price. Clear organization of the information makes such an approach possible.

A second major strength is the effective use

of format and presentation conventions. A cover letter supplies general information and extends the offer of further assistance. The sheet listing basic prices is self-contained. And the additional sheets describing the available printers serves as an appendix that can be consulted as needed but that does not interfere with conveying the core information. If internal approval procedures for the purchase require that the information be shared with others in the organization, the basic price sheet can be copied and circulated, and the sheets on the printers can be held separate. The ability to divide the bid into parts for such purposes is important and is another strength of this winning bid.

Preparing Bids: Guidelines

Our brief analysis of the two sample bids highlights certain features of preparing bids that can be phrased as guidelines. Here are five general ones, followed by two specialized ones:

1. *Be responsive to the recipient's needs by answering all questions, explicit or implicit.* Don't assume that everything in the bid is obvious just because *you* think so. As a precaution, always provide your phone number so that the recipient can ask questions that you didn't think of. Don't use that route, however, as a way of avoiding responsibility for answering questions in the bid itself.

2. *Structure your information strategically to ensure ease of access.* Tables, graphs, and other visuals are especially helpful. Visuals may well carry the central message, with text used to explain or qualify. A table listing all items and their individual and total prices is nearly mandatory. The contrast between the bids in Figures 17–2 and 17–3 illustrates the importance of displaying critical information in a clear visual form.

3. *Be precise and specific.* Even if for convenience you group items in categories in a summary sheet or table, always provide a full description of what you are supplying. An appendix can do this, as we saw in the additional information about printers in Figure 17–3.

4. *Verify the accuracy of all numbers.* Since bids are essentially price quotations, you must be sure that the numbers add up. Many bids fail because the arithmetic is wrong. A reader is justified in a negative response because sloppiness in simple calculations reflects poorly on your ability to do the job.

5. *Use an appropriate format to achieve a neat and polished appearance.* Neatness always counts. It promotes ease of access to the relevant information and at the same time reinforces your image as a careful worker. If a particular format is required by the RFB (as usually occurs in government bidding), follow it scrupulously. If none is specified, follow the form used by your organization. (Information on memo

and letter formats is given in Chapters 12 and 13.) And don't underestimate the value of appendixes as a way of supplying detailed information without obstructing the general flow and the overall structure of a bid.

Two more specialized guidelines emerge from our analysis of the sample bids. The first applies to solicited bids:

6. *In a solicited bid, explicitly justify substitutions.* Even if "equivalent" items are permitted in the RFB, it's your job as a bidder to explain why you selected the ones you are proposing. You have to demonstrate that the substitution meets the specified criteria or offers more (for less, if possible) than the stipulated item. Don't expect the superiority of the substituted item to be obvious.

The final additional guideline applies to unsolicited bids:

7. *In an unsolicited bid, make an extra effort to get the reader's attention.* Recipients of solicited bids have to read them because they requested them. But an unsolicited bid can be disposed of quickly—after all, who asked for it? An unsolicited bid has to capture the reader's attention at the outset to overcome a natural resistance to buying anything.

You can begin by raising the question directly: "Why should you purchase a home security system? Because . . ." Or you can slip into the sales pitch after first calling the reader's attention to a problem: "Every year eight thousand homes in Spokane are broken into when their owners are away. A home security system can protect you when you are on vacation or out of town on business. We offer . . ." Attractive visuals and interest-getting typography and format can also help focus the reader's attention long enough for you to make your bid. If no one asked for the bid, the burden is on you to justify the use of the reader's time and energy to read, evaluate, and—if you've done your job well—accept the bid.

▰▰▰ *Preparing Proposals: A Case Study*

Now let's turn from a bid to a proposal. Figure 17–4 is a proposal written by an agent of an insurance brokerage firm. It addresses a particular problem: A poorly designed benefits plan is costing the JFS Manufacturing Company too much money and is helping the employees too little.

The proposal presents a solution that seems likely to solve the problem. The agent suggests an assessment of company and employee needs and a review of existing benefits programs available from insurance underwriters that will result in the presentation to JFS of a less expensive and more effective plan than the existing one.

The proposer also presents a good case for herself and her company. In the "Record of Service" section, she points to her company's success in designing benefits programs for over one hundred other firms and supplies addi-

REIMBURSEMENT SERVICES

P.O. Box 74 / Moorestown, NJ 08057 / 609-636-3588

November 1, 19xx

Mr. James Simpkins, Sr.
JFS Manufacturing Company
3645 West Broad Street
Camden, NJ 09064

Dear Mr. Simpkins:

I enjoyed our telephone conversation yesterday concerning the trouble
you are having with the benefits program at JFS. The enclosed brief
statement shows how Reimbursement Services can improve the package
to benefit both you and your employees.

The proposal outlines the specific services we offer and indicates our
experience. It also provides a schedule of activities we would conduct for
you.

Please feel free to phone me if you have questions about the proposal. I
look forward to working with you.

Sincerely,

Jennifer Friedman

Jennifer Friedman
Benefits Counselor

Enclosure

FIGURE 17–4. Insurance brokerage proposal (courtesy of Jennifer Friedman).

REIMBURSEMENT SERVICES

PROPOSAL FOR JFS MANUFACTURING COMPANY

Proposal

Reimbursement Services proposes to design an employee benefits program that fits the needs of the JFS Manufacturing Company and costs less than the plan currently in use.

Statement of Problem

In today's market, health care costs are continually on the rise. As a result, employee benefits programs are becoming more important to an organization's efforts to maintain the highest quality employees. Too often these benefits plans are not properly designed and are thus both too costly and of insufficient appeal to employees.

Objective

By first understanding your needs in a health care program, we can develop one that will be most beneficial for JFS Manufacturing. We will then search for this particular type of program at the least possible cost. In addition, we aim to improve the employer/employee relationship through our service of the program. We orient employers as well as employees to the new plan, assist with claims, and educate employees on how their benefits can best serve them.

Procedure

1. We will meet with either you or your benefits coordinator to:
    —assess your specific areas of interest in an employee benefits
       package
    —discuss your philosophy of compensation
2. We will collect information about the JFS Manufacturing Company, including:
       —an employee list
       —employees' birthdates and dependent status
       —copies of bills and enrollment books from present carriers

1

3. We will contact insurance firms that can:
    —provide the program you are looking for
    —insure you at the lowest rates
4. We will analyze the information we receive from insurance carriers.
5. We will present to you:
    —an analysis of your present program
    —our suggestion of a less expensive and more effective employee
    benefits program.
6. We will visit your firm monthly following adoption of a program. We
    will conduct a claims assistance meeting with employees and provide
    each employee with a printout detailing his or her benefits.

Record of Service

Reimbursement Services has successfully designed effective benefits
programs for over one hundred South Jersey firms. A list of clients will
be provided on request. We are experts in the field of analysis and
design. In addition, we have a twenty-four-hour phone number as well
as a staff experienced in handling claims and problems.

Cost to JFS

Our suggestions for a more effective benefits program are free. You pay
the normal cost of the plan to the insurance company, and we receive
from the carrier the usual agent's commission. All of our service of the
plan is also done without charge to you or your employees.

Schedule

Week 1—initial interview
—collection of data
—survey of insurance firms for information
Week 2—analysis of results
Week 3—presentation to JFS

2

tional supporting information about its capabilities. Such evidence suggests the likelihood of success in this case. At a general level of review, then, this proposal is well conceived. It identifies a problem, suggests a solution, and demonstrates the ability to carry through the work. Let's look now at how it is structured.

The proposal includes seven short sections, each labeled. The first, "Proposal," is the introduction, a brief (one-sentence) overview of the proposal itself. The remaining six sections constitute the proposal core:

Statement of Problem: Identification of the central problem to be solved.
Objectives: Transition to the solution section, laying out the specific goals of the work.
Procedure: The method of attack, here given in six detailed steps.
Record of Service: A component that justifies the work and demonstrates the proposer's ability to do the job by citing successful experience and capabilities.
Cost to JFS: The budget section, even though in this case there is no direct cost to the sponsor.
Schedule: Further justification and at the same time an amplification of the procedures section; a week-by-week accounting of what will be done.

This structure works well. The whole proposal is brief. Acceptance of it entails no financial obligation on the part of the JFS company, and thus the financial data need not be emphasized.

One additional feature should be noted. A letter of transmittal accompanies the proposal and provides the necessary logistical information concerning the proposer. Such a letter is common with proposals. This one takes the place, too, of a title page or cover, an element that would be included with longer proposals.

Finally, the proposal coheres. It subordinates information to one unifying sales pitch: a benefits program that will cost the company less and benefit the employees more. Key phrases carry this message: "an employee benefits program that fits the needs of the JFS Manufacturing Company and costs less than the plan currently in use"; "we aim to improve the employer/employee relationship through our service"; "our suggestions of a less expensive and more effective employee benefits program"; "our suggestions for a more effective benefits program." Reiterating the central message unifies the proposal and draws together the elements into a coherent whole.

This is a successful proposal. It addresses the audience's needs, structures information appropriately, and sends a single clear message. It sells.

Preparing Proposals: Guidelines

Many of our guidelines for bids apply as well to proposals, but with this example in mind, let's summarize some strategies for proposals:

1. Clearly identify a real problem. All proposals address problems. In a solicited proposal, the problem has already been assumed. Still, the proposer cannot assume too much but must clearly state the nature of the problem. In an unsolicited proposal, the writer must first establish the problem—*from the reader's point of view.*

An illustration: A large consulting firm responded to an RFP from a university hospital. The management of the hospital solicited proposals to develop a master plan to guide the hospital's development over the next decade. The management was convinced that it faced a serious space problem, and that it needed a rational plan for integrating a new building into its overall scheme. The consulting firm analyzed the hospital carefully and concluded that the real problem was a cumbersome organizational structure, which led to overlapping responsibilities and massive confusion about reporting lines. This problem, the group felt, had to be addressed before the space issue could be considered.

The consulting firm's proposal, however, was rejected. The hospital board saw it as unresponsive to the perceived need for more space. A rival proposal team, which also saw the organizational problems, subordinated the need for organizational change to a plan for physical development and thereby met both the perceived needs of the board and its own (and the other consulting firm's) analysis of management problems.

People who sell cars understand this point. If a customer is interested in high performance, talking about fuel efficiency is fatal to making the sale. If the customer wants "basic" transportation, emphasizing the plush interior won't do. Understanding what the customer wants and pitching the message to that perceived need are as important in writing proposals as in selling cars.

2. Describe a reasonable approach to solving the problem. Once you have identified the problem (the right one, of course), you must propose a reasonable way to solve it. Note carefully that the proposal does not present the solution itself. That step will come later, probably in a report (see Chapter 18), after you have carried out the work described in the proposal. What the proposal provides is a *method,* an approach that will reasonably lead to a solution or answer.

Here is one example. A large insurance company wanted to help the suburban municipality in which its headquarters were located to overcome the pressure on highways created by morning and evening rush-hour traffic. Almost twelve hundred workers arrived at the office for a 9 A.M. start and left at 5 P.M. One way to solve the problem was to adopt flexible work hours to stagger traffic. The company identified the problem clearly and solicited a proposal from a consulting firm for a study to evaluate the effectiveness of flexible hours in solving the problem. Here is the relevant section of the proposal, labeled "Approach to the Problem":

We will administer to all hourly and salaried employees a simple questionnaire (see Appendix) that will determine the likely impact of flexible working hours on the flow of traffic to and from the office. The questionnaire will ask each person to list his or her most likely times of arrival and departure (with information on carpooling) under the proposed policy. We then will code and process these data to prepare a master schedule showing the number of employees arriving between 7:30 A.M. and 9:30 A.M. and leaving between 3:30 P.M. and 6:00 P.M. Based on this schedule, we will evaluate the likely effectiveness of the policy on traffic patterns around the headquarters building.

Our final report will make a recommendation to guide you in deciding whether or not to adopt flexible work hours as a way of solving the traffic problem.

The approach defined here is relatively simple but has the advantage of yielding a good deal of concrete information on which a recommendation can be based. Note that the "approach" section is addressed exclusively to the *means;* it suggests not a solution to the problem, but a reasonable way to *reach* a solution.

3. Show that you can carry out the proposed approach—indeed, that you are the **best** *organization to do so.* A reader legitimately wonders: Can this person (or organization) pull it off? Having accepted the existence of the problem and the viability of the proposed method of attack, the reader now wants to know if *you* are the one to do the job: Do you have the experience and education? The physical resources? The contacts with the experts needed for additional help? The time and money required?

Sell yourself and your organization: people, time, equipment, money, and facilities. Convince the reader. Show any related experience that proves your track record on similar projects.

Preparing Proposals: Structure

Conventional formats help proposal writers to control and effectively deploy information. Company policy on format varies, and as always, you should follow the conventions prescribed by your employer or by the sponsoring agency to which the proposal is submitted. Here we discuss a generalized structure applicable to all proposals—short or long; memo, letter, or other; internal or external; solicited or unsolicited.

This generalized structure includes three components: front matter, proposal core, and back matter. The first and last of these can be quickly described. We will concentrate on the proposal core.

Formal proposals require the same front matter as major reports (see Chapter 20): cover (with title, date of submission, name of sponsor, name of proposer, and the like); executive summary or abstract; and table of contents. Back matter is also similar to that for a report: bibliography and appendixes.

The proposal core focuses on the three guidelines we mentioned: problem, approach, and qualifications or justification. Here is a typical list of headings, similar to those in the JFS Manufacturing Company benefits proposal:

Introduction
Problem statement
Objectives
Solution or method of attack
Justification
Budget

Introduction

The introduction briefs the reader on the main points of the whole proposal and prepares her or him for the reading. It provides an overview of both the substance and the process of the proposal. It aims at a broad audience both in management and in any technical specialty on which the proposal draws.

Problem Statement

The problem statement conceptualizes the basic problem to be addressed. For example, the problem statement in a proposal for analyzing and improving the quality control system of a thread manufacturer might be this:

> The Matthews Thread Company has experienced a 32 percent increase in returned shipments from customers based on unacceptable quality, and this increase is eroding profit margins. An improved quality-control system is needed.

A complex problem may lead to a longer and more detailed problem statement. To show that the problem is recognized within a profession or discipline, the writer may also refer to published literature:

> Economists have been unsuccessful in determining the price elasticity of demand in higher education, a problem that makes tuition setting difficult for colleges and universities that want to predict the impact of tuition on enrollment.

In a solicited proposal, the writer essentially repeats—with appropriate modification and elaboration—the problem as defined in the RFP. The writer can assume familiarity with the technical field: A proposal to accountants can freely use the language of accounting. But because in an unsolicited proposal the writer must first convince the audience that a problem exists, the problem statement is less easy to compose. Often the writer has to move toward the problem through a series of statements that the reader will clearly agree with until the proposal can be brought around to the core of the problem and induce the reader's agreement with that.

Here is the problem statement for an unsolicited proposal:

> Industrial spying costs American business millions of dollars a year. Research is expensive, and when research results are passed to competing firms, the short- and long-term losses can be substantial. Why should your competition gain the benefits of *your* research? To prevent such illegal "leaking" of industrial research results, Securitech has developed a program to (1) audit your corporate research security policy and practices and (2) recommend improvements that will protect your costly investment in research. Our approach is described in Section 1.1 below.

The problem is defined generally but in terms designed to make the recipients of the proposal see its applicability to them. Once they accept the problem as real for them, they are prepared to read further about the means of solving it.

Objectives

The objectives section is a transitional element between the problem and the solution segments. It establishes specific objectives for the proposed work that will lead to the solution of the problem. For example, in the proposal dealing with price elasticity of demand in higher education, the objective might be

> To develop an equation based on historical enrollment and tuition data at XYZ University to predict the effects of tuition changes on enrollment.

Proposals may have one or more objectives. Generally, the objectives should be measurable: to increase the profit margin to 14 percent, to reduce the deficit to 3 percent, to decrease employee absenteeism by 2 percent a month for two years. Whenever possible, make the objectives quantitative: numbers of people, dollars, machines, or whatever.

Solution or Method of Attack

The solution section defines the method of attack that will be followed to solve the problem, such as a review of existing literature, an experiment or set of controlled observations, a "what if" simulation, or an in-house survey. This section answers the reader's question, "How are you going to solve my problem?" It must therefore be detailed and authoritative, stating clearly the actual work that will be done. It is also desirable to provide a schedule linking the parts of the work to demonstrate that everything will indeed come together in the end. For example, the schedule might include three weeks to review the published literature and interview company executives, three weeks to design an appropriate survey instrument, two weeks to interpret the collected data, and one week to summarize and make recommendations. Most schedules are displayed in visual form (see Chapter 8).

A schedule serves two good purposes: It helps the proposer to structure the work to be done, and it convinces the sponsor that the proposer knows his or her business and has a realistic grasp of the problem and the time and energy required to find a solution. The absence of a detailed schedule not only may leave an unstructured task to be performed but may also leave the reader feeling that the writer is vague and unorganized.

Justification

The justification section proves that the writer can do the job. It shows the writer's track record and details her or his resources. Some of the needed information is considered "boilerplate," prepared data plugged in as needed: current detailed résumés of the principal investigators and others; lists of past customers, clients, and sponsors; inventories of computer hardware and software available in your business; statement of finances bearing on the project; management structure. In short, informal proposals, much of this information may already be known and can therefore be quickly summarized. But even when the resources are not detailed in full, the audience must still be persuaded that the writer can do the job.

Budget

The budget gets serious attention from reviewers of proposals because it is really the quantitative abstract of the whole document. The budget expresses in the medium of money everything contained in the proposal and therefore represents a brief summary understood at a glance by expert reviewers. Budget analysis allows them to assess the value they will obtain from you. Reviewers look not for the cheapest proposal but for the one promising the greatest value. An unrealistically low budget is often regarded as a sign that the proposer doesn't understand the problem and may therefore not be able to reach the solution quickly and effectively. An inflated budget, of course, can also be a reason for rejection. In the proposal business, it's a commonplace that noticeably low or high budgets are equally destructive to a proposal's chances of being accepted. The "right" budget is the one that realistically assesses and presents costs.

In organizations that deal extensively with proposal preparation, budget specialists handle the details, and customers or sponsors likewise have budget analysts who review that segment. But the person responsible for the overall proposal still is responsible for seeing that the budget is appropriate and well integrated with the whole package. Even though financial experts may prepare and review the budget, it should be understandable to nonspecialists and should not be a maze of figures requiring the translating capabilities of a CPA.

Preparing Proposals: One Clear Message

The components we have just described may lead you to think of proposals as collections of discrete pieces. In some proposal-oriented companies that observation may be true, as the paste-and-scissors approach dominates when time is short and the pressure is high. But proposals really are unified documents that deliver one clear message.

As sales documents, proposals must make a single point and make it clearly and repeatedly, as advertisments carry to the consumer a single strong image or theme. To work, a proposal must have a pitch, and all elements have to repeat, restate, and emphasize that pitch. In the absence of a clear pitch or message, the proposal dissolves. It loses effectiveness as its separate parts deliver multiple (and perhaps contradictory) messages.

The unifying theme—the big picture—of the proposal can be stated as a simple phrase, as in these examples:

- Cost reduction through improved control.
- Improvement of employee morale through benefits packages tailored to individual needs.
- A better environment that will increase worker productivity.

These are unifying themes around which proposals can be shaped. The theme can be announced first in the title, developed in brief form in the executive summary, previewed in the introduction, and repeated throughout the problem, solution, and justification sections.

Centering the proposal on one clear message—and making that message explicitly apparent to the audience—allows the writer to bring together the segments that comprise an effective proposal.

After Proposals: The Progress Report

Your proposal has been accepted. Now the next stage begins: You carry out the work that the proposal committed you to as the best way to solve the identified problem. The sponsor or customer may simply wait until that work is done; but often, especially in large projects that require considerable time, the sponsor requires one or more progress reports (sometimes called *status* or *interim* or *periodic reports*). These ensure that adequate progress toward the goal is being made. Progress or status reports are effective management tools that help both reader and proposer in validating approaches (and changing them if necessary) and assessing outcomes.

If by law, convention, or special agreement one or more such reports are required, that fact should be mentioned in the original proposal. Even if no formal arrangement for them is made, it's wise to submit progress reports just to remind the client that work is continuing. Such a reminder helps to reinforce the image you want the sponsor to have of you as responsible and dependable. It keeps communication open and builds goodwill.

Progress reports are conceptually simple. They report the progress made so far. They generally have three parts: what has been accomplished, what remains, and what problems or issues require special attention that may not have been originally foreseen. Figure 17–5 is a progress report on the JFS Manufacturing Company project. The first section surveys the work accomplished and is structured according to the original tasks. For each, a brief summary of the work is supplied. The second section indicates the overall status of the project with respect to the proposed schedule. The third section describes the work remaining. The last section presents a summary of the project—what has been completed and what is about to be done.

One feature of progress reports is clear here: The report is closely tied to the original proposal. It refers specifically to tasks and schedule components listed in the proposal. This practice simplifies the organization of the progress report because one need only follow the original structure.

This report does not suggest any problems in the work. That's a happy occurrence, but often things don't go as smoothly as planned. The progress report provides the opportunity to identify problems that have arisen and that may require modification of the approach presented in the original proposal. If needed information is unavailable or if the original estimates proved wrong, the progress report allows an opportunity to point out these matters to the sponsor before the project ends with an unexpected outcome. Sometimes it is necessary to renegotiate proposals based on new facts or interpretations that have developed during the course of the investigation. If it is necessary to make changes, you should alert the customer as early as possible.

In general, progress reports should be brief, factual, and realistic.

REIMBURSEMENT SERVICES

P.O. Box 74 / Moorestown, NJ 08057 / 609-636-3588

November 18, 19xx

Mr. James Simpkins, Sr.
JFS Manufacturing Company
3645 West Broad Street
Camden, NJ 09064

Dear Mr. Simpkins:

The enclosed progress report details my work on the proposed project to design an effective employee benefits program for the JFS Manufacturing Company.

I hope you will find the results to date satisfactory. Please phone if you have questions or suggestions. We look forward to completing the project for you as scheduled.

Sincerely,

Jennifer Friedman

Jennifer Friedman
Benefits Counselor

Enclosure

FIGURE 17–5. Progress report (courtesy of Jennifer Friedman).

REIMBURSEMENT SERVICES

Progress Report for JFS Manufacturing Company

Work Accomplished

Here is an overview of the work to date. I have completed one third of the work on this project.

Task 1: Initial Interview

On November 14, I met with Janet Cunningham, the benefits coordinator for JFS Manufacturing. Janet informed me that the administration is dissatisfied with the high costs of the present group-insurance plan. In addition, JFS is interested in maintaining the best employees through a comprehensive benefits program. They prefer a 100 percent plan but would accept an 80 percent plan if the cost were considerably less and there were other benefits of some significance.

Task 2: Collection of Data

Janet Cunningham also provided me with certain data necessary to our project. The JFS Manufacturing Company's present major medical carrier is Blue Cross of New Jersey, and the present group life carrier is Phoenix Mutual. A copy of the October billing from Blue Cross provided the names, birth dates, and dependent status of employees. Unfortunately, Janet could not find a copy of the latest billing from Phoenix, but she promised to mail me one when the November billing arrives.

Task 3: Information Sent to Insurance Companies

I sent census information to four insurance companies asking all to follow a minimum life schedule and to show me their suggestions for a dental program. I have also asked each insurance firm for specific information as outlined below:

CIGNA—Standard wraparound on Blue Cross with a variety of surgical schedules and deductibles.

Guardian Life—100 percent plan superimposed on Blue Cross 14/20 series and Rider J. with a $100 deductible.

New York Life—Standard 100 percent wraparound plan.

1

Metropolitan—Comprehensive program with a $100 deductible and a $500 out-of-pocket maximum, both with and without first-dollar coverages.

Schedule Status

At the end of the first week, work on this project is on schedule. I am waiting for proposals to come in from the various carriers that have been solicited.

Future Work

When I receive proposals from CIGNA, Guardian Life, Metropolitan, and New York Life, I will analyze each to determine which firm can provide the most effective package at the least cost. Next, I will put together a presentation folder and report to explain my recommendation. This report will be complete with an analysis of both JFS's present plan and the recommended plan. I will then meet with you to explain the programs and answer any questions you may have.

Schedule

Completed———Week 1 —initial interview
                    —collection of data
                    —survey of insurance carriers

Entering———Week 2 —analysis of results
              Week 3 —presentation

2

An honest assessment of where the project stands is desirable for everyone's sake. A proposal involves trust. The sponsor exhibits trust in you, and you in turn show your trust in the sponsor by doing the work as contracted. The progress report, in addition to being the simple transfer of necessary information, is a vehicle for strengthening the trusting relationship that should obtain between sponsor and proposer. It demonstrates that you are meeting your obligation—and that you are therefore not only likely to complete the project at hand but also warrant future support. The specific work of a proposal may be short-term, but the relationship with a customer should be long-term—

that's the essence of good business practice and applies to proposals as it does to any form of business communication.

Exercises

1. Write a request for bid (RFB) for three filing cabinets for your department.

2. Write a bid responding to the RFB you prepared for Exercise 1. Based on your experience as a responder to the bid, would you write the RFB differently? Why? How?

3. Go to the purchasing office (it may be called the business office) at your college and ask if you can have a copy of the guidelines used for preparing requests for bids. Examine them to see what effect on the *writing* of an RFB such organizational policies and procedures have. If your college is government-supported, look in particular for the *legal* requirements and try to gauge their impact on the writer of an RFB.

4. A chain of grocery stores in the St. Louis area sent your consulting firm a request for proposal (RFP) for a study of its employee benefits package. Before you submit the proposal, you are asked to send a one-page outline as a preproposal so the chain can get an early sense of the extent of the project and its likely costs. What form will your outline take? What elements or sections will you include? How much space will you give to each item?

5. Here are some topics on which students in business communication courses have written proposals:
   (a) The organizational structure of a fraternity.
   (b) Campus parking facilities and regulations.
   (c) Computerization of the inventory system in a sporting-goods store.
   (d) The selection of fire-retardant wall coverings for a new motel.
   (e) The financial impact of two-for-one promotions at a video store.
   (f) The effect of colors on the buying habits of men in clothing stores.
For each topic, complete this sentence, which will serve as an introduction to the proposal: "This is a proposal to . . ." Be precise in phrasing the sentence, since it will *control* the entire project and the final document that will emerge from it.

   For each topic, using the one-sentence control statement, prepare an outline of the proposal showing the major elements that the final document will contain.

   What kind of information (see Chapters 4 and 5) will you need to complete the proposal? For example: review of professional literature, observation and experiment, survey, books, and reports.

6. You are working on a year-long project to track the relationship between the market price of Abott Oil Services Company common shares and the market price of the common shares of five other domestic oil producers. The proj-

ect requires massive number crunching, and the week before your first quarterly progress report is due, the mainframe you are using crashes and you lose a great many data. Fortunately, you can reconstruct all the data, but the crash has set you back several weeks in your work. Write a one-paragraph report on this part of the project that honestly relates the problem but that demonstrates to the sponsor your ability to recover and to bring the whole project in on time. Before you begin to write, clarify for yourself the precise communication goal of the paragraph: What are you communicating, and why?

7. As part of a proposal to the U.S. Department of Commerce for a study of the impact of foreign-car imports on employment in the domestic steel industry, you must include a schedule of tasks for the eighteen months you expect the work to take. Prepare the schedule in as much detail as possible. Don't forget these tasks: data collection, progress reports, final editing, and production. There are many others, of course. Try to get them all into a form that will be easily understandable to the sponsor and useful to you as project director.

Business Reports: Strategies

So why are written reports necessary at all? They obviously can't provide timely information. What they do is constitute an archive of data, help to validate *ad hoc* inputs, and catch, in safety-net fashion, anything you may have missed. But reports also have another, totally different function. As they are formulated and written, the author is forced to be more precise than he might be orally. Hence their value stems from the discipline and the thinking the writer is forced to impose upon himself as he identifies and deals with trouble spots. Reports are more a medium of self-discipline than a way to convey information. Writing the report is important; reading it often is not.[1]

This comment from Andrew S. Grove, President of the Intel Corporation, points to three major purposes for reports, from the writer's point of view:

1. To serve as an archive of information.
2. To discipline the writer's thinking.
3. To convey information to readers.

Grove stressed the first and second purposes. Indeed, these goals shape many reports. Here's H. W. Gillett, former president of Battelle Memorial Institute, a large contract research organization, on the researcher's own need to write:

One of the most important reasons for writing reports is because it forces the experimenter to review the project, see whether it is getting anywhere, and to reorient his attack if it isn't. What you carry in your head and have in your notebook will generally turn out to have big holes in it when you once get it down on paper in orderly fashion. Without writing it up, you are not likely to realize the existence of these gaps.[2]

So writing reports serves the writer. Reports often must serve the readers, too. Many reports don't get their work done until they are read and acted on. We can define a *report* broadly as a document that presents information developed during a project. That broad definition includes many kinds of reports. Here are some scales that measure differences in reports:

Goal: to record⟶to inform ⟶ to persuade

Readers: one⟶many

known⟶unknown

---

[1]Andrew S. Grove, "Keep a Watch on Your Most Precious Resource," *The Wall Street Journal*, 12 September 1983, 32.

[2]"The Psychology of Report Writing," *Battelle News* reprint.

Writers: one———→ group

Approach: routine———→specialized

Presentation: informal (often, a memo)———→formal, full dress

Length: one page———→volumes

    This chapter provides an overview of the range of reports on each of these scales. It then discusses some techniques for analyzing information in preparation for report writing and ends with a case study: how to write a case analysis report. Chapter 19 offers guidelines for writing the major segments of a report: the introduction, the middle, and the ending. Chapter 20 discusses the ancillary elements of a full-dress report.

Report Goals

Grove's analysis can be modified a bit to identify different kinds of reports according to their goals:

1. Documentation reports.
2. Information reports.
3. Persuasive reports.

Documentation Reports

All reports, as we saw in Chapter 4, derive from information. That information may occur in the form of facts, observations, interpretations, and/or opinions. Documentation reports are close to the raw data. They are designed to create an archive on a project, to record details. They are highly specific and technical in language and approach and are expressed more in visuals than in words. Brokers' profiles of corporations often fit this purpose, as do rudimentary trip reports and project reports sometimes headed "memo for file" and compiled by writers essentially for themselves.

Information Reports

Information reports have more public intentions. They assist a reader in *understanding* information. Within a company, such reports fit the three communication goals discussed in Chapter 1: definition, control, and maintenance. You write reports to *define* the organization and to articulate its goals. You also write to *control* and monitor activities toward those goals and to *maintain* good housekeeping in the company. Chapter 22 looks in detail at such internal reports.

Persuasive Reports

Persuasive reports aim at action. Their goal is to persuade the readers to do something or to come to some decision. You may write a report that *recommends,* for example

- Formation of an intramural softball league.
- Implementation of a new marketing strategy for a family restaurant.
- Installation of security devices at a shopping mall.

One project may lead to each kind of report. The documentation report may provide the basis for an information report that is later shaped into a persuasive one. In the process of conversion, you shift emphasis, tuck away details, and use different structures for arranging material, as you'll see.

Report Readers

Except for strictly documentary and personal texts, most reports are not complete until they are *read* and understood or acted on.[3] Moreover, most reports, like the solicited proposals discussed in Chapter 17, *respond* to a specific reader request. Someone—often, your supervisor—assigns a project to you. The sole outcome of the project may be a report. In reading the report, then, your supervisor has certain expectations based on the assignment.

Some reports address only one reader—the supervisor, for example. But some address many readers. Sometimes the writer *knows* the reader or readers. Sometimes the readers, or at least some of them, are *unknown.* Reports aimed at many readers may address all simultaneously, and each reader may act or send back comments independently to the writer. Or reports may address readers in sequence. Such reports, as they hop from desk to desk, often gather covering notes and annotations in the margins. The *readers* in effect become adjunct *writers* as they shape a report through an approval route. Moreover, the readers may open the report for different reasons and with different expectations, depending on their role in the organization and their

---

[3] For a discussion of general categories of readers, review the appropriate sections in Chapter 3.

personal tastes and interests. Some skim. Some just look at the pictures. Some read every word and number.

One way to look at a *sequence* of readers is to think of *primary, secondary,* and *immediate* readers roles, as discussed in Chapter 3.[4] The primary reader is the person who requested the report or who is chiefly responsible for acting on any implications in the report. Secondary readers are other people who need to know what's in the report because they will be affected by any changes it implies, but they do not have decision-making power. Immediate readers are those who will pass on the report to the primary reader.

For example, a report from a consulting firm recommending increased funding levels from the U.S. Department of Transportation (DOT) for public transportation in Philadelphia has these readers. The *primary* readers are at the DOT: program managers, financial officers, and the Assistant Secretary of Transportation. Some readers are economists, some engineers, some political scientists, and some political appointees with no background in any of these areas. Before the report reaches the DOT, however, other *immediate* readers at the consulting firm—the writer's boss, other members of the project team, and an in-house editor—will read and approve the report. *Secondary* readers who may respond to the recommendations in the report include other federal agencies, local authorities whose operations may be affected, the press, Congress and other oversight groups that monitor the use of federal funds, and interested bystanders who order the report through the National Technical Information Service, a clearinghouse for government reports.

All readers of a report probably look for some common core of information. But beyond that, readers segment into different groups seeking different information. A report written for many readers, then, has to address both shared and specialized needs. Figure 18–1 shows some writing implications of different audience profiles. The report must be particularly well structured and must be labeled to cue readers about what information will be found where. Appendixes are helpful in siphoning off details in highly technical reports.

Report Writers

You may well write a report by yourself. *You* are in charge of the investigation and *you* are responsible for its presentation. But often, writers in organizations don't write alone. They write as part of a team.

---

[4]This categorization derives from an excellent study of report writing: J. C. Mathes and Dwight Stevenson, *Designing Technical Reports* (Indianapolis: Bobbs-Merrill, 1976).

Question	Answer	Implications
Why is the audience reading this report?	Has to, but isn't really interested.	Make it lively and brief; use introduction to attract interest.
	Will have to summarize its contents for someone higher up.	Write a clear, precise executive summary (see Chapter 20).
	Loves the topic and can't read enough on it.	Provide all the relevant details and don't hesitate to elaborate on interesting points.
What is the audience's level of technical understanding?	High—at least up to yours.	Don't hesitate to use specialized language, and don't overexplain.
	Low—lay audience.	Simplify discussions of technical matters; translate specialized language into clear English.
What can or will the audience do as a result of reading this report?	Take some action.	Clearly focus on the conclusions and the recommended actions; say what should be done and why.
	File for reference.	Be sure all aspects of the issue are covered adequately; don't worry about specific recommendations.
Are there any unique "political" implications that you should be aware of?	Yes—the sponsoring agency already did a study showing contradictory results.	Downplay the differences between the conclusions—but make your own clearly apparent.
	Yes—the sponsoring agency doesn't normally use the approach you did.	Make a special effort to explain why you chose the approach you did—its advantages and so on.
	Yes—Congress has expressed doubts about this project.	Give special attention to the secondary audience (Congress) and try to be especially persuasive.
	Yes—public opinion seems to be against this idea.	Write, for a lay audience, a well-developed defense or explanation of the idea.

FIGURE 18–1. Writing implications of audience profile.

The first step in team writing is for everyone on the team to agree on the report's *goal* and *readers*. That decision may be simple—or it may be the subject of heated debate. Agreement, however, is the basis of good teamwork. Then the team draws up two plans: one for what they will *do*—the tasks—and one for what they will *write*—a preliminary outline of the document. Either plan may be used to coordinate team-work. Each member (designated here by initials) may perform one *task:*

JBC   Preliminary literature search
ABK   Development of the statistical base
PSS   Coordination and information gathering with other teams
SSC   Preparation of visuals
BBP   Writing and production of report

This division assures some degree of coherence in the text because it is *written* by *one* person—presumably the best writer on the team. Or each member may write one segment, as indicated in the plan for the document, with perhaps some joint writing of the introduction and the summary. If that's the division, then some *one* person still has to be responsible in the end for getting the report out the door. Chapter 11 provides further details concerning team writing.

Routine and Specialized Reports

Some reports are a matter of *routine* and are written at certain desig-nated times (for example, at month's end or year's end) and in an approved and required form. They are, in effect, fill-in-the-blank exer-cises, best structured around the form. These include many internal documents, like quarterly activities reports, segments of annual re-ports, trip reports, progress reports, job descriptions, and personnel evaluations (see Chapter 22). The use of creative license in such docu-ments is usually not welcomed.

On the other hand, some reports, although conventional in format, are one-of-a-kind occasions. Such *specialized reports* must match the lines of the material to specific reader goals. The structure is particu-larly significant. It requires more creativity and attention from the writer than filling in the blanks of a routine report.

Informal and Formal Reports

An *informal* report is usually presented in memo or letter form (see Chapter 19). Most of the day-to-day reporting within an organization and between an organization and its customers fits this framework. Such reports are rarely more than five or six pages long.

A *formal* report, on the other hand, is given full-dress treatment;

that is, it is placed in a cover and is accompanied by certain ancillary elements: a title page, an abstract or executive summary, and a list of references if printed materials were used in its preparation. Long formal reports also include a table of contents, a list of figures and tables, appendixes, and perhaps even an index. Each of these elements is discussed in detail in Chapter 20.

Report Length

Reports come in all lengths, from one page to volumes. Indeed, when you are assigned to write a report, one important constraint to clarify is the intended length. Length is an indicator of the amount of detail and the complexity of development required in the assignment.

Preparing the Report

You'll probably find that creating a business report, particularly one that is formal, specialized, long, and meant to persuade multiple readers, is like painting a room. The actual writing, like the actual painting, usually occupies only a small percentage of the total task time. The preparation—stripping, washing, sanding, spackling, taping woodwork, and putting down drop cloths—takes perhaps 50 percent of the time. Cleanup may account for another 25 percent. The painting itself may take, at most, 25 percent. Count on your preparation as taking at least 50 percent of your time in compiling a major report, too. You may become edgy because you feel you are not *writing*. But the words will go on smoothly—and will stick—if you prepare well.

That preparation includes careful collection and analysis of information and careful assessment of the context for writing. In analyzing and generating information for your report, apply these two strategies:

1. Classify your research problem.
2. Develop routine questions.

Classify Your Research Problem

Think about how the problem you are working on might fit into one of the following groupings: problems of fact, problems of means, or problems of value.

When we work on *problems of fact*, we're simply trying to find out *what is* (although the work necessary to find that out may be difficult):

What is the accounting system currently employed at X Company? What is the gross national product of each country in the Common Market? What are current trends in the men's neckwear industry? To answer such questions we require facts. We observe or read about other people's observations. We often count things. The result of such an investigation is usually a documentation report or an information report.

When we work on *problem of means* we require different information. These are *how to* problems. Perhaps we need to design a procedure for assigning computer terminals to project members, a method of paying for a new athletic facility, a management information system for a restaurant, or a benefits package for a small company. A variant is a *why* problem: Why did our profits decline? Why didn't the toothpaste pump sell? Why did our model house attract only five visitors over a two-month period? Such a problem may lead to an information report simply detailing the design or the explanation. But more likely you'll be asked to recommend some solution to meet the need or to overcome the problem. Thus you'll write a persuasive report designed to entice the reader to implement your solution.

When we work on *problems of value*, we often enter a more abstract and subjective realm. Such problems require an investigator to measure something or to determine its relative desirability, usefulness, or importance on some scale. The standard of measurement may be fixed, or developing that standard, too, may be part of the problem.

In a simple form, such a problem is routine. You measure a new commodity against an objective scale: Does this cereal contain the number of grams of sugar indicated on the box? Is the patient receiving the diet specified by the physician? Have you accumulated enough credit hours of the right type to be certified for graduation? You check against the standard.

More complex problems require you to digest (often with the aid of a computer) vast quantities of data and to establish criteria: What are the top 20 NCAA Division 1 college soccer teams in the country this week? The ranking published in *The New York Times* derives from a consensus of the twenty-four members of the regional rating board of the Intercollegiate Soccer Association of America. The board, of course, favors teams that win over teams that lose. But in addition, the members have to consider the difficulties of the schedules of each competitor, the records of competition among teams in the top twenty, the point spread in the scores, and other, more subjective issues. Politics enters. Subjectivity enters—as looking at other rankings for the same week and listening to locker room conversation show.

Value problems, then, require judgment calls. You accumulate every bit of pertinent information you can; screen it through the best, the most specific criteria you (often in consultation with others) can establish; and end up with an evaluation: You rank the soccer teams. You determine the most effective policy for the U.S. Forest Service to implement in controlling avalanches in the western U.S. You select the *best* benefits package for a client company. In your report, you may push that evaluation to a recommendation: You recommend that the Forest Service implement a particular avalanche policy. You recommend a particular benefits package. Your research, then, leads to a *persuasive* report.

Classifying the problem you are working on will take you a long way toward determining what information is pertinent to the report and how the report should be structured to exploit that information.

Develop Routine Questions

Another way to generate and analyze information is to develop a set of questions to ask about the investigation. Journalists, so the story goes, both begin an investigation and check on it with the five W's: Who? What? When? Where? Why? You can also reconstruct the course of your investigation with questions like the following:

1. What question did I ask as I began my investigation?
2. To find an answer, what method did I use?
3. Using this method, what results did I obtain?
4. From these results, what can I conclude?

The answers to these questions provide a rough structure for the report itself: 1. statement of problem; 2. procedure; 3. results; 4. conclusions. Figure 18–2 provides another sample set of questions. Adapt these to each report you need to write.

A Case in Point: The Case Analysis Report

Let's look at how you might prepare and write one common assignment in a management class: the case analysis report. A business *case* describes some slice in time in the life of an organization. Typically the case includes a chronology of significant events, statements by organizational members, and sometimes information about competitors and indicators of performance. Some of the information is relevant to one or more targeted problems, and some is not. Usually the cases are based on actual organizations and events. You may have to provide a

Context

Who asked me to look into this?

Why did they ask *me?*

What brought them into the problem?

Who else knew about this? Who knows now?

Has anything like this happened in the company before?

What was the outcome then?

What limits do I have in solving this problem? Budget? Time? Overlap
    with someone else's responsibility?

What priority does this problem have in the company?

What was I specifically asked to do?

Are there any hidden agendas?

My Response

Where did I look for information?

What chief areas did I study?

Whom did I talk with?

What did I read?

What surveys or observations did I make?

What tools did I use?

What results did I obtain from all this?

My Conclusions

What do the results add up to? Short-term? Long-term?

Do the results show any trends?

How do these results relate to other findings?

Are these results accurate?

Are these results valid?

What tests did I apply to ensure accuracy and validity?

Do my conclusions match my assignment?

Have I overlooked anything I was asked to do?

So What?

In the reader's terms and the organization's terms, how does all this
    matter?

Can I recommend any action? Was I asked to?

Is any further work planned or needed?

FIGURE 18–2. Questions about an investigation.

recommendation for turning the company around. That case analysis is a *report* that you write for your professor or perhaps for some reader mentioned in the case. Good reports *analyze* the situation rather than just *summarizing* the case. Here are some guidelines for writing this special report: the case analysis.

Guidelines for Analysis

1. Read the case quickly for an overview of the situation.

2. Read it again slowly. Begin to assemble the facts of the case. You may simply list the known information, or you may assemble charts to show relationships. On the basis of these facts, begin to note the apparent objectives of the company (or the departments within a company) along with current policies and strategies.

3. Read again slowly; determine the core problem in the case and any subproblems. Classify the problem: Fact? Means? Value? Look for *dissonance.* Look for deviations from a standard. An unmet objective is a problem; so is a discrepancy between the present situation and the desired future position, or between the current role of some individual and the desired action. In looking for problems and their causes, identify the elements in the situation that have to be changed before anything else can be changed. See how this company's problems fit any general set of problems that you've read about in textbooks or discussed in class. Note the *causes* of the problems (but don't just look for scapegoats). Problems usually have complex, not simple, causes. Tie these causes to concepts you've read about, for example, poor planning or inadequate task design. Note any threats to the company's continuing vitality and any opportunities that the company might be missing to enhance its productivity.

4. If appropriate, read other sources to find economic or industry information that provides a setting for the company's situation.

5. Build a framework for selecting and organizing the pertinent information in the case. For example, peg your information to the company's goals and anything that is blocking their achievement. Or look at key individuals. Or examine informal groups and motivation.

6. Once you have identified the chief problem and the subproblems, develop a set of options for solution. Don't be content with just one answer to the problems. Play with various possibilities. In identifying the *options*, assess the organization's strengths and weaknesses and methods for taking advantage of the strengths and offsetting the weaknesses. Note how the organization interacts with its environment and its market segment, note its position relative to the competition, and assess its goals and plans as well as management (capabilities,

range, and numbers), finances, accounting control, organizational structure, production system, and marketing strategies.

7. Then set criteria for identifying the *best* option for action:

Relevance: Does the option resolve the causes identified?

Risk: What is the ratio between the expected gain and its cost?

Economy of effort: Does the scale of the solution match that of the problem?

Timing: Are you changing the vision of the company? Then steam ahead. Are you changing habits? Then move more slowly.

Limitations of resources: Does the solution respect the limits in financial, physical, and human resources?

8. Apply the criteria to the alternatives and prepare a specific set of recommendations for action. The decision you select must be one acceptable to the persons affected. It must be one that will work. Note how the decision will be implemented.

The Report

Most professors set their own constraints on the shape of the final case analysis report. But here is a good general plan:

Summary: Write a short overview of the main causes of the problem and your recommendations.

Problem statement: Briefly identify the problem or problems.

Analysis: Bring together here the best points of your analysis. Do not rehash the case, but pull together the pertinent facts to support your analysis of causes and options and to tie this information to management concepts.

Recommendations: Give your plan for correcting the problems. Such recommendations should be consistent with the analysis; that is, if poor planning was a cause, propose changes in planning, not in structure.

Achieving Report Goals

One engineer in a large corporation defines a good report as one that "goes away." It leaves his desk, goes out to his readers, does its work— and does not return to haunt him. You can't fully control what happens to your reports when they leave you, but control what you can so that the report achieves your own goal and gives the readers what they need in order to accomplish the organization's work.

Exercises

1. Develop a report from a case study that you encountered in a business class. In the class, you may have analyzed the case as a student outsider. Instead, take the role of someone mentioned in the case and write from that person's perspective. Write *to* someone else who is mentioned in the case, or look beyond the case to other possible audiences, either inside or outside the organization. Who would be interested in the information? What leverage might the audience have to *change* something in the organization or otherwise to act in response to your information?

If you work in a group in a course or on a project, write a brief report (two or three pages) to your professor about the group's activities in the project. Assess and analyze each person's behavior and the group's behavior as a whole. Use your understanding of psychology and management theory for the analysis. Look at communication in the group, motivation, leadership roles, goal setting, control mechanisms, and the like. Measure the group's productivity. Then recommend changes (if necessary) to make the group more productive. The professor is your *primary* audience, but assume that you will also distribute the report to other members of the group.

3. Faced with the prospect of writing a report, many students in business communication courses have a hard time choosing a topic. But topics are everywhere.

(a) Use a case from a management or marketing text or from a business communications casebook.

(b) Select a problem on campus. A college or university, of course, is an *organization*—often a complex one. Think of a problem on campus that you could develop into either an *information* report that describes the problem or a *persuasive* report that recommends action. Who is the appropriate person or persons to read the report? Who has jurisdiction over that concern? What *role* will you assume as the writer: Interested student? University employee? Outside professional consultant? Here are some topics; narrow these for a report, or think of others:

Parking
Campus security
Academic calendar
Intramural programs
Athletic facilities for general use
Town–gown relations
Library policies (for example, excessive noise in the library)
Access to computers in dorms and computer centers
Major and minor course requirements

(c) Use your own work experience as a basis for a report. Write to your supervisor, or assume some role other than your real one on the job. Write an internal report or an external one to a customer, a client, or an oversight group (see Chapter 22). Here are some possibilities:

A marketing plan for a restaurant

An advertising plan for a deli

Improved posting and filing techniques for a small business

A motivational program for part-time workers in a store

A better inventory system for a record store

Recommended purchases to start a karate studio or a fitness salon

4. In selecting a topic, *ask questions.* For example, here are some questions to consider:

- What mix of stores is appropriate for a new shopping mall in X community?
- Should the ABC Company move its offices to X?
- What is the best car for X customer?
- What stocks and/or bonds should X client buy?
- Who works for Z Corporation?
- What programs are needed to improve productivity at X Inc.?

5. Construct a *control statement* (see Chapter 6) for an information report and then change the statement to one that would work for a persuasive report. Work through a series of such statements for different topics. For example:

Information report: This report describes current management practices at the XYZ Corporation.

Persuasive report: This report recommends that the XYZ Corporation implement a management-by-objectives program in its home office.

6. In the reference section of the library, look through the *Monthly Catalog of U.S. Government Publications* for the titles of reports on some topic you are interested in. Then locate and read the report. Where does the report fit on each of the scales on pp. 338–39? Or if you have access to a corporate report, measure it on the scales.

Business Reports: Structure and Style

19

Reports work because they make a point—the right point; because they support the point with accurate evidence strategically deployed; and because they express the point and the evidence in a style that readers find engaging and informative. Let's look at how you can achieve a report that works.

Structure

All reports, whatever their individual differences, are composed of three segments: an introduction, a middle, and an ending. Here is advice on writing each segment. At the end of the chapter, you'll find an informal information report on corporate fitness programs that displays the segments working together.

Introduction

When do you write the introduction to a report? You may start there as a way of building your own momentum for composing the draft. If so, you'll probably want to come back to the introduction at the end of your drafting to incorporate whatever changes in structure and information you discover in writing. Many authors, however, start writing in the middle, comfortably expressing familiar material, and then compose the introduction at the end when they've confirmed in prose how the story comes out.

Whenever you *write* the introduction, however, remember that readers often form an impression of an entire project on the basis of the first page or two of the report. Although different readers may read the report itself selectively, *every* reader will probably read the introduction closely. Those pages are critical. You must pull the readers immediately away from whatever occupied their thoughts before reading and set their thoughts on your cause. Reaffirm your goal before you write. Is it to

Arouse interest?

Influence an attitude?

Provide neutral information?

Convey the solution to a problem?

Urge the reader to action?

Begin with something familiar to the reader and gradually move the reader toward the new. Most business reports are directly structured. The introduction covers these topics:

1. The major theme—the big picture (the purpose, conclusion or recommendation, if appropriate).

2. The context (who requested the report and when, the problem that necessitated it).

3. The scope and plan of the following discussion.

The announcement of the report's framework makes it easy for readers to know what to do with the details that will come in the middle.

If you anticipate that the reader will need to be sold on your conclusion or will find a bald statement of your conclusion either threatening or pushy, you may be indirect. Announce the context for the report (who authorized it, what problem necessitated it, what information you were assigned to discover, what limits were placed on your search, and what the plan of the report will be), but withhold your conclusion. Perhaps begin with a narrative of the project. Then gradually, as the middle develops, you'll bring the reader through the analysis and into your main point.

Here's the introduction to an *information* report about the men's neckwear industry. The structure is direct. Each of the three introductory topics is covered.

> The purpose of this report is to furnish executives of the Brooks Shirt Company with the necessary data to aid them in deciding whether or not to manufacture ties.
>
> This information derives from a detailed study into the men's neckwear industry. The information comes from two sources: industry publications and interviews with Philadelphia manufacturers and retailers.
>
> The report covers neckwear trends: types, fabrics, colors, widths, prices, and sales. It looks particularly at the influence of specific designers.
>
> Two limits on the report should be mentioned. First, because the majority of neckwear manufacturers are privately owned, few financial reports and industry sales figures are available, and thus the report does not cover costs. Second, the information compiled from interviews derives from manufacturers and retailers only in the Philadelphia area, one of several segments within Brooks's total market.[1]

This report grew up in the marketing department of a large shirt manufacturer. The president of the company, looking for ways to diversify its product mix, asked the marketing vice-president to investigate a move into tie manufacture. That vice-president asked the supervisor of the author (who was an assistant in the department) to compile the information. The assistant did so. The report was first read by her supervisor, who suggested revisions; then by the vice-president; then

[1] Courtesy of Jane Bacal.

by the president, who suggested other changes; and then by the board. The experiences, education, and interests of each of these readers varied widely, so the information was presented nontechnically.

The author mastered the material, which she displayed efficiently for understanding. She made no recommendations. She avoided technical terms, from, say, marketing, that might annoy or confuse readers with a financial bent. She aimed at comprehensiveness and objectivity.

The report could, of course, have developed in a different shape. It could have become more political, serving other, perhaps hidden, agendas. The marketing vice-president, for example, might have objected to the idea of diversification into ties and might have biased the report accordingly. The president might have been responding in his assignment to a board member he thought was foolish in suggesting ties, and might have told the vice-president, in effect, to come up with a negative report. Another report, based on this one, but signed by someone with the power to make recommendations, might indeed have served a persuasive purpose. Here, however, the report served mainly to compile data on one topic.

The following introduction begins a *persuasive* report. The approach is more *indirect*. It begins with a statement of the problem (rising costs); it then announces the authorization and topic of the report and the five objectives; it then gives the plan of the report. The *recommendation* of a specific benefits package, however, is saved until the end of the report itself.

> With the rising costs of health care, employee benefits programs are becoming more important to an organization's efforts to maintain first-rate employees. Too often, however, these benefits plans are not properly designed and are thus ineffectual.
>
> In response to a request from JFS Manufacturing Company, Reimbursement Services has prepared this report, which analyzes the Company's present benefits program and presents the design of a new and more effective plan. The new plan addresses the firm's objectives and needs in a health care program.
>
> Five major objectives comprise the ideal benefits program for the JFS Manufacturing Company:
>
> **1.** Provide ample protection for the employees while being cost-effective.
>
> **2.** Improve employee morale through the plan's serviceability.
>
> **3.** Use a fair and uniform rate of contribution for the employees.
>
> **4.** Incorporate a master plan to improve and add benefits over time.
>
> **5.** Lend itself to effective communication to the employees.
>
> This report is divided into two main parts: a description of the present program and then an analysis of the recommended program. Each pro-

gram is analyzed in terms of the firm's objectives for an ideal health-care package.[2]

The writer whose introduction you'll read next had several goals in mind for his report. Perhaps the most important was his own coming to grips with ideas and information he'd had around for a long time. The author is a U.S. Forest Service employee who knows a good deal about avalanches and wrote this report for a short course in outdoor recreation. So one reader was the course instructor. The writer knew that the instructor wanted a thorough treatment of the subject, particularly some administrative background as well as the details of the writer's own research. But in addition, the writer used the report as a way to compile all the information he had stuffed into file drawers from fifteen years of dealing with avalanches. He used the occasion of the report assignment to discipline his own thinking and to structure otherwise loose material. Moreover, he considered showing the report to colleagues and his supervisors in recreation management. Thus he included recommendations on policy and programs (while carefully noting in a preface that the ideas expressed were his own and did not reflect an official Forest Service position).

The Forest Service program in avalanche control and public education entails six components:

1. Supervisory Forest Service avalanche hazard forecasters at high-hazard downhill ski areas.

2. Procurement and supervision of military weapons and ammunition used in ski areas and for highway control.

3. Forecasting for highways in selected locations.

4. Regional avalanche-warning programs for back-country users.

5. The Biannual National Avalanche School sponsored jointly by the Forest Service, the National Ski Patrol System, the National Ski Areas Association, and others.

6. Snow and avalanche research.

This report examines the first five of these programs and suggests courses of action that will bring them into conformance with the new Forest Service Manual directive, with general Forest Service policy, and with the realities of tightened budgets in the outdoor recreation function of the Forest Service.

In undertaking this examination we need to address three major questions regarding avalanche policy:

1. In avalanche forecasting, control, and supervision, how will the agency make the administrative transition from the old FSM 2342 pol-

[2]Courtesy of Jennifer Friedman.

icy to the new FSM 2342 policy and maintain high standards of public safety in the process?

    2. How will the agency maintain field people who have the background and expertise to monitor effectively how ski areas and highway departments forecast and control avalanches?

    3. Is maintaining a national leadership position in the avalanche field still an objective of the Forest Service?[3]

Each of these introductions eases the reader into the report by forecasting both the *content* and the *structure* of the whole document.

Middle

Then the middle gives the proof. The middle is further divided into smaller *segments*. The segments must be clearly identified, as not all readers will read every segment. For *routine* reports, the segments follow a predefined course. You fill in the information required. But finding the *best* arrangement of segments for a specialized report may be complicated, especially for long reports. You'll outline, then try a draft, and perhaps you'll hit the *best* plan only after several drafts. The final plan should be simple and obvious for the reader, efficient in conveying the material, and effective in showing your good work. Chapter 6 discusses conventional patterns for writing; let's examine how these fit report writing:

Cause and effect/problem and solution.

Classification and analysis.

Comparison and contrast.

Narrative.

Cause and Effect

One form of *cause and effect* reasoning is a report that bases one or more recommendations on the results of a survey. For example, here is the outline of the middle segment of a report on public transportation in Philadelphia. The authors, advocates of public transportation, anticipate a bias toward private automobiles rather than public means among the report's readers at the U.S. Department of Transportation (DOT) and in Congress. So they have structured the report *indirectly*, with the analysis *preceding* the recommendations:

1. Introduction—mass transit in American cities
2. The Philadelphia Area Transit survey

[3]Courtesy of Scott H. Phillips, U.S. Forest Service.

a. Description of the project
b. Profile of the Philadelphia commuter
c. Energy use in the Philadelphia commuter rail system
d. Costs of the Philadelphia commuter rail system
3. Conclusions concerning energy and economics
4. Detailed recommendations for DOT funding over five years
Appendix A. Raw data/commuter survey
Appendix B. Raw data/comparative costs—rail and private auto

Here's how the structure breaks out in, for example, Segment 2b:

Profile of the Philadelphia Commuter

1. General summary of characteristics: demographics, distance between work and home, frequency of travel, attitudes toward commuting

2. Demographics: age, sex, marital status, educational level, occupation, mean income

3. Distance between work and home (by rail line: Chestnut Hill–West, Main Line, Media, Wilmington)

4. Frequency of travel

5. Attitudes toward commuting

Another form of cause-and-effect reasoning is reasoning from *problem to solution*. Indeed, *problem solving* as a business activity generates many reports. Here's the outline of a problem-to-solution report (for the full text of the report, see Chapter 20). The author began the introduction with a brief description of a problem, then provided his recommendation. He offered the recommendation directly in the introduction because he anticipated no reader resistance. Indeed, the reader would look for the answer first. The middle of the report supports that answer:

Current and Potential Problems in Operation at the Whistling Abalone Restaurant
1. Poor food and liquor inventory control
2. Inefficient waiter service and floor operations
3. Added bookkeeping
Solution: MIS
Advantages of the System
1. Constantly updated inventory
2. More efficient waiter service and floor operations
3. Better bookkeeping

Classification and Analysis

Informative reports, like the Brooks Shirt report and the report on corporate fitness at the end of this chapter, often show the components of some whole or fit the pieces of information into some class. The Brooks Shirt report, for example, followed an *analysis* of neckwear *trends:*

Types

Fabrics

Colors

Widths

Prices

Sales

In Chapter 18, we classified research problems into three groups: problems of fact, problems of means, and problems of value. An *analysis* is not a *summary*. Instead, you cut into your information to see how it works. Your education in business provides you with the tools—like those in the guidelines for case analysis reports in Chapter 18—for cutting.

Comparison and Contrast

In analyzing your information, you may find that the best way to understand it and present it is through comparison. You can peg the comparison to the *criteria* for your analysis. The JFS Manufacturing Company report compares the present and recommended benefits programs as each meets five criteria:

Present Benefits Program
  Criterion 1
  Criterion 2
  Criterion 3
  Criterion 4
  Criterion 5
Recommended Benefits Program
  Criterion 1
  Criterion 2
  Criterion 3
  Criterion 4
  Criterion 5

Of course, you could also compare present and recommended programs along each criterion:

Criterion 1

    Present program
    Recommended program

Criterion 2

    Present program
    Recommended program

But for reasons of emphasis and persuasion, the author wanted to close the middle of her report—and build momentum for her recommendation—with a lengthy description of the new program.

Narrative

A *narrative* retraces an investigation over time. Sometimes that retracing is framed by a series of tasks. Here's a task-by-task arrangement for a report about the organization of a competitive swimming program at a swim club. Just be careful with *parallelism*. Make sure each segment is indeed a *task:*

Preparing the Pool

Hiring a Coaching Staff

Scheduling Practices

Scheduling Meets

Establishing the Parents' Committee

Selecting the Team Roster

    A *narrative* retraces the events in an investigation from Day 1 to its conclusion. But such a structure may be unemphatic, burying a significant result because it occurred on Day 15, right in the middle. Most documentation reports are written as narratives, but those meant to inform or persuade readers usually follow a more reader-based structure.

Combination Plan

Whole reports are often profitably structured in *one* of these conventional patterns, but you may combine patterns. The avalanche report combines some aspects of a comparison (between the present programs and the changes needed for conformance with new directives and conditions) with a discussion of problems and solutions (see Figure 19–1).

TABLE OF CONTENTS

FIGURE 19–1. Table of contents of a report that combines a comparison with a discussion of problems and solutions. Parts II, III, IV, and V are the middle segment (courtesy of Scott H. Phillips).

Ending

After negotiating the hard evidence in the middle of your report, the reader will expect some signal that you are about to finish up, that the discussion is about to come to some resolution. If the reader turns the last page expecting more text, you haven't provided a good ending. You need to wave good-bye.

Like the introduction, the ending is a point of heightened reader attention. It reminds the reader of the main point or points that you've made in the report—a reminder that may be necessary if the reader bogged down in the details of the middle. The ending draws a line and shows once more what all the numbers, all the data of whatever kind, add up to.

In the ending, you return to the introduction, showing the reader that you've proved what you promised to prove. The introduction and the ending should be on the same plane, the same scale of generalization. A long report may end in a summary, but don't feel you *always* need to summarize. You may repeat conclusions drawn from your data and perhaps provide recommendations based on those conclusions. You may hint at what's to come. But don't introduce a whole new topic. If a question was raised in the introduction, the ending makes sure that the reader knows the author's answer to that question.

Here, for example, are the last two paragraphs of the avalanche report. These paragraphs answer the last question that the author posed in the introduction—evidence for which was presented in more detail in the middle.

> Third, we posed the question, "Does the Forest Service still have the objective of maintaining a national leadership position in the avalanche field?" This author believes that the answer to this question is yes. The recommendation made by the Task Force Committee in 1970 is still valid today. However, we must accomplish the leadership objective by placing increased emphasis on a role of public education and training in avalanche awareness and technology transfer in snow and avalanche research. The Forest Service should definitely continue to sponsor Phase 1 of the National Avalanche School (NAS), the classroom session in Reno. Phases II and III should continue to be contracted out to the private sector, with the Forest Service doing a minimal amount of coordination. The tuition paid by the students to NSAA for the avalanche training is sufficient to cover most of the basic costs of the NAS. This one high-visibility effort will do more than any other single activity to maintain a leadership role for the agency. The involvement of Forest Service personnel who manage the school and act as instructors serves to maintain a base level of knowledge, enthusiasm, and involvement, which is fundamental to any continuing program.
>
> In addition to maintaining the national school, the Forest Service

can complete its leadership role by maintaining its snow and avalanche research arm and by continuing to cooperate with the established regional warning programs. Public education and training in avalanche awareness should be the focus and emphasis of the agency in the next decade.[4]

Note how this ending—like most endings—moves back up out of the details of subtopics to the general plane of the introduction—in this case, with a look toward the future.

Style

Select the best structure for your material. Think in terms of *segments*. Then check the *connections* among the segments. Cue your reader to the connections. See that information is properly distributed to visuals or words. Check the sound of your voice coming off the page. Let's look at some of these elements of style.

Cue Your Reader

Report information can get complicated. The *structure*, however, must be simple. That simple structure must be made obvious to the reader. Use headings, of course (see Chapter 6). In addition, look for ways to show direction within the text itself.

1. Provide overview statements for the whole report and for segments:

> This section discusses a third task required in establishing a competitive swim team: arranging the practice schedule.

Use such overview statements to connect paragraphs externally; each develops some point or subpoint mentioned in the overview. Think of paragraphs in sequence. Don't think of each paragraph as a whole new beginning.

2. Provide checklists, where appropriate, for topics you will discuss:

> This report compares information on public transportation systems in the following cities:
> San Francisco
> Miami
> New York
> Houston

---

[4]Courtesy of Scott H. Phillips, U.S. Forest Service.

3. Periodically summarize a discussion before moving on to the next topic:

> Thus retail sales in Chicago and Kansas City have maintained a steady growth curve at the same time that sales in Houston seem to have plateaued. This curve is borne out in each of the leading indicators discussed.

4. Enrich the discussion with cross-references (but don't overuse them):

> This growth curve reflects particularly the changing patterns of worker migration with the declining market in oil and gas (see the discussion of Houston on pp. 8–15).

5. Refer to the big picture in each major segment:

> A second problem that can be solved by the incorporation of a management information system is the added bookkeeping that resulted from our expansion.

Authors, rightly enough, often fear redundancy. They don't want to keep repeating themselves. But one reader rarely reads a whole report intended for multiple readers. Thus, to make sure your point hits home, include it in the introduction, of course, and then repeat it in each major segment so that a reader who reads selectively will make sure to hit on it.

6. Avoid surprises. Where you have, for example, a "finally," make sure that you've earlier clued the reader to expect a series. Eliminate any casual references early in the document that depend on the reader's having read an extended discussion later on. Bring in the extended discussion earlier. Don't present it as if it were new information that the reader is familiar with.

7. Play to reader expectations. In a list of candidate items or systems to be selected, *start* or *end* with the one you are recommending; don't bury it in a middle position, which is unemphatic.

Distribute Information Appropriately to Words and Visuals

A short, informal report may rely entirely on words to carry its information. But many informal reports, and almost all formal reports, particularly long ones, balance the text with visuals. Readers *expect* such forms of presentation and will probably be uncomfortable if too many pages pass without a table or figure. Avoid using a narrative, for example, for financial information; that belongs in rows and columns. Make sure that the information in visuals and in the text is consistent.

Always announce a visual in the text before the visual itself appears. Chapter 8 provides advice on using such visuals as pie charts, line graphs, bar charts, tables, matrixes, drawings, and photographs.

Check the Sound of Your Voice

Some writers feel compelled to be stuffy when they compose a report page. Resist. Here's H. W. Gillett of Battelle on the subject:

> I'm not so much concerned about whether our reports would suit teachers of English literature or rhetoric. If a sentence tells exactly what you mean, it is likely to be good English. Nor need we avoid homely words and phrases or become stilted in our effort to write good English. We should be reasonably dignified but not affected, and if dignity restrains us from saying just what we mean, dignity be hanged.[5]

Gillett pointed to a major problem in reports: They are "stilted," stuffy in language and approach. That stuffiness often reflects group authorship and compromises on language that are necessitated by working as a group. Here's a stuffy first sentence from a student group report:

> In order to effectively judge what is important to the blue-collar workers employed by the Suburban Propane Corporation, it is first necessary to familiarize oneself with the workers as a reference group.

Sometimes the stuffiness results from an attempt to integrate textbook talk with your own voice. Note the failure to integrate in these sentences:

> The management factor that our group executed best was organizing.

> Behavioral competencies, which effective managers need to master, concentrate on the social relationships which are required within a group.

> We used individual interaction as our problem-solving method.

> The workers became overconfident, thus causing dysfunctions in the company's present motivating factors.

In each, the textbook terms—*management factor, behavioral competencies, individual interaction, dysfunctions,* and *motivating factors*—remain undigested. They fail to convey concrete meaning. Review your report, as Chapter 9 suggests, for simplicity and consistency in your voice. Make sure your voice inspires confidence and will allow easy reading and understanding.

---

[5] *Battelle News* reprint, p. 3.

Producing the Report

Like the clean-up after a paint job, cleaning up a report-writing job is important. The writing—like the painting—isn't over when you have finished the draft or the wall. Often you're tired when you're cleaning up, but you need to muster some last energy to assure a good finish.

A simple typing job may finish off the report. But more likely, especially in a corporate setting, you may be sending your report through a sophisticated printer connected to a word-processing system that will allow you a wide choice in design (see Chapter 10). You may be printing up hundreds, even thousands, of copies. These may be bound within a distinctive cover, whose artwork, too, is your responsibility. You'll need to coordinate the text with visuals. These may be available on the same computer system used for word processing, or they may have to be separately produced and then combined with the text.

Look through the design of each page. Check for:

- Adequate white space and consistent margins.
- At least one paragraph break per page.
- No single last lines of paragraphs carried over to the next page.
- Adequate space around figures.
- No headings as the last line of a page.

In general, make sure that your report conforms to any standards set by the reader, particularly in terms of length, the number of copies required, and the required front matter and back matter. Flip through the whole to make sure that the design is pleasing. Once you are satisfied with the prototype, sit back, order up the requisite number of copies, and get ready to distribute them—with pride—to the reader or readers.

A Business Report: Corporate Fitness Programs

Here is a short internal report. It is an *information* report, as defined in Chapter 18. It is *informal* in presentation and was written by a group in response to a supervisor's request. The introduction states the big picture directly. The middle is segmented by analysis. The ending is a brief summary and restatement. Informative headings aid the reader. A table is attached. Note how all the segments of the report work together. Note also that the style avoids stuffiness.

January 15, 19xx

TO: Barbara Williams
FROM: Jim Anderson
          Pete Riley
          Andrea Markenatatos
RE: Corporate Fitness Programs

In response to your question during last month's staff meeting, here's some information concerning corporate fitness programs. More and more corporations are developing such programs; 57 percent of the companies in a recent survey offer health-promotion programs, up from 24 percent five years ago. The Hay/Huggins Benefit Comparison, as reported in *The Wall Street Journal* (25 April 1986, 29) noted the following popular programs within those companies:

Program Type	% of Companies Offering Program
Smoking cessation/drug and alcohol assistance	57
Weight reduction	49
High-blood-pressure control	43
Stress management	43

Companies find benefits in improved employee morale and productivity and decreased health-care costs. The American Association of Fitness Directors in Business and Industry is a professional organization that assists corporations in implementing fitness programs. The association can provide further information, but we hope this brief report gives you enough background to decide if we should consider establishing a program of our own.

1

<u>Overview of Corporate Programs</u>

According to Dr. Jonathan Fielding, a fitness consultant, industry currently spends about $1 billion on such programs (1). Stephen M. Ruff, of Control Data, which has developed software for such programs, sees a "multibillion-dollar potential" for employee health products and services (1). About 20 percent of the nation's corporations have programs (2). That group includes such companies as Johnson & Johnson, Kimberly-Clark, L. L. Bean, Tenneco, IBM, Pepsico, Levi-Strauss, AT&T, and Georgia Pacific. Some programs are addressed only to executives; some reach all workers. Indeed, programs receive union support. Some unions write wellness benefits, like company-paid membership in YMCAs, into contracts.

<u>Program Benefits</u>

The range of benefits cited is impressive, although these are hard to quantify.

1. *Reduced employee health costs,* including the costs of absenteeism, loss of productivity, and insurance protection. Such costs now amount to as much as 25 percent of the total payroll, according to a study by Coopers & Lybrand (1).

2. *Improved hiring and retention of good staff.* Dr. Robert E. Dedmon of Kimberly-Clark, for example, notes that several new hires said the K-C health center figured in their choice of that company.

3. *Improved morale and job satisfaction.* Many corporate spokespersons note that fit employees feel better about themselves and are more productive for the company. Programs aid employees in managing stress and weight and in curbing smoking and alcoholism.

<u>Program Goals</u>

Individual company programs vary widely. Most, however, emphasize *wellness,* that is, good health practices. At a basic level, the programs attempt to meet these goals:

2

1. To assess the fitness levels of employees.
2. To prescribe individual exercise and nutrition programs to achieve fitness.
3. To provide employees with facilities for a low-risk exercise program.

Some programs also provide workshops on nutrition and stress management as well as counseling on alcoholism and drug abuse.

Fitness Facilities

The range of facilities, of course, varies to meet different goals. Some companies provide memberships in health clubs or YMCAs near the office rather than providing facilities on-site. Those with their own facilities provide at a minimum a locker room, showers and toilets, and some space for Nautilus equipment and some Universal weights. Other companies provide extensive facilities: a swimming pool, a sauna, an indoor track, a squash court, and several stationary bicycles, in addition to lockers, showers, and exercise equipment.

Staffing

Program staffing needs reflect the number of people being served and the season. For best results, a center needs a full-time exercise physiologist. In addition, many centers also employ, at least part time, a registered nurse, a physical therapist, and a cardiologist. Adequate supervision is essential to meet the needs of a *low-risk* program. The rule of thumb seems to be one supervisor for twenty participants at any one time.

Fitness Screening

Most screening occurs in three stages: personal history, medical examination, and physical tests. The screening aids in identifying any physical problems and in designing an appropriate exercise regime. Attachment A shows one typical medical examination; Attachment B shows a typical "physical fitness profile" based on a battery of tests.

Program Cost

Obviously, the *cost* of the program is directly related to its facilities and staff. In urban areas, where office space is limited and private health clubs are easily accessible, several companies find it effective to provide memberships, which may run around $250–$850 per year per person. Companies at suburban locations usually provide facilities on-site. Some have rudimentary provisions, perhaps even entirely outdoors. Indeed, "lifetime exercise courses," a series of stations along a path, each suggesting certain exercises, are popular. Exclusive of land costs, such courses cost about $10,000. Equipping an exercise center indoors, with Nautilus equipment and some weights, runs about $15,000, including lockers and showers. The salary for a full-time center director usually runs about $25,000–$30,000.

Summary

In general, then, the range of corporate fitness programs is broad. The potential seems great. Increasing numbers of companies are turning to such programs to enhance worker motivation and thus to lower turnover and improve productivity. Many companies, too, see such programs as good public relations: in a culture currently turning more and more to physical fitness as one of its highest values, the company that also emphasizes fitness is seen as a leader in its field.

References

1. Freudenheim, Milt. "Companies Pour Millions into Programs Aimed at Keeping Workers Well, *The New York Times,* 14 October 1984, 36.

2. Thomas, Patricia. "Bringing the Pleasure Principle to Work," *Goodlife,* May 1984, 52–53.

4

Attachment A: Suggested Medical Examination

1. *Medical History*
   Family history
   Orthopedic history
   Medications
   Risk factors: diabetes, smoking, alcoholism, high blood pressure,
      heartbeat irregularities, and so on

2. *Present Condition*
   Any symptoms (for example, pain)
   Lipid profile: cholesterol (HDL, LDL), triglycerides
   Blood sugar level
   Percent body fat
   Orthopedic evaluation
   Low back evaluation: strength and flexibility
   Lung capacity
   Psychological stress evaluation (Type A personality?)

3. *Exercise Stress Test*
   Treadmill
   Resting EKG
   Blood pressure before, during, and after test

5

Attachment B: Physical Fitness Profile Form
(courtesy of Dr. Robert E. Neeves).

Name _____ Age _____ Sex _____
　　　　　(Last)　　　　　　　(First)

Body Weight _____ lb. (_____kg.)　Percent Body Fat _____

	Raw Score	T Scores	Rating
Muscular strength and endurance			
Grip strength	_____kg	_____	_____
Sit-ups (bent knees)	_____no.	_____	_____
Pushups	_____no.	_____	_____
Flexibility			
Trunk flexion	_____in.	_____	_____
Trunk extension	_____in.	_____	_____
Motor performance			
Agility run	_____sec.	_____	_____
Vertical jump	_____in.	_____	_____
Squat thrusts (30 sec.)	_____no.	_____	_____
Cardiorespiratory endurance Step test (5 min)	Min _____Step	_____HR1 _____HR2 _____HR3	
2-Mile run	_____min	_____	_____
Treadmill Test	_____ml/kg	_____	_____
Bicycle ergometer	_____ml/kg	_____	_____
Blood pressure	_____mmHg	_____	_____
Vital Capacity	_____cc	_____	_____
Percent fat (LBW)	_____lbs		
Scapular	_____mm	_____	_____
Triceps	_____mm	_____	_____
Iliac	_____mm	_____	_____
Umbilicus	_____mm	_____	_____
Thigh	_____mm	_____	_____

6

Exercises

1. Here's the table of contents from a report recommending that a restaurant install a dance floor to increase the customer base in the late evenings. Comment on the pattern of information here. Are the headings parallel? Is the voice that the headings represent appropriate for a report? The primary reader is the manager of the restaurant. But the restaurant is part of a chain, so the vice-president of operations at the chain's headquarters in Kansas City will also read the report and pass it on to the marketing director.

CONTENTS

INTRODUCTION
Dance the Night Away at Tootsie's 1

GIVE THE PEOPLE WHAT THEY WANT
Objectives 1

THE METHOD TO THE MADNESS
Procedures 2

LET'S DANCE
Conclusion 2

IT PAYS TO POLKA
Considerations and Profitability 3

THE MOUNT LAUREL EXPERIMENT
A Comparison 5

CAN'T BEAT THE BOOGIE BEAT!
Choosing a dance floor over alternative methods 6

CONCLUSION 7

2. The following questionnaire was used as the basis for a study of worker motivation in a small retail store. It was administered to all salespersons. Comment on the questions. Then hypothesize the responses and suggest the structure for a report to be written from these data. Specify an audience. Suggest one structure for an *information* report and another for a *persuasive* report.

EMPLOYEE SURVEY QUESTIONS
To Assess Motivation of Sales Employees:
Q1. On most days on your job, how often does time seem to drag for you?
      A1 _____ About half of the day or more

A2 _____ About one third of the day

A3 _____ About one quarter of the day

A4 _____ About one eighth of the day

A5 _____ Time never seems to drag

Q2. Some people are completely involved in their jobs. For others, the job is just one of several interests. How involved are you in your job?

A1 _____ Very strongly involved; my job is the most important interest in my life

A2 _____ Strongly involved

A3 _____ Moderately involved

A4 _____ Slightly involved

A5 _____ Not much involved; my other interests are more important

To Assess Working Environment and Relations with Supervisors:

Q3. When you don't like some policy or procedure on the job, how often do you tell your opinion to one of your supervisors?

A1 _____ Very rarely or never

A2 _____ Once in a while

A3 _____ Half the time

A4 _____ Most of the time

A5 _____ Almost always

Q4. How free do you feel to disagree with your supervisor to his or her face?

A1 _____ I do not hesitate at all to disagree.

A2 _____ I hesitate only a little.

A3 _____ I hesitate some before disagreeing.

A4 _____ I feel I'd better not disagree.

Q5. A. The relations between management and employees at Wrubles are not very strong because management's interests are different from the employees' interests.

B. The relations between management and employees at Wrubles are strong because both groups are working together toward the same goals.

Which of the two statements comes closer to your opinion about Wrubles?

A1 _____ Agree completely with A

A2 _____ Agree more with A than B

A3 _____ Agree more with B than A

A4 _____ Agree completely with B

3. Read this draft of the introduction to a report dealing with a common problem on college campuses (and elsewhere): too few parking spaces. The author was not happy with this draft. What suggestions can you make for revision?

INTRODUCTION

Over the last sixteen years, the university has undergone significant changes. Enrollment has doubled and the number of buildings on campus has also increased. Consequently, the University has had to increase its classroom facilities. New buildings such as McKinley Lab, Johnson Lab, Hobson, and the extension of Gates Library have been added to accommodate the students. However, with the increase in classroom facilities, there has been a substantial decrease in university-provided parking.

The parking development plan for the university is a viable plan and once in operation will alleviate the current parking problem.

Significance/Purpose

As with most thriving universities, parking problems are common. Due to current parking problems the community is suffering in terms of inconvenience and expense. Therefore, to continue growth and stability at the University, an action-oriented plan must be undertaken.

The purpose of this report is to recommend our parking development plan to alleviate current parking problems. These recommendations will alleviate the current parking deficiencies.

Limitations

This report is limited to current parking deficiencies and a proposed recommended parking development plan. This plan indicates what needs to be accomplished, but does not give an economic analysis. For these reasons, a Cost-Income summary is not submitted.

Program Considerations

Among the many important factors to be considered in formulating the plan's parking facility are location, accessibility, land cost, and site geometry. The new parking facility should be conveniently located with respect to campus, thereby, keeping walking distance to a minimum. The site's accessibility to major streets is necessary to maintain efficient facility operation and keep congestion at a minimum.

In selecting locations for the new parking facility, primary consideration must be given to the accessibility of the site to major arteries. The public transportation system must be made readily accessible, convenient, and inexpensive. Among the many important factors to be considered in formulating an incentive plan to entice commuters to utilize public transportation are accessibility and expense.

4. Here is a data dump (see Chapter 6) of information concerning a preservation organization. Sort through these items. Develop several different structures for presenting this information to different readers, for different purposes. You might begin an information report, for example, as follows:

Historic Red Clay Valley Inc. is a not-for-profit organization whose members aim to promote interest in the social and economic history of the Red Clay Valley, to promote the use of parks and other areas of recreation, to preserve and restore historic sites, to establish and operate museums with accompanying educational programs, and to issue publications relating to the Red Clay Valley.

Historic Red Clay Valley Inc—nonprofit
no compensation to officers and board of directors
aims: to preserve historic sites, establish museums
publishes brochures
names of publications
any about other mills?
the mill: latest object of interest
names of officers
membership
history of mill
history of HRCV
financial needs of HRCV
architect's report on structural suitability of mill
biography of Evans
bibliography? Carroll Pursell's book, "Two Mills on Red Clay Creek in the 19th Century"
membership categories—benefits of membership
members' activities—the Railroad connection
acquisition of the mill
estimates for restoration: paint ($2,000), roof ($2,400), reinforce understructure ($7,000), footbridge ($7,000)
where to look for funds for restoration?
volunteer efforts on workdays
picnics for volunteers
junior division of workers
how acquire old milling equipment?
use as a rest area on Kirkwood Highway?
5-acre tract for recreation near mill
educational opportunities—use mill for school groups, teach about early milling industry
other mills: iron, spice, paper, snuff, grist
use for conservation?
education in Indian lore

Business Reports: Ancillary Elements of the Formal Report

This chapter surveys the ancillary elements that surround the text of a full-dress report. Some come before the report proper:

Letter (or memo) of transmittal
Cover
Title page
Table of contents
List of figures and list of tables
Executive summary (or abstract)
Preface
Foreword

Some elements appear after the text:

Appendix
References and/or bibliography
Index

Letter or Memo of Transmittal

The letter of transmittal (a memo if the report is being circulated *within* an organization) allows you to target the report to the reader (see Figure 20–1). Such a device is particularly useful for reports that will circulate to many readers. Moreover, it gives you a chance to talk about the report in perhaps a more informal and personal voice than the report itself allows. In writing the letter, imagine that you are handing over the report. What would you say? How would you like to frame the reading? Some of that cordial conversation belongs in the letter. Consider some of the following:

- Indicate the full title of the report.
- Review the logistics and authorization for the work, with particular thanks to the reader for assigning the report.
- Highlight the content of the report, emphasizing what's of interest to this reader.
- Cite any deviations from the original plan for the project represented in the report.
- Thank people who assisted in writing the report (particularly the reader).

March 3, 1988

Mr. John Bossacco
The Whistling Abalone
12 Ocean Street
Monterey, CA 93940

Dear Mr. Bossacco:

I am happy to submit to you the attached report, which covers the results of phase one of the project I proposed to you on February 1, 1988. The project was to investigate the feasibility of implementing a management information system at the Whistling Abalone. In completing phase one, I have determined the needs of the restaurant and how a computer system can meet these needs.

The report identifies areas of potential improvement and recommends specific features of MIS that can improve the efficiency of our operations.

On the basis of this report, we should be ready for phase two: soliciting bids from manufacturers of specific systems to determine the most cost-effective one for our needs.

I appreciate the cooperation of the managers within this organization who helped me complete this investigation. With their insight I have found that MIS can be beneficial to all the differing operations within the restaurant.

Please let me know if I can be of any further help. I have enjoyed working with you on this project.

Sincerely,

Thomas E. Puglisi

Thomas E. Puglisi

Enc (1): Phase one report

FIGURE 20–1. Letter of transmittal.

- Offer to answer questions about the report.
- Note any need for further study.

Cover

Many organizations have standard covers for their reports. The cover is instantly recognizable to the reader in a stack of other reports and confirms a certain consistency and polish that enhances a company's image through its documents. Specialized reports may be graced with well designed covers whose artwork reinforces the central theme of the text (see the Travelers report at the end of the chapter). As a practical matter, the cover holds the pages of the report together.

Title Page

Every report has a title. It may appear directly on the cover, or it may appear on a title page inside the cover. Some report covers have windows onto the title page through which the title shows. In general, routine reports have routine titles that denote the *function* of the report in the system, often as an indicator of time: "Second Monthly Progress Report," "Annual Report of the XYZ Corporation," "Quarterly Report to Stockholders."

But specialized reports require more substantive titles. The title alerts the readers to the content and the approach of the report, allows the report to be filed in an information retrieval system, and enables the readers to refer to the report. The content title may be augmented by an administrative one (usually just a number) that identifies the report within the framework of a project and a sequence of documents on that project.

The title is often the last item a writer thinks about. The reader, however, encounters it *first*. The title pulls readers into the report (or repels them). So give some attention to the title. You might build a tentative title early in your writing and let that shape the structure of your draft.

Avoid mere generic titles like "Final Report" or "Plan." Avoid, too, titles that give merely a general topic ("Avalanches" or even "Avalanches: Forecasting, Control, and Public Education") if the emphasis is really on the U.S. Forest Service role. Enrich the title:

"AVALANCHES: The Present and Future Role of the USDA Forest Service in Forecasting, Control, and Public Education"

Instead of "Benefits Program" write:

"Improved Employee Benefits Program for the JFS Manufacturing Company"

Avoid dual titles, like "Computers and Inventory Control." Instead, show the *relationship* between the two terms:

"A Computer-Based Inventory Control System for Peters Furrier"

Entice the reader through the title, as in this title of a talk on linguistics by George Lakoff of the University of California at Berkeley:

"Women, Fire, and Dangerous Things: A Guided Tour of What Categories Reveal About the Mind"

But don't try to make the title into an abstract; avoid overly long titles:

"A Six-Year Plan for the Growth and Development of a Required Physical Education Program for Students Who Need to Develop Life-Time Habits of Good Exercise and Reduce Their Exposure to Indolence and Passivity"

Scrutinize the title for possible misreadings and for unwarranted connotations, or misplaced modifiers:

"Comparison of Dried Milk Preparations for Babies on Sale in Seven European Countries" [*Problem:* The milk is on sale, not the babies, but the title is misleading.]

"Views Men Have of Women in Labor" [*Problem:* This report deals with women in the labor force; the term *labor* has an alternate connotation for women.]

"Mothers and Such: Views of American Women and Why They Changed" [*Problem:* the meaning of *they;* how "women" have changed or how "views" have changed?)

Don't promise in a title information you won't deliver in the report. And try to place key identifying terms at the beginning of the title. Save words like "A Report on" or "A Study of" for the end (or eliminate such terms in revision).

Of course, the *title page* displays your report's title or titles. It also provides the name of the author (or the issuing agency) and the name of the reader. It may include a security classification and the date of issue. The title page sets up the content of the report. It also sets up the *style* in its graphic presentation. A physically attractive title page promises the reader a pleasant reading experience. Note the title pages of the sample reports at the end of this chapter.

Table of Contents

The table of contents lists headings from the report. It thus quickly reveals the report's structure. It provides a brief overview of the report's contents and page notations for finding each section. To prepare the table of contents, simply write, in order, each of the headings in the report (several computer programs do this automatically). Preparing the table of contents gives you an opportunity to check once more on the logic of the report, and to see if the segments follow rationally and if the headings indeed give realistic cues to the reader about what's to be found in each section. If you work from a good outline, the outline topics move into the report as headings and then into the table of contents. Figure 19–1 in Chapter 19 and the two reports at the end of this chapter provide model tables of contents.

List of Figures and List of Tables

The table of contents lists the topics of the report's text. The list of figures, as the name implies, provides a guide to the report's figures (see Figure 20–2). The list of tables collects the titles of the report's tables. Even if you have only one figure, list it separately, for ease of reference. Don't list a figure in the table of contents.

List of Figures

Figure 1.   Solar power plant design   7
Figure 2.   Windmill design   9
Figure 3.   Topographic map of resort area   10
Figure 4.   Chart of relative energy costs   11
Figure 5.   Example of vertical-axis rotor   15
Figure 6.   Example of horizontal-axis rotor   15
Figure 7.   Sketch of condominium plan   17
Figure 8.   Sketch of condominium elevation   18

FIGURE 20–2.   List of figures (courtesy of Deborah Rawlings).

Again, in preparing these lists you have one more opportunity to see that each figure or table is well labeled and well located in the text.

Executive Summary

An executive summary condenses the report for a decision maker interested in the main lines of the discussion. The summary tells what the report is about. The summary of an *information* report collects the main points, stripped of supporting evidence. The summary of a *persuasive* report includes a brief discussion of the problem that led to the investigation, the writer's objectives, and an overview of the context. The summary also highlights the significance of the work and, if action is called for, defines the action and the actors. Figure 20–3 is an executive summary for an information report; Figure 20–4 is the summary of a persuasive report.

The report itself provides such specific details as the pool dimensions, the placement pattern of lane ropes, specifications for the nonskid surfaces on the starting blocks, and the colors of the uniforms. The summary suppresses these details to show instead the general hi-

Because of increasing demand from club members, a competitive swimming program has been established at Newtown Park and Swim Club. To implement the program, several steps have been taken. The pool has been prepared for competitive swimming, and the necessary equipment has been purchased. A coaching staff, consisting of a head coach, an assistant coach, and a diving coach, has been hired. A practice schedule and a meet schedule have been arranged. In addition, a parents' committee has been formed to organize swim meets and to hold fundraisers. Several fund-raisers have been planned for the coming season. Finally, we have prepared a roster of team members and a budget. With these tasks completed, the Newtown Swim Team is ready to begin its first competitive season.

FIGURE 20–3. Executive summary for an information report (courtesy of Karen Dunlap).

Because over forty complaints have been filed with the City of Newark concerning excessive delays at the intersection of West Park and Orchard Road, Lt. Jeff Townsend, Traffic Adviser, asked me to recommend a more efficient means of regulating traffic at that intersection. The traffic signal was installed at that intersection in 1971, and since then, traffic has more than doubled. After investigating the rationale for the 1971 installation, I collected new traffic-count data through field observation, interviewed residents of the area, and then developed two solutions:

1. Use a pretimed signal only during rush hours and change to flashing (red on Orchard, yellow on West Park) at all other times: initial cost, $150; maintenance cost, $100/year.
2. Install a semiactuated signal: initial cost, $3,900; maintenance cost, $300/year.

A cost–benefit ratio analysis shows that both solutions are economically feasible. In terms of gas saved, the first would pay for itself in eleven days; the second, in about two years. But in terms of safety, the second solution provides more control at the intersection during off-peak hours. Thus I recommend that Solution 2—installation of a semiactuated signal—be implemented.

FIGURE 20–4. Executive summary for a persuasive report (courtesy of John C. Volk).

erarchy of topics covered in the report. If the reader is confident in the writer and is assured about the status of the investigation, he or she may not even read the report.

The term *executive summary* usually refers to the summary of a corporate or government report or of a proposal in a business setting. Another term, *abstract*, is usually used for scientific and technical summaries in academic settings, as well as in professional journals or the proceedings of meetings. Summaries tend to be longer than abstracts—perhaps 20–30 pages for a 300- to 1,000 page document, whereas abstracts rarely exceed 200–300 words.

To write the summary, work from your outline or table of contents, which should indicate your chief topics and their sequencing. Many writers find that creating a summary *before* they settle in to compose a whole document aids them in the final writing. They know how the story comes out. A summary also helps direct the team in a multiple-author project. Keep these suggestions in mind:

1. Include the control statement from the parent document.

2. Include the most important second-level assertions.

3. Omit minor details, even if (especially if) they are cute.

4. Make sure the summary is readable without reference to the parent document.

5. Use complete sentences.

6. Eliminate any redundancy and weak connectors. Reduce paragraphs in the original to sentences, sentences to phrases, phrases to single words.

The summary is a major business tool. In these days of inflation in prose (as in other segments of life), the executive summary quickly leads the reader to the main points. Supporting information may be conveyed in the report itself for the record but may hardly be read.

Preface

Some reports, and many books, include an introductory statement from the author called a *preface*. The preface serves some of the same functions as a letter of transmittal; it allows the author to converse with the reader of the report perhaps more personally than in the report or book itself. The preface often includes an overview of the author's intention for the document. The preface to the avalanche report whose introduction and table of contents we saw in Chapter 19, for example, noted that the opinions expressed in the report were those of the author and were not official U.S. Forest Service policy. Sometimes an author discusses his or her work in creating the document and in overcoming any special problems and acknowledges people who assisted in the work.

Foreword

Like the preface, the foreword is an introductory item for a report or book. It, too, is not essential to the understanding of the document but provides context. Forewords are usually not written by the author of the report. Instead, they are written by someone who validates the importance and credibility of the report.

Report Proper

Behind whatever front matter you consider appropriate for the report, you place the report proper—the text itself: introduction, middle, and ending. This is the heart of the report. Chapter 19 discusses the report proper in detail.

Appendix

As the name implies, an appendix contains material *appended* to the report. It comes *after* the report proper. The section may also be called an *attachment* or *exhibits*. Such material supplements information given in the report, often providing greater technical detail and more extended mathematical or verbal discussion than is considered warranted in the report itself. It's often the most highly technical section of the report. It functions, in effect, mainly to document conclusions for the record. Usually, appendixes are read only by the intrepid or by those who question the report's conclusions and methods.

Here are some forms of information that may conveniently be attached to a report:

- The full text of a questionnaire whose results are summarized in the report itself.
- Complete derivations for formulas highlighted in the text.
- An earlier report on the project that this report modifies.
- Detailed rules and codes that served as the legal basis for applications discussed in the text.
- Figures that form the basis for discussion in several places in the text or that are foldouts or otherwise unusual in size.
- A glossary of terms, abbreviations, or symbols used in the report.
- Letters to the author concerning the information covered; the letters may be quoted in part in the report.

Figure 20–5 shows a glossary. You may include one or many appendixes. Each one should be labeled and numbered (or lettered). Titles for all appendixes, along with their page numbers, should be included in the table of contents.

Glossary
MICROCOMPUTER APPLICATIONS

Word-processing programs facilitate creating and editing written documents. They may also work with devices that produce high-quality results, some of which can produce many different fonts (e.g., bold, italics, different size letters) in a single document.

Word-processing programs are available on personal and large computers. Personal computers have the advantages of being under your control and of not being slowed down by others' work. Some people find the programs available for personal computers easier to use than the programs available on larger computers.

Large computers are able to handle larger texts and can produce printed results on many different devices, including letter-quality printers and laser-page printers, which can produce a mix of fonts.

Statistics programs for data analysis used in an academic environment are available on mainframe computers. Many of these programs are widespread and well known (e.g., SAS, SPSS). They provide many different statistical routines whose results have been thoroughly tested. Until recently, the statistical programs available for personal computers were not of the same quality as the ones for larger computers. They did not perform the same range of functions, nor were their computational methods thoroughly tested for soundness and accuracy.

More advanced programs are becoming available for personal computers. These are often scaled-down versions of programs available on mainframes. They generally require a powerful personal computer—one that has a high-capacity fixed disk and lots of main memory. They are also very expensive.

Data-base programs facilitate the collection and retrieval of information (e.g., bibliographies). Well done programs are available for all sizes of computers. The size of the computer may limit the volume of information that the computer can handle. The program itself may impose limits. No single program is suitable for all needs.

FIGURE 20–5.   Glossary of microcomputer applications (courtesy of Academic Computing Services, University of Delaware, 1984).

Spreadsheet programs give the user an electronic analogue of an accountant's spreadsheet. One can, for instance, enter columns of numbers and tell the computer to add them or to take the average. One of the most useful functions of these programs is to recalculate automatically all values whenever the numbers on which they are based change. Spreadsheet programs were developed for personal computers before they were made for mainframes. They work well on personal computers because they are highly interactive.

Programming languages permit a person to write his or her own programs to tell the computer what to do. Dozens of languages are available for both mainframes and personal computers. Each language is better for some kinds of tasks than for others. For instance, BASIC is good for writing quick, short programs. COBOL is good for business problems. FORTRAN is good for engineering and scientific calculations.

Graphics programs allow one to create graphs, charts, diagrams, and pictures on the screen and on paper. Some programs are interactive and easy for nonprogrammers to use; others are designed for programmers. Some programming languages, such as IBM PC BASIC, have graphics commands built into them.

References and/or Bibliography

Many reports derive from the author's own observations and conclusions, but sometimes a writer also works from the literature and needs to acknowledge these printed sources. That acknowledgment, in the form of notes or a list of references, is attached to the end of the report. See Chapter 5 for a detailed discussion of the methods for compiling a list of references or bibliography and for documenting a text.

Index

For very long reports, particularly reports to be segmented into volumes and read by many readers, you may need to prepare an index that will let each reader find information on a topic of interest without having to read the entire report. Many computer programs can compile an index of key words automatically. If you don't have access to such a program, then read through the text with note cards by your side. Jot one key term on each card as you go through, alphabetize the cards as you jot, and note page references for each page on which the term occurs. The process is rather slow and tedious, but remember that you want your reader to *find* what he or she needs, by the term under which he or she will look for it.

Pagination

Every page must be accounted for, although the number of the title page is not usually printed. Sometimes, to ensure completeness, numbers are given in the form, "page 2 of 15," with the first number indicating the sequence of pages and the last indicating the total number of pages in the document. Most commonly, the number is printed at the top right of the text page, with the number for the first page of the introduction centered below the text of the first page. But practice varies. Again, adhere to the standards of your organization.

Report Page Numbers

Title page	i (not printed)
Subsequent front matter	ii,iii, etc. (printed)
First page of report proper	1
Subsequent pages	2,3,4. . .
Appendix	Arabic numbers in sequence with the body of the report; every page is numbered (sometimes appendix pages are numbered separately by appendix, for example, A-1, A-2, etc.)

Student Report[1] : A Management Information System for a Restaurant

The owner of the Whistling Abalone, a resort-area restaurant, moved his operation to a larger space to accommodate increased business. But he was afraid that the move might exacerbate some already-existing operating problems and might bring other problems as well. So he

[1] Courtesy of Thomas E. Puglisi.

asked the report's author, who is a waiter at the restaurant in the summers and an accounting student during the school year, to identify the problem areas and to recommend procedures to streamline operations. The student took on the task and wrote the report reproduced here. His letter of transmittal for the report is Figure 20–1. He wrote a letter, rather than a memo, because at the time he mailed the report he was at school. The owner decided to install the system recommended in the report. The report is reproduced on pages 391–401.

Front Matter and Introduction to a Corporate Report: The Travelers[2]

For the Travelers Insurance Companies, a major insurer headquartered in Hartford, Connecticut, one direction of corporate interest has been the concerns of older Americans. Corporate spokespersons have addressed this issue in national symposia; some marketing materials also develop the theme. Within the company, the Personnel Research unit was asked to investigate opinions of employees 55 years or over concerning their future work and retirement preferences. We have reproduced here the front matter (cover, title page, executive summary, table of contents) and introduction of the resulting report. The survey is an information report. It does not advocate a policy concerning retirement but provides evidence that might then be woven into a persuasive report at another level in the organization. It is mainly an internal document although it was also distributed externally to readers interested in the issues of the older worker. The front matter and introduction are reproduced on pages 402–06.

[2]Courtesy of Travelers Insurance Companies.

A MANAGEMENT INFORMATION SYSTEM
FOR BETTER INVENTORY, SERVICE, AND BOOKKEEPING
AT THE WHISTLING ABALONE RESTAURANT

Submitted to: John Bossacco
The Whistling Abalone
12 Ocean Street
Monterey, CA 93940

Submitted by: Thomas E. Puglisi

March 3, 1988

TABLE OF CONTENTS

LIST OF FIGURES

EXECUTIVE SUMMARY

The Whistling Abalone has recently moved to a new location in Monterey, California. The transition to a larger space, with doubled seating capacity, has already revealed problems in the current pattern of operations and will undoubtedly create further problems when we move into full capacity this summer. John Bossacco, owner of the restaurant, asked me to identify these problems and to recommend a solution.

The increased volume of food and liquor has resulted in poor inventory control. Moreover, the large size of the restaurant has impaired waiter service and floor operations in general. Another problem is the added amount of bookkeeping that has come with expanded operations.

These problems must be resolved before the vacation season begins in May. The purpose of our move is to expand our business and to improve our already good reputation. Problems like those mentioned will undoubtedly hurt our reputation if not corrected immediately.

I recommend the use of a management information system (MIS) at The Whistling Abalone to correct our problems. A simple system can solve all those problems mentioned and provide other useful features for our bright future.

INTRODUCTION

Our move over the winter to a larger building has greatly expanded the operations of The Whistling Abalone. In making this move, we cannot compromise the quality of our service and thus our reputation.

As is common in any business expansion, we have been experiencing some operating problems, particularly poor food and liquor inventory control, less efficient waiter service and floor operations in general, and added bookkeeping.

John Bossacco, owner of the restaurant, requested that I identify the problems caused by our expansion. This report summarizes the needs we identified and recommends the installation of a management information system (MIS) that will make our operations more efficient, will lower costs, and will enable us to provide even better service. Such a system should allow us to be in top condition when we begin our busy tourist season in May.

This report is divided into three sections. The first section details the problems caused by our expansion. The second provides an overview of a management information system. The third shows how the system can solve each of the problems identified.

CURRENT AND POTENTIAL PROBLEMS IN OPERATION

To identify the needs resulting from our expansion, I interviewed the kitchen manager, the bar manager, and the bookkeepers. Each commented on changes in his or her specific operation. I also observed floor operations in the dining room to determine problems with waiter service. After the interviews and observations, I researched MIS in current trade periodicals to determine the features of MIS that are applicable to The Whistling Abalone.

Inventory Control: Food

Our new restaurant has twice the seating capacity of the former one; thus we have been serving about twice as many dinners compared to this time last year. The increased number of dinners served has greatly increased the volume of food inventory that we handle. Becky Anderson, the kitchen manager, has found keeping track of the inventory manually to be inefficient. Items are often either understocked or overstocked. If the restaurant runs out of an item, that dinner cannot be served, and guests complain. If an item is overstocked, it often spoils, increasing costs. Becky also suspects that certain kitchen employees have been stealing food. The present system is not accurate enough to indicate the amount of pilferage or the identity of the pilferer.

Inventory Control: Liquor

Our present system lacks any control over the inventory of liquor at the bar. David Smity, the bar manager, has a running count of the liquor delivered to the restaurant, but he has no way of determining the quantity that should be left at the close of business each evening. He spends over ten hours weekly attempting to keep an accurate total of the amount of liquor we have in storage. He suspects that the waiters may be giving away drinks to friends and regular guests. He also thinks that the bar boys may be taking a bottle now and then after work. The information provided by the present manual system is often inaccurate and is usually available too late to indicate any causes of shortages.

Waiter Service and Floor Operations

Since our move to the new restaurant, some of our guests have complained of poor service. The waiters note that the increase in size has required them to walk much farther to do their jobs. The bar and the kitchen are distant from each other and from the dining room. Waiters have to walk more than three times as far to the bar and the kitchen as at the former restaurant. These added steps can slow down even the best

2

waiters and greatly impair their service. The extra time spent walking is time spent away from the table. As a result, there is less time to provide the personalized service The Whistling Abalone is known for.

The waiters and the cooks have also had problems communicating. The waiters try to minimize the number of trips to the kitchen; as a result, they are often late in picking up their dinners. The cooks get angry when the food cools; the guests aren't happy, either. Moreover, if the cooks aren't sure about an order, the waiter is rarely around to clarify it. This lack of access to the waiters also causes the cooks to be angry. The animosity between cooks and waiters is getting worse. Both parties have individual objectives, and neither is willing to compromise.

These problems decrease the quality of our service and of our food. The Whistling Abalone's reputation is based on gourmet dinners and excellent service. We cannot afford to blemish our reputation at such a crucial time as our recent move.

Bookkeeping

The increase in the size of our business has also increased the amount of bookkeeping. Ann Stone, bookkeeper, figures that the accounting tasks involved in payroll, inventory invoices, and accounts payable alone are enough to keep her and her assistant busy all week.

In addition to these tasks, she is responsible for recording all the information from dinner checks each night. She must record the number of each dinner, appetizer, dessert, and drink served by manually going through each dinner check. While she does this, she also checks for waiter mistakes in calculations. This method was adequate at the former restaurant, but with the increased size this method has become tedious and inefficient. Ann and her assistant are both working overtime.

THE SOLUTION: A MANAGEMENT INFORMATION SYSTEM

A reading of several restaurant journals and discussion with experts in MIS have turned up several systems used by other restaurants to meet many of the needs that The Whistling Abalone now faces. Two excellent sources are cited at the end of this report. Figure 1 shows the variety of reports available from such a system.

For purposes of explaining the features of MIS, assume that our system will be composed of an electronic cash register (ECR), a small personal computer, and two remote-site printers. (Specific software and hardware for The Whistling Abalone will be selected in the second phase of this research, but this setup is common in restaurants of our size.)

When the waiter receives an order, he takes it to the cashier. The cashier punches the order into the ECR. The following then occurs:

1. The drink order is automatically sent to the bar and is printed on the remote-site printer there.
2. The food order is sent to the kitchen and is printed on its remote-site printer.
3. The entire order is sent to the computer, and each food and drink item is recorded in its memory.
4. The ECR neatly prints the dinner check to be presented to the guests when they leave.

Figure 2 illustrates this process.

ADVANTAGES OF THE SYSTEM

The system aids in solving each of the problems we identified.

Constantly Updated Inventory

When the order is entered into the ECR, the computer records each food and drink item. The computer automatically subtracts from inventory the

Figure 1. Some Reports Available from a Restaurant MIS

About menu items
- current inventory
- break-out of ingredients used and their availability
- shopping list (continuously updated) of ingredients needed
- comparison of vendor prices per ingredient
- total sales
- sales recorded by hour, day, week, month, year
- recipes

About customers
- individual tally for each check
- demographic information
    - peak meal times
    - table turnovers
    - percentage of guests ordering from each menu category
    - total number of guests broken out by hour, day, week, month, year, or by menu category

About operations
- sales and profit figures
- waiter scheduling
- spread sheet scenarios for setting menu item prices and categories to achieve a profitable menu mix

5

Figure 2. System Overview

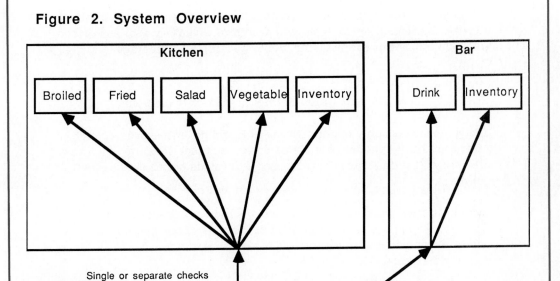

items that are ordered. Moreover, the computer can be programmed to know every ingredient of each dish. When a certain dinner is ordered, the computer subtracts from inventory each ingredient in that dish, right down to the last half-teaspoon of salt.

The computer can also be programmed to subtract a certain number of ounces of liquor or mixer for each drink. If a Beefeaters and tonic is ordered, two ounces of Beefeaters and four ounces of tonic are reduced from inventory totals.

The system thus provides a constantly updated total of food and liquor inventory. At any given time, the bar manager and the kitchen manager

6

can compare the computer's inventory total with the actual totals in storage. These tighter controls will facilitate inventory reordering and will help to prevent overstocking, understocking, and pilferage.

More Efficient Waiter Service and Floor Operations

The waiter makes only one trip to the ECR and his entire order is placed. After that, he simply has to time his orders and pick them up when they are ready. The time saved can be used to provide better service for his guests.

Communication problems between waiter and cook are also eliminated. The order is printed in detail in front of the cook; thus discrepancies and potential confusion are prevented. The waiter need not enter the kitchen to place his order.

Better Bookkeeping

Many of the bookkeeper's tasks can be facilitated with the use of this system. Because each item ordered is recorded in the computer, Ann need not record information manually from the dinner checks each night. Mathematical errors are eliminated because the electronic cash register prices each item and totals the bill. Elimination of these tasks alone will save the bookkeepers at least twenty hours per week.

Programs are also available to compute the payroll, to keep records of accounts payable, and to keep track of invoices. These features will greatly reduce the bookkeeper's burden and will save on labor costs: we are now paying Ann and her assistant for twenty hours of overtime per week.

CONCLUSIONS

This investigation has led to the following conclusions:

7

1. *Inventory.* The most crucial and costly problem we face right now is poor inventory control. The costs of overstocking, understocking, and pilferage can cut into profits considerably in the restaurant business. A management information system can substantially improve our inventory controls. The availability of updated inventory totals is crucial to prevent unnecessary inventory costs.

2. *Service and floor operations.* The service at The Whistling Abalone is one of our main attractions. The recent decrease in the quality of our service must be corrected. An MIS will allow waiters to spend less time on the logistics and more time on service to customers.

3. *Bookkeeping.* The amount of additional bookkeeping associated with our recent expansion has been a great burden on Ann Stone. Keeping accurate records of operations is crucial in any business. An MIS can alleviate a large number of small but time-consuming bookkeeping tasks. Eliminating the manual recording of items served will be a major benefit to the bookkeeping operations. Computerizing other accounting functions will also reduce the work load.

RECOMMENDATION

Based on these conclusions, I recommend that The Whistling Abalone implement a management information system that has the following capabilities:

1. Keeping accurate and updated inventory records.
2. Providing automatic ordering of both drinks and dinner items to ease the waiters' ordering tasks.
3. Providing record-keeping and accounting functions to facilitate bookkeeping.

REFERENCES

Farrell, Kevin. "Skeeter's Restaurant: A push-button operation," *Restaurant Business,* 1 June 1980, 148–150.

Farrell, Kevin, and Denise M. Garbedian. "Banking On Management Information Systems, *Restaurant Business,* 15 May 1981, 69.

REPORT OF RESULTS

The
Travelers
Pre-Retirement
Opinion
Survey

THE TRAVELERS

THE TRAVELERS PRERETIREMENT OPINION SURVEY

REPORT OF RESULTS

Prepared by:

Lloyd D. Marquardt, Ph.D.
Personnel Research

Alice R. Gold, Ph.D.
Corporate Marketing

January, 1981

i

SUMMARY

In August, 1980, Chairman of the Board Morrison H. Beach announced that Travelers was initiating a National Leadership Program designed to address the needs and aspirations of older Americans. One aspect of this effort is the development of programs for Travelers own older employees.

The Preretirement Opinion Survey was designed to solicit opinions of employees aged 55 or over which would be helpful in designing future Company programs. Seventy-nine percent of those surveyed responded.

The following highlights the major findings of the survey:

. Only 12-14% of those surveyed had already done a considerable amount of preretirement planning.

. Sixty-eight percent expressed an interest in attending voluntary group preretirement planning sessions. A majority (65%) preferred the sessions during working hours. Only 22% preferred that spouses not attend. The remainder either desired spouses' attendance (36%) or had no preference (42%).

. Twelve percent plan to retire before age 62. Twenty-two percent plan to continue working past the age of 65. However, of those 62 and over who were surveyed, the percentage planning to work past 65 increases to 43%.

. Reasons given for working beyond age 65 are largely economic, although some plan to continue for the enjoyment of work.

. Of those surveyed, 85% expressed an interest in some form of paid employment after they retire. The majority (53%) would prefer part-time employment with The Travelers.

. Forty-one percent said they would consider retiring earlier if part-time work were available.

. Working fewer days per week is clearly the most preferred part-time schedule.

. Thirty-nine percent indicated an interest in pursuing a second career. This interest was lowest among weekly employees (32%) and highest among officers (56%).

. Only 9% of those surveyed chose volunteer work as their first preference after retirement. An additional 40% had some interest, but not as a first choice.

. Twenty-three percent were very interested in increased time off for volunteer work as retirement approached.

ii

TABLE OF CONTENTS

1

INTRODUCTION

In August, 1980, Chairman of the Board Morrison H. Beach announced that Travelers was initiating a National Leadership Program designed to address the needs and aspirations of older Americans. One aspect of this effort has been the development of programs for Travelers own older employees.

In order to help design these programs, a survey was conducted of employees who were nearing retirement. The survey covered a wide range of topics relating to retirement plans and the desire for postretirement work.

This report details the findings of the survey. The findings are grouped into three topics - retirement planning, early versus late retirement, and working after retirement.

A copy of the survey questionnaire may be found in Appendix A.

Procedures and Instructions

If all else fails . . . read the instructions.

A *report*, in whatever form, concludes an investigation or some phase of an investigation. Another important document in an organization is a *procedure*. A procedure tells the reader how to do something or how to behave. Such a document may also be called *instructions*, or *a directive*, or *guidelines*, or a *performance aid*. This chapter discusses how to write an effective procedure.

You will write procedures for readers both outside and inside your organization. Good customer or client relations, for example, depend on clear instructions: No matter how valuable your product or service is, it will not satisfy unless the customer or client can *use* it. Moreover, good procedures are an important management tool. They limit and focus an employee's tasks and responsibilities; a bank, for example, prepares a procedure to guide internal auditors as they conduct audits of branches; a fast-food chain issues guidelines for its employee crew's dress and behavior.

Procedures vary in length. A few lines of instructions often appear at the top of a form. A memo may instruct employees about how to sign up for vacation. A letter to students may instruct them about registering for classes. Full-page or several-page inserts boxed with equipment tell readers how to assemble and install what's in the box. Extensive manuals and guidebooks, some in volumes, describe procedures for operating and maintaining major machines and systems or for performing complex tasks.

Many readers get a knot in their stomachs when they face a set of instructions. You've undoubtedly read instructions, perhaps with the same knot in your stomach. You often read them under duress—by the side of the road with other cars whipping past as you try to assemble the jack to change a tire. Sometimes instructions are recreational, but more often they mean *work*, the beginning of a job. Even if the result will be pleasurable, however, opening a set of instructions means you'll have to do something new, and doing something new often causes anxiety. You have to pay attention. For a writer, creating a clear set of instructions is a demanding task, made more so because, if the instructions are good, they *appear* to be simple.

Of course, you often describe a procedure orally, but you will need to write the description when:

- You don't have direct access to the person who needs the instructions and thus cannot converse with him or her.
- The procedure is difficult.
- Many people will need to perform the procedure.
- You require a record to check your performance against.

This chapter discusses three types of procedures: step-by-step instructions, manuals, and behavioral guidelines.

How to Ski

Let's look first at instructions in a recreational context. The passage in Figure 21–1 is clearly aimed at the beginning cross-country (x-c) skier. It *encourages* the beginner with an opening picture of millions enjoying the sport. At the same time, it cautions that mastery will take time. It then offers "hints" for the first day. Each hint starts a short paragraph of explanation. Most of the hints are in short sentences. Each is framed in an imperative form of the verb and in parallel form (see Chapter 7 if you need a refresher on style): "start out," "go out," "stop," "be sure," "dress." The author's voice is soothing and inspires confidence. He addresses the reader directly as "you." He creates a picture in our mind of expert skiers and reminds us that they were beginners once, too. His diction is casual: "traipsing," "slogging," "deep stuff," "knows the ropes," "warmly in the pants division." His advice is crisp and authoritative without intimidating us.

How can *you* tell someone how to do something? Let's look at some strategies.

Getting Ready to Write

First, if often helps to be well versed in the procedure yourself. John Caldwell, for example, the author of Figure 21–1, was a former Olympic skier who had spent more than thirty years teaching the sport. But even if you don't have thirty years' experience, you may write a procedure based on reading, interviews, and some quick learning. You also need to set specific, measurable goals for your instructions. And of course, you must assess the user's prior knowledge of the process and likely habits in using the procedure.

Learning the Procedure

Sometimes the expert—like Caldwell—writes the description. At other times, someone else writes. That person gathers information from the developers or owners or performers of the procedure, from standard sources, or from descriptions of similar procedures in a series and, on the basis of interviews and readings, writes up the procedure.

Millions of people in North America are enjoying x-c: skiers touring in deep powder in the high country, or backpacking on skis through the forest, or traipsing across a pasture, or even racing like the wind along a well-packed trail. However, don't be misled into thinking you are going to reach these heights first time out. Remember, all those skiers in the pictures started out just like you: they all had a first day. And perhaps it wasn't so easy for them, either. But they probably used discretion, took some simple precautions, and came back eager for more. Here are a few hints that may help you:

Start out skiing in tracks. This will make everything much easier for you. Slogging through deep snow is heavy work for anyone and it makes learning to ski quite difficult. After you gain experience you will enjoy the deep stuff more.

Go out with a friend, an instructor, or someone who knows the ropes. Follow his lead.

When you begin to tire, stop. You may discover muscles in your lower legs, for instance, that you never thought you had. They can tire rather quickly just from trying to maintain your balance. After a few times out, though, you'll be amazed and pleased at how much you progress.

Be sure your equipment fits and is in good shape. Nothing is worse than trying to ski with skis that don't slide or are too long and awkward, or with boots that twist around in your bindings, or with boots that are too big and don't give you good control over your skis.

Dress warmly in the pants division, using long underwear if it's cold. Wear several light shirts, including a wind-breaker, and shed them according to the weather and your level of exercise.

FIGURE 21–1. Tips for those first times out (*Source: Cross-Country Skiing Today*, by John Caldwell. Copyright © 1978 by John Caldwell. Reprinted by permission of Stephen Greene Press, a wholly owned subsidiary of Viking Penguin, Inc., p. 64).

Whether your sources are your own experience, interviews, or books, master certain information:

What *materials* and *tools* are necessary to perform the procedure?

What are the *time* constraints?

- What is the *range* of possible steps or actions?
- What is the *best* sequence of steps or actions?
- What are the necessary *precautions?*
- Where can a user find *further information?*

Materials and Tools

First, clarify whatever materials and tools are necessary. The materials are the resources, the ingredients that will be transformed in the process—like the chocolate chips before they become the basis of chocolate chip cookies (see Figure 21–12). The tools aid in the transformation. Remember how you once (perhaps even now) tried to get a toy up and running? Most of the *materials* probably came in the box—the parts of a helicopter, for example. But another material, batteries, might well have been missing—the object of midnight searches in convenience stores. As a writer, make sure you know all the materials that will be needed and can alert the reader to them early in the procedure. Examine the required tools. If you are writing about a particular piece of software, learn in advance what hardware it is compatible with, along with requirements for memory, terminal type, and the like.

Time

Assess how long the process should take. Steps in some procedures are pegged to the calendar. For example, readers may have to abide by closing dates for certain financial transactions or filings. Waiting periods may also be necessary. Account for the process time.

Range of Steps or Actions

Sometimes there is only one way to do something. When you ask several individuals about how *they* complete the procedure, they all list the same steps or activities. But often you find, as you read about the process and talk with performers, that you can reach the same goal by different routes. Collect instances of how the process can be performed. At this stage, develop a list of steps, including alternate routes. Isolate trouble spots and look for shortcuts.

Best Sequence

If appropriate, while you are researching the procedure you may want to try it out yourself. You'll gain confidence for writing that will translate into credibility in your instructions. You may not be the best performer. Indeed, many people who know how to do something well are unable to show others what they know. But you do need to analyze well what an expert performer does. Some sophisticated computer programs are now applied to this task, particularly in analyzing the actions associated with certain athletic activities, like the forehand kill shot in racquetball.

In testing out a procedure yourself, based on reading and interviews, establish a critical path to the goal of the procedure—the steps that absolutely must be taken in a specified sequence. Along the way, sort through alternate approaches.

Necessary Precautions

It's important to keep people safe while they work. Although someone faces fewer safety hazards filling out forms in an office than working with explosives in a laboratory, still, flag any possible dangers in the procedure. Less drastically, note where one might go wrong, and derive correctives.

Further Information

Particularly for long or complicated processes, compile a bibliography of sources for further information about details of the procedure. For example, if you are writing a guide to using a word-processing program in a business writing class, you will gather your information from such references as the operator's guides to the computer hardware, the user's manual for the operating system that the hardware runs, and the manual for the complete word-processing package. You'll then list these manuals as references for your readers in the class.

Setting Goals

The central goal of any procedure, of course, is "to instruct." But as a goal, this is hard to measure. How will you know if your instructions have worked? How will the reader know?

Instead, state goals as actions. And state goals in either individual terms or organizational terms. Note, for example, what the reader should know or should have produced at the end of the process. Here are two goals statements:

> When you have finished filling out this questionnaire, you will know:
>
> Your strengths
>
> Your weaknesses
>
> Your most probable career path

> This dress code tells you how to dress every day on the job to match the clean, neat, well groomed look our customers expect.

Sometimes the goal of a procedure statement is to enhance profitability and efficiency in the organization. In creating an insert to be mailed with claims forms, for example, a company may aim to reduce the number of incomplete or incorrectly filled out forms by a certain percentage. You might also write a procedure to reduce (by a specific number) the calls to a customer hotline.

Targeting the User

The goal, of course, depends on the reader. Procedures must work for the particular reader. Their failure is immediately obvious: The reader can't follow the instructions. Making assumptions about the user is tricky. An elaborate discourse on running a machine won't work if the reader can't find the on/off switch. A reference manual on a printer hooked up to a computer won't work if the manual doesn't note the presence of a reset button—one of the first things to push if the printer stops.

As with any marketing project, establish a baseline for your target users. Interview a sample of potential clients or customers. If your company has a toll-free telephone number to handle questions on the procedure you need to describe or on similar procedures, then record those questions for a period to make sure your description covers those most frequently asked. Moreover, you need to guard against telling the reader *everything*. Instead, tell only what the reader needs to know to achieve the specific goal you have set.

Different tasks have different degrees of difficulty. For the task you are describing, assess the prerequisite skill level and clearly target the description only to those capable of achieving the skill. Make sure that a process you design for beginners does not include any individual steps that can be accomplished only by experts, as a beginner's trail on a ski slope should include no expert pitches (unless, of course, you provide a beginner's bypass).

Envision, too, the reader as he or she reads. Some readers merely skim the instructions at their desk or in the field before plunging into the project. Some consult the procedure only in times of trouble. Even the most conscientious readers usually do not read straight through; to write the instructions assuming that the reader will begin on page 1 and continue uninterrupted page by page is to deny reality. Readers read and perform interactively. You'll need to accommodate their reading habits in the document's design.

Writing Three Types of Procedures

Once you have analyzed the process and have got a bead on the user, you should be in good shape to draft a procedure. Let's look at three different types of procedures. First, we'll examine the most common:

a *set of steps* in chronological order devised to achieve some goal. Second, we'll look briefly at guidelines for writing *manuals* that show how to operate a system or some equipment— and how to get out of trouble if the system or equipment does not operate. Third, we'll look at statements concerning employee *behavior* meant to carry out organizational policy.

Step-by-Step Instructions

Figure 21–2 is a procedure to be used by crew persons at McDonald's to fill a customer's order. It is specific and concrete; it anticipates questions.

Figure 21–2 works. It's easy to know how to act after reading it. Figure 21–3, however, caused confusion. It's a company's procedure statement "for obtaining approval for purchase of computers for administrative use."

The vice-president of operations circulated this procedure in a memo to all company employees. Each division had different equipment. The vice-president wanted to establish a standard to prevent duplication in systems, to increase compatibility, to ensure integrity of the data base, and to reduce cost through centralized purchasing. These are worthy goals, but the brief statement raised many questions.

First, the procedure glosses over the question of *who* within a division initiates a request. The McDonald's procedure clearly addresses the crew person at the register. Here, however, one senses that the initiator is the division head, but the route for requests within a division is unclear.

Second, the specific documents that trail the applications process are not designated. The company is large. Information submitted to anyone on the wrong forms is considered not submitted. But the form is not specified. And what does "makes justification" mean in practical terms? Can I apply orally, as the proposal will occur in a meeting? What gets approved (in Step 2, "Upon approval")? In Step 3, how do I "obtain funding approval"? Step 3 also discusses first "purchase requisitions" and then "requisition." Are these two different forms?

Third, several specific steps are ambiguous. For example, what will the Information Center do in its "two-week feasibility study"? Why two weeks? Is this the length of the study itself? Or will the division submit a list of documents written in a two-week period to determine frequency of use and therefore eligibility? In Step 4, who receives the items? Purchasing? Does *received* mean when I have them in my hands in the division?

This procedure serves neither the general reader who simply wants an overview nor the reader who wants to order equipment. It fails to

SERVICE: SIX STEPS

1. GREET EVERY CUSTOMER: "Good morning" or "Hi." Just saying, "Can I help you," is not a greeting. Be enthusiastic and smile. You never get a second chance to make a first impression.

2. TAKE THE ORDER: "May I help you please?"
    a. Listen attentively and do not interrupt the customer.
    b. Note only one item of suggestive selling.
    c. Explain delay (if applicable in case of grill).

3. ASSEMBLE THE ORDER: REMEMBER TENDER LOVING CARE AND ACCURACY.
    a. If tray is needed, assemble and put on counter.
    b. If everything is ready, use the fastest possible assembly.
    c. Handle cups by sides only.
    d. Be sure all drinks are filled, clean and capped.
    e. Select proper bag. Do not pop bag open.
    f. Bag food only if EVERYTHING is ready.
    g. Place sandwiches in bottom, fries on top.
    h. Pick up no more product than you can handle.
    i. Take items from right to left.
    j. Pick up fries from side, not from top.
    k. Double fold top of bag neatly and place logo (McDonald's emblem) toward the customer.

4. PRESENT THE ORDER: Slide tray or bag toward the customer.

5. RECEIVE PAYMENT: "Sir, your order will be $1.42, please."
    a. Call out sale and amount given you ("out of five").
    b. Place bill on register ledge until sale is completed.
    c. Count change to yourself, then into the customer's hand.
    d. Do not count coins, just bills.

6. THANK CUSTOMER AND ASK FOR REPEAT BUSINESS: "Thank you, sir, and come back again."
    a. Be polite and enthusiastic and remember to SMILE.
    b. Put bill in register and close the drawer.

FIGURE 21–2. Workable procedure (courtesy of McDonald's, Dukart Management Corporation).

1. Division contacts Computing Services Information Center to schedule meeting to discuss applications.

Division makes justification for purchase, which must include location of equipment and personnel who will use equipment. Division must plan to allow necessary time for training or self-education of these personnel. For word-processing equipment, the Information Center will conduct a two-week feasibility study.

2. Upon approval, Information Center submits to Division the hardware and software configurations with prices.

3. Division prepares purchase requisitions and obtains funding approval and sends requisition to Information Center, which then forwards it to Purchasing.

4. When all ordered items have been received, Division contacts Information Center for installation and assembly.

FIGURE 21–3. Unworkable procedure.

include the reader. Readers need to see themselves performing the process as they read. They need to translate the description immediately into action. Instructions, then, must be concrete. Otherwise, readers will have to spend extra time turning abstractions into some scene with them in it.

Part of the problem lies in the "business voice" that resounds through the procedure. Note the telegraphic style ("Division contacts Information Center"), the vagueness ("makes justification for purchase"), the passives ("when all ordered items have been received"). The vocabulary is indeed loose. "For installation and assembly" may be redundant. The phrase may also reverse the normal order; you will probably assemble the equipment before you can install it.

In revising these instructions, the writer should first *target* the audience better. As it turns out, only division heads can order computers for administrative use. So a specific procedure should be sent only to them.

Second, procedures work best when the writer addresses performers directly in imperative verbs. The following sentence is flat:

Failure to comply with tag-out procedures could result in injury to personnel and damage to equipment.

It gains in emphasis when expressed in *you* form:

> If you fail to comply with tag-out procedures, you could injure yourself and others and damage equipment.

Third, the writer should clarify the *sequence* of steps that the verbs represent. Authors need to imagine the reader, sitting at a desk and wondering what and to whom to write. Here's a revision of one section of Figure 21–3 (note the use of the imperative "send"):

> To justify your request, send the Information Center a brief statement (no more than three pages double-spaced). Include the following information:
>   **1.** What will you do with the equipment? (Give a general overview of the tasks now performed manually that you will assign to the computer.)
>   **2.** Where will you house the equipment?
>   **3.** Who will use the equipment (number of users and their job titles)?
>   **4.** How will you train these people?

Because a process occurs over time, most process descriptions are ordered chronologically. After an introduction that highlights the purpose of the procedure and that provides the context for the description, the steps are listed as the reader would perform them, one after another. Recipes follow this order (see Figure 21–12). So do most office procedures as in Figure 21–2.

Manuals

The manuals that accompany hardware or software, however, pose other levels of difficulty. We should say right off that manuals are big business. A manual may cost from $200 to $1,000 a page and from 3 percent to 10 percent of a company's total expenses. When their production lags behind the production of the items they document (a common occurrence), that lag can cost thousands of dollars a day. Moreover, up-to-date manuals are essential to the safe and effective operation of any equipment. By one estimate, the U.S. Navy alone has 200,000 manuals that must be kept up to date, but because of the difficulties in keeping current, 25% are out of date.[1]

Broadly speaking, there are two types of manuals: *standard* manuals that arrive with the item or system and serve all customers and *custom* manuals written for specific applications or customers. Because of the need for updating, manuals of either type are often con-

[1] Ron Winslow, "Technical Manual Production Finally Enters Computer Age," *The Wall Street Journal*, 21 June 1985, 29.

tained in a 3-ring binder so that customers can insert new instructions when items change. Tabs or other designators allow readers to find their way easily to the section they need. A good index is critical.

Manuals serve one or more of the three goals for documents that we discussed in Chapter 3. Let's review, for example, some of the standard documents that typically accompany a software package. First, an operating manual *records* the system. It is written from the system's point of view and notes, in technical and thorough detail, all of the system's specifications and capabilities. It is thorough and usually heavy.

Several other documents aim to *inform* the reader about how to use the system. Standard documents include, for example, a tutorial that runs through the basics of loading and using the program for a first-time user. The tutorial may also include exercises; it sequences instruction from easy to more difficult functions. Some of the instruction may be on-line as well as on paper. (Increasingly, too, video-tapes meet this need.) Often, customers rewrite the tutorials and other instructions for their own special applications. In addition, the software producer may provide a reference card listing appropriate commands and a template to place on the keyboard as a reminder of functions and keys.

More and more software houses are becoming aware that the documentation they provide is a key to selling the system—perhaps the major key. So they are developing documentation that *persuades* the reader as it informs. They are paying attention to design and avoiding the colorless, dense, margin-less, small-type pages of traditional manuals. Drawings help. So do instructions that are written not from the system's point of view as *capabilities* but from the user's point of view as *actions*. Here is a list of capabilities:

Line Format

Character Set

Constants

Variables

String Expressions and Operators

Numeric Expressions and Operators

Note how that list contrasts with a list of action steps:

Writing with Word Frames

Calculating with Spreadsheet Frames

Making Numbers Graphic

Figures 21–4 to 21–8 show the cover and sample pages from a well designed and persuasive guidebook introducing one software program, *Framework* ®. Figure 21–4 shows how the cover graphically emphasizes the idea of "frames." Figure 21–5 is the table of contents. Note the large typeface and several action statements as headings. Figure 21–6 shows a typical title page of a segment; all such pages are in similar form, with lots of white space and clean lettering. Figure 21–7 is the first page of the text, with a boldly displayed page number for ease of reference. The page facing the first page of text in each chapter also has a drawing (see Figure 8–21 in Chapter 8) that reinforces the message and provides aesthetic interest. Figure 21–8 shows a page of instructions. Running footers on the left pages give the name of the software; those on the right, the name of the producer.

In considering the content and design of a manual, producers must understand how different cultures learn. For American readers, this means putting an overview of each system or function before the details. For readers from other cultures, the approach must be different—one reason that simple translation of manuals rarely works. Japanese readers, for example, learn better through a more gradual introduction to the parts before the whole. A manual for Japanese users of the Apple IIc computer begins with a fairy tale, complete with four-color illustrations and other introductory material that is meant to reduce fear and build confidence.[2] Then sections discuss distinct functions. The authors designed the manual like a traditional Japanese dinner: All the food is placed on the table at once, and the diners eat the courses in any order they choose.

Behavior Guidelines

In addition to process descriptions and manuals, you may have to write instructions for general *behavior* on a job to put corporate policy into practice. Figure 21–9 is a procedure for dressing and personal appearance ("dress code") that supports the McDonald's goals statement quoted in part in Chapter 22. In its simple language and details, the statement is well tailored to an anticipated readership of young people, particularly students.

Designing the Procedure

As we've suggested, the *design* of a set of instructions is at least as important as the text itself—perhaps even more important. A crowded

---

[2]"Writing User Manuals for Japanese Readers," *Simply Stated*, The Document Design Center, American Institutes for Research, Washington, D.C., July, 1985.

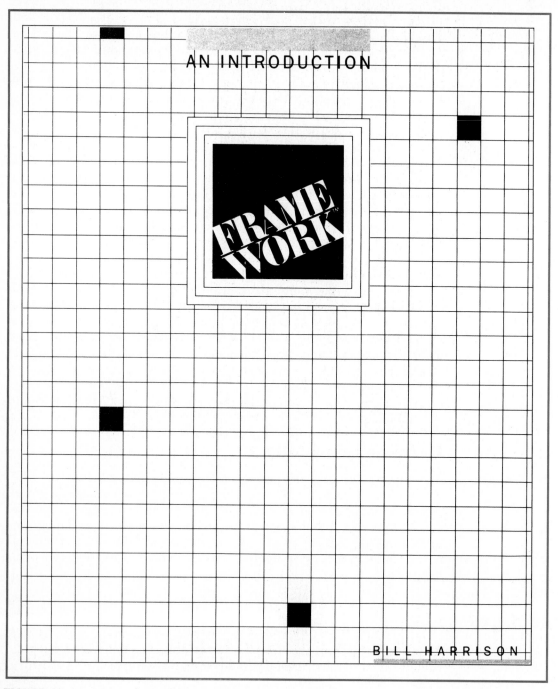

FIGURE 21–4. Cover of a well designed introductory guidebook to a "work processing" program called Framework (tm) (*Source:* Bill Harrison, *Framework ®: An Introduction*, Culver City, Calif.: Ashton-Tate Publishing Group, 1984. © Ashton-Tate, 1984. Used by permission).

CONTENTS

PART I:	**PRESENTING FRAMEWORK**	
Chapter One	A Framework for Mindwork	**1**
Chapter Two	Capabilities of Framework	**9**
Chapter Three	Working with Framework	**33**
PART II:	**FRAMEWORK OPERATIONS**	
Chapter Four	Framework ABC's	**47**
Chapter Five	Dynamic Outlining	**81**
Chapter Six	Writing with Word Frames	**105**
Chapter Seven	Calculating with Spreadsheet Frames	**141**
Chapter Eight	Making Numbers Graphic	**193**
Chapter Nine	Managing Information with Database Frames	**211**
Chapter Ten	Assembling and Outputting Frames	**229**
Chapter Eleven	Connecting to Outside Sources	**247**
PART III:	**APPLICATION EXAMPLES**	
Chaper Twelve	Thinking with Framework	**275**
Chapter Thirteen	Constructing a Client Database	**285**
Chapter Fourteen	Building Business Spreadsheets	**297**
Chapter Fifteen	Creating Compound Reports	**333**
PART IV:	**LOOKING AHEAD**	
Chapter Sixteen	Exploring the FRED Programming Language	**351**
APPENDICES		
Appendix A	Connecting a Printer to Framework	**365**
Appendix B	Using Framework Utilities	**367**
Appendix C	Changing the Framework Default Settings	**369**
Appendix D	Framework Error Messages	**371**
INDEX		**373**

ASHTON-TATE

FIGURE 21–5. Table of contents. © Ashton-Tate, 1984.

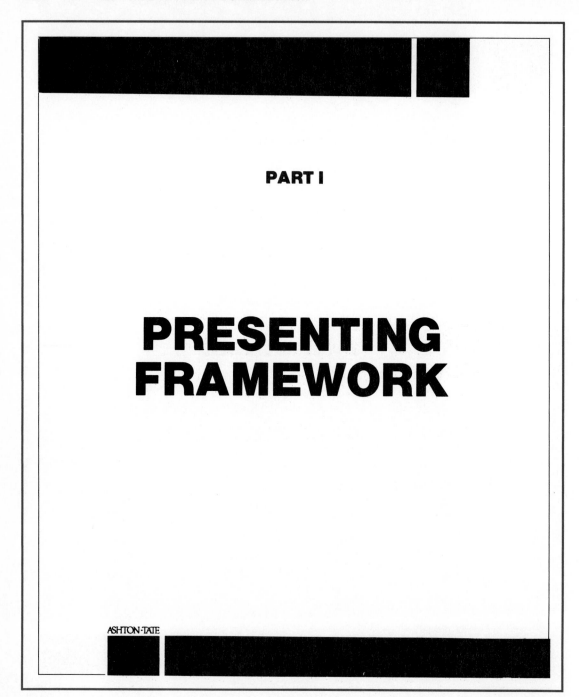

FIGURE 21–6. Title page of a segment. © Ashton-Tate, 1984.

1

CHAPTER ONE

A Framework for Mindwork

Frames are like scratch pads of the mind.

Framework by Ashton-Tate is a super-fast, professional *work* processing system. It multiplies the personal productivity of professionals, managers, and other information workers by applying the power of the personal computer to the essential information processing and communicating tasks that are central to virtually all professional work. These tasks include:

- compiling, sorting through, and analyzing information
- making calculations
- organizing ideas
- writing
- editing
- preparing, printing, communicating, and storing text, tables, and graphs

ASHTON-TATE

FIGURE 21–7. First page of text. © Ashton-Tate, 1984.

WORKING WITH FRAMEWORK | 39

ELECTRONIC SPREADSHEET

To build an electronic spreadsheet, you must first decide how many rows and columns to have. You enter these settings into the appropriate options on the CREATE menu and they will remain there until you change them.

The spreadsheet process begins when you select the Spreadsheet option from the CREATE menu. A frame like this appears:

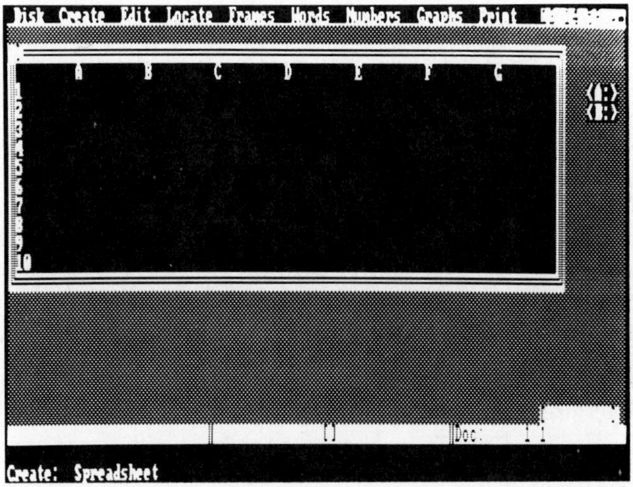

The spreadsheet frame reflects the settings you entered for the number of rows and columns. If the spreadsheet is too large to fit on the screen, move the cursor all the way to the right edge and bottom edge of the screen to see the columns and rows that run off the screen.

The spreadsheet frame is laid out differently from the word frame. You'll

ASHTON·TATE

FIGURE 21–8. Sample page of instructions. © Ashton-Tate, 1984.

NEATNESS COUNTS AT McDONALD'S

We have learned over a long period of time that our customers like a crew with a clean, neat, well-groomed look. This means:

Dress Code for Males and Females

A. Males

    1. Dark, clean, hard-soled shoes.

    2. Hair must be above collar, back and neat on the sides. Sideburns will not be permitted to grow long and bushy. No beards.

    3. McDonald's crew uniform will be worn, including a crew hat *and* name tag. Aprons will be worn on grill. Hats will be issued once a week. If you feel the uniform must be replaced because of wear, you must see a manager.

    4. Hair must be kept under the hat.

    5. All buttons on the shirt must be buttoned except for the top button, and proper personal hygiene standards must be followed.

B. Females

    1. White, nonskid soles or saddle shoes (brown and white) will be worn *and* kept clean and polished. Shoes must conform to uniform. We recommend white nurse shoes for looks and for comfort.

    2. Hair will be neatly combed and tied back if it is long.

    3. No excess or gaudy jewelry will be permitted. Makeup must not be worn to excess.

    4. McDonald's crew uniforms will be worn, including a crew hat and a name tag.

    5. Fingernail polish is unsanitary for the grill people.

    6. Only white sweaters may be worn. All buttons on blouse except for the top one must be buttoned.

    7. Proper personal hygiene standards must be followed.

Remember, your name tag is part of your uniform. A lost name tag will cost you 50 cents.

FIGURE 21–9. McDonald's dress code (courtesy of McDonald's, Dukart Management Corporation).

page layout and small print tighten the knot in the reader's stomach. The procedure looks unwelcoming, intimidating. To ease the reader's lot, design the document for both clarity and attractiveness, as in Figures 21–4 to 21–8.

Throughout the text, in both words and graphics, build in cues that indicate steps and allow the reader to move back and forth between text and action. Make it easy for readers to find their place again. Here are some points to watch, particularly as you revise your draft:

1. Headings. Consider using headings that describe *action*, in verb form, rather than mere noun titles. Or use questions as headings. Use first- and second-level headings, but avoid subdivision beyond the second level. Choose a design that highlights the headings and lets them clearly segment the text.

2. Indentation. Write procedures in short sentences and short paragraphs. The document is a place for isolated units of meaning that a reader can easily check off. The white space for indentation builds the reader's confidence and paces the reading. There is little room for the more leisurely discussions that occur in long paragraphs.

3. Numbering. Sometimes, you'll want to number steps—again, for ease of reference. The numbers also provide a way for the reader to keep score; the reader can mark progress as he or she moves on to steps with higher numbers.

4. Layout. Don't crowd the page. Encourage reading and remembering with a pleasing design. Choose a typeface and a type size that will accommodate the readers. For example, a text aimed at the elderly is best composed in a fairly large type size. Avoid using all capital letters (some people read these as a reprimand). If you need to warn the reader about a particularly dangerous step, make that warning stand out from the rest of the page. Allow adequate margins for the reader's own notes.

Composing with Visuals

Many procedures are drafted first *visually*. Then the writer adds words to explain. A visual can summarize an entire procedure in one whole picture, as in the flowchart shown in Figure 21–10. The chart both *documents* the procedure for writing reports in the author's organization and *instructs* report writers about the procedure. Words can only describe the segments.

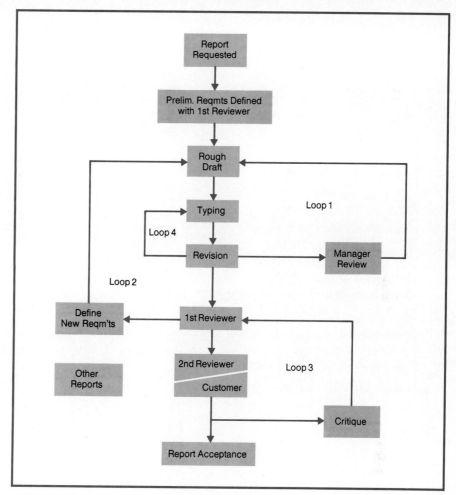

FIGURE 21–10. Flowchart of report production.

Visuals also motivate a reader. For some audiences, cartoons and other drawings provide welcome relief from the tediousness of the procedure.

Novice users may respond particularly well to visual analogies. For example, one word-processing program uses icons to instruct. The user is told to consider the entire screen a desk. Then icons represent actions: a trash can for something the user wants to delete, a folder for a file, and the like. The analogies simplify the understanding of tasks performed electronically by the system.

Some instructions, particularly those that must serve several lan-

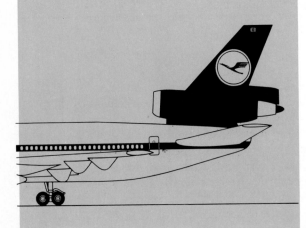

FIGURE 21–11. Instructions for an international audience (courtesy of Lufthansa German Airlines).

guage communities or those addressed to children, are almost entirely visual (see Figure 21–11). Moreover, instead of a document, you may elect to use a videotape of someone performing the procedure as a method of training new users.

Testing the Procedure

Writers probably revise and rewrite procedures more often than they redo other documents. The instructions have to work.

Validation and Verification

You may not get rid of every bug before you issue a procedure, but try to spot as many as you can. *Validate* and *verify* the procedure. Both reviews are tests of *performance*.

A procedure may fail because of inaccuracies in the content. For example, a manual may lack information concerning a last-minute enhancement in a new product. To validate the procedure, check it for accuracy.

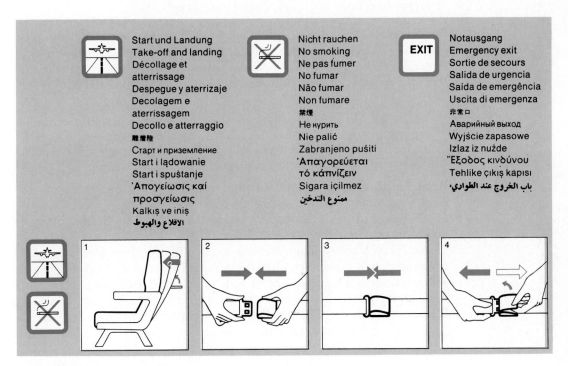

FIGURE 21–11. (*continued.*)

A procedure may also fail because of ambiguous language, insufficient detail, confusing format, or confusing visuals. To verify the procedure, test it on yourself, although as an informed user you may overlook what others may find troublesome, and particularly the ways in which someone may go wrong.

A better route is to test the procedure on a sample of users before you issue it widely. Watch them and ask them to comment aloud as they work through your statement. Or devise a questionnaire to determine their ability to read and follow the instructions or to remember the steps.

In general, revise to *simplify*. Tell the users only what they need to know—no more. If you really feel that a wholesale explanation of the system is in order, consider placing such a description in an appendix. Build in examples—the examples you may gain only as you test the general statements in your draft. Listen when readers comment, "Does that mean . . . ?" Make sure to include any necessary cautions (like reminding someone to unplug a toaster oven before cleaning it). You might also warn readers about any common mistakes in following the procedure and provide ways out of them.

Your Voice as an Instructor

Finally, read through your procedure to hear how your voice comes off the page. Check your style and tone. It's easy to preach or to chide. Instead, put yourself in the reader's shoes. C. Northcote Parkinson (author of *Parkinson's Law*) noted:

> Bad instructions are sometimes deliberate, arising from some muddled motive, the desire to humiliate, the desire to reveal somebody's stupidity, the desire to show that the coming disaster was not our fault. In such instances the will to communicate is absent. More often, however, the will is there, but the imagination is not.[3]

Being imaginative requires, in part, rethinking the process from the reader's perspective and escaping from the "business voice." Figure 21–12 pokes fun at that voice, but this parody works because it's not far from what one reads every day in offices.

And watch your biases. Here is a set of instructions from a student newspaper at a university in Philadelphia. The school's basketball team was playing in a tournament in Salt Lake City, Utah, and the editors were giving advice on how to get there. The approach is fine: The text defines the intended readers (in the first paragraph) and then gives the routes. Note, however, the change of scale—from minute instructions

---

[3]"Parkinson's Law of the Vacuum (or, Hoover for President)," *Forbes*, 12 May 1980, 138.

For those government employees and bureaucrats who have problems with standard recipes, here's one that should make the grade—a classic version of the chocolate chip cookie translated for easy reading.
Total Lead Time: 35 minutes.

Inputs:
1 cup packed brown sugar
½ cup granulated sugar
½ cup softened butter
½ cup shortening
2 eggs
1½ teaspoons vanilla
2½ cups all-purpose flour
1 teaspoon baking soda
½ teaspoon salt
12-ounce package semisweet
chocolate pieces
1 cup chopped walnuts or pecans

Guidance:

After procurement actions, decontainerize inputs. Perform measurement tasks on a case-by-case basis. In a mixing type bowl, impact heavily on brown sugar, granulated sugar, softened butter and shortening. Coordinate the interface of eggs and vanilla, avoiding an overrun scenario to the best of your skills and abilities.

At this point in time, leverage flour, baking soda and salt into a bowl and aggregate. Equalize with prior mixture and develop intense and continuous liaison among inputs until well-coordinated. Associate key chocolate and nut subsystems and execute stirring operations.

Within this time frame, take action to prepare the heating environment for throughput by manually setting the oven baking unit by hand to a temperature of 375 degrees Fahrenheit (190 degrees Celsius). Drop mixture in an ongoing fashion from a teaspoon implement onto an ungreased cookie sheet at intervals sufficient enough apart to permit total and permanent separation of throughputs to the maximum extent practicable under operating conditions.

Position cookie sheet in a bake situation and surveil for 8 to 10 minutes or until cooking action terminates. Initiate coordination of outputs within the cooling rack function. Containerize, wrap in red tape and disseminate to authorized staff personnel on a timely and expeditious basis.

Output:
Six dozen official government chocolate chip cookie units.

FIGURE 21–12. A bureaucrat's guide to chocolate chip cookies. (*Source:* Susan E. Russ).

about leaving Philadelphia to the broad scale used for the rest of the country. The distortion is clearly funny—like the Steinberg cartoon map of New York City that shows the limited vision of residents of one part of the country. But be wary of unintentional—and thus harmful—distortions when you write.

There are undoubtedly some of you out there who want to go to Salt Lake City, and who are

(a) immune to auto sickness.

(b) not independently wealthy.

(c) not particularly interested in your classwork.

The solution—drive. In your own car, or in a Hertz special. It only takes 48 hours, and the directions are simple.

Take Spruce Street over the South Street Bridge and make a left on the Schuylkill Expressway (I-76 West). Stay on this road for an eternity, all the way through Pennsylvania and into Ohio.

When you get to Youngstown, I-76 turns into I-80 (the Ohio Turnpike). Stay on I-80, even when it becomes the Indiana Turnpike.

Stay on 80 when it goes past Chicago.

Past Des Moines, Iowa.
Past Omaha, Nebraska.
Past Lincoln, Nebraska.
Past Cheyenne, Wyoming. Cheyenne, Wyoming!

The next big town is Salt Lake City. You can't miss it.[4]

Writing That Works

The final test of a good set of instructions, of course, is that the reader can follow them. Increasingly, researchers are studying *how* people learn for clues about how best to design instructions. The Document Design Center of the American Institutes for Research is one of the leaders in this field.[5] You read instructions almost every day. Try to read them not only for what they say, but for tips about how they are designed. Keep those tips in mind as you write instructions for others to follow.

Exercises

1. Here are two descriptions of the registration procedure at a university. They are general descriptions intended for a brochure about the activities of the records office, so they differ from other models we have seen of instructions intended for performers rather than for those simply interested in an overview. How do they differ from each other? Do they give the same details? Can *both* be accurate? Which would be easier to follow, if indeed you needed to register for classes?

---

[4] *The Daily Pennsylvanian*, 21 March 1979.
[5] For information about the Document Design Center and its excellent newsletter, *Simply Stated*, write to the Center, American Institutes for Research, 1055 Thomas Jefferson Street NW, Washington, DC 20007.

A
REGISTRATION PROCEDURE

Preregistration:
    1. Preregistration forms are mailed to all undergraduate and graduate students, by the Records Office.
    2. Students wishing to preregister return the completed form to the Records Office within two weeks.
    3. After all forms are received, class request lists are compiled by the computer. A list for each class is made that contains the name of every student who requested the class.
    4. The class request lists are then sent to the individual professors. The professors then "red-line" or eliminate any students who are not qualified to take the course (i.e., students who do not have the proper prerequisites or who are not in the proper department).
    5. After the lists are returned to the Records Office the remaining students on the lists are assigned a point value as follows:

Freshman	100
Sophomore	200
Junior	300
Senior	400

The student's total number of credits earned is added to the class specification points to determine each student's point value.
    6. After the point values are assigned, each class is filled with students in order of point value, until the class limit is reached.

Drop-Add and Late Registration:
    1. Students who did not preregister or who didn't get a class through preregistration can add classes at the beginning of the semester through the drop-add system.
    2. Drop-add forms are filled out exactly as preregistration forms are except that drop-add forms require a professor's signature for each class.
    3. After the drop-add form is signed by the professor, the student is added to the class, and a point value does not have to be determined.

B
REGISTRATION PROCEDURE

    Each current full-time student is given a two-week advance registration period. The students are given a blue form, which is used only for requesting up to seventeen credit hours. Statistics show that only eighty percent of the students advance register.

After the forms are collected and stamped, they are processed into a computer. The computer stores the information in its memory by social security number, not by first come, first serve as commonly believed.

Then the process of trial assignment begins. This is when the computer scans through its tapes and assigns the requested courses. Each student is given a number through a point system which is obtained by the number of earned credit hours multiplied by four-hundred points for a senior, three-hundred points for a junior, etc. The students, with the highest number, get priority in course selections.

The computer scans the first gridded box and determines if the particular class is opened and then enrolls the student. The following boxes are processed the same way and then the computer continues downward in numerical order.

Finally, the student gets his program and only receives three courses when a student requested six. The reason for this is because of a procedure called red-lining. Red-lining occurs when a student requests a course but he is not in that major or doesn't have the prerequisites needed. For example, it is very difficult to obtain a communication or business course if you are not in that particular college.

The student must now drop/add which is in the hands of the individual professor. The faculty decides how many students they will offer the class to. If there is room, students can add the course; this is a first come, first serve process.

2. Comment on the *style* of the following instructions, from a university faculty member telling readers how to get from the university to his home:

Drive east on Route 2 (Kirkwood Hwy.). Turn left on Polly Drummond Rd. (first left turn after Red Hill Nursery sign). Drive up the hill for about a mile, then turn right onto Linden Hill Rd. at the *second pair* of flashing yellow lights (bypassing Polly Drummond Plaza in the process). Turn at the second right turn, where a small black-and-white English Village sign marks the way. Follow the winding road until you see another English Village sign, where you turn left into a declivity. Keep right until you pass the tree in the middle of the road, then turn left around a sharp hairpin curve down another declivity. Look for two brown dumpsters fronting an elevated walkway leading to Jill Hall (adjacent to the woods). Walk right in and go up to the top floor, #17, last door on the right. If lost, call 737-8661. (It sounds complicated but I find my way home nearly every night.)[6]

Could you draw a map from these instructions?

3. Write a set of instructions to tell a reader how to go from some Point A to some Point B. Assume that the reader knows nothing about either location. Use no visuals. Then change the conditions. *Use* a visual. Assume a reader who is generally familiar with the area, and with one location, but not with the other. What differences appear in the instructions?

4. Choose one of the following topics. Then write a procedure on the subject, using at least one visual. *Before* you write, define these constraints:
   1. The audience and assumptions concerning their prior knowledge.
   2. The purpose of the procedure.
   3. Your point of view: A set of instructions? A reference description? A narrative of how *you* did this once?

Topics:
   • What to do when your car won't start.
   • How to get access to a computer on campus.
   • How to make a hoagie (submarine, grinder—whatever you call a long sandwich with various meats in it).
   • How to cure a headache.
   • How to sell something (select one thing you know something about).
   • How to read a corporate annual report.

5. As a class project, collect instructions from different household or office devices, preferably instructions in multiple languages and with pictures. How do these differ: Size? Shape? Devices for courting the reader? Visuals? Forms of address (*you?* generalized?)? What makes them easy or hard to read?

6. This chapter discussed problems in writing instructions for different cultures. Review several sets of instructions with multilanguage origins. Note word usage, of course. Often, such usage is a source of humor, as in a translation of *hydraulic ram* as "water goat." But beyond this literal level, note any differences in structure or assumptions about the reader that are inherent in this sample of English-language instructions for devices manufactured abroad.

[6]Courtesy of Ted Billy.

Documents of
the Corporation

[The company] grew up in an environment of extensive planning, detailed corporate manuals and endless memos.[1]

So far in this part of *Business Communication*, we've looked at the major *forms* of business communication: memos, letters, bids, proposals, progress reports, business reports, and procedures. This chapter takes a different perspective. It looks at business documents as they do the work of a corporation. First, it discusses *internal* documents that meet the three organizational goals discussed in Chapter 1: definition, control, and maintenance. Second, it discusses the *external* documents that circulate to customers, shareholders, the government, and the public at large. This chapter, then, reviews and augments the rest of this part of the text in the context of the corporation.

Internal Documents

The array of documents required to trail every decision or action in an organization may baffle an office newcomer. In general, the larger the organization, the more numerous the forms and the standard documents, and the more likely that items will be known by acronyms or numbers understandable only to the initiated: a "PIN," a "16-J-18," a "Form 52-X." Although many of these documents may seem designed more to prevent work than to enable it, still some are critical. Let's look at the most significant ones.

Documents That Define

At the highest level, documents codify the very meaning of an organization. They identify goals and strategies, set an agenda for action, and shape an image that governs the organization's life. Let's look at three forms:

1. Goal statements.
2. Policy statements.
3. Plans.

Goal Statements

Goal statements are sometimes called *strategy* or *mission statements*. They tell in general terms what the organization is and what it aims to accomplish. Figure 22–1 presents the mission statement of Metro-

---

[1] Monica Langley, "Bell Battles: AT&T Marketing Men Find Their Star Fails To Ascend as Expected," *The Wall Street Journal*, 13 February 1984, 1.

Metropolitan Hospital is a private, not-for-profit organization established to provide medical care for the residents of the Tri-County area. It offers three levels of service: emergency treatment, basic diagnostic and surgical care, and—through its Metropolitan HomeCare Facility—long-term nursing care for the elderly.

Metropolitan Hospital seeks to provide the best possible care in all categories at the lowest cost consistent with sound medical and fiscal practice. It is committed to personal service, attention to individual patient needs, and courteous professional relationships with its clients.

People make Metropolitan Hospital work. Therefore Metropolitan is people-oriented in its employment practices as in its medical service. It aims to help its employees at all levels to develop their skills and abilities to the highest level they are capable of and provides support services to help all employees reach their maximum potential as individuals and as providers of health care. Relationships among employees at all levels are governed by professional courtesy and with the ultimate goal of making Metropolitan a truly caring institution.

FIGURE 22–1. Mission statement for Metropolitan Hospital.

politan Hospital (METHOP). The statement segments levels of service and emphasizes the hospital's "people orientation," both toward patients and toward employees. Many mission statements are mere exercises in jargon—the "stuffy talk" we noted in Chapter 7. But Figure 22–1 avoids the twin traps of pomposity and vagueness.

The mission statement sets a direction. It establishes a big picture and a corporate style that then reverberate through each employee and corporate action. Figure 22–2 is another goal (or mission) statement— from the McDonald's Corporation.

Policy Statements

Policy statements translate goals into behavior. They address personnel issues (hiring, firing, promotion, and compensation), corporate social responsibility, the use of company facilities for nonbusiness purposes, or advertising and promotion standards. Figure 22–3, for example, provides a policy statement on patient relations derived from Metropolitan Hospital's mission statement: "committed to personal service,

OUR OBJECTIVES

Our philosophy is really very simple, but making it work takes the best effort of everyone on the team. Our prime objective is

TO SATISFY THE CUSTOMER

The customer is the most important factor in our business. We do this by giving the best QUALITY, SERVICE, CLEANLINESS, and VALUE

Q   McDonald's reputation for quality is internationally known. We are especially unique because the highest quality standards are maintained at very reasonable prices. We use the finest available products and carefully developed formulas. But all of this can be lost without your help. Always check the products you prepare or serve. If they are not right, do not serve them and tell your manager. One of the keys to quality is Tender Loving Care—''T.L.C.'' All our efforts can be lost if you crush or drop a sandwich. Handle all products with ''T.L.C.''

S   Quality and Cleanliness are wasted without fast, courteous service. A smile does as much to bring a customer back as the best food in the world. And remember—the customer is the most important single factor in our business. Courtesy is always easier if we remember the GOLDEN RULE: ''Treat everyone, especially the customer, the way you want to be treated yourself.'' The customer appreciates courtesy and appreciates speed. Sometimes it is hard to give them both at the same time, but that is what makes McDonald's unique.

C   Cleanliness is like a magnet drawing customers to McDonald's. Our stores must be spotless at all times, both inside and out. Only through the best efforts of everyone will that happen.

V   Value is a subjective judgment by our customers—how they view the product received in relation to the price they pay for it. Value is the combination of a quality product served quickly and courteously in a clean environment. Only by maintaining the highest standards of QSC will our customers view McDonald's as a true value.

OUR EMPLOYMENT POLICY

It is the policy of McDonald's to offer employment and promotional opportunities to the most qualified individuals and to establish a Wage and Salary Program consistent and equitable for all employees.

Further, it is the policy of the company to prohibit actions or practices which would discriminate in the implementation of the above or general personnel programs for reasons of race, color, age, creed, national origin, or sex. We are an Equal Opportunity Employer.

If you have any questions about this policy, please contact your Store Manager.

FIGURE 22–2. McDonald's goal statement (courtesy of McDonald's, Dukart Management Corporation)

Metropolitan Hospital is committed to dealing with its patients and their families in a courteous and professional manner that ensures maximum attention to individual needs consistent with the overall goal of providing excellent medical care. To achieve this goal, the staff of the hospital should at all times treat patients and their families with respect and with sensitivity to their emotional needs. Adult patients are always addressed as Mr. . . . or Ms. . . . Children are called by their first names. Staff should avoid becoming too familiar with patients and families or developing personal relationships that interfere with professional standards of treatment. Staff should not allow personal attitudes toward patients to obstruct the professional delivery of health care. Patients or families with special emotional problems or social difficulties should be referred to the counseling staff, which provides specialized psychological help. All patients and families should be treated equally and fairly; favoritism shown to individual patients or families is counterproductive to the effective operation of the hospital.

FIGURE 22–3. Policy statement on patient relations for Metropolitan Hospital.

attention to individual patient needs, and courteous professional relationships with its clients."

The policy statement provides guidelines for action: Be sensitive and respectful, address adults as Mr. or Ms., don't become emotionally attached to patients, refer special problems to counseling, treat everyone equally. The statement is not a *procedure,* as we discussed in Chapter 21. A procedure is a more specific set of rules and regulations for behavior to carry out a policy. For example, Figure 21–2, in Chapter 21, describes the correct procedure for handling orders at McDonald's to carry out the policy of customer service, and Figure 21–9 provides the dress code to carry out the policy of cleanliness. The METHOP policy statement might be broken out into a specific *procedure* for checking patients into the emergency room—a procedure that would put the guidelines in the policy statement into practice.

Plans

A third type of document that defines is a plan. Most organizations have general plans, sometimes called *business plans* or *strategic plans,*

Because our people are our major asset, the hospital regards staff development as a function of the highest priority. To encourage it, we will create a position of *assistant director of personnel for staff development* and will hire the best qualified person for that position. He or she will be charged with developing a master plan for staff development in consultation with divisional and departmental supervisors. A budget for this function will then be developed and submitted to the board for approval. The Staff Development Program should become operational within nine months, pending Board approval.

FIGURE 22–4. Plan for human resource development for Metropolitan Hospital.

as well as detailed operating or tactical plans. These general plans convert mission statements into broad agendas for action. Figure 22–4, for example, shows how Metropolitan Hospital's concern for people gave rise to a strategic plan for human resource development. This brief *plan,* part of a large planning document, outlines an approach to meet a goal (creating the new position of assistant director) and attaches a deadline for action.

Documents That Control

Once the destination and the direction are set, markers are needed to assess progress along the way. *Control documents* monitor the route toward the goal. We can identify two forms:

1. Operational plans.
2. Routine reports.

Operational Plans

METHOP's strategic plan for staff development crates a new assistant director's position. That's fine. But what specific programs will that person oversee? Another level of plan is needed: an operational or tactical plan that provides specific guidelines for action.

Operational plans contain quantitative measures. They establish schedules. For example, the Niblex Snacks Company, which manufactures and sells salty snack foods, has established as one linchpin in its strategic plan the need to maintain its return on investment (ROI) at 18 percent. To achieve this goal, Niblex requires that profit margins for its Niblex brand must be 28 percent. To achieve that goal, Niblex has determined that unit costs must be maintained at 50 cents per package. Thus the operational plan is as follows:

> To maintain acceptable profit margins to meet corporate ROI goals, direct unit costs per package of Niblex must be held at a maximum of 50 cents. Unit labor cost should be 35 cents, and materials cost 15 cents.

The statement is precise, concrete, unambiguous—like a good statement in any operational plan. It should leave no doubt in the mind of the reader about how to carry out the plan.

Routine Reports

To keep management informed about how plans are being carried out, and in general about how life in the corporation is moving toward its goals, routine reports are written. Such reports contain financial information, along with data on sales, inventory, and production. They are usually brief and short on the amenities—the writer assumes a common framework with the reader. Figure 22–5 is a routine periodic update in a memo from Niblex. This brief memo provides the vice-president with enough information to assess whether the division's operations are meeting goals. Every month, Saunders submits such a memo. Indeed, many routine reports are pegged to the calendar; an employee may be required to write every week or every month on her or his work. Such reports help management to keep control of the company's movement toward its goals.

When work requires an employee to leave the office, then another common form of routine report documents the time away: *the trip report.* Such reports let management know what was learned. They also serve a secondary function in documenting expenses as part of audit requirements and personnel practices. Chapter 12 provides a model trip report. Most reports cover these topics:

1. The reason for the trip.
2. Logistics (date, time, locations, and people met with).
3. Expenses (with attached receipts).
4. Results (sales made, contacts developed, and future actions needed to reach the intended goal).

Niblex Inc.
Production Department

To: C. Blake, VP Operations
From: J. Saunders, Production Supervisor
Date: April 2, 19XX
Subject: Manufacturing Cost Data, March

Units produced	897,000
Labor Costs	$322,800
Material Costs	$135,600
Average Unit Cost	$ .511

Both labor and material costs per unit exceeded division goals, resulting
in a 1.1-cent-per-unit overage. Labor costs were increased by the snow
emergency on March 7, which reduced the work force by three persons
that day. Material costs were affected by an increase in the price of salt.
Both these problems were one-time and should not recur. We are
making every effort to lower direct unit costs this month to compensate
for the performance during March. Our year-to-date figures remain
within the 50-cent-per-unit goal, despite the March problems.

FIGURE 22–5. Routine up-date report.

Documents That Maintain

Finally, many documents keep the house in good shape. The company
needs to order supplies, hire employees, and describe daily activities.
We can identify three major types of maintenance documents:

1. Operating procedures and rules.
2. Personnel documents: job descriptions and performance evaluations.
3. Employee relations documents.

Operating Procedures and Rules

Every organization lives by rules. These rules, or operating procedures, govern such housekeeping functions as purchasing, building maintenance, security, property control, parking, and facilities use. Most large companies, hospitals, government agencies, and fast-food chains have operating manuals that include all such rules and regulations. These are commonly updated regularly to reflect policy changes. Their aim is clarity. As we saw in Chapter 21, such procedures must be written to the level of the intended reader and should contain illustrations and perhaps sample forms.

Personnel Documents

Many operating-procedure statements govern the behavior of personnel: hiring, firing, promotion, compensation, schedules, vacations, coffee breaks, and dress codes. Such procedures are one form of personnel document. Here are two other important forms: *job descriptions* and *performance evaluations.*

Job descriptions.   As the name implies, job descriptions are documents that describe the requirements—in terms of responsibilities, personal characteristics, and reporting lines—of positions within the company. Before METHOP could hire an assistant staff director, someone (probably the staff director) had to write a description of the position and gain approval of that description. Abbreviated forms of the description appear in advertisements soliciting applications for the position. Figure 22–6 is a job description.

Performance evaluations.   Clear and specific job descriptions ease the employee's task in fulfilling the job and ease a supervisor's task in evaluating an employee's performance. Indeed, another important personnel document is the performance evaluation, which is a formal review of employee behavior and achievement during a given time. Evaluations are standard in large organizations and are becoming common in smaller ones. The growing concern about people as the core of business reinforces the importance of evaluations.[2] Moreover, outside agencies are increasingly intervening in corporate affairs: Evaluations often provide the basis for corporate actions that are subject to judicial or agency review or individual legal action. Thus, for positive and negative (protective) reasons, organizations take performance evaluations seriously. Most documents result from conferences with the em-

---

[2] For further details about performance evaluations, read Carol Hymowitz, "Bosses: Don't Be Nasty (and Other Tips for Reviewing a Worker's Performance)," *The Wall Street Journal,* 17 February 1985, 29.

Metropolitan Hospital

Job Description

Position: Correspondence Secretary   *Reports to:* Director
Department: Medical Records   FT_____ PT_____
Grade: 5   *Signature of Supervisor*_____ Date_____

Qualifications:

Education: High-school graduate or equivalent.
                   Accredited Record Technician [ART] preferred.

Experience: Minimum 2–3 years in medical records.

Other: General secretarial skills. Minimum 40 wpm. Ability
                   to work independently and assume responsibility.

Physical: Must be able to pass METHOP physical exam.

*Area of
Responsibility:*   Processing all requests for medical records.

Duties: Receive, review, and process all requests for medical
                      records information according to prescribed
                      guidelines.
                   Process subpoenas for medical records.
                   Answer telephone inquiries regarding how to request
                      information and the status of a request.
                   Maintain Release of Information Log.
                   Follow up problem requests.
                   Maintain communication with business office
                      regarding requests from insurance companies and
                      HMOs.
                   Perform other duties as assigned by the Director or
                      designated representative.

FIGURE 22–6. Job description (courtesy of Jeanne Romanic).

ployee, often before the report is written, and almost always after, to confirm the conclusion and to allow for clarification and dissent.

Such evaluations should not be broad pictures ("Helen is a good worker"; "Rex must do better next year"); rather, they should be classified ratings in agreed-on areas of performance. Some organizations use forms that call for numerical ratings and/or comments in dozens of categories of behavior. Some forms are more open-ended. Figure 22–7 is a discursive evaluation; Mark Dornberg is evaluating Rick Heinz in accordance with a format requiring ratings in five areas and general commentary in three others.

Employee Name: Rick Heinz
Employee Title: Clerk/typist II
Evaluator Name: Mark Dornberg
Evaluator Title: Supervisor, Accounts Payable

Date: June 18, 19xx

I. General Background

Rick Heinz joined this department on September 5, 19xx, and has worked in the capacity of clerk/typist II since that date. He has reported to me since he joined. Rick had six months of part-time experience as a typist before coming here and worked ten to fifteen hours a week at a fast food restaurant while completing high school. He is a high-school graduate and last fall began taking a night course in business at the community college. He types 45 wpm and has recently begun to use our wp and electronic mail system. He's enrolled in a vendor's course next fall to increase his skills on that machine. Rick does all my regular typing, including correspondence and reports; is responsible for filing all documents in the office and is assisted in that job by a part-time secretary; and organizes the office routine (handles vacation schedules, fills out personnel attendance records, takes orders for coffee breaks, and so on).

II. Perceived Weaknesses

Rick is hesitant to accept new responsibility. He seems too comfortable with his routine and avoids new tasks that might require more of him.

FIGURE 22–7. Performance evaluation.

He seems content to continue in his current job, though at my urging he is taking courses part time at the community college. I hope he will be inspired to reach for more in his current position or to seek a more responsible one here. He lacks ambition. A second problem with Rick is that he is somewhat rigid in dealing with the office routine. He gets angry if the other secretaries don't follow "the book." He likes things to be cut and dried. Maybe this is another reflection of his lack of commitment, as doing things routinely means he doesn't have to extend himself.

III.   Perceived Strengths

Rick does his job accurately, thoroughly, and on time. He follows directions carefully. His typing is accurate. His filing is always correct, and he supervises our part-time secretary efficiently. Rick is pleasant and friendly and enjoys generally good relations with the office staff (but see above on one point). I think Rick has real potential in business, and I am encouraging him to pursue a career more seriously. His current position is really below his capabilities.

RATING	Superior				Inadequate
	5	4	3	2	1
Skills		x			
Business habits			x		
Personality			x		
Initiative				x	
Overall performance			x		

Even experts disagree on what constitutes an ideal performance evaluation. Some argue for an entirely quantitative rating; others argue for totally open-ended narratives; and others advocate various mixes. In general, however, most agree that the evaluation should be concrete, honest, objective, and careful.

Concrete. The evaluation should be concrete, directing an employee's attention to a particular point that can be corrected. Instead of "Inattentive to detail," the evaluation should note, "Fails to complete purchase orders in normal company fashion and neglects to maintain attendance records of subordinates."

Honest. Honesty doesn't require brutality, but it does require that the writer avoid fudging, obscuring, and equivocating. Lies are terribly easy to detect. They show someone shirking responsibility for helping employees to overcome weaknesses and build on strengths. And lies can get the writer into deep trouble if a real personnel problem develops.

Objective. In *rating* someone, a writer is often tempted to *judge* that person. The line between rating and judgment, after all, is pretty fine. But good evaluations hold the line. For example, instead of noting, "Ms. McCauley fails to behave in a manner consistent with the high tone expected in this office," a good evaluation notes, "Ms. McCauley should refrain from chewing gum, playing the radio loudly, and eating at her desk, as these activities detract from her professional image."

Careful. Performance evaluations are organizational tools. But they can also figure in disputes that may reach outside the organization to government agencies or the courts. Writers need to keep such potential secondary audiences in mind. Even inside the company, managers are rated by their supervisors on an ability to evaluate employees and hence develop them. Moreover, someone who consistently writes positive performance evaluations and then recommends the person for a low raise or (worse) termination is going to have to explain the inconsistency to someone—certainly the employee, perhaps even a judge. One value of performance evaluations is that they document employee behavior that may lead to adverse actions. Periodic written evaluations that consistently point to major weaknesses and report no progress in overcoming them represent helpful support if it becomes necessary to demote or to fire someone, particularly if those evaluations are reinforced by other evidence—like coworker complaints about Ms. McCauley's gum chewing or radio playing.

Employee Relations Documents

Keeping employees informed about company news, especially people news, is an important step in making sure that the organization is functioning at its maximum—and that everyone knows that it is. Large organizations have staffs devoted to the publication of in-house newsletters and magazines and the circulation of notices concerning promotions, hirings, reassignments, awards, and recognition.

External Documents

We've examined *internal documents* in light of the particular organizational purposes they perform. *External documents* are more easily grouped according to the audiences they address. Most serve the common purpose of making the organization look good. They both inform and persuade.

Let's look briefly at documents produced for four audiences: customers, shareholders, the government, and the public.

Documents for Customers

We're already seen many documents addressed to customers: sales letters, responses to complaints, collection letters, proposals, and bids. Correspondence with customers and business proposals may originate in any of several divisions of the company. In a large company, a marketing department may oversee the care and feeding of customers, particularly advertising, product announcements, and sales brochures. Those functions may require a multimillion-dollar budget.

In a small organization, a simple typed notice may suffice, as in Figure 22–8. Woody Hermann, the owner, is concise and direct. Considering its audience, this simple notice, tucked under a windshield wiper, conveys the right message.

Figure 22–9 shows a more sophisticated customer-relations document. *Energy News You Can Use* is an insert that accompanies monthly bills sent by Delmarva Power. Richard G. Hofmann, Managing Editor of Delmarva Power, saw this insert as a major factor in improving the utility's customer acceptance rating from 49 percent in 1982 to 71 percent in 1985.

To Our Valued Customers:

Beginning in August, Woody's Garage will be providing complete service on Hondas, Toyotas, and Datsuns. We have hired John Politz to supervise work on Japanese automobiles. John has had years of experience and will be happy to discuss your automotive needs.

Thanks for your continuing patronage. Please tell your friends about our new service.

FIGURE 22–8. Service announcement.

ENERGY NEWS

YOU CAN USE

Call Us ... We Can Help

What should you do if you can't pay your Delmarva Power bill by the date it's due? Call your district office right away.

When you call your local office, a customer information specialist will talk with you about your situation and work with you to help you avoid service disconnection.

We realize that you may be worried about the possibility of your service being disconnected. Our customer information specialists will be happy to help you find a solution to your problem.

What can we do to help you?

We may be able to set up a credit extension to help you avoid service disconnection. We also offer other programs. They include:

■ **Installment Payment Plans:** We may be able to arrange an installment payment agreement for you. The amount of the install-

ments is based on several factors including the amount of the unpaid balance, your ability to pay, and your past payment record.

■ **Budget Billing:** We can set up a budget billing plan for you. This program allows you to pay a fixed amount each month. Your account is reviewed quarterly and payment amounts are revised if necessary.

■ **Social/Service Agency Referrals:** Our customer information specialists can refer you to community and government agencies that may be able to help you with various energy assistance programs.

If you would like more information about any of these programs, call your Delmarva Power office.

What Did Santa Bring You?

Santa delivered many VCR's, microwaves, televisions, and other appliances during the holidays. Here's a guide to give you a sense of how much these appliances cost to operate.

Appliance	Typical Wattage Rating	Estimated kWh Used/Month	Approximate Cost/Month*
Videocassette Recorder	150	9	90¢
Microwave Oven	600	9	90¢
Color Television	200	40	$4.00
Hair Dryer	1200	9.6	96¢
Automatic Coffee Maker	1200	18	$1.80

*This cost is based on 10¢/kWh. The price you're paying for electricity is less than this. We rounded the number to help make your energy budgeting easier.

FIGURE 22–9. Customer service insert (courtesy of Delmarva Power & Light Company).

Documents for Shareholders

Government agencies, nonprofit organizations, and profit-seeking organizations that are privately owned need not worry about reporting to shareholders. They may have analogous constituencies (voters, in the case of government agencies, for example) to whom they are accountable and for whom they must therefore provide information and with whom they must cultivate a good image. But here we're concerned with publicly owned corporations, which must, as a legal requirement, report certain basic financial and marketing data to shareholders every quarter. Securities laws stipulate minimum reporting requirements: income statement, balance sheet, sources and uses of funds, statement of accounting principles, notes on valuations, research investment, foreign currency effects, and so on. Although some corporations comply at only a minimal level, firms that have many stockholders almost always dress up these statements.

While quarterly reports are usually brief and straightforward, *annual reports* are dressier. They represent the company's best occasion for communicating to its owners what it is doing and why. The report aims to bolster the investor confidence needed to maintain stock prices and to make the company an attractive one for potential owners as well. Increasingly, annual reports have become critical marketing tools, the special assignment of investor relations offices or groups within public relations departments. These reports are often handsomely designed, with color photographs and graphics.

Occasionally, publicly held companies need to communicate special news to shareholders, for example, a takeover bid from an unfriendly source that requires shareholder resistance, a major new product that will improve the company's financial prospects, a change in top management, or the results of litigation that may affect the company's stability. These messages typically come as *letters from the chief executive officer* and follow a letter structure and style (see Chapter 13).

Many large companies also produce newsletters or magazines directed to shareholders. Their goal is to make the shareholders feel positive about the company, to encourage continued ownership and further investment, and to create an attractive company image. Some of these, like *The Lamp*, produced by the Public Affairs Department of Exxon Corporation, rival the publications of commercial presses in graphic design and readable reporting.

Documents for the Government

Business leaders often complain about government regulation. But whatever their feelings, they must communicate with federal, state, and local government agencies. This is just part of doing business in a democratic society. Reports to agencies may be regular or occasional.

Regular reports include the 10K forms that have to be filed annually with the Securities and Exchange Commission (the core of the annual report) and similar documents filed with state agencies. In addition, companies write periodic compliance reports on affirmative action agreements, reports on health and safety standards, and statements concerning the status of retirement and benefit programs governed by statute.

Occasional reports vary, depending, of course, on the particular need. One is the Environmental Impact Statement (EIS), which must be submitted when a company proposes some action that can affect the natural environment. Building a new highway, for example, requires the submission of an EIS, as does the construction of a factory in a marsh or the extension of a water and sewer system to a new subdivision.

Documents for the Public

Companies communicate with the public at large mainly through advertising. The advertising may be broad-based, like billboards on highways, or targeted, as in direct-mail solicitations (see Chapter 16). In addition, companies produce documents concerning special events, publish brochures on topics related to their major product or service, and write press releases. The range of possibilities is wide. Let's look briefly at a few examples.

Some public relations writing in corporations follows up on events, particularly if a problem has arisen that needs to be turned into an opportunity. One case in point: A large land-development company invited opinion leaders from an East Coast city to the grand opening of a corporate office complex. But on the day of the event, one of the worst rainstorms in history stalled over the area, turning the site into a mudfield.

People's clothes got wet and many shoes were ruined. The company, however, turned this negative item around and made it the theme of the follow-up mailing. Under a bold heading, "Mudslide Hits Malvern and You Were There," the company sent this message, accompanied with pictures of muddy shoes and people dancing barefoot in the mud, and with a shoe-care kit:

> At Rouse & Associates, we have a reputation for unforgettable parties. But our May 26 "Today and Tomorrow" party, celebrating the new Great Valley Corporate Center East, was more unforgettable than most.
>
> The tent was beautiful, the food and drinks were wonderful, and spirits were high. But let's face it—our shoes took a beating.

Well, we're sorry about that. So sorry, in fact, that we've created this special shoe-care kit for you and everyone else who braved the mud. Keep it handy at your office . . . or when you travel . . . or for the next time we throw a party![3]

Informative brochures are another form of public relations document. Figure 22–10 shows the cover of a brochure, "The Economics of Energy," produced by the Informationszentrale der Elektrizität-swirtschaft e.V., in Frankfurt, West Germany. It aims to educate the public at the same time that it displays the utility's own careful conduct of its business.

The goal of a press release (or a series of releases) is to promote goodwill with the media and to maintain name recognition. A release may cover such events as the appointment of a new president, the promotion of a key employee, the acquisition of another company, the sale of a division, the expansion of a plant, the resolution of a legal action, an invitation to an open house, the sponsorship of a softball team, or the sponsorship of research. Figure 22–11 is a press release announcing a promotion.

Old hands at press releases—both writers and readers—would recognize the style and content in Figure 22–11 immediately, even without that "For immediate release" tag line. It's obviously positive—about Blakely, about Tatum, about British Classics. It includes a quotation (perhaps real, probably something invented by the writer). It gives the company's background. It identifies a contact person for follow-up questions and confirmation. Such releases find their way to local newspapers and radio and TV stations; they also go to trade publications and alumni offices.

Writing and circulating press releases is, of course, a specialized function typically falling to people who have an eye for media events and know the right people in the media. Trained and experienced public-relations people cultivate contacts in the press, arrange for special tours, schedule press conferences on major news, and generally develop the publications program that ensures that the company's image will be kept broadly and positively in the public eye.

The Corporate Communication Environment

This chapter began with a quotation about a company that grew up in an environment of paperwork: "extensive planning, detailed corporate

---

[3]Used by permission of Rouse & Associates.

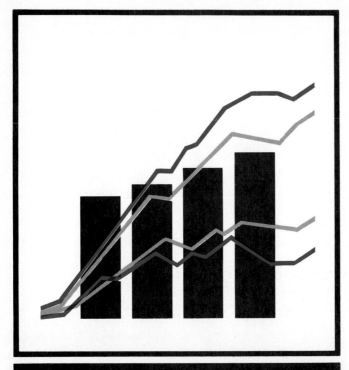

FIGURE 22–10. Brochure cover (courtesy of IZE, Frankfurt, West Germany).

British Classics
Lakewood, Louisiana

For immediate release:

British Classics of Lakewood, Louisiana, announced today the promotion of Henry Blakely to the position of President and Chief Operating Officer.

Mr. Blakely joined the company in 1978 as Sales Manager after fourteen years in the automobile sales field throughout Louisiana. A native of Dallas, Texas, he graduated from Rice University in 1962 with a degree in Business Administration and served in the U.S. Army in Germany as a Staff Specialist in purchasing. Mr. Blakely is married to the former Julie Watts. He is a member of the Rotary of Lakewood and served as director of its Youth Sports Activities Program. He owns and services several classic British sportscars and is active in the Sports Car Club of America.

Mr. Blakely said, "I am honored by my appointment as President of British Classics and look forward to working with the very dedicated staff of this great company and with our many customers nationwide. I pledge to continue the excellent service that has been the hallmark of British Classics under my predecessor, Ryan Tatum. Our company has a great future."

Mr. Tatum retires from the presidency after eight years and will continue to live in the Lakewood area. He remains a director of British Classics.

British Classics, founded in 1960, imports British Leyland and other fine automobiles from the United Kingdom. It offers sales and service on all makes of British cars, including Jaguars, Rovers, Austins, and the popular Land Rover and Range Rover four-wheel-drive recreational vehicles.

Contact: Henry Lukens, Public Relations, 504-636-3588

FIGURE 22–11. Press release.

manuals and endless memos." Sometimes the paper chokes corporate growth. But most of the time, some paper is necessary to get the company's work done, both to meet inside purposes and to convince outside audiences that the company works. In this chapter, we've toured several of these forms rather briefly. Perhaps after this initial visit, you'd like to spend more time with some of these forms. Do so. Browse through annual reports or other corporate statements in your college or university library. Or if you work in an office, read through the files to see how your company does its paperwork—and how you can perform that work to the company's benefit, and your own.

Exercises

1. Here is a "market comment" from the director of research at a brokerage house. (You'll recognize the first sentence from Chapter 9). Assume that the author has asked you, a new member of the Statistical Department, to revise this draft to be sent to clients. Refer to the Handbook at the end of this book and to Chapter 9 for advice:

Those that give credence to the January market barometer, that is whatever way the market goes in January, so will be its overall direction for the year, the prospects are not promising. For the month of January, the Dow Jones Industrials lost 38 points and the Dow Jones Transportation Index lost 45 points in the same period. This was accomplished on record volume of over 2.2 billion shares in the New York Stock Exchange for the month of January.

All this volume does not make the brokers ecstatic for it is on the down side and could indicate movement of capital to the sidelines and into short-term interest bearing vehicles.

Adding to market watchers woes was the disturbing news that an AFC team won the Super Bowl. This theory holds that should a NFC, or an original NFL team now in the ARC wins, the S&P 500 will rise, and will decline when an old AFL team wins. Its accuracy quotient of forecasting advances and declines are between 94 and 100 percent.

To put the recent decline into more perspective, since the 1984 high point established in the first week of January until February 3 close, the Dow Jones Industrial Average has slumped 92 points.

A number of views have been proferred as to the whys and wherefores of the market drop. The most prominent reason is the feeling that the economic recovery has been showing signs of slowing. Yet, on Tuesday the Index of leading economic indicators showed an increase for the month of December of 6/10 of 1%. Others cite the budget deficit which has been targeted at $180 billion for the year, and estimates of higher deficits through 1989. This has become ammunition for the anit "supply siders" who are clamoring for a tax increase and lower military spending to reduce the deficit. The financing of the deficit by Treasury borrowing will put pressure on interest rates, many feel.

The one shining light in the market has been overall strength of the oils as the takeover fever still pervades. Getty 123 ½, Gulf 54 ½, Unocal 36 ¼, Texaco 39 ½, have been strong for the past month.

Market Appraisal

It would appear that the selling which has picked up in recent weeks could soon ease up. There have been indications from the administration that there could be some budget pruning and some income tax changes. A move toward a fixed rate of 25%-30% for all seems to be gaining momentum in Republican and Democratic circles. There also seems to be an intensifying clamor for a less restrictive money policy by the Fed. We would view positive actions in this regard as favorable for the market.

Intermediate term we view the market favorably. We believe that there will be numerous profit making opportunities in the market between now and the fall with now being a buying opportunity. It is our belief that the election year market will swing to and fro as the political trends are divined. We continue to recommend purchases in the auto, bank, chemical, drug, retail, steel and utility stocks.

2. Turning complaints (or mistakes or bad luck) into opportunities is an art, perhaps, more than a skill. But good communicators are marked by such an ability, as we saw in the statement about the mud-slide party. Think of a recent event where something went wrong, or imagine such a situation. Then create a news release or a customer bulletin that turns the problem around.

3. Consider how you would state the *goal* of your college or university. Where would you look for a goal statement? In the catalog? As a group project, write such a goal statement. While you write, consider how you would measure achievement of the goal, that is, how you would make the statement *operational*.

4. As a team, analyze and then summarize a corporate annual report. Other teams will summarize the same report. Note any discrepancies in the summaries. Is the report deliberately evasive? Does it contradict itself? Do the pictures and the financial data tell different stories? Does the auditor's letter contain any cautions about the company's financial health?

5. Collect a sample of brochures from various companies and public agencies. Note their strategies for presenting material. Who is the intended audience? What level of language is used? What *voice* does the author write in (see Chapter 7)? How much real information is given relative to the number of words and visuals used? How is the document designed? Is it easy to read?

PART

The Process and Forms of Communicating Orally

Talking and Listening to Meet Communication Goals

In this part of *Business Communication* we look at strategies for goal-oriented talking and listening to match the advice you read earlier concerning goal-oriented writing. Of course, we should say right off that not all talk is instrumental. Not everything you say is meant to get work done. Indeed, much goodwill in an organization depends on small talk, the kind of chatting about the weather and baseball scores that smooths a friendship or serves as a prelude to more directed discussion. A good manager is adept at small talk, particularly at knowing what topics fit which people and when small talk is and is not appropriate.

But here we emphasize talking that works. In this chapter, we examine some basics. In Chapter 24, we look at the most interactive occasions for going public with your ideas: telephone conversations, interviews, and meetings, including teleconferencing. Chapter 25 focuses on the full-dress business presentation.

Deciding to Talk

Consider these situations:

- You're concerned about a coworker's attitude toward her job. You consider sending her a note, but you reconsider and walk down the hall to talk with her.

- You're not sure which of several marketing strategies would be best for a new product that your company has developed, so you ask the product developer, another marketing person, and a secretary who has a great consumer's knack to meet in your office to forge an approach.

- You've submitted a proposed reorganization plan for your division. Your boss asks you to come in and talk about it.

- You're a broker for an investment firm. You've bought a list of potential clients, and you're going to call them to solicit business.

- Your division's sales have been lagging. You call in the salespeople to motivate them to sell more.

- Every quarter, you present a five-minute overview of the financial standing of your group to the group's administrators at their quarterly meeting.

- You've applied for a job, and now the company's college recruiter wants to talk with you about your application.

- You're a banker, and your former fifth-grade teacher asks you to visit his class because they are studying banks.

In each of these situations, you decide (or someone else has decided) that the communication goal is better served by talking than by writing—or, in some cases, by talking *and* writing. Let's look at some criteria for making such decisions.

First, sometimes you talk with people as a preliminary to writing. You interview sources of information for a report, you check out political positions before drafting a policy statement, and you hold a meeting to gain consensus for a decision and a plan of implementation.

Second, you may talk with someone when a brief discussion seems a faster and easier way of conveying simple information than a memo, or when you need a quick response. "Most executives . . . hate reading the reports, memoranda, and letters that choke their in-baskets, hate reading the stuff almost as much as they hate writing it," noted one writer for *Fortune*.[1] Many communication problems lend themselves to more simple solutions through talking.

Third, you talk through a problem in a meeting to profit from the synergy that comes with group thinking. You brainstorm together to develop a marketing strategy that perhaps no individual alone could have hatched. You meet to form a consensus decision that every member of the group can support.

Fourth, you talk and listen when the message requires a personal touch. Through conversation, you build and enhance a personal relationship. In writing, you address a *real* reader, of course. But *as* you write, the reader is usually only a fiction, someone you imagine. You may have a picture of the reader or readers in your mind (even in a frame on your desk), but the picture is only a representation. As you *talk*, however, you share a room or a hallway or some space in a park with the person or persons you are talking with. Those persons are *real*. Emotionally charged messages are often best conveyed personally—like firings and hirings—with a later written follow-up. You may need a personal meeting to *persuade* someone to buy something or to believe you. Your presence lends credibility. You meet with your boss to convince her of the appropriateness of the proposed divisional restructuring you sent along in a memo earlier. The college recruiter wants to see how the potential applicant acts, how he presents himself. So do bosses: "In making decisions, executives tend to give more weight to concrete examples, concretely presented, than to assemblages of fact abstractly pitched. What is more concrete than Smoking Joe Junior Executive up there really making the numbers come alive. . . ?"[2] Fifth-graders may want to *see* a banker. The salespersons in your division

---

[1] Walter Kiechel III, "Office Hours: The Big Presentation," *Fortune*, 26 July 1982, 98.
[2] Kiechel, p. 98.

may want to shake your hand. A client corporation may want to meet the architect to whom they'll entrust the design of their new headquarters.

Depending on your own personality and the situation, the prospect of face-to-face meetings may either attract you or send you to your pencil. At the extremes, some occasions demand writing, and some occasions demand speaking. You must *write* to create a permanent record. Writing transcends time. You also must write anything that readers will use for reference or anything that requires great detail. The written record further allows different readers to read selectively and to reread matters of importance. Talking doesn't last. Moreover, a writer gains one great advantage in writing over those who speak: the possibility of revision. You can examine and reexamine statements to make sure they say exactly what you mean. When you talk, you can't take back your words. The writer has more *control* over the information and the presentation than the speaker. Speakers can be interrupted. Speakers can be surprised.

On the other hand, *talking* meets other goals better than writing. Documents, for example, are not interactive—and there are times when interruptions and surprises are welcome in communication. Talking *is* interactive. Through talking you share ideas and build agreement. Moreover, as we have seen, you use your presence in a room, with other people, to defuse or build the emotional charge in a message, to sell an idea or a product, to confirm your credibility, and to incite others to action. The head of the sales division calls in salespersons less to inform them about lagging sales than to use a discussion of that problem to engage their energy to sell more. The session builds enthusiasm and forges the goal.

Certain occasions *demand* either talking or writing: You're required to attend a meeting, you're requested to participate in an interview, or you're assigned to write a report. But often you have a choice. Decide to write or talk based on a sense of your own strengths and your management style. Some managers prefer the sidelines, using memos to convey information, calling few meetings, and scheduling few interviews. They write and are written to. Others are motivated only by the presence of people. They are more apt to stop by your office to converse about some problem or topic than to send you a memo. You may write to them. But you'll get action only when you stop by their office.

Deciding to Listen

Talking, as we've mentioned, is *interactive*. The flip side is *listening*. When you decide to talk, you must also decide to listen. You must further decide to listen when others choose to talk. Listening is not just a passive condition. It's an activity. Here are some guidelines for active listening.[3]

First, *listen accurately*. Hear the message as the speaker sent it. That probably seems simple, but many people don't hear well. In part, failure to receive the message may result from physical difficulties: noise in the room, the speaker's mumbling, or the listener's hearing loss. But more often listeners miss messages because they are thinking only about themselves, because they are biased toward or against the speaker, or because they miss cues, either verbal or nonverbal, to key points and evidence. Instead, as you listen, try to construct the big picture of the message as it is being sent. Relate it to what you already know. Jot down key words (but don't try to write down everything the speaker says). Reconfirm main points afterward with the speaker. Question any points that seem controversial.

Second, *listen analytically*. Confirming the message is the baseline of listening. But because talking and listening are interactive and personal, the process is more complex. The ground of the discussion shifts. You negotiate and build on what the other has said. Listen not only for the message, but also for the speaker's *intent*. Analyze particularly any *covert* intent. When your boss says, "You're looking tired. Why don't you take a few days off," is her real intent to tell you that you are not working up to her expectations? Intending to find out about your extracurricular activities an interviewer asks, "What sports do you participate in?" You are active in clubs, the theater, and musical groups, but not in sports. If you assess the real intent as "extracurricular activities," then you'll respond, "I'm not very active in sports, but would you like to hear about other extracurricular activities I participate in?"

Sometimes, of course, what people say *is* what they mean. As a listener seeking covert intentions, you may misread a signal. Someone who says, "People like you impress me with your ability to get work done," may intend a compliment. A listener sensitive about her age may hear, however, "You're surprised because you think someone my age can't do *anything*."

In looking for covert intent, be aware enough of your own biases and pressure points not to attribute to others your own lack of self-confidence.

A speaker's intent is often signaled by the connotations of the words he or she chooses. Analyze, for example, a speaker's use of jargon. If a speaker drags out terms from a professional language different from

[3] For an excellent discussion of listening in a managerial context, see Allan A. Glatthorn and Herbert R. Adams, *Listening Your Way to Management Success* (Glenview, Ill.: Scott, Foresman, 1983).

yours, is he trying to impress you? To intimidate you? Or is he just displaying his own laziness in not adjusting the language to your needs? In addition, analyze a speaker's choice of slang or coarse usage. Is she deliberately trying to offend you? Is she trying to validate her own toughness? Analyze any evasive language a speaker uses. Civilized behavior often requires a certain degree of evasion and ambiguity. Not all misunderstanding is bad; some light misunderstandings even enrich relationships. On the basis of your feel for the context of the discussion and for the speaker, weigh evasions and assess whether to let them go or to question them.

In general, then, *evaluate* the message, and on that basis, formulate your *response*.

Third, *listen ethically*. By this, we mean: Be sensitive to the other person's needs and individuality and withhold judgment. Give the person time to develop a point. Don't interrupt. Don't pry—but don't close off any possibility for someone to talk with you. Let's restate here, as in Chapter 1, one guideline for ethical behavior: In all your dealings, leave the other at least as well off.

Productive Talking and Listening

One problem in listening well—and talking well—is that so much happens simultaneously. You have to listen accurately, analytically, and ethically *all at once*. These difficulties are compounded as the differences between you and the person or persons you are talking with increase. You may build these differences into barriers to communication. But to achieve your goal—a goal that, by definition, can be achieved only *through* others—you must at least accommodate to those differences. At best, you'll benefit from them. Let's look at three potential differences between you and the people you talk with and listen to: a different gender, a different culture, and a different point of view.

A Different Gender

Researchers are discovering that gender stereotypes create real, if invisible, barriers to effective communication among men and women. In the traditional stereotype, men are "objective, rational, independent, ambitious, and responsible; women, subjective, intuitive, emotional, dependent, and accommodating. Authority roles require men; women serve as helpmates."[4] In blind experiments with identical evi-

[4] F. Geis, M. Carter, and D. Butler, "Seeing and Evaluating People," Office of Women's Affairs, University of Delaware, 1982.

dence (essays, or inventions, or dossiers), evaluators routinely rate as superior the evidence attributed to males.

In another type of experiment, a position at the head of the table in a group including both sexes conferred leadership on the man but failed to confer it on a woman.[5] Women who take charge in corporate circumstances are perceived as "cold, unfeminine, aggressive, abrasive, and arrogant," although researchers have found that similar behavior by males is described as "objective, efficient, ambitious, decisive, and self-confident."[6] In discussions, men tend to interrupt women and to set the agenda more than women interrupt men or establish discussion topics.[7] Women's interruptions, moreover, are more likely to be seen as violating a norm of subservient behavior, whereas men's interruptions are encouraged. In general, women's speech tends to be descriptive and "superpolite" rather than direct and informative, with more questions and signs of uncertainty.[8]

The stereotypes and the patterns of behavior are changing. But many very decent people are trapped into behavior that prevents them from listening accurately and benefiting from the insights of others. Look beyond the stereotype to the person sitting at the conference table.

A Different Culture

Look beyond cultural stereotypes, too, that warp understanding. Whenever some people go somewhere new, even if only to the next department, or to another level of management, they often regress to childhood. They feel clumsy and liable to make mistakes. Even little things—perhaps *particularly* little things—loom large: You get lost in another company building. You can't figure out the pay telephone in a Glasgow, Scotland hotel lobby. How do you know what coins to insert? What does the beeping sound mean? Why can't the person you hear on the other end hear you?

Feeling childlike inhibits your ability to act as an adult among other adults. A certain self-confidence is necessary for you to accept differences in others without either cowering or rudely imposing. The unselfconfident may take refuge in rank or national origin as a way to avoid

[5] N. Porter and F. L. Geis, "Women and Nonverbal Leadership Cues: When Seeing Is Not Believing," in C. Mayo and N. Henley, eds., *Gender and Nonverbal Behavior* (New York: Springer Verlag, 1981).

[6] N. T. Feather and J. G. Simon, "Reactions to Male and Female Success and Failure in Sex-linked Occupations: Impression of Personality, Causal Attributions, and Perceived Likelihood of Difference Consequences," *Journal of Personality and Social Psychology* 31 (1975), 20–31.

[7] For example, see J. A. Piliavin and R. R. Martin, "Effects of Sex Composition in Groups on Style and Social Interaction," *Sex Roles* 4 (1978), 281–296.

[8] See, for example, Robin Lakoff, *Language and Women's Place* (New York: Harper & Row, 1975).

contact with a person. Chapter 28 discusses international communication in more detail, but let's mention a few constraints here.[9]

One of the most deeply rooted cultural senses is the sense of time. American business behavior places a premium on punctuality. You attend a meeting *on time* or suffer group censure. Indeed, times for meetings are fixed and specific. In other cultures, the times are more advisory. In Japan, for example, people can acceptably arrive at a meeting several minutes before or after a suggested time simply because the traffic is unpredictable. In some South American countries, attendees arrive half an hour or more after the appointed time as a measure of courtesy, somewhat in the way that an American host would not expect guests for a 7:30 P.M. dinner party to arrive much before 7:45. The duration of a meeting also varies among cultures. Americans tend to measure in minutes and hours, with a premium usually given for brevity. Most meeting places have clocks; most attendees have watches. In Saudi Arabia, the measure may be a day or an evening, with pauses for ceremony. A simple work-change order that would require perhaps ten minutes in an American meeting may require eight or ten hours. In going abroad, you need to set more than your watch to local time. You need to set your behavior and expectations from others differently.

Similarly, different cultures have different senses of personal space. Some authorities suggest that Americans tend to stand about seventeen inches to twenty inches apart in general social dealings. Italians and Latin Americans tend to stand closer; the Japanese, farther apart. Backing off from an Italian to achieve your own space may send a message of rejection and may hinder communication.

Acceptable posture and gestures in discussions also differ. Japanese executives may sit up straight, arms balanced on a chair's armrests, as befits persons of good education and balance. They may find offensive the slouching posture that an American may feel appropriate for a discussion. We say a lot by the positioning of our bodies and need to be aware of how these statements translate in different settings.

Moreover, different cultures display different ways of listening and learning, of processing messages. American business in general tends to emphasize the *product* of a meeting: a contract signed, a sale completed, a plan endorsed, information conveyed. The meeting or training session moves linearly toward that goal. A brief hello, and then it's down to business. Other peoples, like the Saudis, value the *ceremony* perhaps more than the product. The product indeed becomes a kind of

---

[9]For further insight into international communication, see "Going International," film/video series produced by Copeland Griggs Productions, 3454 Sacramento Street, San Francisco, CA 94118.

by-product of the maintenance and cultivation of an ongoing relationship. The business information is only one strand in a fabric of discussion woven with social ceremonies.

A Different Point of View

In addition to gender differences and cultural differences, you have to communicate across differences in point of view. Conflicts occur daily. The company's goals—and your own goals—depend on your ability to manage conflicts and to learn from criticism.

Managing Conflicts

The first rule in managing conflicts is to recognize that some are inevitable. Look for them. Avoid glossing over differences.

The second rule is to recognize that conflicts rarely have only a single cause and a single resolution. Listen to bosses, peers, or subordinates who express different opinions or hint at problems, even vaguely. Listen analytically to what people *say* is wrong and to how stories about the conflict differ. Sift through the issues to focus on the causes, and then deal with each cause.

That said, here are some brief guidelines for responding when someone is in conflict with you.

1. Don't pick fights. As a function of listening analytically, weigh the importance of the differences in information or point of view that you hear. If the difference is trivial, let it go. Avoid a spiral of ever-escalating conflicts on trivial issues.

2. Postpone discussion when the other person is angry. When, for example, you deliver an emotionally charged message that angers the other person, give that person time and space to compose himself or herself. Suggest another meeting later on—and arrange it. Give the other person room.

3. Look for areas of agreement. Although conflict is inevitable, it is also limited. Rarely do two people disagree on everything. In a discussion, look first for a point of agreement that can maintain a relationship through the later, and lengthier, statements of disagreement. One simple technique: Restate someone else's position in your own words before you question it. At least then you can agree on the *statement* of the issues.

4. Demythologize. Many conflicts occur because people address each other as roles or genders or representatives, not as people. They perceive situations as immovable wholes, not subject to intervention or change. Sometimes one person, for only vaguely perceptible reasons, will become another's nemesis. You know you can't talk to X without getting angry. You know that every time you're in a certain office you get upset. You've never got anything straight on a Friday the thirteenth. Such myth making, the creation of individuals and events that are larger than life, blocks reason and thwarts communication. Try to deal with people as the individuals they are.

Learning from Criticism

Recognize, first, that *everyone* is criticized at some time. You are not alone. Criticism is needed if we are to zero in on problems and construct correctives.

Second, listen analytically to the criticism. Be critical about criticism. Assess your relationship to the critic and any hidden agenda that the critic may have. *Attribute* the impulse to criticize. A critic may snarl simply to show his or her own discomfort, to vent his or her own peeves, to mask a lack of self-confidence, or to forestall any counter criticism. That criticism has nothing to do with you. On the other hand, some criticism has real content. Evaluate its source. Do his or her interests conflict with yours? What does the source have to gain from criticizing you? What's the source's track record for sizing up other situations? Try to strip the criticism of any emotional response it invokes in you and to place the message in the context of what you already know. Learn what you can. Request supporting details or evidence if necessary. Then suggest a corrective—or ask the critic for suggestions—and end the discussion on a joint look to the future.

Final Word

Ineffective communicators see all the differences as so many *hindrances* to getting their work done. Effective communicators play to these differences as yet more opportunities both for personal satisfaction in mastering something new and for professional satisfaction in achieving some mutual goal with another person or other persons.

Talking and listening will be an important part of your job. Cultivate an ability to perform each activity well—and to determine which occasions demand each. Figure 23–1, "When's the Best Time to Stop Talking," emphasizes the need for brevity and quiet, too, in a relationship. In the next two chapters, we provide a routine for handling the most common situations. Don't just trust your intuition, good as that may be. Bolster that intuition with some strategies that will help you to achieve your intended purpose, and that will make your discussions *work*.

When's The Best Time To Stop Talking?

Probably
now.
A story is
told about
FDR when he
was a young
lawyer.
He heard his
opponent
summarize
a case before
the jury
in eloquent,
emotional,
but lengthy
appeal.
Sensing the
jury was
restless,
FDR is reported
to have said,
"You have heard
the evidence. You
have also listened
to a brilliant
orator. If you
believe him, and
disbelieve the
evidence, you
will decide
in his favor.
That's all I have
to say."
He won.
Overstate
and bore.
Understate
and score.
When a baseball
umpire says,
"Strike three!"
He doesn't have
to add "Yer out."
That's what
strike three
means.

How we perform as individuals will determine
how we perform as a nation. FREE: If you would like
an 8½″ × 11″ reprint of this message, write to
Harry J. Gray, Chairman and Chief Executive Officer,
United Technologies, Box 360, Hartford, CT 06141

FIGURE 23–1. Advice about talking—and listening. Used by permission.

Exercises

1. As a participant in a meeting, observe not only *what* is being said, but *how*. Note how the leader establishes a tone and a procedure. Are these appropriate? Does the meeting get out of control? Who interrupts whom? What signals an interruption? If the meeting includes members of both sexes, do you notice any differences in their group behavior?

2. Here's a list of some categories into which we classify people. (You can, of course, add any others.) As a group exercise, draw a verbal picture of each of these (see the example). Be specific. Does everyone agree? Speculate on the origins of these stereotypes:

Jock attributes: hangs around locker rooms, chews gum, wears warm-up suits and athletic shoes, stares a lot, . . .

Nerd	Italian
Workaholic	Irishman
Hacker	Macho man
Preppy	Drunk, junkie

3. Talk with some international students at your school about their expectations in conversations and particularly their sense of what's *different* about talking with Americans, in an American setting.

4. Several best-sellers over the last few years have exploited the notion of classifying people—by whether or not they eat quiche, dress like preppies, or eat smooth or crunchy peanut butter. Set up some stereotypes or categories yourself; then sort the people you know into them. What's the principle of classification? Can you *predict* any behavior based on the categories?

Phone Calls, Interviews, and Meetings

We're finding that many people do their most creative work outside the direct office environment—in the hallway, the dining room, wherever they can gather. So we have been paying more attention to nurturing those spaces and getting away from a total concentration on cosmetics and the work station itself.[1]

That's how an architect who specializes in office design describes his work. Much of what he designs for is *discussion*, those formal or informal occasions when people get together and exchange information and ideas. Discussions occupy a good portion of a professional's day. This chapter provides an overview of items to keep in mind when you talk with others. Much of that talk will involve just one other person or a small group. It will require a good deal of give and take, an ability to listen as well as to talk and to read cues in the person's behavior as well as words.

When you talk with someone on the phone, or even more dramatically, when you meet with another person or with a group, behavior often says more than words, pictures, or numbers. Within any one organization, you may find different norms and values that must be accommodated. As we have seen, those differences are intensified when you go abroad, even if you speak the same language as the people you are visiting. In this chapter, we review some strategies for behaving well as you communicate through phone calls, interviews, and meetings.

Phone Calls

"Call me."
"I'll call her about that."

Business couldn't run without telephones. To emphasize this fact, one cartoonist reversed the typical office picture: On the desk chair is a telephone; at the left side of the desk where a telephone would be sits a small man, cross-legged. Indeed, for many professionals, the telephone runs the day. It links people, of course. It also links machines. Facsimile machines accomplish the transfer of documents across telephone lines. A researcher in Waldenburg, Switzerland, for example, can dial a journal editor in Cleveland and feed an article into a Fax machine; it will be received and printed out in the editor's office almost instantly. Modems turn telephones into data entry ports for computers. As we shall see, telephones and computers also link up in tele-

---

[1] Ed Freidricks, Managing Principal of the Los Angeles office-design firm of Gensler & Associates, as quoted by Stephen MacDonald, "The Desk Set: Well-Designed Offices Are Harder to Achieve in the Age of Technology," *The Wall Street Journal*, 9 January 1985, 1.

conferencing networks through which people in remote locations can converse across the miles, sometimes aided by graphics and even full-motion video images of each other. Telephones also anchor powerful telemarketing projects. In these, targeted customers or clients are contacted one by one for surveys, sales promotions, or fund-raisers. Such marketing can be broad-gauged, as in solicitations for the alumni fund or the National Trust for Historic Preservation. Or it may consist of a support group of highly trained specialists who answer questions on a specific product, like the user-assistance lines for purchasers of computer software.

Whatever the sophisticated enhancements, however, good use of the telephone requires basically the same two practices we've seen before: Define your goal and attend to the expectations and needs of the other (or others) on the line.

Before you call someone, clarify *why* you are calling. Don't simply reach for the phone in the murk of the problem; take time to sort through what you need from the person you are calling. A business call is a form of work, a fact reinforced in many law firms, for example, when lawyers dial in the client's billing account number as they dial the telephone number; a computerized system automatically tracks the client's cost for the call. Formulate questions. Sometimes the questions will be highly structured, as in a telephone survey. But even for informal calls, set a strategy for moving through the information you need. Gather whatever evidence—files, previous correspondence, data sheets, tax forms—you think may be required in the course of the call. Have pencil and paper handy.

Then, call. Establish your identity briefly but in adequate detail to alert the respondent. Ask if this is a convenient time for a call. People often pick up the phone on the run—few people are able not to answer a phone call— and they may not be able to talk with you at that time. It's common courtesy, when you are invading someone's privacy, at least to ask for permission.

Convey your message or ask your questions, again briefly. Take notes on the person's responses while you talk, and verify any potentially controversial or ambiguous information at once. A misunderstanding may cause you to talk at cross purposes. Moreover, it may be hard to get hold of the person again after you hang up.

Close the call clearly. Confirm the next step in the project under discussion or otherwise indicate that the call is at an end. Don't just stop. Listen for cues from the respondent. It's sometimes hard to get out of a phone call if the other person seems to want to keep talking. Some people invent an external reason for cutting the discussion, like remarking that there is someone at the door. But it's best if you can peg the closing to some comment of your own or the respondent's that finishes off at least this segment of a continuing discussion, for example, noting that you'll call again with suggested dates for a meeting. End on a note of courtesy rather than just business.

When someone else calls you, make sure you understand the person's name and organizational affiliation. For future reference, write these down as you hear them. If you suspect that the call may be controversial or that you may want to look up some information before you continue a discussion, then tell the caller you'll call back. Don't be abrasive. Simply note that you've been caught at a bad time. Take the person's number, do your checking, and then call back.

Avoid revealing too much in a phone call, particularly to a stranger. Of course, never reveal anything until you've verified the caller's identity either by asking for information that will establish credentials or by calling someone back who has called you. Don't be too hasty to point out shortcomings in your company or in people you're being asked to comment on. Determine the proposed use for any information that you'll give before you give it.

Interviews

You'll use the phone often during a business day to gather and confirm information. You may also call someone to persuade him or her to buy a product, a service, or a concept. Sometimes, too, people use the phone to conduct an interview, particularly when a tight deadline or the distance between the two parties makes an in-person interview difficult. Certain communication goals, however, require a formal interview in person. In Chapter 5, you read guidelines for *information-gathering* interviews.[2] Chapter 27 gives advice on being interviewed as a candidate for a job. Here, you'll find some guidelines for conducting interviews in general.

Routine interviews, which are usually scheduled in advance, last generally from a half hour to an hour. Particularly intense job interviews, like those for upper-management positions or for spy work, may last for days. Whereas telephone calls and hallway conversations may be subject to interruption by anything more important that comes along,

---

[2] Here are the 7 guidelines for conducting an interview to gather information in the course of a project:
1. Select the interviewee carefully.
2. Arrange the interview in advance and at the interviewee's convenience.
3. Prepare for the interview.
4. Have a plan and some specific questions.
5. Make a record of the interview.
6. Thank the interviewee orally and in writing.
7. Treat the interviewee with the utmost respect.

an interview implies some buffer from any but the most serious interruptions.

Usually, an interview engages just two people at a time: One has initiated the interview and controls its conduct; the other responds. Interviews may occur between colleagues at the same level, but often the two people come from different levels in the organization: a supervisor and a member of the group, a recruiter and a potential employee, a student and a professor.

The *location* of the interview often affects its conduct. Sometimes that location is out of both the interviewer's and the interviewee's control. Many interviews are conducted in hotel rooms during professional meetings, with interviewees meeting each other as they go in and out the door. Perhaps even more occur in offices. But when you can *choose* the location of an interview, think about avoiding hotel rooms or offices. These carry associations that could jeopardize the interview. An office, in particular, bears signs of authority that may intimidate the visitor. If you do need to meet in an office, try at least not to let the desk separate you from the interviewee. Move to the side. At best, choose a neutral and perhaps friendlier setting, like a conference room. You might also try to meet in a corner of the cafeteria or a restaurant, as long as you can ensure privacy and adequate quiet for discussion.

Set the Stage

Begin the interview with some small talk drawn from whatever you know about the interviewee's interest. As part of that discussion, too, you might ask about how the interviewee would like to be addressed, if you don't already know. The standard in most American corporations is the use of first names, but if the tendency in your corporation is toward titles, then use them. If the interviewee is European, you should pay particular attention to titles.

Early in the interview ask open-ended questions to establish a level of discussion. These require more than a yes or no answer and may suggest areas the interviewee considers important. Starting too specifically may cause you to ignore an important topic.

Ask Questions

Ask both general and specific follow-up questions:

• Avoid questions with built-in biases, such as, "Don't you think this job will really be too much for you?" or "Wouldn't your interest is skiing make it hard for you to live here in the South?"

- Don't waste time quibbling over items of fact. Suggest that you'll look the item up later on, or ask the interviewee to look it up and report back.
- Unless it's really important, don't dwell on negative information. Interviewees have trouble enough remarking on negatives about themselves. Let the information pass calmly.

Pay Attention

As you listen to the interviewee, think:

- How does this information compare with information from others?
- Do you really understand, or are you just nodding to be polite?
- Is the interviewee focusing on important matters or wandering into trivial territory?
- Is he or she self-confident? Hesitant?

If your mind wanders, consider *why* it's wandering. Are you bored because you've heard all this before? Or because this information seems far removed from what you need? Take steps early in the interview to correct your boredom:

- Ask the interviewee to repeat what he or she said when your mind started to wander—and ask early enough to retrace the line of discussion.
- Cordially suggest another line of response.
- If the comments seem vague, ask for examples.
- Rephrase key issues to confirm your understanding and encourage his or her elaboration of those points.

Take Notes

Note-taking helps to keep you alert and active as a listener. Moreover, good notes provide an essential and accurate record of the interview.

- Don't note only negative information. Take notes from the beginning. Otherwise, your note-taking may intimidate the respondent into silence.
- Reread the salient points from your notes at the closing to ensure agreement on main points.
- After the interview, review the notes to clarify any items that seem unclear and to add any information needed to make the notes a good record for later reference.

Negotiate Disagreements

Sometimes, interviews unearth points of disagreement. If so:

• Hear the other person out. Don't just cut off the discussion.

• Ask questions that clarify the issues at hand.

• Try to state the other's point of view in your own terms, and ask him or her to do the same.

• Perhaps suggest coming back to that topic later, and switch to a different one.

• Admit any mistakes promptly.

• End the interview if your differences seem for the time irreconcilable, and then later, take the initiative to set up another meeting. Perhaps send along something in writing that may reconcile the differences.

Conclude Gracefully

As you opened the interview, finish it on a bit of small talk. Don't be abrupt. Perhaps make reference to the future: another meeting, a date for notification of the results of the interview, documents you will send or that the interviewee should send to you.

Meetings

Many managers put "meetings" at the top of their lists of the greatest time-wasters ever. However, studies show that most managers spend around 70 percent of their workday in meetings. Meetings *can* be productive if they derive from clear goals and are conducted efficiently.

One way to classify meetings is to sort them by *function:* regular and specialized. Regular meetings parallel in many ways the goals for corporate documents, particularly *control* and *maintenance*, that we reviewed in Chapter 22. Like these documents, the meetings keep the routine of the company going. They occur at scheduled intervals, generally with the same attendees. Specialized meetings are called to match a particular, one-of-a-kind need. They are often set up to solve a problem. We'll return to this classification shortly.

Another way to look at meetings is to examine the *structure of the group*. Sometimes the group is determined by the direction of communication. *Lateral groups* are gatherings of colleagues at the same level. *Vertical groups* reflect the chain of command and may be quite large, for example, a whole division. *Lateral-diagonal groups* are gatherings within or among departments. Group structure may also reflect the pattern of leadership. Occasionally, all group members are appointed; they then select their own leader. More often, a leader is appointed along with the members. Group reporting lines also vary: In a *centralized group*, the members communicate with each other mainly through the leader or through a reporting hierarchy. In an *open group*, members address each other directly.[3]

In general, *regular* meetings tend to reflect a centralized group structure. Individual tasks and reporting lines are well defined. *Specialized* meetings usually require a more open group structure. Such meetings may address the corporate goal of *definition*, that is, policy setting and long-range planning. They are also useful in solving problems and in arriving at a consensus on a new product or a merger. The meeting's purpose is best served when the group members are well informed and well motivated toward the goal and when they communicate frequently with each other. Given these differences in purpose and structure, then, here are some guidelines for meetings, to be adjusted to individual circumstances.

Regular Meetings

Regular meetings accompany the day-to-day course of the organization. Thus a finance committee meets every quarter, a division staff meets every month, all the waiters and waitresses gather for an hour every Friday morning. Policy changes are announced, grievances heard, or plans arranged. The caller of the meeting may circulate an agenda in advance, noting the topics of discussion and the names of those responsible for reports (see Figure 24–1 for the agenda of a regular meeting of the advisory board for preserving a historic grist mill). Often the sequence of the meeting simply follows conventions. Each attendee, for example, reports briefly, and those reports spark the conversation.

Regular meetings serve an important role in monitoring corporate activities, providing early warnings of any problems, and keeping people informed. In terms of our communication model, they aim most frequently at *understanding*, although, of course, they sometimes lead to action. They also enhance the sense of identity and common purpose in the group. They maintain goodwill. The trap in such meetings is small talk and gossip. The convener of the meeting has to have a keen sense of when small talk should be allowed and when it should be (gracefully) turned off.

---

[3]For more detailed insights into communication in groups, see H. J. Leavitt, "Some Effects of Certain Communication Patterns on Group Performance," *Journal of Abnormal and Social Psychology* 47:46 (January 1952), 38–50.

Greenbank Mill Associates
A Division of Historic Red Clay Valley
605 Greenbank Road • Wilmington, Delaware 19808
(302) 998-8991

G.M.A. Agenda - March 13
8:00 p.m. Sid Craven's House

   I. Minutes of December and February meetings.

  II. Finance Report (Hank Tillson).

 III. Discussion of Insurance Coverage (Hank Tillson).

  IV. Eagle Scout Project (Manning).

   V. Landscaping (Manning).

  VI. Cost Figures (Craven).
     A- Water course (mill race, flume, etc.)
     B- Water Wheel
     C- Flooring
     D- Painting
     E- Installation, doors and windows
     F- Water and sewage
     G- Additional inside work (bathrooms, apartments, heat, AC, etc.)

 VII. Funding for F - G above (Manning).

VIII. Plans for March 23 & 30th (Craven).
     A- Equipment (trailer, truck, back hoe, etc.)
     B- Work teams
     C- PR? (Bill Frank?, N.J.?)

FIGURE 24–1. Agenda (courtesy of Greenbank Mill Associates).

Here are some guidelines for conducting regular meetings:

1. Plan.
2. Move the meeting with dispatch.
3. Close on a positive note and close promptly.
4. Circulate accurate minutes.

Plan

Your planning may be informal, particularly if your group meets frequently and has standard roles. But you'll probably want to compose at least a brief agenda—more detailed for more formal meetings. Preparing an agenda forces you to consider pertinent topics and to assess the amount of discussion necessary for each topic. Circulating the agenda also alerts the participants to bring whatever materials are necessary for the discussion. Keep to appointed times, or announce the meeting well enough in advance to allow the participants to adjust their calendars. It may be a prerogative of power to have others at your command whenever you need them, but it's a sign of respect for others and their work to provide sufficient notice.

Some legitimate emergencies do arise, but at least 80 percent of your meetings can be scheduled a week or so in advance to allow others some control over their calendars. If it looks as if you have too much on the agenda for one meeting (keep meetings under two hours), then schedule two brief meetings. An unworkable agenda will undermine your credibility.

Move the Meeting with Dispatch

Allow some slack time for civility and make sure that everyone has a say. But move. By definition, almost everyone at a "regular" meeting knows the others and their biases, so don't let the discussion dissolve into reruns of old battles. Keep to the topic.

Close on a Positive Note—and Close Promptly

In closing, restate a main accomplishment or summarize briefly the main points discussed. Don't let people drift off from the meeting one by one; conclude on time, while everyone is present. Note, if necessary, any further meetings to be scheduled or follow-up steps to be performed.

Circulate Accurate Minutes

The minutes reconfirm the main actions and actors of the meeting, and they remind the participants of any future tasks that came from the meeting.

As a record, the minutes contain the following information:

- The time and place of the meeting.
- Names of the chair and participants.
- Chief topics and their disposition (as based on the agenda).

• Future actions required, with the names of the people responsible for the actions and a schedule for evaluation.

Specialized Meetings

Specialized meetings are both more open in structure and more directly instrumental. Although they may aim at understanding, they often lead to action. Many managers (and others) appoint a committee (and thus initiate a string of meetings) when they don't know what to do otherwise to solve a problem. Such a meeting, in computer terms, is the *default option:* What happens when you don't specifically design a response. Instead, make sure a meeting is the only way to achieve your goal, for example:

• When you need a group's collective ideas to design a corporate policy decision or to define a problem.

• When you need to announce a major change that would otherwise be the subject of an extensive (and time-consuming) rumor network.

• When you seek consensus on a project or a problem.

• When you need to resolve a dispute.

Include only those people who really must be there. Don't send blanket invitations out of a misguided fear of leaving someone out. Select the best.

Some of the guidelines for regular meetings apply to specialized ones, particularly meetings making announcements. But often the environment is different. There's no agenda, just a goal, for example, the selection of a new computer system.

State the Objective

First, clarify the purpose of the meeting. Presumably, this step was achieved *before* the meeting, but make sure each participant understands the objective in the same terms. Perhaps state the objective as "How might we . . . ," filling in the particular purpose.

Define the Problem

Then focus the problem. Watch for these traps:

• *Hasty negation:* "The benefits package doesn't work." This statement fails to define the problem. Dig into some questions: What are the components of the package? What information do you have about its functioning? Who has reported problems?

- *Hasty solution:* "We need to increase payments in the dental plan." Increasing payments is one solution, but perhaps not the *best* solution, to problems in the plan. Instead, state the problem in a way that encourages thinking about alternate solutions: "The dental plan seems to cost more than the benefits warrant."
- *Hidden agenda:* "Let's review inefficiencies in the benefits package." This statement may hide another agenda item: "I don't like Peter Jones, Vice-President of Human Resources Management, who instituted the plan." Be candid in focusing on the real issues.

Generate Solutions

The best approach to problem solving in a meeting is *brainstorming*. Let the discussion leader record ideas, either on paper or, better, on a blackboard or flip chart that everyone can see. Make sure that everyone contributes. Allow people to build on each other's ideas. Seek abundance. Defer judgment.

Evaluate the Solutions Against Criteria

Then, evaluate. Some common general criteria are practicality, economy, acceptability, ease of implementation, and simplicity. Allow debate; don't settle too early on one solution.

Arrive at a Decision

Talk out each alternative until you reach agreement on eliminating all but one. Use data to convince. Allow a mechanism for the expression of strong dissenting opinions. Make sure, once consensus is reached, that the holders of minority opinions are given a positive role in the final implementation.

In a brainstorming meeting, everyone should participate. Use direct questions to draw in someone who looks bored or angry. If necessary, stop someone who seems to be talking too much by posing a general question to the whole group.

Visuals in Meetings

One excellent way to move a meeting along is through visuals, particularly overhead transparencies. Many business leaders could not conduct a meeting without them. Indeed, as evidence of the effectiveness of visuals, let us cite one study that's especially interesting. In the study, conducted by the Wharton Applied Research Center at the University of Pennsylvania,[4] MBA students participated in specialized group

---

[4]Chris Shipley, "Graphics Influence Decision-Making at Business Meetings," *PC Week* 2:8 (26 February 1985), 21–22. For a full report of this study, see *How to Present More Effectively—and Win More Favorable Responses from More People in Less Time* (St. Paul: 3M Audio Visual Division). The study was sponsored by 3M.

meetings to achieve a consensus decision on whether to introduce a new product. Two speakers presented identical information to two different groups, but one speaker made specific reference to transparencies and one only wrote notes on a white board. Each group then discussed the recommendations and later filled in a questionnaire concerning the decision.

More of the group that saw transparencies decided for the recommendations than those in the group where the recommendations were not presented on an overhead. Moreover, the participants perceived the presenter with the transparencies more favorably than the presenter in the other group. The participants were also able to make their decisions and to achieve consensus faster when transparencies were used. The use of transparencies, then, can often move a meeting along in the direction set by the presenter. Particularly now that graphics are easy to produce through computer programs (see Chapter 8), consider using such a tool in your meetings.

Teleconferences

Business people spend a lot of time *in* meetings and in traveling to and from them. The travel also consumes a lot of money. Many companies are looking to technology to achieve some of the advantages of meetings without the travel time and expense. One technical solution is *teleconferencing:* Three or more people at two or more locations communicating electronically.[5]

Teleconferencing takes various forms, from the simple to the sophisticated. At the simple end is *audio-only* teleconferencing, which is, in effect, a conference call, perhaps with amplification so that several people in a room can hear. In the middle, *audiographic* teleconferences allow for the transmission of charts and diagrams; in some systems, these can be developed interactively among participants through an "electronic blackboard." At the sophisticated end are *full-motion video* conferences that require specially wired rooms and allow people in such rooms across the world to see and hear each other.

In addition to saving the time and money associated with travel to meetings, teleconferencing has other advantages. For example, it prevents "information float," the time delay associated with simply calling a meeting. Information can circulate and garner responses rapidly. Moreover, some people feel that teleconferences tend to be more open—

---

[5] For a survey of teleconferencing practices, see Janet Cote-Merow and Jeremiah Goldstein, "Teleconferencing: Everything You Wanted to Know," *Communicator's Journal* 1: 3 (September–October 1983), 24–28.

and less polarized—than face-to-face meetings. Teleconferencing works particularly well for routine decision-making among people who are remote from each other at different plant sites, but who have met before. It's also used for training and for political campaigns. Physicians use teleconferencing for difficult diagnoses, drawing on a bank of experts in the field.

As a supplement to in-person meetings, then, teleconferencing has a bright future. It serves a lot of everyday purposes, freeing time and money for convening the participants in one place when an in-person meeting is required.

Getting Together

Any guidelines for phone calls, interviews, and meetings must be bent to your own style and environment and to the clues you receive from the people you are talking to. But our discussion provides a place to begin. As the new person in an organization, observe closely and intelligently how the leaders behave. Take to heart your organization's common practices. Ask questions. Withhold too domineering a presence until you've had a chance to see what passes for acceptable behavior. Listen.

Finally, good intentions *do* count. Most people worry about committing irreversible gaffes—saying the wrong thing or being caught in an inappropriate gesture. Gaffes can cause problems. But if your approach to a discussion is an honest and humane one, there is not very much that can't be overcome with good humor and the passage of time. The guidelines will help you get going. Your own integrity, and your respect for other people, will carry you through.

Exercises

1. Try a brainstorming session to solve a problem that a group you are a member of faces. For example, use brainstorming to arrive at an analysis of a case in a management or business policy class. Or brainstorm a solution to a problem in some club you belong to. Be particularly careful to define the problem well, to generate abundant solutions, and to evaluate them against appropriate criteria. Make sure that those who hold minority opinions are given a role in implementation that makes them feel part of the final decision.

2. Keep a log of notes on each phone call you receive for one week. Record the date and time of the call, the caller's name, the central message, and any action required from you because of the call. If you're a student, lots of your calls may be personal ones, but keeping a log is a good habit to cultivate for

your days in an office. The log there can become a significant document in its own right as a basis for reports.

3. Watch your own telephone behavior over the next several weeks (although it's obviously difficult to talk and watch at the same time). How do you open and close the discussion? How much time do you tend to allow for small talk before getting to your point? Are you comfortable with pauses? How, in particular, do you close off a conversation when the other person seems to be talking too much?

4. If the topic for your report in a business communication or marketing class is appropriate, try a telephone survey. Establish a questionnaire (see Chapter 5). Call the respondents. Is interviewing over the phone different from interviewing in person? What special requirements are there in your questions or procedure?

5. Visit a teleconferencing site at a local corporation, if such a site is easily available. Talk with administrators of the site about the company's use of technology in communication.

6. In our discussion of visuals, we noted a study concerning the increased effectiveness of meetings as a result of the use of overheads. The study was sponsored by 3M, which produces audiovisual equipment. Does that sponsorship affect the reliability of the study? Why or why not? Consult Chapter 4 as you consider your decision.

7. Divide your class into groups of about five people each. Take one class period for each group to discuss some campus issue and to propose a new policy or procedure concerning that issue. All the groups should discuss the same issue. The result of the discussion should be a brief (no more than one page) statement of the proposal (see Chapters 17, 21 and 22). During the next class period, have a spokesperson for each group present the group's statement. Then compare the statements. Discuss in a general session *how* each group arrived at its statement.

> *Some general issues:*
> Class registration
> Student evaluation of faculty
> The grading system
> The college or university policy on alcohol
> The student activities budget

Business Presentations

25

Respondents to surveys often rank "making presentations in public" their number one fear, greater even than the fear of nuclear war. Yet professionals in business make presentations every day: around a conference table, in a meeting room, in a classroom, in studios and auditoriums. In the United States alone, more than 55 million people attend an estimated 26 million group presentations annually, according to a survey by the American Management Association.[1] "There are the people who do the work, and the people who present it," observed the chief executive officer of a *Fortune* 500 company. "Often it's the presenters who get the credit, and the promotion."[2]

Your organization—and your own career and self-confidence—will benefit if you give effective business presentations. This chapter outlines a routine for you to try, both as an individual and in a group. With practice, you'll certainly become at least a competent speaker. Who knows? You may find that you *enjoy* performing. Let's examine each step in the routine outlined in Figure 25–1.

Preparing

"The more you sweat in advance, the less you'll have to sweat once you appear on stage," advised George Plimpton.[3] You'll boost your confidence and achieve your purpose if you take time in advance to plot your strategies.

Analyze the Audience

Your talk must work *for your listeners.* Start your preparation by analyzing their needs and expectations. Ask the following questions.

Are the listeners *insiders?* Then you can assume some common vocabulary, motivation, and background in the topic. Be prepared for interruptions if you are addressing your superiors or peers; you have less control than when you address subordinates. *Outsiders?* Clients, sponsors of research, customers, government officials, the town council, or a fifth-grade class may ask to hear you. Assess their context for understanding your topic. Adjust your vocabulary to their level. Is some information restricted only to certain audiences? Don't be the one to divulge an earnings chart to the wrong people.

Who are the *key people?* While not ignoring anyone in the audience,

[1]"Graphics a Popular Tool at Corporate Presentations," *PC Week* 2:8 (26 February 1985), 26.

[2]Walter Kiechel III, "Office Hours: The Big Presentation," *Fortune,* 26 July 1982, 98.

[3]"How to Make a Speech," an advertisement of the International Paper Company copyright 1981.

Preparing

1. Analyze the audience
    Are they insiders or outsiders?
    Who are the key people?
    Why are the participants attending?
    How many people will be there?
    What do they know about the topic?
    What is the audience's attention span?
2. Clarify the logistics
    Length? Time of day? One of a series of speakers? Room arrangement? Distractions? Audiovisual equipment?
3. Set your goal
4. Gather information
5. Organize your talk
    Introduction (opening)
    Middle
    Ending
6. Prepare visuals
7. Practice

Presenting

1. Expect to be nervous
2. Open with vigor
3. Control your voice and mannerisms
4. Talk *with* the audience
5. Control the visuals
6. Don't read
7. Preserve the ending

FIGURE 25–1. Checklist for a business presentation.

find out in advance if there are key people whose needs must be addressed. Don't let them suddenly pop up in a question-and-answer period and surprise you. Although you might think you'd prefer *not* to know that the CEO is planning to attend your talk, flying blind can be just as scary and much less productive. Once you accommodate yourself, you have more time to prepare strategies before the talk to exploit the CEO's presence for your own ends, too.

Why are the participants attending? Are they being forced to attend? Did they volunteer? Have they been singled out as people with some deficiency that you're being brought in to correct? A coerced audience may well be grumpy. Your talk, particularly its opening, will have to entice them to listen, will have to soothe them. Angry people are notoriously poor listeners.

How many will be there? You may not know how many people to expect, but try to estimate. Your talk can be fairly informal and conversational if there are ten or fifteen; you can plan for lots of audience involvement. With larger groups, however, such involvement is more constrained; you'll probably have to plan to do most of the talking.

What do they know about the topic? Presumably, you're giving the talk because they do not know what you know. You'll tell them something new. But that new information will be within a context of the known. Find that context for this audience: their educational level, their experience in the field, their roles within the organization. Can most of them read a balance sheet? Do they understand fund accounting? Levels of understanding may, of course, differ within an audience. You'll hope that the differences will not be great and suggest, if possible, to the organizer of the talk the need for some grouping within the audience. If you must address a varied group, then aim at the middle. Provide supplementary material, in the form of handouts, for those who may not be up to speed. Include a question-and-answer period to tailor comments to those on the fast track.

What's the audience's *attention span?* Once they get going, lots of speakers find the sound of their own voices intoxicating, and they go on and on. Twenty minutes may seem like five. For the audience, however, that twenty may seem like forty. And forty minutes of your talk may be more than they wanted. Few of us can really concentrate for more than five or ten minutes at a time. So plan your talk in short modules for delivery of information. Build in some device—a new visual, a summary statement, or an anecdote, depending on the topic— to rekindle interest. You can assume a longer attention span among professional accountants, say, than fifth-graders, but be aware at each level that attention will drift.

Clarify the Logistics

Some of the drift may derive from the environment of the talk. A recent advertisement for *The New York Times* shows a very small man reading the paper amid the chaos of Times Square. The caption notes,

"Every message is at the mercy of its environment." Yours will be, too. Control what you can.

Know in advance *how long* you are supposed to talk and prepare for that length. Your self-confidence will suffer if you run over a time limit and have to be cut off. That embarrasses the audience, too. But prepare *enough*. If your talk is scheduled for forty-five minutes and you last only five, those forty remaining minutes will hang very heavy.

Adjust your remarks to the *time of day* for their delivery. Everyone has a slightly different biological clock, but within a business environment, certain patterns usually obtain. Expect alertness early in the morning. (Such alertness differs radically from the clocks that operate in most university classrooms, for example, where the early classes are usually the sleepiest.) Expect a lull after lunch. Expect fussiness near the end of the day as listeners, particularly in a commuter environment, anticipate making the train or the carpool home. Expect that listeners will want to be entertained in an after-dinner talk. Presentations are scheduled all day long; be aware of your audience's psychological time at the hour for your presentation.

Will your talk be part of a *series?* With practice, you'll be able to adjust to most situations, particularly when you hear the speaker before you saying what you had intended to say. But prepare: Know if others are talking and find out their topics and approaches to carve out new territory for yours. If you are to be first, build in some introductory matter unnecessary for those in the middle. If you are last, anticipate the possibility that others will run over and you'll have less time.

If possible, visit the room you'll be speaking in and determine the limits of its *arrangement*. Can you move the chairs for a role-playing exercise in groups? Will the participants need to talk with each other as well as listen to you? Then try a U or a circle arrangement. Will you lecture? Then arrange the chairs in rows, one behind another.

Be alert to potential *distractions*. Does a train run by every fifteen minutes, obliterating voices? Does sun glare wipe out the image on the screen in the early morning? Will the sound of voices in the next room come through the movable partition between the rooms? Compensate for what you can't control—by knowing you'll need to pause for the train, by closing the blinds, by asking the audience to sit on the quieter side.

Check on audiovisual (and other) *equipment*. Do you need a podium? Do you need a table in the front of the room to display an architect's model of the new office complex you are going to explain? Most conference rooms have overhead projectors, but don't assume that and show up with fifty transparencies to give a talk in the one room that does not. Does the room have a slide projector? And what kind?

Don't arrive with carousels for a Kodak if the room contains other equipment. Is the room equipped with a rear-screen projector? Many people have sat drumming their fingers in a conference room while the speaker reversed all his or her slides for rear-screen projection. When time has been tight, we've even sat through whole presentations in reverse, with the speaker nervously translating every slide label. Find out the limits of the equipment *in advance*.

Logistics seem like simple matters, and they are, when they work. Good logistics are transparent. Problems in logistics can be devastating.

Set Your Goal

Good logistics should accommodate your goal in speaking. Business presentations, like writing, serve two broad goals: to inform or to persuade. But because of the interactivity of a presentation, each of these goals takes on a special significance. In *informing*, you may simply announce or report information. You may also *instruct* the audience to do something while you are there to aid and correct. In *persuading*, you may sell a product or service, or you may encourage consensus on an issue and rally support. That goal can only be achieved *through* the audience—that's why you are talking. Clarify your goal in the audience's terms. For example, assume that a supervisor has asked you to "review the year-end profit picture" for a finance committee. By *picture*, does he mean that you should look to the future? How far? A five-year plan? Ten years? Or by *picture*, does he mean a look backward to trace a graph of profits over the past year? How detailed should you be? Should you consider profitability in light of patterns for the industry as a whole? Many speakers have found themselves thwarted in presentations because they expected to give one kind of talk and the audience expected to hear another. With a document, a reader can pick and choose among sections in order to find what he or she needs, but a talk doesn't allow that option. Settle the goal in advance.

Gather Information

Then gather the information that will meet that goal. This step is often simple, particularly if your presentation is based on a document already in hand, like a major report or proposal. You may, however, need to collect some additional information that's become available since the report was completed. Appropriate information is perhaps contained in financial or operations records you keep as part of your regular routine. Or you may need to interview associates, make some phone calls, or read through some back issues of business publications to cull the data that will prove your point. See Chapter 5 for details about this step.

Organize Your Talk

Arrange your information to match your goal. Even the most seasoned presenters rarely go into a presentation cold. Plan. When your goal is to inform, be direct. State your goal and provide an overview of your main point. Then give the subpoints and the supporting evidence. Then restate the main point. The folklore for such an approach runs: "First you tell them what you're going to tell them, then you tell them, then you tell them what you've told them."

When your goal is to persuade, consider an indirect approach. Begin perhaps with a discussion of the problem, and then alternate solutions—arriving at your own point only when you think the audience has been brought around to agreement. Encourage questions and discussion early to build consensus. Figure 25–2 shows a large-sheet outline form for organizing a talk in support of a proposal for research and development. Note the division into modules of time. As you talk, you can see if you're running behind and cut from the middle while preserving your ending. The form also encourages you to think of visuals as you plan. Visuals are important; just resist the temptation to think that simply arranging your visuals is the same as making a plan.

Like a document, a presentation has three main sections: an introduction (opening), a middle, and an ending. Let's look at some features of each.

Introduction (opening)

Open the talk strongly. Draw the audience's attention, set the topic and pace of the talk, and establish your authority and credibility. The audience will size you up in the first few minutes. Show them that they should listen. Here are some attention-grabbers to try:

Analogy   Here's a sports one (from Fran Tarkenton):

> The moment the ball is snapped, the quarterback needs the skills of involvement, goal-setting, feedback and reinforcement—the same ones that work in business.[4]

The analogy also announces the themes of the talk to come: "involvement, goal-setting, feedback, and reinforcement," each to be touched on in that order.

---

[4]As quoted by Joseph Durso in "Scouting: A Little Help," *The New York Times*, 17 January, 1985, B-12.

Key message: Before you start outlining, write a single-sentence statement of the key message here (the thesis). Refer to it as your "baseline" as you develop the outline. Divide the paper into two-minute or smaller segments, depending on the length of the presentation. (Good average maximum: ten minutes) Titles and sketches of visuals are an integral part of the outline.	
Beginning Purpose: To capture audience's *attention* and stimulate *interest* in what is to follow by hinting at possible *benefits* for the audience (be sure to *translate features* of your approach, team, experience, etc., into *benefits* for the audience) Calculate time needed for effective introduction Detail introduction; then detail conclusion Slide 1 Title, Sketch	Continuation Slide 3 Don't plan on using more visuals than you can handle effectively. Rule of thumb: average one visual per two minutes Have backup visuals ready for question–answer period after presentation
Middle Purpose: To gain confidence and create desire for your product, approach, etc. Organize the presentation *around the visuals;* tentative selection of visuals should be one of the early steps in outlining. Sketch visuals selected; then select cue words for help when you're discussing each visual. Organize the middle of the presentation to follow the introduction and support the conclusion Slide 2 Title, Sketch	In addition to discussing the problem and the approach to the solution, it's good to touch on: —*Why* your aproach will work. —Alternatives to your approach. —*Why* your approach is superior. Some goals: —Raise audience confidence—show flexibility. —Raise questions about viability of competitive approaches. Slide 4 Title, Sketch Slide 5 Title, Sketch
Don't plan a more detailed presentation than you can handle effectively in the time allotted to you; if appropriate, rely on reference to handouts, documents, etc., for details. Don't try to make more than three subpoint in addition to your main point.	*Conclusion* Purpose: To propel the audience's thinking into the future when they've accepted your proposal; restate the benefits of your approach. Sometimes a summary is OK for a complex presentation; however, future orientation is generally better than past orientation for the conclusion. Calculate the time necessary for an effective *selling* conclusion; add this to the time required for the introduction; subtract from the total time allotted to you. This remainder is all that's available for the body of your presentation.

FIGURE 25–2. Large-sheet outline for a persuasive presentation (courtesy of Dolores Landreman, Battelle Columbus Laboratories, Columbus, Ohio).

Startling statistic   You might try dazzling the audience with numbers, for example:

> "Did you know that 80% of the students who sign up for dormitory space fail to get their first choice?"

Quotation   The authority you quote should be significant to both you and the audience, and the statement should be pithy:

> As Tipp O'Neill is fond of saying, "Politics is mostly a matter of timing."
> Earl Weaver, former manager of the Baltimore Orioles, sums up managing in one sentence: "A manager's job is to select the best players for what he wants done."[5]

Joke or cartoon   Jokes and cartoons can draw attention, but make sure that the opener's tied in with the presentation. Otherwise, you will be left without a bridge to the information to follow. Jokes, too, depend on a certain chemistry in the teller that connects with the chemistry of the group. Jokes don't transfer reliably from one group to another, and after the punchline, you may find yourself staring at a whole bunch of somber faces.

Announcement of topic   For a direct talk, announce your topic, preferably in terms of benefits to the audience:

> By the end of today, you'll know how to get a short document in and out of our new word-processing system—and you'll have a document to show for it as well.

Authorization   "The chairman asked me to talk with you today about . . ." Invoking the chairman establishes your own credibility and sets the bounds for discussion. One reporter noted about a Cabinet officer who lacked power, "Without authority he has no voice." An appeal to authority may set the course for your voice.

Indirect opener   When your goal is to enlist the audience's support and to persuade them of something, you may use a more subtle opener. You could begin with the call to action, or with a discussion of your preferred solution. But that might seem too heavy-handed. People might feel forced. Instead, you lead them by degrees to your conclusion—and to feel indeed that your conclusion is *their* conclusion. We're more convinced by our own ideas than by someone else's, so the goal of such a strategy is to make the listeners think they came up with the solution.

---

[5] As quoted by Thomas Boswell, *How Life Imitates the World Series* (New York: Doubleday, 1982), 153.

The opener, then, sets up the problem (perhaps with a startling statistic).

Middle
The middle works out the implications of the opening. In arranging material to enlist support, consider this plan:

- Criteria for a solution.
- Candidate solutions.
- Elimination of all but the solution *you* support.
- Enlistment of audience's aid in the solution.
- Description of the new situation with the solution in place.
- A call once more to action.

An indirect opening and plan may be effective for news you think the audience may find upsetting, particularly news about changes. Most of us resist change to some extent. Many presentations announce changes; the presentation form is used rather than a memo because the information becomes, perhaps, more humane and less threatening in a room than on a page. Deal with the audience's discomfort right from the start, but build in time to develop the proof that will justify or explain the change. Here's one opening:

> I know many of you have read reports in the media and heard rumors on the street concerning the impending takeover of our company. You are understandably uneasy about how such a change in organizational structure, should it occur, may affect your own positions here. Let me provide you with some information that's not in the media or on the street to inform you about the company's real position and your options with us.

Then come the information and the encouragement for support.

A *direct* report is built hierarchically. First, announce the main point. Develop each subpoint with facts, statistics, examples, and reasoning. Avoid too many details; they are hard to remember. Build in frequent transitions rich in reminder words: not just *third,* but "The third problem we considered was . . ."; not just *next,* but "our next step was to . . ." Listeners don't have the luxury of going back to reread your talk. Summarize periodically to return drifting minds to your main track. Reinforce each transition and each main point with a visual.

Ending
Asking "Are there any questions?" is one way—but not the *only* way—to end a talk. Indeed, it's often not the best way. Although many inse-

cure presenters take refuge in the line, it shifts emphasis and control, at a psychologically critical time in the talk, away from you and onto the audience, which may or may not be ready to take up the burden. Often an audience is not ready, and the talk thus dribbles out into an embarrassing silence.

Instead, keep control at the end. End positively and strongly. If the audience is going to pay any attention at all to you, they will do so most predictably at the beginning and at the end. Use that attention to bring home your main point—twice, at least. Prepare for the ending with some cue: "finally," or "in summary," or "I'd like to end with one thought." Or perhaps return to the visual that began the presentation to show where you and the audience have arrived. Here are some other techniques for ending strongly.

Action You might stress some action needed. The call to action may be rather formulaic:

Again, I'm pleased with the profitability picture. Keep up the good work!

Or it may be specific:

Now that you are familiar with at least the basic commands and functions of the word-processing system, try it out in your offices—this afternoon. Don't wait.

If you're a particularly forceful manager, you might add:

By Friday I'll expect to receive a word-processed memo from each of you simply noting that you're on the system.

Summary You may summarize briefly.

We are, indeed, then, likely to be taken over by Short Line Express, a step that will assuredly aid the company in seeking its long-term goals. But in the short run, we'll have to adapt to changes in our operations and some minimal reductions in staff. The long-term picture, however, looks bright for all of us.

Striking image You may end with a particularly striking image. At a college athletic banquet, the speaker, stressing the theme of scholar-athletes learning in the classroom as well as on the field, ended this way:

With your fine education, you'll be ready for even more challenges in your careers and your personal lives after the air goes out of the soccer ball.

In your opening, as in the introduction to a document, you forecast the plan of your talk. In the end, you show the audience that you have completed that plan. You may simply end on the last major point. Led to expect that ending, the audience will rouse itself to attention. You can show once more the slide listing the topics to be covered and note that you are now through. You may ask for questions. Turning off the projector gives the final punctuation.

Prepare Visuals

Organizing your visuals goes hand-in-hand with organizing your talk. Some people, indeed, *start* with the visuals and build the talk from there. Figure 25–3 describes the most common forms of visuals in business presentations.

Your goal for the talk, your budget, the audience's expectations, the logistics of the presentation site, and the professional skills available to you in preparing visuals will determine the visual form you select. Use visuals to:

- Present information.
- Cue the audience about the plan of the talk.
- Reinforce the main points.
- Give the talk polish.

Chapter 8 discusses visuals in detail. Here, let's briefly review each of these purposes.

Present Information

Charts, graphs, photographs, and drawings can provide the data that support your main points. Let the visuals compensate for the difference between your rate of delivery, which is probably about a hundred words a minute, and the audience's rate of understanding information, which is much higher. The audience can absorb details from the visual while you highlight its significance or items of particular interest. But avoid too much detail. About ten lines of text are enough. Simplify the complete tables and charts from your data collection to emphasize major trends. For presentations to multinational (and thus multilingual) audiences, exploit the possibilities of visuals to explain concepts across language barriers.

Cue the Audience

A reader can skim a whole text to learn the big picture before reading in detail. A listener doesn't have that luxury. Use visuals to make the plan obvious. Bring back an introductory visual (as in Figure 25–4) each time you move from one subpoint to another.

Form	Speaker/Audience	Advantages/Disadvantages
Overheads	Faces	Room remains lighted; overheads can be both prepared in advance and written on during the presentation; easy to rearrange at last minute and to recall in a question session; easy to produce. Hard to see at a distance; resolution is often not precise for photographs.
Slides	Faces	High image resolution; good projection in large rooms for large groups; capable of dramatic artistic and emotional effects. More difficult to produce than overheads and more difficult to arrange at last minute; room must be dark.
Flip charts	Faces	Easy to move around; may be used for spontaneous jottings during a talk or prepared in advance—in part or completely; room remains lighted. Less polished than overheads or slides; the speaker must have good handwriting.
Blackboards	Turns back	Easy to use for spontaneous notes or may be prepared in advance; often available; room remains lighted. Informal; hard to see at a distance; may become messy; the speaker must have good handwriting; speaker must turn away from audience to write.

FIGURE 25–3. Common forms of visuals for business presentations.

Confidentiality of the Medical Record

1. *The Record Itself*
   What is its purpose?
   Who owns it?
   Who is responsible for it?
2. *Primary Users*
3. *Other Users*
4. *Individual Patient's Use of the Record*

FIGURE 25–4. Vugraph overview of a presentation (courtesy of Jeanne Romanic).

Reinforce the Main Points

Write the main points on a blackboard or a flip chart. Or show a slide with a list of recommendations to reinforce your views in the audience's mind and to increase the likelihood that the audience will support them. Concentrate on key words rather than full sentences. Write any potentially unclear terms. Because listeners cannot usually *see* what we are saying, they may hear something other than what we intended. We may say *measurability;* they may hear *measure ability.* We may say *serial attacks;* they may hear *cereal attacks.* Of course, the context may make the words clear, but write on a visual or a board the key words for the discussion.

Give the Talk Polish

In this visual age, audiences generally *expect* visuals to create and maintain interest. Some very informal presentations do without, but most occasions demand them. Indeed, good visuals can often make even a mediocre presenter memorable as the source of good information. Making good visuals has become easier, thanks to graphics packages that run on personal computers and produce output easily transformed into transparencies. Just avoid becoming a graphics junkie. One veteran advises that you select the slides you think you absolutely need, then cut that number by half. Keep a consistent lettering style, format, and color choice throughout your charts. Make sure all the visuals work *together.*

Practice

You can't sit at your desk, look over your notes, and go through your thoughts on the matter in exactly the same time that it will take you to give the presentation. Instead, stand up and say your talk: to an audience of friends, if you can round them up; to a videotape recorder, if one is available; in the room reserved for the actual presentation, if possible; in the shower, if necessary. Time yourself and cut (or add) what's necessary to match the time allotted—or, better, a little under that.

As you practice, too, become aware of any distracting mannerisms and correct them. A videotaped session aids greatly in identifying these. Do you push up your eyeglasses, or tug at your sweater, or play with your hair, or shake loose change in your pocket? Do you cling to the lectern as if to life itself, your white knuckles visible symbols of fear? Any of these mannerisms will draw the audience's attention away from your talk.

Some acting coaches, who also coach corporate executives, recommend a practice technique called *split-focus concentration*. Try giving your talk while you go through some other activity that you're comfortable with (one of our students, a basketball player, dribbled a ball while he practiced). Then, when the time comes to talk, so the coaches say, you'll be relaxed with your body and able to use appropriate gestures.

Practice with the equipment you'll be using. Make sure you can find the on-off switches. Try placing transparencies on an overhead right-side-up. Make sure you can focus them and that the audience can read them from their seats. Practice where you'll stand so that you won't block the screen.

While you're practicing with the visuals, proofread them once more. A spelling error or an error in parallelism is bad enough when the letters are a quarter-inch high on a sheet of paper. Such errors look particularly bad when projected to four or five inches.

After the practice, ask your friends for their comments, and evaluate yourself. But don't be too harsh. Correct what's correctable. Let the practice build confidence.

Presenting

With your message prepared and practiced, you'll be in good shape for the presentation.

Expect to Be Nervous

As you walk to the front of the room, or as you clear your throat at the conference table in the time after someone introduces you or calls on you and before you begin, expect to be nervous. Even the pros are. Use your nervousness; let your good preparation turn nervousness into energy once you get going.

Pause when you arrive at the podium or after you've been announced. Look at the audience. Take a breath.

Open with Vigor

Then, open with vigor. If you haven't already been introduced, introduce yourself. Announce your title if you're giving a formal talk. Deliver the first sentences that you learned and practiced.

Control Your Voice and Mannerisms

You have to do several things at once when you talk: Think about your information, control your voice, and use gestures effectively. That's why planning and practice help; you can work on each of these in isolation so that, when the time at the podium comes, you can relax. A tense speaker leads to tension in the audience. A speaker who is comfortable makes the audience comfortable. Stand confidently, neither draping yourself over the podium nor bracing stiffly as if waiting to be shot.

Enunciate clearly. Vary your vocal pitch and pace. Adjust your volume to reach the back row. Don't rush. Nervousness often translates into speeded up delivery. If you know you're apt to speed up, deliberately slow down. Don't drop internal syllables or the words at the ends of sentences.

Talk with the Audience

While you speak, look at the audience, not at the ceiling and not out the window. They are in that room, not reading you at a desk, because their presence matters. Acknowledge that fact. You might pick out several people in different parts of the room to look at. These may be your friends or just individuals who seem to be listening and who thus will encourage you. Select people in different parts of the room so that you include the whole room in your talk. Be particularly careful not to look only at the chief authority in the room. Students are often guilty of this: While talking to a class, they look only at the teacher, and the rest of the group rightly feels left out.

Control the Visuals

A speaker's own visuals may pull her or him away from the audience. Your visuals should *connect* you to your audience, not bar you from them. Yet many speakers are known more by their backs than their faces. As we've seen, one of the chief advantages of overheads is that they will work with the lights on while you face your listeners. Don't violate that advantage by turning to the screen. Instead, if you need to point out a feature, point to the transparency as it sits on the projector. You can also, of course, *write* on the transparencies as you talk— and look up from time to time as you write. Make sure your body is not blocking the audience from seeing the screen.

Don't let the visuals take over the presentation. Remember that *you're* the presenter. It's very boring for an audience when the only continuity in the talk is a repetition of the phrase "This slide shows . . ." Subordinate the visuals to a theme, and keep talking while you change slides and vugraphs. Don't read the visuals *at* the audience. Don't get ahead of your visuals. Some presenters keep moving along their outline, forgetting that they have slides to illustrate specific points. Then they must, in effect, backtrack through the slides to catch up at a point whose slide they remember.

If your presentation depends on extensive numerical data, as part of a financial review, for example, make sure you have a visual for the most important numbers. And don't just put all the numbers on one slide and start reading from the top. The audience can read (silently) faster than you can read aloud. If you feel they should have the numbers for later reference, provide a handout. In your talk, focus on what's most controversial or important.

Don't Read

Don't read the talk from the visuals. And don't read the talk from your notes or a script. "If you write out your remarks, it's an insult to an audience. It shows that your first priority is to protect yourself against them," notes one expert. "They sense it. If you just have a few notes on a scrap of paper, you'll walk away with more friends. They'll think, 'Hey. He's honest.' "[6] The only exception to this rule is the prepared statement, developed with legal counsel, that has to be read verbatim. In highly sensitive political or legal contexts, you may well have to

---

[6] Bill Veeck, as quoted by Boswell, 288.

read to avoid repercussions. But such circumstances are not the norm. Normally, talk from your notes, which may be on a pad of paper or on note cards, whichever you find most comfortable.

At many professional meetings, colleagues read papers at each other, and the response is a predictable sleepiness, as when parents read to children at bedtime. You'll be more likely to keep your audience alert, and to achieve the response you desire, if your presentation has a certain spark of spontaneity.

Preserve the Ending

If, as you march through your talk, you find you are running out of time, then cut from the middle, not the end. Preserve your ending. The audience will pay attention to that. *Use* the attention to ensure that you will reach your goal. Don't make your audience feel responsible or guilty about your running out of time:

> This is just too big a topic to cover in the short time you've given me here.

> Is my time really up? Well no wonder I'm running over—there's no clock in this room.

Worry about the extent of the topic or the clock *before* the presentation, and negotiate changes. But once you are under way, make the best of whatever's around you. End on a positive note—and a note of goodwill. If you feel that, indeed, some important information has been sacrificed, then you might offer to send along supplementary material.

Managing Group Presentations

This routine for preparing and presenting talks works for both individuals and groups. But group delivery requires a few added steps:

In *gathering information*, assign particular topics according to who is the expert on each. Meet to discuss the general theme *before* you head in different directions, so that the information follows the same track. (See Chapter 11.)

In *planning* the talk, agree on a sequence of topics. Let the most effective presenter provide the introduction and the conclusion.

Before *delivering the talk*, establish the format. How long should each person speak? How will the presentation move from one speaker to another? What common form will the visuals fit? Who will project the visuals? How should you dress? What signaling system will the group leader use to alert a speaker who is running overtime? Who will moderate the questions? Who will answer the questions? Where will the presenters sit or stand when they are not talking?

With good preparation, a group report will flow smoothly. Otherwise, it may dissolve into lots of people bumping into one another.

Dealing with Questions

When the talk is over, smile, gather your visuals, and return to your seat. On some occasions, the ending is marked by applause. If so, savor this as your just reward for a fine performance.

Many business presentations, however, particularly those aimed at informing the audience, end in a question-and-answer period. If the talk was informal, you may have answered questions during the presentation. Questions for more formal presentations are usually held to the end, sometimes until after a series of speakers has had a go at the podium.

Clarify with the organizer of the talk *in advance* the routine to be followed for a question period. How much time will be allowed? Who will moderate? What people in the audience will be most likely to ask questions? What are their biases? In many organizations, certain individuals have a track record for certain kinds of questions. It's nice to know this in advance: the person who always brings up a situation of forty years ago, the person who likes to tell stories regardless of the topic of the talk, the person who has never met a young person she likes. An organizer who also moderates the question period can be a great ally in negotiating among the questioners and keeping people on track.

Here are a few guidelines for question-and-answer sessions.

First, don't assume that everyone in the audience has read any information you sent ahead of time. Some will have read it; if the questioner seems familiar with the material, then answer on that basis, while still gently clueing the others in on the context.

Second, always repeat the question, preferably in a short form if the question was asked in a long one. In that way, you'll be sure that everyone in the audience has heard. You will also gain time to think about the answer. You may be able to turn the question slightly in a direction that you want to emphasize, even if that direction wasn't exactly implied. Of course, the questioner may not let you get away with this, but it sometimes works. You can't anticipate every question, but be prepared for the most likely ones. Hold some transparencies in reserve.

Third, if you don't know the answer, don't guess. And don't let a belligerent questioner supply you with an answer to which you acquiesce, only to have the questioner pull the rug out from under you by saying that that is *not* the right answer. Instead, admit that you don't know. Offer to find out the answer. Ask the questioner for an address that you can send it to—and then send it.

Some questioners ask only to hear their own voice in the room. They simply want to register their presence. Gently acknowledge such questions for what they are and try to nudge the questioner to silence. That may be difficult, particularly if you are the questioner's junior, but some good humor and sensitivity will preserve your control and win you the audience's appreciation, too.

Fourth, guard against highly particular questions that will take the discussion on a tangent away from the talk and away from the main interests of the audience as a whole. Answer briefly, and then agree to talk with the questioner at greater length after the session.

Finally, don't let a question period linger too long. When the pace of questions has died down, and no more seem immediately forthcoming, don't prolong the session artificially. Close. Offer, if that's possible, to talk with people individually if they'd like to ask more specific questions. Try to use the last question as a springboard back to the main theme that your entire presentation was designed to establish.

Knowing how much to leave to a question-and-answer period depends on your own style as a presenter. Some people are much better in answering questions than in giving a formal talk. These people should speak briefly and move quickly to the questions. Those better at showmanship may want to leave only a short part of the allotted time for questions. In answering questions, listen well, so that you know what's being asked, and answer forthrightly.

Relaxing and Enjoying

In the end (note how that phrase shows we are coming to the end of the chapter), try to relax a bit and enjoy performing. It's probably scarier to *think* about speaking in public than to do it. The key ingredient is respect for the audience. This means that you prepare well, that you treat them well (as adults, if they are adults), and that you work within the agreed-on limits of logistics. In each presentation, display enough self-confidence to carry through positively and in a spirit of goodwill, even if your host mispronounces your name, even if you arrive at the conference room to find a different brand of projector from the one you had specifically requested.

You do have something to say, and saying that, to an appreciative audience, can mark a high point in a career.

Exercises

1. A small-scale industry has developed around people's fears of making presentations. Many consultants offer coaching services for executives. Many authors have produced "how-to" books. One organization even publishes a monthly newsletter, *The Executive Speaker*, devoted to speech making (P.O. Box 2094, Dayton, OH 45429). From your bookstore or library, collect examples of advice on making speeches. What seems to be a core of advice? Where do the experts differ?

2. As a way of hearing your own voice, read aloud some paragraph from a paper you have written. Does it sound the same as when you read it silently in your own mind? Do you notice any problems in reading—like a repetition of *s* sounds or lengthy sentences that keep you from breathing naturally? If you read into a tape recorder, you can listen to your own voice *after* you speak.

3. The best way to learn to give a talk is to give a talk. Look for occasions to do so, in your business classes and your business communication class. If you are particularly nervous, you may want to enroll in a public-speaking class, or join a chapter of Toastmasters International, an organization whose members meet frequently to give and listen to talks and thus improve their skills.

4. In addition to giving talks, it's helpful to see yourself as you deliver them. Videotaping makes this easy. An audiovisual center at your school or company probably has videotaping equipment. Arrange to give a talk, and then, on tape, to see yourself as others see you.

5. Use your final report in a business communication class as the basis for an oral presentation to the class. As part of the exercise, first change the audience. For example, if the report addresses a supervisor or a client on the job, address the presentation to the class itself. What differences in emphasis and content are dictated by that change in audience? Select some aspect of the report to develop in the presentation. You can't read the report, and you can't give all the details. You may be either more general or more particular. For example:

> *Final report:* A Junior Golf Program for the Basking Hills Golf Course (addressed to the manager of the club).
> *Presentation to the class:* How to watch a golf game and not be bored.

> *Final report:* A Rotation System for Waitresses at the Lazy H Restaurant (addressed to the restaurant's owner).
> *Presentation to the class:* A time study of a waitress during one evening at work.

> *Final report:* Investment Potential for the Simplon Corporation in Ecuador (addressed to the financial vice-president).
> *Presentation to the class:* Method for financial analysis of South American countries.

Speaker:

Date: Scale   1 Inadequate
                                  3 Adequate
                                  5 Distinguished

CONTENT

Effectiveness of introduction   1 2 3 4 5

Identification of problem/focus   1 2 3 4 5

Obviousness of organization   1 2 3 4 5

Use of appropriate evidence   1 2 3 4 5

Effectiveness of ending   1 2 3 4 5

Overall content   1 2 3 4 5

DELIVERY

Posture and presence   1 2 3 4 5

Energy and vigor of delivery   1 2 3 4 5

Timing   1 2 3 4 5

Eye contact   1 2 3 4 5

Voice   1 2 3 4 5

Language   1 2 3 4 5

Use of visuals   1 2 3 4 5

Overall delivery   1 2 3 4 5

Special weaknesses:

Special strengths:

Control statement:

FIGURE 25–5.   An evaluation form for an oral presentation.

Timing
Started _____ m.   Well timed _____
Stopped _____ m.   Too long _____
Time _____ min.   Too short _____

Organization
Gave suitable introduction:
                    Yes _____   No _____
Topics discussed in logical order:
                    Yes _____   No _____
Interrelationships of topics:
Made clear _____   Obscured _____
Fairly clear _____
Closed effectively _____   or just ran down _____

Manner
Presented paper by:
Talking without notes _____
Talking from manuscript or notes _____
Reading manuscript _____

Looked at audience:
All of the time _____
Part of the time _____
Never _____

Effort to gain audience attention:
Enthusiastic _____
Casual _____
Complacent _____

Mannerisms:
Relaxed and moved easily _____
Stood rigidly _____
Moved excessively _____
Clutched lectern _____
Hands in pockets _____
Nervous efforts _____

Gestures:
Impressive _____   Distracting _____
Natural _____   None _____

Speech
Enunciation:
Distinct _____   Heard by all _____
Fairly distinct _____   Partially heard _____
Indistinct _____   Seldom heard _____

Phraseology:
Concise _____   Descriptive _____
Too brief _____   Generalized _____
Verbose _____   Vague _____
Used extraneous transitions ("er," "ah," etc.)
                    Yes _____   No _____

Delivery:
Smooth _____   Appropriate emphasis _____
Jerky _____   Periodic inflection _____
Too fast _____   Monotone _____
Too slow _____

Visual Aids
Quantity: Too many _____   Adequate _____
           Too few _____

Quality:
Well composed _____   Lucid _____
Superfluous detail _____ Legible _____
Confusing _____   Illegible _____

Presented: Too fast _____   Suitably _____
            Too slow _____   Convincingly _____
Visual aids (would have been)   (were)
A hinderance _____
Helpful _____
Exceptionally good _____

Discussion-Rebuttal
Attitude toward
   Questions: Replies:
Receptive _____   Logical and convincing _____
Indifferent _____   Acceptable _____
Antagonistic _____   Evasive _____
                     Irrelevant _____
No discussion held _____

General
Have you a clear idea of the speaker's theme?
                    Yes _____   No _____
Was she or he convincing to you?
                    Yes _____   No _____
Did she or he hold the attention of the audience?
                    Yes _____   No _____
Was this an exceptionally good presentation?
                    Yes _____   No _____

Comment: _____

FIGURE 25–6. Another evaluation form (reprinted with permission from The Institute of Electrical and Electronics Engineers, Inc.).

6. Figures 25–5 and 25–6 provide two evaluation forms for oral presentations. When you next listen to a talk, use these guidelines for determining what went wrong and what went right. Take notes to apply to your own presentations. And then, when you give a presentation, evaluate yourself on these scales. (See pages 511, 512).

PART **IV**

The Job Search

Résumés and Cover Letters

One way not to begin a job search is to postpone and concentrate on today. Or you can worry a lot. Or you can hope that someone else will take care of it all for you, while you daydream about a brilliant career.

A better way, however, is simply to get started. Don't think of the job search as a mythic quest. Instead, work in increments. For a time, think of the search as your job. Here are seven checkpoints to consider. Each is manageable. Each can be enjoyable.

1. *Self-inventory.* Think about yourself and what you want to do.

2. *Market inventory.* Inventory the market of available and enticing positions and companies.

3. *The résumé.* Prepare a one-page fact sheet that details your skills and experience in the market's terms.

4. *Recommendations.* Ask appropriate people to write letters of recommendation (sometimes called *letters of reference)* for you.

5. *The cover letter.* Send your résumé with a letter that targets it to a specific potential employer. You may write to several companies; each deserves a tailored letter.

6. *Interview.* Talk with potential employers.

7. *Follow-Up.* Respond to offers and, sometimes, to rejections, too.

This chapter offers advice on checkpoints 1 to 5. The interview and the follow-up are covered in Chapter 27. Chapter 15 discusses how to write letters of recommendation. Chapter 22 describes the writing of job descriptions.

Self-inventory

The job search begins with you. Figure out what you want to do on the basis of what you have accomplished, what interests you've shown, and what skills you have developed. Sit down and write the answers to questions like those shown in Figure 26–1. Don't just *think* the answers; write them.

Market Inventory

While you're checking on your own interests, you'll also want to check on the market. Let's look at some sources of information.

1. What decisions have you made in the last year? Can you see any pattern in them? What do they show about your priorities?

2. What would you do (besides sleeping) if you were given an extra day in a week? What do you enjoy doing?

3. Do you work better alone or on a team?

4. Do you like to take charge or to follow directions?

5. Do you like to take risks or to avoid risk?

6. What working conditions do you prefer? Inside or outside? Can you tolerate noise, or do you need quiet conditions?

7. How do you reward yourself when you've done something special?

8. What circumstances make you feel happy? What, on the other hand, frustrates you?

9. Do you meet deadlines easily? Do you work well under pressure?

10. What are your greatest achievements? What skills were needed to achieve them?
    Gathering and analyzing data?
    Getting other people to work?
    Fixing things?
    Seeing patterns where others see chaos?
    Speaking or computing in various languages?
    Operating any special machinery?

11. Think of your courses in high school and college. List the most important ones. Selecting what you consider most important will help you profile your interests. What did you do best in? How have your courses prepared you for the career you are interested in? Given another chance, would you take different courses?

12. How will you know you are successful? What do you note as signs of success in others?

13. Do you weigh job satisfaction or salary more heavily?

14. Do you gravitate toward new ways of doing things, or are you more comfortable with a known routine?

15. Where would you like to be next year? What do you see yourself doing at 10 A.M. one year from today?

(continued)

FIGURE 26–1. Self-inventory checklist.

16. Where would you like to be in five years? Write a brief statement about what you want to be. You may have a narrow focus:
- I want to work for a Big Eight accounting firm in Denver as an account manager whose responsibilities gradually (but rapidly) increase so that in five years I'm a vice-president.

Or you may see yourself in a broad range of positions:
- I'd like a job offering a lot of contact with the public.
- I'd like to work in a small, entrepreneurial company aggressively marketing an innovative product.

Newspapers

Check the job listings. Usually these are classified by type of job. Discover them in:

- Local papers where you are in school or would like to settle.
- National papers (like *The New York Times* and *The Wall Street Journal*).

Career-Planning Office

Your college or university probably has one or more people who assist students in their job searches. The office will usually maintain a file of potential employers and a library of books and newsletters about employment, like the *College Placement Annual,* which publishes a current listing of employment opportunities on a regular basis. In addition, private career-planning consultants provide such services on a fee-paying basis. Such consultants may be listed in the yellow pages or in the classified sections of newspapers. Private employment agencies also assist in the job search. If you engage the services of such an agency, however, clarify *in advance* the extent of their services, the fee scale, and the method of payment. Sometimes employers pay, and sometimes *you* pay.

Professional Job Listings

Government agencies and various professional societies maintain job listings that they publish or circulate on some regular basis. Check, for example, the U.S. Bureau of Labor Statistics's *Occupational Outlook Handbook* or *Career Index*. *Working for the USA* and the *Federal Career Directory* discuss work with the federal government specifically. English departments are familiar with the Modern Language Association's *Job List*. Some professional societies also publish job listings as a regular feature in national and local magazines and newsletters. Others, like the International Association of Business Communicators, maintain a telephone hotline of available positions. A few concerns (perhaps their number is growing) offer computerized job listings, mainly for jobs in high-tech companies. Subscribers access the listing on their terminals and can reply instantly (and electronically) if they are interested.

Information About Corporations

Chapter 5 discusses in detail sources of information about corporations. Read up about companies that do the kind of work you'd like to be part of. Check, for example, Dun and Bradstreet's *Million Dollar Directory* or *Middle Market Directory* and *Poor's Register of Corporations, Directors, and Executives*. Check the annual reports, company magazines, and other publications of any company you'd like to apply to. Information about specific companies will aid you in sorting through career possibilities; it will also serve as good preparation for an eventual interview.

State and Federal Employment Offices

Government employment offices provide listings of job openings and opportunities and can also help in a job search. Check on the agencies in your area in the blue pages of the telephone book.

Word of Mouth

Talk with friends who work for companies that interest you. Talk with recent graduates from your school in your major to find out what they are doing and what companies they recommend. Ask former supervisors if they know of available positions. Talk with professors. Read jottings on bulletin boards.

You may also engage in what one authority calls "informational interviewing."[1] Ask someone who performs the kind of work you'd like to do if you can talk with him or her about that work and about the expectations for those who do the work. Talk with your parents, your aunts and uncles, and their friends. In the search, no one is out of bounds. As you are shopping around, sometimes a lead into one job will send you on a detour to another. Be willing to spend time talking to people ("networking") who may not be able to help you directly, but who may be able to send you to those who can.

The Résumé

With notes in hand about who you are and what's out there, you're ready to enter the market. Some people enter bizarrely and boldly—particularly people in marketing. One person handed out his résumé at rush hour to arriving commuters at Grand Central Station in New York City. A Chicago copywriter put a coupon on her résumé, offering five dollars from her first paycheck to anyone who put her on the payroll. A man who wanted to work for a TV network displayed his résumé on a billboard across from the network president's office.

But even if intriguing, such gimmicks are both costly and dubious. They rarely work. Instead, assemble two standard documents that will send you into the market: a résumé and a cover letter. In this section, we look at the résumé.

A résumé simply pulls together the most important information from your self-inventory in a format that makes easy reading for potential employers. That format is not universally dictated. The major *goal* of the résumé is to persuade an employer to interview you. The résumé also serves as a reference during the interview and reminds the interviewer about you after the interview. To achieve those goals, you can select one of two forms: *chronological* or *functional*. The chronological is the most common. As the name implies, such a résumé lists your education and work experience, job by job, in chronological order. A functional résumé arranges your experience in terms of the *skills* you can present. Figures 26–2 and 26–3 are chronological résumés. Figure 26–4 is a functional résumé. First, let's discuss the *content* of the résumé. Then we'll discuss *design*.

Content

Figures 26–2, 26–3, and 26–4 show what you usually include in a résumé. Let's discuss how you develop that information from your own self-inventory.

---

[1] Richard N. Bolles, *What Color Is Your Parachute? A Practical Manual for Job-Hunters and Career Changers* (Berkeley, Calif.: Ten Speed Press, 1984).

SAMANTHA MACDONALD

134 Clark
Laramie, WY 82070
(307) 451-8788

EDUCATION

University of Wyoming
B.S. in Business Administration with emphasis in marketing management
(expected June, 1989)

Dean's List
Attended computer seminar that examined operations and applications of IBM
personal computers. Actively participated in marketing research projects.

EXPERIENCE

Elaine Powers Figure Salon, Laramie, WY
Service Consultant. Instruct aerobic dance and exercise classes. Develop
advertising campaigns. Sell membership programs and weight loss products.
10/88 to present

Bank of Wyoming, Central Marketing Department, Cheyenne, WY
Marketing Research Assistant. Analyzed present and potential markets for
new and existing products and services. Interpreted secondary research findings.
Entered and manipulated research data for statistical analysis. Evaluated current
and potential branch sites. Extracted data for market share reports and the
analysis of market penetration. Assisted product managers with requests for
ongoing research data. 6/88–9/88

University of Wyoming, College of Commerce and Industry
Microcomputer Lab Instructor. Instruct faculty and students in use of IBM
personal computers. Correct accounting assignments. Work with the following
software:

VisiCalc	Visitrend Plot	Lotus 1-2-3
WordStar	Peachtree Accounting	

1/87 to present

Sid's Pants. Worthington, OH
Sales Clerk. Provided product information and buying recommendations to
customers. Arranged merchandise floor plans. Assisted in inventory control.
Handled cash transactions. Summers 1985, 1986, 1987

BACKGROUND

Tutor economics and mathematics. Member of Business Students Association and
College of Commerce and Industry Council. Intramural athletics. Interests include
jogging, tennis, and travel. Willing to relocate. References available on request.

FIGURE 26–2. Chronological résumé.

MARTIN ALLENQUIST

College address (until June 1): 906 Syphert/Ithaca, NY 14850
Permanent address: 210 Halsey Ave./Jericho, NY, 11753/516-432-9655

Objective	A position in internal auditing with a large multinational organization in which I can combine my accounting skills with my knowledge of different languages and cultures.
Education	B.S. in accounting, Cornell University, 1990. Courses in managerial accounting, cost accounting, business law, finance, operations management, and marketing. GPA 3.5 out of 4.0. Earned 75% of college expenses.

Experience

Summer 1987	**POM Recoveries,** Syosset, NY. Posted financial statements by hand and on computer.
Spring 1987	**Publisher's Clearing House,** Port Washington, NY. Sorted checks, processed magazine orders, and validated contest entry forms.
Summers 1984, 85, 86	**Camp Thistle,** Rabbit Lake, NY. Organized games, taught swimming, and supervised campers.
Activities	Cornell University Marching Band (3 years), intramural soccer and baseball.
Personal	Born September 17, 1969. Have traveled widely and attended schools in Switzerland and England. Willing to relocate.
References	Available on request.

FIGURE 26–3. Chronological résumé.

Andrea P. Corbisiero

Current Address

2705 Edouard Montpetit #16
Montréal, Québec H3T 1J6
514-674-6516

Home Address

120 Lake Sundance Crest, S.E.
Calgary, Alberta T2J 2S7
403-522-7811

OBJECTIVE

To work directly with customers in designing systems for a small computer software firm.

EDUCATION

Bachelor of Commerce (Management), 1988; specialty in Management Information Systems, McGill University.

> Specialized course work included Management and the Major Corporation; Organization and Personnel Behavior; Market Analysis and Evaluation; Computers and the Corporate Future; extensive study in COBOL, PASCAL, and LISP.

SKILLS

Organizational Planning

Supervised the planning and administration of a University-wide weekend seminar focusing on the importance of computers in education (1–2 March 1987). Delegated authority to staff of ten, acted as liaison with visiting corporate executives, and maintained all accounts for budget of $8000.

Computer

Assisted in the development of a computer program to improve scheduling of classes in appropriate-sized University classrooms. Worked closely with University programmers in debugging program during first week of classes.

Developed computer simulation program for advanced marketing course to aid students in evaluation of strategies.

Well versed in several languages and in programs for data base and financial management (including Lotus 1-2-3). Experience on both mainframe (DEC and IBM) and IBM personal computers. Surveyed internal computer use as part of a summer intern program at the Kendal Corporation, Boston, Mass., USA (Summer, 1986). Assisted with developing a management information system for inventory, Dominion Textile Inc., Montréal, Québec (Summer, 1987).

Communication

Excellent communication skills developed through coursework in English and French and as a writer for the quarterly newsletter of an organization of business students. Interviewed local executives for feature articles and wrote a column on "Financial Facts." Fluent in English and French.

INTERESTS

Enjoy sailing, downhill skiing, and racquetball.

REFERENCES

Paul P. Fuller, Professor
Department of Management
McGill University
Montréal, Québec H3C 3G1

Joanna L. Johnston, Professor
Department of English
McGill University
Montréal, Québec H3C 3G1

Mark Ostrik, Manager
Management Information Systems
Dominion Textile Inc.
1950 Sherbrooke Street West
Montréal, Québec H3H 1E7

FIGURE 26–4. Functional (skills) résumé.

Name and Address

You provide your name and address to identify the résumé and to allow a potential employer to get in touch with you. Figures 26–3 and 26–4 provide two addresses: campus address (called *campus* or *temporary* or *current address*) and home address. Include a phone number, with the area code.

Objective

If you can state your objective clearly, and in at least modestly concrete terms, as in Figures 26–3 and 26–4, then go ahead. Show what you want to *do*, not what you want to *be*. Many résumé readers comment that they like to see a clear statement of goals:

- A supervisory position in production or quality control.
- A position in research and development or in technical service, either within the company or in the field.

Sometimes, however, you can state your goal only generally:

- An entry-level position in the business world.

If so, then omit the objective statement. The omission will not count against you, but a vague or wide-eyed statement will. One disadvantage of being too specific is that you may reduce the number of positions you seem to be qualified for. However, if you create your résumé on a word processor, you can pop statements in and out to tailor them to particular jobs.

Education

Most recent graduates will find that their education is the major selling point. Should you include high school? Perhaps, if you feel the school's identity comments well on your own identity or if you want to note special awards or achievements there. But certainly once you finish college and move to other degrees or experience, you should drop the high-school notation.

In both the chronological and the functional résumé, list the college (or colleges) you have attended. Indicate any degree or degrees you have received or expect to receive, with the date of graduation and the years of attendance. Avoid obscure abbreviations. You might list important courses, with grades if they are good. Again, avoid internal codes: "BU 441," "E 215." Instead, use course titles: "Business Policy," "Written Communications in Business."

Design a category for "percentage of college expenses earned" if the percentage is high. That figure shows your keen motivation. (On the other hand, don't develop that category and note "0%" if you received a free ride.) Indicate scholarship aid if appropriate. You don't need to detail the amount.

Also create a category for honors and awards if you have evidence to display, and identify the awards. If you won the "Golden Shovel Award" for the best sophomore in marketing research, you'd better tell a reader the meaning, lest he or she interpret the shoveling differently.

Experience and Skills

Here's where the chronological and functional approaches differ. In *preparing* to write, draft a list of all your jobs: delivering papers as a kid; later, cooking at a fast-food restaurant, clerking at the local deli and at a clothing or sporting-goods store, vending on the boardwalk, or lifeguarding at a neighborhood pool.

What, you ask, does all this have to do with a career in marketing or accounting? Plenty. Think about what you did in each job and what you learned. Did you have any specific responsibilities? Did they change? Did you have any part in making them change? Can you quantify the results of your work (dollar amounts earned in a summer painting job, the number of customers served, the percentage increase in sales, the area covered, the number of tables at a restaurant where you were the sole waiter)? Did you write any reports or other documents on the job? How much time did you work each week? Did you operate any equipment? Were you able to work on your own? Don't forget your experience in internships, cooperative education programs, or campus activities.

Then, decide on an approach. Choose a *functional* approach if your experience is limited or somewhat scattered, both in kinds of jobs and in amount of time in the work force, or if you are shifting careers or are well along in your career. Incorporate your experience under skill labels like "communication," "management," "supervisory," and "proposal preparation" (see Figure 26–4). Make sure that all the labels are parallel and don't overlap.

Otherwise, use the more common *chronological* approach shown in Figures 26–2 and 26–3. List the title, employer, and dates for your jobs, but don't let your description end there. Describe what you did and what you learned, with particular emphasis on increasing responsibilities and an ability to work without close supervision. Note the skills you developed and your track record as a self-starter. Quantify the description wherever possible, and use active verbs. If you worked with computers on your jobs, be sure to note that, including information about the hardware, the software, and the languages you became proficient with. You might want to group a series of summer jobs.

Personal Information and Interests

Use the résumé to emphasize your strengths. Affirmative action guidelines caution against revealing such personal information as birth date and marital status, but you may if you like. If you speak another language, mention it, particularly in an application for a job with a multinational organization. Mention computer literacy, an extensive travel record, and extracurricular activities. Indicate whether you are willing to relocate. In the end, try to see from an interviewer's perspective the picture of yourself you paint. Noting involvement in group activities like sororities or fraternities and in such "corporate sports" as football, racquetball, and downhill skiing indicates a team player. Listing together such hobbies as long-distance running, mountain biking, cross-country skiing, and vegetarian cooking may suggest more of a loner personality.

References

Note the names and addresses of references who will speak or write on your behalf. Make sure, of course, that you check with all of them *before* you list their names. Three or four names should be enough. If you are printing up several copies of the résumé, you may not want to list the names; instead, you may select different references for each position. That's fine. Just note that references are available on request or indicate that you have a dossier of reference letters on file with your college placement center.

General Content and Style

Before printing it, reread the résumé as a whole to see that there are no red flags, nothing that will raise unwanted questions. Readers are reading to *eliminate*. Don't give them anything to go on. Of course, make sure that there are no errors in spelling or grammar. You *will be* eliminated if there are.

In addition, look for anything that might be read to your disadvantage. If, for example, you have always lived in New England, and all your education has been there, a reader at a corporation in Phoenix may automatically eliminate you as a poor risk in a new geographic environment. Meet that potential misreading head-on by including a notation that you are willing to relocate (perhaps even go so far as to indicate your desire to move to the Southwest). As a married woman with four children you are proud of, you might note those children and their names and birth dates on the résumé. But think again. A potential employer may circle that notation and wonder, "When would she have time to work for *us?*" *You* know you can do it; don't raise the issue.

The time for commentary is later, in the cover letter, and particularly in the interview. Keep the résumé simple and honest. Don't puff. Don't provide opportunities for misreading. Stick to the facts.

Design

The design of your résumé is as important as its content. Most readers will give your résumé no more than a minute's reading to make the initial cut. It has to *look* good and provide instant access to the information that the reader most needs. Figures 26–2, 26–3, and 26–4 provide different models of good design. Try different typefaces. Don't crowd the text on the page. Suit the design, of course, to the market you'd like to enter. If you are interested in advertising, your résumé should show flair and creativity. An architect applying for a position with a design-oriented firm produced a résumé on gray paper with dark blue type. His name and address, with no capital letters, was written along the left margin so that the reader needed to turn the résumé to read it. Applicants to a Big Eight accounting firm, however, should probably stay with white or slightly off-white 8½″ × 11″ paper and a traditional format and type. If your résumé is *too* slick, the packaging may work against you. Keep things simple. If a word-processing system is available to you, that's probably the best solution to production. But don't overdo. The author of the résumé in Figure 26–5 became the victim of all the types his computer could muster. Control yourself.

Recommendations

In your résumé, you provide statements about what you have done. Letters (or phone calls) of recommendation provide outside evidence to support what you can do.

Select your recommenders, your *references*, to reflect your own best attributes. You'll probably want to ask your adviser or major professor. You may also ask a supervisor who can describe your work habits. If you have been active in a campus organization, you might ask an adviser to that group for a letter. Obviously, it's best if the reference is known to your potential employer. A good source strengthens the force of a good comment.

Some suggestions:

First, *before* you give a potential employer a reference's name, check with him or her. *Never* use anyone's name without asking. And make sure that the potential recommender will write you an enthusiastic letter. One student recommends this technique: She asks a potential recommender if he or she could write a positive letter. That question offers the recommender an out. If the response is something like "I could write you a letter, but frankly all I remember is your grade. After all, it was a large lecture course," then the student thanks the professor and leaves. You don't need lukewarm letters.

‗‗

OBJECTIVE: To obtain a supervisory position in bank card collection with opportunities for advancement in management.

EXPERIENCE:

120 DAY COLLECTOR

From July 15, 1986 to present was collector in charge of half of the premium Plasticard portfolio of the largest "Silver" card issuer in the world. Maintained the highest standards of quality while exceeding goal three months in a row by collecting 50% of my accounts (figures adjusted for bankruptcy) within 30 days.

PART-TIME COLLECTOR

Started as 30-day part-time collector in January 1985 with Surcharge Plus Bank N.A. and was promoted to 90-day part-time collector a year later. Continued to develop advanced collection techniques and shared responsibility for collection of 45% of $2.5 million in April 1986. Again promoted in May 1986 to the only part-time charge-off collector at Surcharge Plus Bank N.A. Took on added written communication with card holders, gained charge-off experience in the highest rated charge-off unit in the industry. Also executed a bankruptcy prevention program that saved Surcharge Plus Bank N.A. $75,000.

TRAINING:

Directly assisted in the creation, execution, and maintenance of a comprehensive bank-card-collection training program. As a part-time collector was the first employee to be released of collection responsibilities to train new full- and part-time collectors. *Trained twenty collectors within six months in use of SSBBAA computer system and collection method and policy.*

EDUCATION:

McGough University. BA in Political Science, including courses in

Government and Business	Consumer Credit Lending
Public Administration	Macroeconomics
Organizational theory and Administrative Behavior	

REFERENCES: Available upon request

FIGURE 26–5. A too-busy résumé. This résumé was prepared on a personal computer with an excellent choice of typefaces, but the author failed to control his choices. The design is crowded; type size gets smaller in every section and thus reading is difficult. (The author's name is omitted.)

Second, in asking for a letter, provide the potential recommender with your résumé, a brief statement of goals, and a description of the job you are applying for. Your interest and willingness to talk with the recommender will probably be reflected in the letter. The more precise and definite the letter of recommendation (see Chapter 15), the more convincing.

Third, consider setting up a dossier with your college placement office. If you do, a recommender will not need to write a letter for each job you are applying for. In special cases, however, you may want to select a particular reference for the job and ask for a tailored letter.

Cover Letter

The resume provides the facts. To show how these facts support your application for a particular job, you write a cover letter addressed to a specific reader and organization. In the letter you aim to persuade the reader to invite you for an interview. Use both an ethical appeal in your style and attention to detail and a logical appeal in the selection and arrangement of your evidence. Consider incorporating the AIDA approach: Attention, Interest, Desire, and Action (see Chapter 16).[2]

Here is a letter that fails to persuade:

Dear _____:

This communication is relative to inquiry reguarding the possibility of either immediate or future employment with your institution or firm.

The applicant is skilled in communications and in management. He has five years' experience in a fast-food chain with ever increasing responsibilities serving many customers.

His academic training consists of a BA degree in Political Science as well as course work in managment.

The applicant is 22 years old, in excellent health, and can furnish superb references and credentials within two days for your review and consideration.

Available for immediate employment, interim appointment, or personal interview. Detailed resume and data on request.

[2]For insight into what personnel officers look for in the cover letter, see Barron Wells, Nelda Spinks, and Janice Hargrave, "A Survey of the Chief Personnel Officers in the 500 Largest Corporations in the United States to Determine their Preference in Job Application Letters and Personal Résumés," *The ABCA Bulletin*, June 1981, 3–7.

The letter is stuffy in style ("this communication," "The applicant," "relative to"). That letterly voice fails to introduce the applicant as an individual. The letter also includes misspellings: *reguarding, managment.* Any misspelling instantly calls the writer's professionalism into question and negates an ethical appeal. Moreover, the letter was sent as a photocopy and was not in any way tailored to a particular "institution or firm." It *told* the reader something about the applicant but failed to *show* any real evidence to encourage the reader's interest in the application.

Instead, let's look at some ways to incorporate AIDA into a cover letter.

Attention

Get attention directly in the salutation and later by using the reader's name whenever possible. If a name is not included in the job announcement, call the company to get the name of the personnel director, or check a standard source. People pay more attention when they are addressed by their name than when addressed only by their role. Get attention, too, by designing your letter well, with adequate margins, good spacing, and a pleasing typeface. Use good-quality paper. For a marketing or advertising position, you might try a clever approach. One applicant, for example, began his letter at the *last* line on the page and wrote up. He said the letter reflected his willingness to start at the bottom. Some letters begin with an attention-getting question:

> Do you need a hard-working self-starter to show your customers every benefit of the VisoLene System?

In choosing an attention-getter, think of the reader. Many readers might find upside-down letters upsetting.

Interest

That opener may simply establish your central selling point *in the reader's terms,* as a way of creating interest. The selling point may be your education, your experience, or both. Choose whether you want to emphasize a single skill or your versatility. For example, note your experience in connection with the product:

> As a committed user of IBM personal computers and a tutor in our university IBM microcomputer laboratory, I am writing to inquire about becoming a participant in your management training program.

Or with the reader's company:

Because of my experience and education in agricultural economics and management, I think I can be an asset to Perdue Inc. as you maintain your strong position in the industry.

Or with the reader's goals:

Are you looking for a sales representative with a degree in marketing and a good technical background in chemistry? You'll find my academic qualifications and personality are well suited to a career in pharmaceutical marketing with your firm.

Be positive. Avoid implying that you'll tell the company how to run the business:

Last summer, I worked for Pediatrics Associates Inc., which uses your office systems. I became very familiar with all the trouble you have with those systems, their lack of reliability, and difficulty of use. I'd like to apply for a job with you to straighten these things out.

Don't be selfish. Avoid a flat announcement of your availability:

In June I will receive a BS degree in management from XYZ University.

"So what," a reader may well respond.

If you feel that the reader is conservative and expects a low-keyed, traditional opener, then begin by noting where you found out about the job. An announcement:

I am writing in response to your advertisement in the June 4 issue of *The Deseret News.*

Or a person:

John Maier, my major professor in the Department of Accounting at Utah State, suggested that I write to you concerning your opening for an entry-level accountant.

Don't begin with a request for an interview. Save that for later, after you've convinced the reader that you're worth interviewing. Make sure that someplace in the first paragraph you have applied for a position. Call the position by whatever name you found in the advertisement or heard from your source:

I am writing to apply for your position of sales trainee.

Desire

Then, provide the evidence that will persuade the reader to interview you. Use a *logical* appeal. Match your qualifications to the position. Indeed, let the position announcement structure the presentation of your main selling point. Here's an ad:

If you have strong analytical skills, are project-oriented, have the ability to work on your own, and are looking for a position where you will participate in and contribute to the decision-making process in both the operations and the strategic planning areas, this may be the position for you.

A response would provide evidence derived from education or experience in each category:

- *Analytical skills:* Courses? Reports written? Problem-solving in summer jobs?
- *Project-oriented:* Marketing or other projects in classes? Group assignments? Development of schedules for summer work?
- *Work on own:* Employer comments about your independence? Independent study credits? Entrepreneurial summer activities?
- *Decision making and operations and strategic planning:* Courses in planning? Team work? Case study analyses?

Here's one paragraph from a response to an advertisement for a management trainee in an investment banking company:

> At college, I have taken many courses in financial management in which I learned stock and bond evaluation, dividend analysis, asset management, and tax policy. Each course required extensive case analyses and practical problem-solving. High grades in the courses indicate my strengths in these skills necessary to do well in your position. In my work with Z Bank Inc., I gained experience in using several computer programs for stock analysis and can bring that experience, too, to your firm.

Refer to the résumé, but don't just rehash it. Don't editorialize; *show* the reader what you can do, don't just *tell*. Avoid exaggeration:

> My extensive course work in marketing and my highly successful summer work experience in a gourmet shop of the highest quality have prepared me for an outstanding career in marketing. If your opening is commensurate with my own needs, I might be available for an interview.

You want to show that you speak the language of corporate employers, but extensive jargon or stuffiness will probably backfire.

Action

The action you seek is a request for an interview, at which time you can persuade the prospective employer in person. End by asking for the interview, restating your interest in the job—and thus closing the sale. Anticipate the question of *when* you could attend an interview by providing a time frame:

> It would be a pleasure to visit you for a personal interview at your convenience. The best times would be a Monday or Wednesday between one and five, but I could arrange another time if necessary.

You might also retain a bit of control over the situation by saying that you will call the reader in another week or two:

> I will call you in two weeks to arrange a convenient time to discuss career opportunities at Philip Morris.

Avoid the letterly voice throughout, but especially in such endings as these:

> Thank you for your time. I look forward to talking with you.
> I hope to hear from you soon.

Instead, tailor the ending to the sales approach of the rest of the letter:

> I would like to use my background in both marketing and chemistry to represent your firm and to contribute to your strong growth trend. Please call me for an interview at your convenience. I'm eager to be part of your team.

Model Letters

In writing the letter, keep in mind the "you attitude" you read about in Chapter 13. It's tempting to simply describe yourself. Resist. As you reread the draft of your letter, look at the opening word of each paragraph. If it's *I*, you may be in trouble. Reverting to "the applicant" won't solve the problem. Instead, shape the letter *in the reader's terms*.

In the following letter, Jenny Smith uses the hospital's advertisement to frame her response. Here is the advertisement (EOE, by the way, stands for "Equal Opportunity Employer").

> Graduate Hospital is seeking highly motivated therapists and certified PT assistants for our 310-bed acute care teaching hospital with a 20-bed rehabilitation unit. Rehab experience is a plus but not required. Case loads will vary. You must be eligible for PA licensure. New graduates are welcomed to apply. Excellent salary and benefits. Send résumé to Rhonda Pappero, Graduate Hospital, Personnel, 19th and Lombard Sts., Philadelphia, PA 19146. EOE.

Smith's letter is addressed to Ms. Pappero:

Dear Ms. Pappero:

Because of my academic work and experience in rehabilitation, I can be an asset to your Physical Therapy Department as described in *The Forum*, May 12, 1987. I am applying for a therapist's position, especially working with young people and with stroke victims of all ages.

The opportunity to work with a varied case load in a teaching hospital, particularly Graduate Hospital, excites me. I hold a BS degree in biological sciences from American University and am a recent graduate of Beaver College's graduate program in physical therapy. I am eligible for PA licensure. Because I am a recent graduate, my experience to date has been clinical rather than job-related, but I have worked directly with both young people and geriatrics in an internship program at the Moss Rehabilitation Center.

The enclosed résumé details my qualifications. At your request, I will be happy to furnish letters of reference that will inform you of my reliability and skill both as a student and as a therapist.

At your convenience, I will be pleased to talk with you. I look forward to learning more about the challenges of rehabilitation medicine and to discussing the role I can play in maintaining the excellent work of Graduate Hospital.

The letter establishes "highly motivated" credentials with words like *excites* and *challenges*. It praises Graduate Hospital. It notes Smith's education, experience, and eligibility for licensure. It mentions the name of the Moss Rehabilitation Center, where Smith interned, because that hospital is also located in Philadelphia and is thus known to—and probably respected by—the reader. The letter emphasizes a broad interest in rehabilitation that reflects the "varied case load" statement in the advertisement.

In the following letter, Susan Hughes describes her personal travel and language skills in the terms of a potential employer at a travel agency. She knows about airline and ground schedules. That knowledge translates into time that Bowman can save in not having to train Hughes. The details, too, about countries visited and study abroad show enthusiasm about the specific job—much more than a bland statement: "I am an enthusiastic traveler." The agency Hughes is writing to is located in Washington, D.C. Hughes writes from Lawrence, Kansas, so she explains her willingness to travel to Washington for both an interview and eventual relocation.

Dear Mr. Bowman:

Having traveled extensively during the past several years, I was pleased to read in the September issue of *Professional Traveler* that you are seeking to expand your staff. With my knowledge of much of the United States and several foreign countries, I would like to contribute to maintaining your excellent reputation as you expand your operation.

Currently, I am a student at the University of Kansas and will graduate with a double major in Spanish and business administration. I will be studying in Madrid for five months this spring and would enjoy relocating to Washington after graduation.

Traveling is one of my main interests. I have traveled through a majority of the continental United States and have visited the United Kingdom, South Africa, Brazil, Spain, Mexico, and Guatemala. I have a good knowledge of airlines and ground transportation, gained both as a hobby and during part-time employment with a local agency that serves the university community.

The enclosed résumé lists my qualifications. I will be in Washington during my spring break, April 6–10, and would like to talk with you, at your convenience, during that time, to discuss how I can contribute to your organization. I'll call you in two weeks to see about arranging an appointment.

In the following letter, Rich Hartman writes to an elementary-school principal because of a suggestion from his track coach. The name of the coach is the point of connection with the reader in the first sentence. Note how Hartman uses the ends of Paragraphs 2 and 3 to state his experience in the reader's terms. He shows his knowledge of children by quoting numbers (sixty) and specific names of programs (HAP). He also establishes his own credentials as a runner. His selling point: He's a runner who has been well coached and who also works well with children:

Dear Mr. Myers:

My track coach, Pete Phillips, recently told me about openings in your extracurricular program at Skyline. I am particularly interested in applying for the position of head coach of the boys' track team. I hope you'll agree that my qualifications suit me well for this post.

This past summer, I taught mathematics, in morning sessions, to sixty seventh-graders in the Higher Achievement Program (HAP) at Logan High School. Twice a week, in afternoon sessions, I demonstrated the basic skills of track and other sports to these same students. HAP has provided me with invaluable experience in dealing with boys and girls about the same age as students in your school.

I have been running track myself at various levels for fourteen years. During this time I have worked closely with five excellent head track coaches (including Pete, of course) and have observed their training techniques. I'm certain I can develop these techniques into a working, successful program at Skyline.

Highlights of my track career and other pertinent information are outlined on the enclosed résumé. I'd like to come to Skyline to talk to you about working with you and your students to develop a strong track team.

Although it's best to address a specific reader, at times you will need to respond to a blind advertisement in a newspaper. Such advertisements avoid the mention of a company name. Instead, the company is referred to by qualifiers: "a major Fortune 500 firm located in New York City," "a rapidly growing West Coast financial services organization," "an expanding real-estate-syndication firm doing public offerings on real-estate-income programs." The advertisements request response to a box number at the newspaper. Companies use these blind ads sometimes to keep their own employees from knowing that the company is seeking new workers or to keep job seekers from beating down their doors. In your response, of course, do not write "Dear Box 62." Also avoid "Dear Sir or Madam." Instead, after an inside address to the newspaper, begin your message directly:

Box 52
c/o *The Wall Street Journal*
420 Lexington Avenue
New York, New York 10170

Now that I have received high marks in my management information systems and programming classes and have completed a summer as a systems analyst for a large organization, I'm ready to be the "experienced, creative business programmer" you advertised for on March 17.

As you send letters maintain good records. Keep copies and establish a control sheet with columns for the date you sent a letter, the date you received an acknowledgment, interview dates, dates of follow-up letters, and the like.

Finally, keep in mind that the reader's job is also on the line when he or she decides to interview you. Particularly in large companies, if you make the initial screening, your letter will be sent along with the blessing of the person you wrote to in the first place. Your letter should make him or her also look good.

On Your Way

With your résumé and letters in the mail, and with recommenders lined up, you are on your way to interviews and the career beyond. You may be anxious while you wait to hear. Everyone is. But people *do* find employment. If you wrote to the right person, you'll probably receive a response. Relax a bit and get ready for the interview stage, which we describe in the next chapter.

Exercises

1. Comment on these opening paragraphs of cover letters:

   Working with people has always been a challenge to me; people are all so different and unique.

   Because of my retail experience previously with the Radio Shack Company and various other positions closely related to communication, I feel amply qualified for the retail clerk position within your store.

   I am writing in response to your recent advertisement in *The New York Times*. After reviewing the job description, I feel that I am qualified for the position.

   Because of my concentration in biology and chemistry in college and my desire to gain practical lab experience in industry, I feel that I would be beneficial to your summer intern program.

   When I first became acquainted with W. L. Gore & Associates, Inc., through your colleague and my friend, Ronald Bove, I was tremendously impressed by the innovativeness of W. L. Gore and its unique lattice-structure organization and philosophy. As the years have passed, I have followed the Gore Association in the news, so now that I am approaching my final year at the university, I find that I would like to become part of its organization.

   Upon reviewing my academic and work experience, I am confident that you will find, as I have, that my qualifications are well suited for the position of marketing researcher as advertised.

I am very interested in securing a position with First Chicago Bank. Recently, you posted a position for a credit analyst that would eventually lead into a position in the Commercial Lending Department.

In a brief discussion with Ed Stella, Dr. Ken Lomax learned about a possible opportunity with your company in the area of irrigation. As a senior in agricultural engineering technology at Western State University, I am currently seeking a full-time career appointment.

Experience is considered the best and most complete teacher, as it is only through experience that one can gain a thorough understanding of the task at hand. In light of this, I offer a full academic year of experience as a consultant in the microcomputer lab at the University of The Middle West. In the microcomputer lab, I have worked extensively with packaged software, including word-processing programs.

2. Comment on any "red flags" or errors in expression in these descriptions of "experience" from résumés:

Resident assistant. Handled general floor maintenance. Presented educational and social programs to residents. Counselled students and provided information about university services.

Waitress, College Hall. Coordinated detailed preparation and service of university and local business banquets.

File Clerk, Johnson Real Estate Agency, Kearny NJ. Maintained the organization of property listing files used by all county realtors, in accordance with the market changes.

Johnson Luggage, Oak Brook Terrace, IL. August 1981 to August 1983. Closed and opened store, night deposits, customer service, and inventory.

Sales Assistant, IBM, Stokely, FL.
    Responsible for the follow up and control of IBM's entire line of microcomputers. Duties include: demonstration of hardware and software to groups and individuals, hardware maintenance, keep customer contact to ensure satisfaction (1/85 to present)

Waiter-clown, Ground Round, Waterville, TX. Gain experience working with people and handling cash.

Laborer. Public Works, Ridley Township, OH. Worked on the "road crew" fixing and sprucing up public facilities.

Offered position as student tour guide.

3. Comment on any problems in expression in these sections under "Education" in a résumé:

Completed courses in Industrial Psychology, Independent Study dealing with worker evaluation and motivation, Learning and Motivation, and Behavioral Statistics, as well as general courses in computer science, business communications, and economics.

Have passed BU614, BU661, E451, MU687, and A111.

Expected date of gratulation: 1989

4. Comment on these job-objective statements:

—Acceptance into health care administration with a future of advancement.

—Buyer in the purchasing department with an opportunity for advancement in management.

—Systems Engineer, specializing in computer-related work that will best use my educational background in the field of finance and personal computers.

—Management-level position as liaison between the business and patient care aspects of a moderately sized health-care facility.

5. Revise the following letter:

I am responding to your advertisement for summer employment which was found in the February 28 edution of *The Journal News.* As a junior, majoring in Computer Science at Macmillan University, I believe that my education, combined with my previous experience, have provided me with the qualifications for this position. Enclosed is a resume for your review.

The educational backround presented in the resume provides me with both a well-rounded programming experience and a complete liberal arts curriculum. In addition, my two years of data processing work experience has sharpened my technical skills and has given me experience in dealing with people on a one to one basis. I also have had experience using the IBM PC and its compatible software.

I am available for an interview during my spring break. Thanking you for your time and interest and hoping to be hearing from you in the near future, I remain

Sincerely yours

6. Pages 542–45 show two functional résumés. Comment on their design. Suggest strategies for revision. Write a revised version of each, inserting current dates where appropriate.

FUNCTIONAL RÉSUMÉ A

Professional Objective: Computer programmer who does simulation and modeling with use of graphics.

Education: BSAS, Computer Science Information, June 19xx, The University of X.
Business Admin. Minor, Dean's List, GPA in major 3.43.

Skills: <u>Problem Solving</u>
Developed new accounts receivables program for collecting bad debts.

Helped set up a different approach to get new students interested and involved in a religious group on campus.

Organized a new filing system to keep more accurate records of company's accounts receivables, helped to collect money before bills got too old.

<u>Communication</u>
Corresponded with numerous people as secretary of Lutheran Student Association, both by telephone and letters.

Frequent use of phone conversation with customers who had overdue bills, included handling some irate customers.

Conducted group workshops at dinner meetings and retreats on such topics as Expression of Anger and Forgiveness.

<u>Organizational Planning</u>
Planned local and regional retreats, including securing speakers and organizing weekend agendas.

Planned social activities such as dances, semiformal, and tournaments as a member of the Campus Planning Board.

(continued)

Experience: Accounts Receivable Personnel, CompuCorp, Logan UT. Responsible for setting up new system for the Rocky Mountain Area (5/xx—7/xx).

Bookkeeper, Freedman Motor Service, Durango, CO. In charge of entering credits and debits, balancing books, and making and recording bank deposits.

FUNCTIONAL RÉSUMÉ B

SKILLS

1. Proficiency in planning, writing, and editing business and technical documents, news releases, research reports, and interpretive papers.
2. Ability to communicate orally.
3. Ability to think creatively and to implement new ideas.
4. Ability to work constructively with a group over a period of time.
5. Ability to direct the activities of others in group projects.
6. Ability to share knowledge and skills.
7. First-aid skills.
8. Ability to learn new ideas and skills rapidly through both oral and written instruction.
9. Ability to travel, to adapt to new cultures, to function on my own without parental or community support.

RELATED TRAINING AND EXPERIENCE

1. o Will graduate June 19xx with a degree in business administration.

(continued)

○ During a five-week internship with the Cheyenne County Personnel Department, produced annual report for the Personnel Board and report summarizing my statistical research on a special project.
○ News editor for high-school newspaper.

2. ○ Gave oral presentation on managing personnel resources to my organizational and management behavior class.
○ Gained poise, confidence, and speaking skills while acting in school plays.

3. ○ Helped found an undergraduate chapter of the International Association of Business Communicators.
○ Started peer advising program for business majors.
○ Started children's acolyte service at church.
○ Choreographed for dance performances.

4. ○ Member of the university dance ensemble, university outing club, intramural sports, Girl Scouts.

5. ○ Directed short play for a literature class.
○ Advised undergraduate officers of the IABC chapter on leadership.
○ Dormitory government representative.
○ Held several offices in high school.

6. ○ Tutor for freshman accounting course.
○ Summer counselor and swimming instructor at Girl Scout camp.
○ Spanish teacher for elementary-school program.
○ Sunday school, Bible school teacher.

7. ○ Worked summers as lifeguard.

8. ○ Worked part time as library clerk and waitress.

9. ○ Spent a semester in England, studying and traveling.
○ Familiar with French and Spanish language and culture.

(continued)

HONORS AND AWARDS

Dean's List, University Honors Program, Rotary Club Service Award,
Teacher's Association Scholarship, First-Class Girl Scouting Award,
Student of the Month, second runner-up in County Junior Miss
Pageant, nominated for People to People Student Ambassador
Program, President of National Honor Society.

7. Here are two chronological résumés. Revise them for better format and emphasis:

CHRONOLOGICAL RÉSUMÉ A

Peter P. Smith
17 Hyde Dr., Apt A
Mountain View, CA 94043

JOB OBJECTIVE:
Challenging position in business/financial management that will
provide an atmosphere conducive to growth and achievement and one
where initiative will be welcomed.
EDUCATION:
University of X
B.S. in business administration with concentration in finance.
Strong background in accounting and business economics. This
program reflected the demand for management capability in every field.
EXPERIENCE:
5/xx–8/xx General Motors Assembly Division, X town CA
Rear-retractable seat-belt operator in the Soft Trim Department.

(continued)

Served as a reliable member of the production team; performed routine testing of components. Emphasis was placed on GM's compliance with the Motor Vehicle Safety Standards Act.

5/xx–8/xx County Country Club, Y town, CA
5/xx–8/xx
Held two positions simultaneously. Waiter in the clubhouse dining room, consisted of such duties as waiting on members for luncheons, dinners, banquets, and poolside occasions. Greenskeeper duties included engineering and maintaining an eighteen-hole private golf course. Tasks carried out were those such as irrigation, planning, landscaping, greens cutting, both pool and tennis-court upkeep.

5/xx–8/xx Pals Cabin Restaurant, Z town CA
Pantry worker, responsible for general food services (cooking and preparation) and managerial assistance in the 75-table restaurant, maintaining beverage and food stocks. Supervised with coordination of others brunches, banquets, and private parties (business meetings, personal celebrations, and community club events).

ACTIVITIES:
University of X
Member of the Business and Economics College Council and Business Student Association. Involved in the Residence Hall Government.
Member of the Delta Upsilon chapter of Delta Phi Delta National Fraternity. Positions include Corresponding Secretary (responsible for correspondence with national fraternity, community, alumni, and parents, writing necessary documents), Pledge Educator, Rush Chairman, Greek Week Representative, and Outstanding Pledge.
Participated in intramural football, waterpolo, basketball and softball.
Member of the University of X Marching Band.
INTERESTS:
Participating in football, golf, camping, and music, and tinkering with automobiles.
REFERENCES:
Available on request.

CHRONOLOGICAL RÉSUMÉ B

Hobbies/Interests: Sports, running, and the outdoors.

Honors: Physical Education Honor Student.
Dean's List three semesters.
Highest GPA for a semester: 3.69 (4.0 basis).
Class rank in physical education: seventh.
Overall GPA: 3.20 (4.0 basis).
X High School: two years letter winner in field hockey and softball.
X High School: top field hockey scorer in a season.

Courses: Skills and Techniques in Field Hockey: 4.0 (4.0 basis).
Psychology of Coaching: 4.0 (4.0 basis).
Coaching Tennis: 4.0 (4.0 basis).
Coaching Softball: 4.0 (4.0 basis).
First Aid and Athletic Training: 4.0 (4.0 basis).

Education: B.S. in physical education and health; expected graduation date: June 19xx

Experience: *County Summer Youth Program*

Summer 19xx, xx   Lunch monitor: duties included delivering lunches, maintaining lunch counts, and interviewing workers.

Winter 19xx   *County Parks and Recreation Basketball League*
Head basketball coach: duties included coaching and instructing boys' basketball team, ages 8–12 (volunteer).

Spring 19xx   *X High School softball "B" Team*
Head softball coach: duties included coaching and instructing girls ages 10–14.
In the spring of 19xx, I will coach the "A" team (volunteer).

Professional Memberships: APHRED.
DAPHER.

References: Will be furnished on request.

8. Revise the following cover letter, written by the author of Résumé A in Exercise 7, in answer to this ad:

ADVERTISEMENT

Financial trainee—Large financial services organization, headquartered in the Southeast, is seeking an aggressive trainee to learn its financial operation. Write to Mr. Anthony Seone, Your Broker, Inc., P.O. Box 37, Atlanta, GA 30307

Mr. Anthony Seone
Your Broker, Inc.
P.O. Box 37
Atlanta, GA 30307

Dear Mr. Seone,

Your September 15 ad in the *Wall Street Journal* described your need for a finance trainee at Your Broker. I am very interested for this could be the opportunity I seek in the area in which I'd like to begin my finance career.

Through my program at the University of X, I have much acquired knowledge, understanding and skill essential to Business finance. With a strong, sound educational backgrond in Finance, Economics and Accounting I will best contribute to your firm because of my interests in this field.

I believe my employment background can also be utilized by your Broker. My ability to be responsible, reliable and willingness to work will benefit your firm.

After reviewing my resume, I hope you will find me qualified for a position with Your Broker, Inc. I can assure you of my value. If you desire any additional information or references please contact me. Your consideration is appreciated, and I look forward to talking with you.

Very truly yours,

Peter P. Smith

Enclosure 1

The Employment Interview . . . and Beyond

27

549

The goal of your résumé and your letter, and of your clever search of the market, is to obtain an interview. In the interview, you convince the employer that you are the best candidate for the job. In addition, you learn about opportunities that the company can offer *you*. An employment interview can take many forms. Some are brief, cordial, highly positive. Some are deliberately stressful. Some require only conversation. Some require tests. They may occur at the potential employer's office, at an interview site maintained by a college or a university, at a hotel during a professional meeting, at a restaurant, or even over dinner at a potential employer's home. Each occasion, of course, requires specific responses.

In Chapter 24, we provide general guidelines for behaving well in an interview. These apply to an employment interview as well. This chapter expands on guidelines for this specific form of interview.

A word of warning: Don't be afraid that the interview requires you to be somebody you are not. It's not an exercise in acting. It's not a competition for perfection. Neither you nor the potential employer will be served by your masquerade, even if you do manage to carry it off. The employer will expect long-term behavior from you that you might find uncomfortable, and you'll lose the opportunity to find out if your long-term self could really flourish in the role the company would like you to perform. So be honest. That doesn't mean, of course, "Be sloppy," or "Be self-defeating." It means prepare well so that you can display your *best* self.

Before the Interview

Don't go into the interview cold. Do your homework. Find out about the company interviewing you. Study its annual reports; read current issues of *The Wall Street Journal* and other newspapers and business magazines; talk with the company's employees. Know enough background to ask specific questions about the position or about projects that the company is now undertaking. You might even bring a list of questions with you to the interview.

Imagine, too, some questions that the interviewer may ask you. Figure 27–1 lists some common ones.

The Interview Itself

Unless you are very unusual, you will be nervous before and during the interview. Expect that. Good preparation will build your confidence, but you'll have to share control during the interview with the

For openers:
Did you have any trouble finding the company?
How's your [fill in the blank] team doing this season?

About your education:
What's your favorite course? Your least favorite course?
Do you think your grades really reflect your understanding of the field?
Why did you decide to go to [fill in the name of your college]?
Why did you major in [fill in your major]?
How did you finance your education?
Do you plan to do graduate work? In what field?
Did you live in a dorm during college? A fraternity or sorority? An
   apartment? How did you decide on those living arrangements?
Were you active in any extracurricular activities? Sports?
What college project interested you most?

About your work history:
How did you spend your summers during college?
What was the most satisfying job you ever held? Why?
What have you learned from all the jobs you've held?
What makes a good boss? Tell me about the best boss you ever worked
   for. The worst?
What is your salary history?
What are your salary expectations for this position?

About your career plans:
Tell me about yourself.
What do you see yourself doing in five years?
What are your greatest strengths? Weaknesses?
Do you prefer working on teams or working alone?
How will you measure your own success?
Are you willing to travel? To relocate?

About the interviewer's company:
Why do you think you'd like to work for us?
Do you know people who work here?
What division of the company most interests you?
How did you find out about this position?

For closing off the discussion:
When could you start work?
What else would you like me to know about you?

FIGURE 27–1.   Some questions interviewers often ask.

interviewer. You can't just recite a memorized text. You can, however, bring with you items that support your credentials, including a copy of your résumé (just in case the interviewer doesn't have one at hand) and perhaps a portfolio of your writings or other work.

The interviewer will introduce himself or herself. Remember that name and use it in the interview. Follow the interviewer's lead in the conversation while still keeping a fix on your own goals through the process of questioning and clarification. Stay alert. Answer questions directly. *Listen.* Don't respond to the question you wished the interviewer had asked—but to the real question. And don't talk too much. Interviewers like to hear themselves talk, too.

Most interviews are fairly smooth, humane endeavors. But sometimes, through inattention or a deliberate attempt to create stress, interviewers make malicious comments or ask embarrassing questions. Respond to these for what they are: clues to your possible future with that company. They may reflect the company's lack of interest in you. So be it. Or, more significantly, they may reflect something about the *interviewer* and his or her sense of self and role in the company. If you are really serious about the company, try to talk with someone else to confirm or correct your impression. The conduct of the interview may point to political or other problems at the company that suggest you would not be happy there.

By law, interviewers should not ask about your age, marital status or spouse's employment, children, religion, national origin, or political preference. If such questions are raised, you can simply decline to answer. That refusal may, indeed, *enhance* your image with an interviewer who is looking for someone who will take a stand. You may feel, however, that declining will eliminate you from a position you are seriously interested in. It's up to you to decide what you'll reveal about yourself. In general, don't reveal anything negative about yourself early in the interview. For the most part, interviewers form rather firm impressions within the first five minutes or so. A negative item that occurs late in an otherwise pleasant interview is not likely to change the interviewer's picture.

Often an interviewer's last question is "Is there anything you'd like to ask me about the job?" Ask something—don't let the interview end on a whimper.

After the Interview

After the interview, both the interviewer and the applicant still have work to do—more, of course, for the interviewer. The interviewer compiles data from several interviews to continue the selection process.

Often, a second round of interviews will be in order for a smaller group of the most promising candidates.

As an applicant, you can gently remind the interviewer about yourself while he or she is making those decisions. Send a brief note to reiterate your interest in the position. Enclose any further documentation of your credentials that may have been requested. Here is the text of a follow-up letter.[1]

I enjoyed talking with you yesterday at the Career Planning and Placement Office here. You only increased my already great interest in working for Premier Systems.

As you requested, I've enclosed a copy of the article on software houses that I mentioned. It appeared in last Tuesday's issue of the *Triangle*, our bi-weekly campus newspaper. It mentions Premier Systems on the second page.

Again, thank you for taking the time to talk with me yesterday. I look forward to hearing from you.

Deciding

You'll probably participate in several interviews in the course of your job search. Compare information from all the interviews as well as from your background reading. Here are some elements to check for:

The Organization
    Salary and fringe benefits
    Size
    Reputation for employee support
    Financial position
    Anticipated growth and mergers
    Facilities

Job Description
    Opportunities for advancement
    Criteria for performance evaluation
    Amount of travel
    Routine versus innovative work

Supervisor(s)
    Style of work compared to your own
    Opportunities for mentoring
    Political position within the organization

[1] Courtesy of Kitsel Outlaw.

Location
    Convenience to where you'd like to live
    Commuting patterns
    Cultural and recreational benefits

Weigh these elements according to your own priorities. Many Europeans, for example, find Americans distressingly job-oriented; Americans will move wherever they are asked to in order to find the *job* they want. In Europe, however, one is more likely to favor *location;* one looks for some job in a place (like Vienna) where one would like to be. What's more important to you? Your potential relationship with a supervisor may also be the key. You may be looking for someone who can "mentor" you through the complexities of promotion, particularly in a large organization, and who can show you how best to achieve your professional potential.

Accepting an Offer

The person who interviewed you, or the personnel department of the company, may make you an offer. The offer may come over the phone, with a follow-up letter explaining the details. Or you may receive a letter with the initial offer. Reply promptly to the offer. If you need more time to think about the offer, say when you plan to give an answer. You may need to negotiate that time.

Saying yes to a job offer is easy. Briefly express your pleasure and your acceptance, show the employer you're eager to work for them, and confirm the starting date and any other conditions of employment necessary, as in the following letter:

I happily accept your offer of employment as Assistant Product Information Analyst in the Product Integration Department, reporting to John Port.

As you recommended, I talked with Mr. Port. He answered a few questions I had about the position before I made my decision. I have informed him that I will be accepting the job, and we agreed on June 17 as the starting date.

Thank you for sending me the description of the benefits package. The completed health survey is enclosed.

If you need other information from me or if you have further information for me, please write or call. I am looking forward to working for Premier Systems.

Declining an Offer

Saying no is more difficult. If possible, discuss why you need to decline. But don't antagonize; you may want to work for that company sometime in the future. Here is one model:

Thank you for your offer of employment with Premier Systems.

As you suggested, I talked with Mr. Jackson about the specific job description. After reviewing the information he gave me concerning the work load in conjunction with the final salary offer, I'm afraid I won't be able to accept your offer.

I would be happy to reconsider this position in the future if you do indeed decide to raise the salary. Premier Systems remains a most attractive place to work, and I hope you will keep me in mind.

Again, thank you for your consideration. I regret that I won't be joining you at this time.

Responding to a Rejection

If your interview does *not* result in a job offer—if the company calls or writes you to say they've hired someone else—you still have one more communication task if you are seriously interested in the company: Write to acknowledge the refusal. You may be angry or hurt, but don't let those feelings override professional strategy. Close out your file with the company on a positive note of your own by sending a letter that expresses your regret in not getting the job but that reconfirms your interest in the company and in any future openings. They may then remember you well and write or call again. Here is a brief letter:

Thank you for your letter of July 8. I, too, am sorry that you do not have an opening for me at this time.

I did enjoy talking with you and learning more about Premier Systems, which remains very attractive to me. I hope you'll keep me in mind for any future openings.

Closing the Search

In *Rosencrantz and Gildenstern Are Dead*, one character comments: "Every exit is an entrance someplace else." The job search process, too, represents both an exit (perhaps only a temporary one) from your career in college and an entrance into a career elsewhere. The process is marked by several checkpoints, each requiring communication, both oral and written. This chapter and Chapter 26 have surveyed some communication strategies that will meet your needs. Assemble your own portfolio of models, both those you write and those you read, to guide you as well.

Exercises

1. Check into the career-planning or placement office at your school or college to see what brochures or guidelines they produce to assist students in job searches and interviews. Several schools also maintain a library of videotapes, including mock interviews and presentations about companies that recruit frequently there.

2. To develop your interviewing skills, *practice* with a friend. Assume the role of interviewer yourself, and then ask the friend to assume that role. Try to outwit the other. See what happens with uncomfortable questions. You might also want to videotape the session.

3. Assume that Premier Systems, a producer of software for data management in small businesses, is interviewing you. The interviewer seems pleased with your credentials, particularly your knowledge of personal computers and your experience as a tutor in a microcomputer laboratory on campus. She'd like to hire you as a sales representative who will travel to various businesses demonstrating the product and then train office personnel in its use. In the interview, she asks you to sketch out your approach to sales and training in a two- or three-page memo that you'll write on the spot. Your sales pitch will be directed to the office manager, who then must convey it to the head of the company. The training session will address secretaries. Remembering your business communication course and the need to consider the audience, along with guidelines for writing procedures (see Chapter 21), write the memo. Time yourself in your writing; you have half an hour.

4. Assume that the First National Bank of Lincoln (address: One Bank Place, Lincoln, NE 68583) has offered you a position as a junior auditor. Write to accept the position. Write another letter declining the offer for some reason, for example, the benefits package or your acceptance of another job. Maintain goodwill in this letter.

PART V

The International Dimension

Communicating in
the Global Economy

(1)選輯範圍仍分為：(A)黨政人士(B)各級民意代表(C)學術界、教育界(D)科技、工程界(E)文化界(F)工商界、金融界(G)自由職業（包括律師、會計師、醫師、建築師。）等七大類。

(2)人數視實際情形而定，大致在一千二百人左右。

(3)預定民國七十四年(1985)六月間出版，用高級道林紙以平四版精印，豪華精裝壹鉅冊計壹萬本，除國內銷售外，至少以三千部透過國外代理商銷售至世界各大圖書館及資料機構。

四、景仰 閣下 在 學 術 界 極負盛名，其卓越成就為世人所景仰，頃經本書編輯委員會遴定為選輯對象，用特專函奉達，即請 察照惠賜個人簡介（以年齡、籍貫、學經歷暨生平得意事蹟、成就及著作為主，由於篇幅關係，請以一張稿紙六百字為限。）連同玉照貳張（請選最近所攝二吋半身光面黑白照片，背面請書明現職、姓名），掛號寄交臺北市重慶南路一段九十四號六樓本局編輯部收。

五、檢陳簡介傳記樣張一份，敬請參閱並俞允賜辦共襄盛舉，仍懇於本年三月十三前將稿件及玉照擲下，以利早日付排製版，至深感禱。

臺灣中華書局股份有限公司

常務董事兼總經理 熊 鈍 生 敬啟

彰，特函請　迅賜擲寄簡介及玉照以便早日編輯出版，至希　俞允共襄盛舉。

說明：一、查本局鑒於歐美日本著名出版公司歷年來發行各行各業「名人錄，WHO'S WHO」，資料蒐集

之廣，出版種類之多，嘆為觀止。揆其出版動機，多在宣揚各界知名之士生平勤奮工作具

有卓越之表現，堪為後世楷模，籍其傳記簡介，選輯成冊俾供查考。此類書籍之銷售遍及

全球，舉凡政府資料部門、各大公私立圖書館，以及在工作或業務上有查閱各類人事資料

必要者，大多購備典藏，由於經常連續性之印行出版，其具有歷史性之參考價值，自不待言。

二、我中華民國近年來由於中樞賢明領導，各界知名人士卓著貢獻，形成經濟繁榮，民生富足

，社會安定，全球有識者為之側目，譽為近代發展中國家政經奇蹟，頗堪自慰。此項成就

皆我各界卓越領導知名人士在其本身崗位多年來努力有以致之，其功誠不可沒，茲為使其

優良事蹟，載諸典籍，宣揚中外以示表彰起見，爰仿歐美先進國家前例，以嚴謹、審慎之

態度選輯「中華民國當代名人錄（WHO'S WHO IN THE REPUBLIC OF CHINA）」一書問世。

三、本書自民國六十七年（1978）十一月下旬出版以後，迄今已在海內外銷售九千餘部，各方讚

譽，本局深受鼓勵，乃於民國六十八（1979）年六月間再出版第四册，茲以事逾數載，新人

輩出，迭據海內外人士熱烈反應以頗多遺珠之憾，似宜繼續編印，以應需要。爰決定於民

國七十四年六月間續編第五册出版，茲仍按前例訂定出版計劃如次：

臺灣 中華書局股份有限公司

台灣中華書局 （ ）

受文者　蕭家駒先生

副本
收受者

批　示

擬　辦

發　日期
文　字號
　　附件

用樣張一份

主旨：本局已編印出版『中華民國當代名人錄（WHO'S WHO IN THE REPUBLIC OF CHINA）』豪華精裝四鉅冊問世，事逾數載，新人輩出，迭據各方熱烈反應，認為頗多遺珠之憾，頃決定於七十四年六月間續編第五冊出版，以應需要。目前正再廣泛蒐集各界知名人士傳記簡介資料，素仰 閣下服務國家社會有卓越成就，為世人所景仰，業經審慎決定納入名人錄中，俾能宣揚中外，以示表

If you received in the mail the document shown on pages 562–64, you would very likely be perplexed. To begin with, you may not recognize what kind of document it is. Although you can probably figure out that it's written in an Oriental language, you may not know that it's Chinese. Can you read it? Is it an invitation to sell a product? An advertisement? A notice that you won a trip or inherited a fortune from an unknown relative? Should you respond? How?

Few Americans would be able to understand and respond easily. But if you're in business, you can expect to encounter messages, oral and written, in languages and forms that are unknown to you. The prospect is both a little frightening and quite exciting. You should be prepared to deal with such situations, however, since business is already global in orientation and rapidly becoming even more so.

Throughout this book, we've mentioned frequently the international dimensions of business communication. This chapter is devoted exclusively to communicating in the global economy, a prime challenge of today—and the future. It's at once a problem and an opportunity—with barriers to overcome and excitement to enjoy.

In this chapter, we first survey some of the reasons for becoming internationally aware. We then look at some problems in international communication, including two brief case studies. We conclude by outlining three strategies for communicating in the global economy.

Before you begin, you might want to know about that odd-looking document. It's a letter sent from Taiwan to participants in a research conference asking for information from which to prepare a directory. It includes a form to be returned with the requested data. It's a routine business letter of the kind you can expect to receive as you function in the world economy.

The Global Dimensions of Business

The world of business is growing larger and is shrinking at the same time. It is growing larger because world trade has expanded dramatically and has made national boundaries nearly irrelevant. It is shrinking because travel and communication, aided by technology, provide businesspersons direct and indirect contact with other parts of the world cheaply, quickly, and effectively.

Even if you are not yourself directly involved in international business, you cannot avoid the evidence of its existence—and its significance. *The Wall Street Journal* devotes two pages of its second section every day to regular coverage of international business news. (It also publishes special editions targeted to specific parts of the world—the Far East, for example—so that people doing business there can stay informed globally.) *Business Week* has a similar regular section on international business. Reports on currency exchange rates and the activities of international equity markets regularly appear in most nationally oriented newspapers in the United States, and features on aspects of international business are common. As a student of business, you should, of course, stay familiar with the global dimension through regular reading of such sources.

Doing so will remind you that we live in a global economy. From the U.S. perspective, international business may be looked at from two dimensions: American involvement in other economies, and the involvement of others in the United States. Through various legal and financial structures, American businesses are heavily represented around the world. In 1984, over 3,200 U.S. firms had over 21,000 subsidiaries and other affiliates in 120 countries. Our investment abroad has grown dramatically. In 1960, for example, U.S. private investment in other countries amounted to $49 billion. By 1970, that figure had more than doubled, to almost $120 billion. In the next decade, U.S. investment abroad increased over 400 percent, to about $517 billion in 1980. And in 1983, the figure was $775 billion—spectacular growth by any standards.

Much of this investment is through multinational companies (MNCs), large and organizationally complex firms that have branches or subsidiaries throughout the world, all connected financially and operationally through headquarters in one country. Many MNCs are based in the United States, but others are anchored in Europe, South America, and the Far East.

These foreign-owned MNCs reflect a second facet of the global dimension of business: the heavy investment by other countries in U.S. businesses. Sometimes we parochially assume that the path of influence is one way, with U.S. business interests dominating in other countries. Not so. To illustrate, here's a random listing of well-known "American" businesses that are fully or partially owned by business interests outside the United States, mostly European: Budd Company, Miles Laboratories, Grand Union, A&P, Shell Oil, and Lipton. The growth of foreign investment in the United States has roughly paralleled that of the United States abroad, rising from $41 billion in 1960 to $782 billion in 1983. About 2.5 million people in the United States are now employed by firms owned wholly or in large part by foreign companies.

Whether direct investment in the United States on the part of international MNCs will accelerate or decline is hard to predict, since future investments relate to interest rates and perceptions of investment safety; but it is clear that large parts of the U.S. economy are owned and operated from outside, just as U.S. companies own and operate large parts of the economies of other countries.

Becoming aware of the nature of international investment and direction makes some people nervous. Americans like to think they control their own business life and regret the passing of their primary role in the world economy. Europeans have always been sensitive to the Americanization of their cultures brought about by heavy U.S. investment and the popularity of products and services traditionally associated with the United States: Soft drinks and fast food are frequent targets of ire. Even language is affected; for example, the French shop at *le drugstore*. Third World nations resent economic imperialism from the developed world and strive for local ownership and control of productive enterprises.

None of us, however, will have our way. The internationalizing of business will not be reversed. The key word in business (as in military-political affairs) is *interdependence*. Business functions cannot be carried on in geographic isolation. Local economies tie into national economies, and national economies tie into an international economy that makes individual countries components rather than free-standing economic systems.

It is precisely this economic interdependence that makes communication so critical in the global economy. The definition, maintenance, and control functions of business discussed in Chapter 1 are performed globally. Hence communication, which as we have seen throughout this book makes possible the successful completion of business functions, must be international in orientation. Just as business success requires communication skills, so international business success requires international communication skills.

But what are "international" communication skills? Like management, communication is generic, common across different organizations and different countries. In other words, defining a communication goal, encoding a message to a receiver, and responding to the receiver's feedback so that the purposeful transfer of information occurs are elements common to all communications. Thus we can say that good international communication is, at one level, no different from any version of communication. But at the same time, communication across distances and cultures requires different emphases and special attention to certain elements of the communication act.

In the rest of this chapter, we highlight those aspects of communication that take on special significance in the international context. The focus is on you, the individual communicating with other individuals in different parts of the world. The overall structure and basic functions of business do, of course, differ somewhat in the global economy from the local or national economy. But at least from the perspective of business communication, the stress is on the individual writer or speaker. *You* have to communicate internationally. *You* have to be a global citizen.

Common Problems in International Communication

It's easy for communications to go wrong. All too easy. And communicating internationally increases the risks because the variables are greater and the circumstances more complex. We've looked briefly at the magnitude and significance of international business. That survey should remind you of the importance of functioning globally in your business career. Now we want to discuss some of the specific communication problems that can occur as you do so. These problems result from differences that exist between the senders and the receivers of messages and that can disrupt the communication process or, at the very least, make it less than maximally efficient.

You need to be aware of four fundamental differences that can affect international business communication: differences in space, time, language, and culture. We'll look briefly at each.

Spatial Separation

Spatial separation introduces serious communication barriers, regardless of whether the communication is across national borders. If you're in the same room with a colleague, you can send a message in a few words or with a gesture. If you're in Hong Kong, and your colleague is in Cairo, a gesture is out of the question and a few words won't do.

Four specific results flow from the physical distancing of sender and receiver that characterizes international communication. First, no direct exchange is possible. If you need Report 27 that is on your colleague's desk, and her desk is ten feet from yours, the exchange can be direct: You can go and pick up the report. Separation in space precludes direct exchange. You must communicate, that is, use words and pictures to convey the message that will achieve the intended outcome of understanding or action on the part of the receiver.

Second, spatial separation eliminates the possibility of nonverbal communication, which plays a strong role in business. Gestures that indicate frustration, pleasure, or anger convey information only if they are observed. If you're face to face with a colleague, gestures work, but if you're not, gestures lose significance. (Notice your telephone behavior—you probably display emotions through gestures even when the person you're talking to can't see them.) To some extent technology can compensate in international communication—videoconferencing preserves the possibility of using gestures, for example. But as a practical matter, the spatial separation that accompanies international communication effectively precludes nonverbal communication.

Third, spatial separation induces a shift to different media and to a higher level of formality in communication. Whereas a note might convey a message when you are separated from a colleague by a few doors or floors, a formal memo may be required if you're communicating from Warsaw to Rome; an interoffice memo might be replaced by a formal letter; and so on.

Finally, spatial separation affects feedback, which is critical to effective communication. The gestures that communicate to a sender that the message isn't being understood are not possible if sender and receiver are physically separated. Hence the sender must anticipate more and must try to send the message clearly the first time, knowing that feedback may not come at all, and that if it does come, it will take longer. Although teleconferencing does provide an opportunity for immediate feedback that is otherwise not possible when the sender and the receiver are physically separated, the experience is simply different from when the two are in the same room. When feedback takes a written form—a memo or letter sent in response to an original message—immediacy is clearly lost. Letters have been known to chase each other around the world, each asking for clarification of the last one sent. International communication need not go only in one direction, but the spatial separation between sender and receiver does greatly diminish the effectiveness of, if not always the opportunity for, feedback.

Differences in Time

Like differences in space, differences in time affect business communication. Letters, memos, and reports that are written and mailed or otherwise physically carried from sender to receiver are obviously unaffected by time differences. Telephone calls, teleconferences, and real-time communication via computer networks (where the medium is "written" but instantly transmitted) are directly influenced by time differences. Also affected in different ways are face-to-face business meetings that occur between persons who have just crossed time zones to be together.

The problems that arise from time differences are well illustrated by recent events in Spain. In preparation for joining the European Economic Community (the Common Market), the government of Spain moved to abolish a Spanish custom: the siesta. The workday in Spain had followed this pattern: offices and shops open from around 10 A.M. to 2 P.M., siesta time from 2 to 5 P.M. (with workers leaving their place of employment to go home for a meal and a rest), work again till around 8 P.M., and rest and dinner (around 10 or 11 P.M.) at home. The government's action in trying to put, first, its own and, later, all commercial offices on a nine-to-five workday offended and enraged many Spaniards, for whom the siesta is an ancient and cherished custom. The change was introduced to ensure that the Spanish workday would coincide with that of the other member countries of the EEC. How could bankers in Brussels or salespersons in Paris call their counterparts in Madrid at 9 A.M. or 3 P.M. if the country was basically closed? Membership in the Common Market meant that Spain had to adopt the business hours that prevail throughout Western Europe.

On a smaller scale, time differences regularly have an impact on business communication. Currency traders in New York have to be available when Zurich calls—even though it's mid-morning in Zurich before most New Yorkers wake up. Stock brokers in San Francisco cannot place orders on the New York Exchange in the afternoon because the people in New York have gone home. The salesperson based in Florence who wants to talk to her boss in Chicago will have to place the call after her own work hours. People who make frequent calls across time zones or who plan international teleconferences find it convenient to keep a map with the world time zones handy at all times.

Once the contact is made across the zones, of course, the time differences cannot be ignored. If you have had your second cup of coffee and are sitting at your desk in New York ready to go, remember that the person you're talking with in Glasgow may be anxious to get out the door after a long day of work. You need to remind yourself consciously of the time in which your receiver is living and to accommodate the tone, pace, and substance of your call accordingly.

The same caution is needed when you do business in person in another part of the world. If you arrive in Frankfurt at 10 A.M. local time after a (for you) overnight flight from Philadelphia, you might be tempted to take advantage of the full day ahead of you by scheduling a round of meetings or sales calls. Don't. If your European operations manager is arriving at 2 P.M., don't drag him into a 5 P.M. meeting; his body will still be operating on European time, and he will want more than anything to get to bed. Experts say that for each time zone you cross, it takes your body one full day to accommodate completely. Few business travelers have the luxury of allowing three, much less eight, days to make up for the time changes of a typical transoceanic flight, but it's wise to allow at least a day for your biological clock to begin to adjust to the wall clock in the place where you've just arrived. Drooping eyelids and fuzzy speech are only symptoms of the disorientation that the international traveler experiences; fuzzy thought is a bigger problem, and communicating with business colleagues always requires sharp thinking and the capacity for quick response.

Differences in Language

Differences in space and time are complicated in international business communication by what many regard as the greatest impediment: differences in language. Few Americans speak or read a language other than English, whereas a great many Oriental, European, and South American businesspeople have made a point of speaking English in addition to their native language, and often others as well. One of the reasons for our national failing is that we inhabit such a vast continent that it is possible to go through life without having to know a language other than English. Europeans live on a continent comprising many small countries and representing many languages. If you grow up in that environment, the need to acquire multiple languages is obviously great. Air travel and telecommunications advances have shrunk the world of communication, and now we all inhabit a multiculture, multilanguage world. Because of technology, we all now live close to speakers of other languages and therefore must do what Europeans have in the past to become capable in languages other than our own.

The effect of language differences on international business communication ranges from the obvious to the subtle. Obviously, negotiating a deal in the Middle East between Japanese-speaking and Arabic-speaking businesspersons is difficult. Less obvious is the effect on communication that comes from language differences rooted in culture. Language is a product of culture and reflects it. It's one thing to speak or read a language, quite another to grasp the nuances that the language captures in subtle ways. If you join a native business partner for a cup of coffee in Vienna, you probably know enough German to order *kaffee*. But the Viennese have at least seven words for coffee, each one referring to a clearly different product; *kleiner brauner*, for example, means an espresso coffee served with milk, whereas *einspanner* is espresso topped with whipped cream. The language captures the Viennese passion for coffee. Literacy in German is no substitute for growing up in Vienna, which makes possible, in this instance, a much more realistic use of the language itself.

Cultural Differences

The fourth and most fundamental difference between sender and receiver that can obstruct international business communication is cultural. *Culture* means the sum total of the knowledge, values, beliefs, customs, and practices within a given society at a given time. We are all products of our culture, and culture shapes what we do and how we look at the world. One example will clarify this concept. Americans are notoriously informal, relaxed, and casual. When they travel abroad, they often stand out because of their casualness of dress—wearing an open shirt and no jacket on the streets of London, for example, whereas the English, at least until very recently, have almost universally dressed more formally. Americans quickly employ first names: "Hi, I'm Jack. Good to meet you, Joan." Europeans tend to be much more formal, more "correct" or "proper" in dress, language, and basic habits. These are cultural differences, and they can impede communication. Many of the English will keep calling you "Mr." or "Miss" long after you call them "Henry" or "Mary," and the difference grates on them and therefore makes communication more difficult.

Differences in dress and manner of address are apparently superficial, but they do reflect deep differences in attitudes that must be recognized when one is dealing across cultural lines. Culturally determined attitudes toward some of the critical variables of business communication are specifically discussed in Chapter 23 with respect to oral communication.

At a deeper level, the attitude toward work and toward one's position within an organization varies from culture to culture and can cause communication problems. Americans typically pursue individual career interests, moving from job to job to achieve "advancement." The Japanese, by contrast, tend to be loyal to their employing organization and regard it as an extension of family life. Career mobility is largely internal in Japanese business, and much slower than in America. People don't typically move from firm to firm in pursuit of personal advancement. The rewards associated with work are also different. In the United States, salary is frequently of great importance, and money is the lure used to recruit new staff. In Japan, pay differentials among levels are much narrower, and salary itself is seldom a determining factor in hiring and promotion decisions.

These differences affect communication in obvious ways. An American manager in a Japanese subsidiary must know that motivating Japanese employees requires an understanding of their values, that money plays a smaller role, that loyalty is paramount, and that the organization functions in a familial role. Similarly, Japanese managers working in the United States should understand that the people they have responsibility for have different attitudes toward work and their relationship with the employing organization.

Such understanding takes effort. Edwin O. Reischauer, economist and former U.S. ambassador to Japan, stated the case well: "The Japanese have learned our language and our way of business and know our regulations. Our businessmen go over there very naively, without learning the language or way of life. So we're trying to achieve something without working very hard at it."[1] As business becomes even more international, such hard work will have to continue to be directed at overcoming the potential communication problems caused by differences in space, time, language, and culture. In the next section, we'll look closely at two examples of the impact of cultural differences on business communication.

Communication Across Cultures: Two Case Studies

 ## Alan Lane Writes to a New Manager

Alan Lane grew up in South Carolina and worked in several textile mills before ultimately acquiring his own, which after twelve years of hard work he built into a small, privately controlled company that operated six profitable plants in the southern United States. To take advantage of England's membership in the Common Market, he recently bought a yarn mill in Newcastle, England, whose products can be sent to other Common Market countries without the duties that would be attached to goods manufactured in the United States. Following the acquisition, Lane spent three weeks in Newcastle meeting the workers, reviewing operations, and making plans with the local management. When he had returned home, he wrote a letter to Stanley Martin, the plant manager, whom he intended to retain (see the letter in Figure 28–1).

Lane's goal—the intended outcome of the communication—is clear: He wants Martin to hire from among the plant's current staff for the two new positions, choosing people with direct work experience in production. This goal is culturally conditioned, a product of Lane's own experience in American business, where

"hands-on experience" and "promote from within" are buzzwords—and, by the way, principles that have served Lane well in his own rise from worker to owner.

How will Martin, who is English, respond? To understand how the message will form in his mind, we need to think from the perspective of Martin's cultural conditioning. In England, education and job advancement are still heavily influenced by the class system. Jobs are class-related: Workers are workers and managers are managers, and there is limited upward mobility. Working one's way from the factory floor to the president's suite (as Alan Lane did) is an American idea. The English don't regard such mobility as common.

The goal in Lane's mind is conveyed clearly through his language, in which there is no ambiguity. Martin shares that language, but the message that forms in Martin's head as the communication unfolds will take slightly different shape because Martin's cultural conditioning is different from Lane's. Martin can probably grasp the meaning, but he has to do some cultural—not linguistic—translation to put it into his own context.

Lane's letter also reflects other cultural

[1] As quoted by Nicholas D. Kristoff, "Japan Trade Barriers Called Mainly Cultural," *The New York Times,* 4 April 1985, A1.

CON-TEXT
Office of the Chairman

April 22, 19xx

Stanley Martin
Plant Manager, Newcastle

Dear Stan,

I enjoyed my visit to Newcastle and am looking forward to our work together.

I know from the visit that you share the view I have always had of the importance of people in the Con-Text organization. People are always our top priority—the key to our business success. That's why promotion from within has always been our practice. I'm personally very proud of the number of shift supervisors and even plant managers (three, in our six U.S. plants) who rose through the ranks from the mill floor.

Stan, to make sure that this spirit prevails in our Newcastle operation, I want to start a system of promotion from within that will make sure we develop our management talent from the pool of loyal workers we already have. My managers need hands-on experience and close knowledge of workers, gained from the inside.

I hope you'll bear this in mind as you staff the two new management positions we discussed, director of quality control and accounts supervisor. Let's draw on our own first!

Good to see you! Let me know how we're doing over there.

Warm regards,

Alan

FIGURE 28–1. Alan Lane's letter.

differences in what is, after all, a common language. American informality is well known. Notice the informal greeting ("Dear Stan,"), the use of the familiar in the letter itself, and the informal closing and first-name signature. Mr. Martin is used to being called Mr. Martin, and he thinks of his boss as Mr. Lane. Obviously both Lane and Martin will have to make adjustments in their language use and expectations to deal with each other across the (relatively small) cultural barrier that separates two English-speaking nations.

 ## Maxine Wells Makes a Request

Maxine Wells has been in charge of international accounts at Dandly Advertising for two years. During that time, she has developed language skills that she first acquired as a foreign language major at Middlebury College. She can readily correspond in French, German, and Spanish with her colleagues at the Paris, Hamburg, and Madrid branches of Dandley. To prepare some material for a meeting at the New York headquarters, Wells wrote in German a quick memo to the director of the Hamburg office (Figure 28–2). An English translation of the memo is presented in Figure 28–3.

The request is brief and almost casual. It is typical of interoffice correspondence in American corporations. Wells's goal is clear: to get an informal report on the current status of the Rorbach account. But Wolfgang Strauss's cultural perspective puts the goal into a different context when the message forms in his mind. Germans are well known for attention to detail and regard for authority. In response to this simple request for an update on

---

AN: Hr. W. Str.
    Direktor, Hamburg
VON: M. W.

Wir sind dabei, die Akten des Rorbach Kontos auf den neuesten Stand zu bringen. Könnten Sie uns bitte so bald wie möglich den Kontostand senden, und zwar mit genauen Rechnungen und einer Schätzung der zu erwartenden Transaktionen. Ich versuche, einen Bericht zusammenzustellen und benötige etwas mehr Information, als mir hier zur Verfügung steht. Danke für Ihre Hilfe. Wenn Sie nächsten Monat hier sind, werden wir uns in einer Sitzung treffen, um zukünftige Schritte in dieser Angelegenheit zu beraten.

FIGURE 28–2. Maxine Wells's memo.

```
INTEROFFICE

TO:     Wolfgang Strauss
        Director, Hamburg
FROM:   Maxine Wells

We're trying to update the files on the Rorbach account. Could you send
me a status report on the account at your earliest convenience, with
details on billings and a rough guess as to the future activity we can
expect? I'm trying to put together a report and need a bit more
information than I have here. Thanks for your help. We'll get together
next month when you're here for the meeting to discuss what direction
we ought to take on this matter.
```

FIGURE 28–3. English translation of Maxine Wells's memo.

the account, Strauss wrote a ten-page report, with three appended tables listing all billings and expenses since the account was opened two years earlier. His report covered every aspect of the Rorbach account and went far beyond what Wells needed. Why this failure in communication? Strauss's cultural conditioning led him to form a different view of the intended outcome from the one Wells had in her mind when she wrote the memo. She should have tried to adopt his perspective, and he should have tried to adopt hers. Neither was wrong, but both could have been more aware of the cultural differences that inform senders and receivers even when they use a common language.

Strategies for International Communication

We've seen how things can go wrong in international communications. Now let's look at what you can do to ensure that things go right. There are three broad strategies for becoming an effective communicator in the global economy:

- Make yourself a global citizen.
- Use technology.
- Be a good communicator.

Make Yourself a Global Citizen

To communicate internationally, you must think internationally. You must develop both a broad international perspective, trying to avoid the narrowness of regional or even national viewpoints, and a specific competence in the culture and language of other nations. Formal and informal education provide the means of becoming a global citizen. If you don't have a second language, acquire one. If you have one, acquire more. Take advantage of being a college student to learn languages. Which ones you choose depends on your interests and how you see your business career developing. European languages are popular choices because of the close historical ties between the United States and Europe. Spanish is a good possibility not only for its international use but because it is really the second language of the United States. Doing business in Florida, Texas, and California may require knowledge of Spanish. Oriental languages are harder for Westerners to acquire but are highly useful as trade with Japan has been extremely strong and economic relations with China are developing rapidly. A petroleum engineer will certainly find that a knowledge of Middle Eastern languages strengthens one's career prospects.

Americans like to take comfort in the fact that English (really, American English) is the international language of business. True, it is. But that fact in no way reduces the desirability of acquiring—and using—another language. The specific choice of a language (or languages) is probably less important than it may seem to you now. You can't predict where your career will take you, and you will always have the opportunity later to learn a language that is of immediate use if you are assigned to a country where English is not spoken. There are two advantages in learning a language now, in college, regardless of what that language is. First, developing language skills will make it easier for you to acquire specific languages later. You become a language learner, and that will help later when you find you need to develop competence in a particular language for business use. Second, learning a language—any language—exposes you to another culture, and learning about other cultures is in some ways even more important than learning the language.

Tables 28–1 through 28–6 present some basic business and conversational phrases in six languages. Many guidebooks are available that provide similar "cookbook" lists. Such tables and guides are useful, although they are not a real substitute for acquiring a language.

Formal education in another culture need not even be based on language study. Take advantage of the opportunity to study the history, literature, and art of other nations while you are in college. Look for courses in the humanities and the social sciences that focus on other cultures that interest you or that might be directly relevant to a career

TABLE 28–1. Business Expressions/ *Japanese Common Expressions*

Good morning	Ohayo gozaimasu
Good evening	Konban wa
Good night	Oyasuminasai
How are you?	Ogenki desuka
I'm pleased to meet you.	Hajimemashite
Do you speak English?	Eigo hanasemasuka
I don't speak Japanese.	Watakushi wa nihongo o hanashimasen
Can you help me?	Onegaishimasu
What's your name?	Onamae wa nan desuka
My name is _____.	Watakushi no namae wa _____ desu
Thank you.	Arigatō gozaimasu (dōmo)
You're welcome.	Dōitashimashite
Yes/no	Hai/iie
Goodbye	Sayonara
Please	Dōzo
Airport	Kūkōjyo
Business Terms	
Business	1) Bijinesu 2) Shigoto (work, job, business) 3) Jigyo
Money	1) Okane 2) Kinsen (monetary) 3) Shōbai (buying/selling)
Bank	Ginko
Credit card	Kurejitto kado
Letter	Tegami (regular letter) *or* Shojyō (written document, business letter)
Memo	Memo
Computer	Konpyuta; Pasokon (personal computer)
Telephone	Denwa
Telex	Terekkusu

goal. Informal education—that is, education beyond the classroom—can also help. If your college offers study trips or a semester-abroad program, try to enroll. Spend a summer hiking in South America. If you have the choice, go skiing in Kitzbühel rather than Aspen. And cultivate friends from abroad. Almost every college in the United States enrolls students from other countries. Look on them as resources. Strike up friendships, get invited to dinner, and take an international student

TABLE 28–2. Business Expressions/ *Chinese Common Expressions*

Good morning	zǎo āng
Good evening	wǔ āng
Good night	wǎn āng
How are you?	nǐ hǎo ma
I'm pleased to meet you.	wǒ hěn rǒng shìng něng rèn shè
Do you speak English?	nǐ huì shuō yīng wén mā
I don't speak Chinese.	wǒ bù huì shuō ẑhōng wén
Can you help me?	Chǐng nǐ bāng ge mǔang; Lǎo jà
What's your name?	Chǐng wèn guì shìng
My name is _____.	wǒ shìng _____.
Thank you.	shìeh shìeh
You're welcome.	bú shìeh
Yes/no	Shè, duày ; bǔ shè, bǔ dua
Good-bye	ẑàijàin
Please	Chǐng
Airport	fēi jì tsǎng
Business Terms	
Business	shāng yèi
Money	jīn chían
Bank	yín háng
Credit card	shìng yùng kǎ
Letter	shìng
Memo	gōng hán
Computer	dìan nǎu
Telephone	dìan huà
Telex	dìan pào

to a baseball game so you can find out how sports are played elsewhere.

Even informal efforts to become familiar with other cultures can have pragmatic value in developing a résumé that will make you marketable, and certainly listing on your résumé languages that you can speak and courses in international relations that you have taken will strengthen your claim to a job with international dimensions. Employers increasingly look for language competence and broad cultural awareness as they select potential new managers to strengthen their own position in the global economy.

TABLE 28–3. Business Expressions/ *Spanish Common Expressions*

Good morning	buenos dîas
Good evening	buenas tardes
Good night	buenas noches
How are you?	¿Cómo está usted?
I'm pleased to meet you.	mucho gusto.
Do you speak English?	¿Habla el inglés?
I don't speak Spanish.	No hablo el español.
Can you help me?	¿Puede ayudarme?
What's your name?	¿Cómo se llama (usted)?
My name is _____.	Me llamo _____.
Thank you.	Gracias
You're welcome.	De nada
Yes/no	sí/no
Good-bye	adiós
Please	por favor
Airport	el aeropuerto

Business Terms	
Business	el negocio
Money	el dinero
Bank	el banco
Credit card	la tarjeta de crédito
Letter	la carta
Memo	la nota/(el) memorando
Computer	la computadora
Telephone	el teléfono
Telex	el telex

Use Technology

Technology is in large part responsible for the internationalizing of business—air travel and telephone links and satellites have all contributed to "shrinking" the world. It's therefore reasonable that you should learn to exploit technological innovations to improve your ability to communicate internationally. Telephones, visual teleconferencing via satellites, and computer networks that afford instant contact with distant cities are obvious technological tools for the business

TABLE 28–4. Business Expressions/ *German Common Expressions*

	German equivalent
Good morning	Guten Morgen
Good evening	Guten Abend
Good night	Gute Nacht
How are you?	Wie geht es Ihnen?
I'm pleased to meet you.	Es freut mich, Sie kennen zu lernen.
Do you speak English?	Sprechen Sie Englisch?
I don't speak German.	Ich spreche kein Deutsch.
Can you help me?	Kŏnnen Sie mir helfen?
What's your name?	Wie war lhr Name?
My name is ———.	Ich heiße ———.
Thank you.	Danke
You're welcome.	Bitte sehr
Yes/no	ja/nein
Good-bye	Auf Wiedersehen
Please.	Bitte
Airport	der Flughafen
Business Terms	
Business	die Wirtschaft (economy)
Money	das Geld
Bank	die Bank
Credit card	die Kreditkarte
Letter	der Brief
Memo	das Memo; die Notiz; die Mitteilung
Computer	der Computer
Telephone	das Telefon, der Fernsprecher
Telex	das Telex

communicator. Earlier in this chapter we discussed some of the problems that can occur when one uses such tools, but the problems are minor compared to the advantages they offer.

Whereas it may take a week for your report on paper to reach Chile, you can have instant contact by telephone or can put the content of the report on the computer network so that your boss there can read it immediately after you finish it in Miami. If three accountants in New York need to discuss a problem in the financial data that have

TABLE 28–5. Business Expressions/ *Arabic Common Expressions*. A key to the symbols: caps = velarized; 9 = glottal fricative; 8 = uvular fricative; ( ) = synonym; *d* = *th* in *the;* : = long vowel; ? = glottal stop.

Good morning	SaBa:H ilxeyr
Good evening	masa:? ilxeyr
Good night	tiSBaH 9ala xeyr
How are you?	keyf Ha:lak
I'm pleased to meet you.	?ahlan wa sahlan
Do you speak English?	biti9raf inglizi
I don't speak Arabic.	maba9rafš 9arabi
Can you help me?	mumkin tisa:9idni
What's your name?	?ismak ?eh
My name is _____.	?ismi _____.
Thank you.	?aškurak
You're welcome.	9afwan
Yes/no	la/na9am
Good-bye	ma9assla:ma
Please	min faDlak
Airport	maTa:r

Business Terms

Business	maHal (mašru:9) tuja:ri
Money	fulu:s (nuqu:d)
Bank	bank
Credit card	ka:rt bila:stik
Letter	xiTa:b (jawa:b) (maktu:b)
Memo	muḍakkara
Computer	kumbu:tar (?a:la Ha:sba)
Telephone	tilifo:n
Telex	talli8ra:f

come in from Bombay, it's not difficult to arrange a conference call or even a teleconference with the appropriate managers in India, so that all questions can be answered at once without the delays inherent in sending letters back and forth.

Of course, technological tools can't substitute in every case for direct contact or for formal documents written on paper and bound in covers. The use of these tools is seldom cheap, and there are obvious barriers to communication built into each, as we have seen. But the wise use of various forms of technology can help you overcome the

TABLE 28–6. Business Expressions/ *French Common Expressions*

Good morning	Bonjour.
Good evening	Bon soir.
Good night	(You wouldn't say this . . . just "bon soir")
How are you?	Comment allez-vous?
I'm pleased to meet you.	Enchanté(e)—extra "e" for feminine
Do you speak English?	Parlez-vous anglais?
I don't speak French.	Je ne parle pas français.
Can you help me?	Pouvez-vous m'aider?
What's your name?	Comment vous appellez-vous?
My name is _____.	Je m'appelle _____.
Thank you.	Merci *or* Merci beaucoup = (thank you very much)
You're welcome.	A votre service
Yes/no	oui/non
Goodbye	Au revoir
Please	S'il vous plaît
Airport	L'aéroport
Business Terms	
Business	Des affaires *or* La commerce
Money	L'argent
Bank	La banque
Credit card	La carte de crédit
Letter	La lettre
Memo	Le memo
Computer	L'ordinateur
Telephone	Le téléphone
Telex	Le télex

problems that occur when you must communicate business information over great distances and from one culture to another. New tools are being developed all the time, and the international businessperson certainly should make a point of learning about them and evaluating their potential contributions to global communication.

Be a Good Communicator

This sounds like begging the question, but the fact is that being a good international communicator really starts with being a good communicator—period. The greater the obstacles to communication, the more you have to work at overcoming them. Communicating in the global economy merely highlights the need for good communication principles and habits.

Getting a firm grasp on your communication goal is always important. It's especially so when you have to communicate that goal to someone who speaks a different language, thinks from a different cultural perspective, or lives halfway around the world.

Encoding the message appropriately is even more critical when the intended receiver will have to translate it into his or her native language. Precision in word choice, clarity of sentence structure, control of paragraph development, and effectiveness of overall organization acquire special significance in international communication. When sender and receiver don't share a language or culture, the observation that if you can be misunderstood you will be achieves a higher level of significance. Communicating internationally demands clear and concise prose, informative and well-integrated visuals, and a controlled and well-paced structure. All communication does, but communicating globally puts a premium on the basic skills.

Every chapter in this book is a chapter on international business communication. To put it simply, to communicate internationally means, first and foremost, to communicate well.

Exercises

1. Here are some common business terms in English. Find the equivalent word or words for each in Japanese, Spanish, German, and French. Start with dictionaries, but don't neglect fellow students from other countries where these languages are spoken:

> depreciation
> marketing
> balance sheet
> inventory
> spreadsheet
> chief executive officer
> point of sale
> quality circle
> line of credit

2. Interview an international student at your college about the differences that he or she perceives in business practices in the United States and his or her country. Ask especially about practices that relate to communication. Based on this interview, suggest ways that an American planning to do business in that country can prepare for the experience.

3. Obtain the instructions or directions that accompany a product made in a non-English-speaking country. Watches, toys, and small electronic devices are good examples. Do the instructions work? That is, can you use the product based only on reading the instructions? Why or why not? Does it appear that the instructions were written in another language and then translated into English? If so, edit them so that the English sounds more natural.

4. Assume that you are a marketing manager for a new brand of "all-natural" toothpaste that is to be sold in France. What do you need to know about the French before you can begin to develop a promotional campaign for the product? How will you acquire this information? Write a memo outlining the campaign that you think will be successful, especially noting *cultural* differences between the United States and France that your campaign is taking into account.

5. You have been assigned to prepare a training manual for clerical workers in your company's newly opened office in Aberdeen, Scotland. You are to base the manual on an existing one developed for the Los Angeles headquarters clerical staff. As the language is the same, you don't have to worry about a translation. Based on cultural differences, what changes, if any, do you anticipate you might have to make in the manual for the Scottish employees?

6. Mary Hernandez has been asked to handle the logistics for a meeting of the international sales force of the Larson Paper Company to be held in Aspen, Colorado. Sales representatives from Brazil, Hong Kong, Egypt, and the Netherlands will attend. She has been told that all of the representatives have been in the United States before, but that most will be bringing spouses and family members who have not been here. To orient the families to American culture and to the company, she wants to have a briefing session. What should she tell them about the United States and about corporate life here in a forty-five-minute meeting? Prepare an outline of her presentation, showing the main topics she should address.

Handbook

Business Communication emphasizes how to set up your writing so that your prose is *right:* efficiently composed and effectively read. Sometimes in the process, however, errors do crop up. Chapter 9 discusses general strategies for revising troublesome drafts. This brief handbook notes some quick guidelines for detecting errors—"error messages" like those you receive on a terminal when the computer can't read your instructions—and correcting them. Be aware of signs that indicate a reader may have trouble deciphering your message. (The page numbers in parentheses indicate sections of the text that cover the item in more detail.)

In addition, the handbook provides generally accepted conventions of punctuation, abbreviation, capitalization, and number use. Such conventions vary from organization to organization; if the group you are part of adheres to different usage, observe its guidelines. Finally, the handbook notes some frequently misused words and phrases and the correct usage.

Error Messages

1. Faulty Agreement

A sentence's subject must agree in number with its verb. A pronoun must agree with its antecedent (the noun it substitutes for). Check in revision to make sure that intervening words have not caused you to pull the sentence elements out of agreement. Some rules often violated:

* Connective phrases like "together with," "as well as," and "in addition to" do not change the number of the subject:

   A list of courses, along with the names of all instructors and the locations of all classes, *is* attached. [The subject is *list,* a singular.]

* A collective noun takes a singular verb when the group is thought of as a unit and a plural verb to emphasize the individuals in the group:

   The number of case studies assigned is large.
   A number of case studies were analyzed in class.

* When *or* or *nor* connects two or more subjects, the verb agrees with the noun closest to it:

   Neither the accounting firm nor the internal auditors were responsible.
   Neither the internal auditors nor the accounting firm was responsible.

● Singular verbs are required by such singular pronouns as *another, anybody, anyone, anything, each, either, everyone, everybody, everything, neither, nobody, nothing, one, somebody, someone,* and *something:*

Each of the teams has its own style of play.

● A pronoun must have a clear antecedent with which it agrees in number:

Error: A manager should not interview a subordinate in *his* or *her* office. [*Whose* office?]
One correction: The manager's own office is not the right place in which to interview a subordinate.

2. Fragments

A fragment is a group of words that looks like a sentence, with a capital letter at the beginning and a period at the end, but that lacks an essential sentence element—a subject or a finite form of a verb. Some fragments are acceptable for emphasis:

You'd think that after fifty hours at the terminal, you'd have a working program. *Wrong again.*

Most of the time, fragments are errors that mislead the reader and indicate a careless author. Avoid them in formal writing:

Error: The reason being that industrial growth did not outpace the inflation rate. [This statement lacks a finite verb, that is, one that shows person and tense.]
One correction: The reason is that industrial growth did not outpace the inflation rate.

Error: A position that has forced him to be insensitive, cold, and calculating to his staff. [This statement also lacks a finite verb.]
One correction: The position has forced him to be insensitive, cold, and calculating to his staff.

Error: A business system that enables us to manage discrete product flows from the supplier to the store shelf in a way that will bound off people and systems and manage by standards so that a means is in place to concentrate and focus resources and assets in arenas where significant rates of change are required in 1989 and beyond to establish an enduring competitive position. [This statement, from a management consultant, lacks a verb, and lacks good sense and meaning, too.]

3. Lack of Parallelism (p. 169)

Items in a series must be equal in logic and in expression. The *logic* of the series is governed by an *enumerator term,* either expressed or understood. The *expression* of the series is governed by the first item, whose form must be followed in all other items:

Error in logic: Medical services that are not available from the college clinic include X rays, cuts and lacerations requiring sutures, broken bones, and any ailment requiring hospitalization and surgery. [The announced enumerator term here is *medical services.* X rays fit, but then the list shifts to *injuries* rather than services—without telling the reader.]

Error in logic: There is to be no smoking, eating, or beverages in the conference room. [The implied enumerator here is "unacceptable behavior." Logically, the third item should be *drinking*, but the writer felt that this word suggested a ban only on alcoholic beverages; soda drinkers might not think it applied to them.]
One correction: Do not smoke, eat, or drink any beverages in the conference room.

Error in logic—faulty comparison: This new power line should improve overall efficiency of the system and decrease fuel costs because the Whitemarsh district will now be supplied with nuclear power from the Peach Bottom nuclear power plant that is connected to Plymouth Meeting instead of fuel oil. [The sentence intends to compare two sources of power for the Whitemarsh district: nuclear power and fuel oil. But the balance is lost with the phrase "instead of fuel oil."]
One correction: This new power line will allow the Whitemarsh district to operate with cheap nuclear power from the Peach Bottom plant rather than with more costly fuel oil; it will thus improve the overall efficiency of the system and decrease cost.

Error in expression: He was first in peace, first in war, and he held first place in the hearts of his countrymen, too.
Corrected: He was first in peace, first in war, and first in the hearts of his countrymen.

Error in expression: Argentina (Ar) and West Germany (WG) have met nine times, including three times in World Cup (WC) competition. The results:

- First round, World Cup, Malmö Sweden: West Germany 3, Ar 1, June 8, 1958.
- July 16, 1966—WG 0, Ar 0, WC first round, Birmingham, England.
- Feb. 14, 1973—Munich, WG 2–Ar 3.
- At Buenos Aires, June 5, 1977, WG 3, Ar 1
- WG 2, AR 1 at Berlin on Sept 12, 1979.
- Ar 2, WG 1, at Montevideo on Jan 1, 1981.
- Argentina and WG in a 1–1 draw at Buenos Aires, March 24, 1982
- Ar 3 and WG 1 at Düsseldorf on 9/12/1984.

● WG 2 and Ar 3 in the final of the World Cup, Mexico City, June 29, 1986

Inconsistencies in abbreviations, punctuation, number use, dates, place names, and the order of elements are corrected in the following table, which is much easier to read and allows a better comparison of the results:

Argentina and West Germany have met nine times, including three times in World Cup competition. The results (* designates winner):

Date	Place	Argentina	W. Germany	World Cup
June 8, 1958	Malmö, Sweden	1	*3	First round
July 16, 1966	Birmingham, U.K.	0	0	First round
Feb. 14, 1973	Munich	*3	2	
June 5, 1977	Buenos Aires	1	*3	
Sept. 12, 1979	Berlin	1	*2	
Jan. 1, 1981	Montevideo	*2	1	
March 24, 1982	Buenos Aires	1	1	
Sept. 12, 1984	Düsseldorf	*3	1	
June 29, 1986	Mexico City	*3	2	Final

4. Misplaced Modifiers (pp. 168–69)

Modifiers that limit the meaning of another word should be located in the sentence close to that word. Misplacement may well distort the meaning of the sentence:

Error: Smith questioned just how much security is required to prevent terrorism at the outset of this meeting. [Meeting participants discussed terrorism; they didn't expect an attack there.]
One correction: At the outset of the meeting, Smith questioned just how much security is required to prevent terrorism.

Error: Many arrests were possible because a suspect was observed stealing through a lookout booth. [Security agents *observed* through a lookout booth; the sentence seems to indicate that the suspect stole something by putting a hand through the booth.]
One correction: Many arrests were possible because agents used a lookout booth to observe suspects in the act of stealing.

Watch particularly how words like *only* change the meaning of a sentence as they move about. Each of the following sentences has a different meaning:

The board has established guidelines regulating *only* the age of the swimmers competing in the league.
Only the board has established guidelines regulating the age of the swimmers competing in the league.
The board has established guidelines regulating the age of *only* the swimmers competing in the league.
The board has established guidelines regulating the age of the swimmers competing *only* in the league.

Some humor—at the author's expense—may result from misplacement:

My client has discussed your proposal to fill the drainage ditch with his partners. [Poor partners!]

5. Dangling Modifiers

A dangling modifier is usually a verbal, often at the beginning or the end of a sentence, that denotes an action of which the sentence's subject is not capable. Like a misplaced modifier, a dangler can be the source of unintentional humor:

I saw the owl *driving down the road.* [Presumably the owl wasn't driving.]

The mouse was caught *using the trap.* [To catch the homeowner?]

After trudging through alder thickets, muskeg, and rain-swollen marshes to reach the railroad, the big diesel came into sight almost immediately. [Comments one reader, "Footsore, but glad to see rails again."]

When making a sundae, the chopped toppings are sprinkled over the ice cream. [The *toppings* don't make the sundae, except in the sense of making it delicious.]

Here are some other danglers and corrections:

Error: Made of 100 percent cotton, styled in two of cotton's favorite fabrics, the special stone-washing process has left these shirts feeling wonderfully soft. [The subject of this sentence is *process.* The modifying phrases beginning with *made* and *styled* express actions that a "process" can't achieve. The modifiers dangle. They should be attached to *shirts.*]
Corrected: Made of 100% cotton, styled in two of cotton's favorite fabrics, *these shirts* have further been made wonderfully soft by the stone-washing process.

Error: Driving down the streets of the suburbs, nothing looks out of place.
One correction: A drive down the streets of the suburbs reveals nothing out of place.

Another correction: As I drive down the streets of the suburbs, I see nothing out of place.

Error: After placing the order, the food was promptly delivered.
Corrected: I received my food soon after I placed the order.

Error: In order to organize the cash flow problem, new procedures were needed to keep track of spending.
Corrected: To organize the cash flow, we needed new procedures to keep track of spending.

6. Shifts in Point of View (pp. 167–68)

Point of view is the author's way of looking at a subject in a sentence, a paragraph, and a whole document. In the whole document, consistency in point of view requires careful control of the logic of the presentation. At the sentence and paragraph level, consistency requires the careful control of pronouns, voice (active and passive), and tense.

Shift in number: An accountant plays many roles. They quantify the value systems of the company. They keep records of expenditures. An accountant also makes sure expenditures and receipts are recorded according to generally accepted principles. [This paragraph shifts from *an accountant* to *they* and back to *an* again. The subjects should be consistently either singular or plural.]

Shift in person: Warning! Don't park in unmarked spaces. Violators will be tagged and towed at *your* expense. [This warning, on a parking receipt, shifts from *you* to *violators* and then back to *you*—but with the second *you* covering *all violators*, clearly not what's meant.]

Shift in person: Managers should attend the meetings if you want to.
Corrected: Managers should attend the meetings if *they* want to.

Shift in tense: No sooner had the meeting ended than the president *arrives.* [The sentence sets up actions in the past and should continue in that tense.]
Corrected: No sooner had the meeting ended than the president *arrived.*

Shift in tense: First, we sent the form to the computing office. They look it over and approve it. Then, with their approval, we sent it on to purchasing, which sends it out for competitive bidding. [These sentences mix the past tense (what we *did*) with the present (what these offices *do*). Each approach is fine separately, but the author should choose either the *present* tense consistently, to show the general routing of the form, or the *past* tense consistently, to show what happened with this one form submitted in the past.]

Shift in voice: The president rushed us into writing the report, and we were asked by him to present it Wednesday. [The sentence shifts from the active, "rushed," to the passive, "were asked."]

Corrected: The president rushed us into writing the report and asked us to present it Wednesday.

Shift in voice: "Category killer" stores are described in a *Journal* article, and the article discussed Ikea as one such store.
Corrected: A *Journal* article describes "category killer" stores and discussed Ikea as one such store.

7. Shifty or Missing Subjects

When an author changes subjects in midsentence without telling the reader about the substitution, confusion often results.

Shift in subject: Pizza Headquarters promises to deliver its pizzas within thirty minutes after placing an order; otherwise, it will give the purchaser a discount. [The subject is *Pizza Headquarters*, but the *purchaser* places the order.]

Omission of subject in second clause: On January 6, the ABC Board of Directors declared the regular quarterly dividend of 12 cents per common share payable on January 29 to shareholders of record January 18 and is enclosed. [Problem: *What* is enclosed?]

8. Mixed Metaphors

Figurative language is useful, particularly in documents for popular audiences, but the images must be consistent. Be careful to analyze the roots of clichés:

Mixed metaphor: Planning has blossomed and percolated during the past decade and now occupies an important niche in the public eye. [This sentence derails on inconsistent images: *blossom, percolate, niche,* and *eye.*]
Mixed metaphor: The investor fell victim to a window of opportunity.

Punctuation

Punctuation helps an author tell a reader how to read the discussion: What belongs with what and what needs to be emphasized or subordinated. It paces the reading. Like words themselves, punctuation is an element of an author's style. Here are some generally accepted rules for punctuating. But within guidelines for *correctness,* an author makes personal choices to achieve clarity for the reader.

The Comma

Commas are relatively soft marks of punctuation used under certain circumstances to separate one part of a sentence from another or to enclose a sentence element. In current practice, good authors tend to use commas sparingly.

Use a single comma:

1. To separate two independent clauses in a compound sentence when the second clause begins with a coordinating conjunction *(and, but, or, for, nor, yet):*

> Magee set a still-untouched record of 2,242 career points, and he was a Boston Celtic draft choice in 1963.

Omit the comma if the two clauses are short:

> He is handsome and he is wise.

2. To set off introductory phrases and clauses:

> After reading the proposal, the sponsor fainted.

3. To separate items in a series of more than two:

> The writers' poll routinely came up with these college soccer teams as the best in the country: Hartwick, UCLA, American University, University of Virginia, Indiana, and Clemson. [Note: Practice varies, but in general in business writing, a comma is used before the final *and.*]

4. To separate two or more adjectives, each of which modifies a noun independently:

> durable, cool, breatheable wear [Test: Use a comma if you could logically place an *and* between the adjectives.]

5. To separate the year from the month and day, and the state from the city:

> September 17, 1985 [But "17 September 1985" and "September 1985."]

> Acton, Maine

6. To indicate the omission of a word or phrase:

> The accounting department brought coleslaw; logistics, ham salad.

Use a pair of commas:

1. To enclose interrupters and parenthetical expressions:

> I will, of course, be happy to come to your office for an interview at your convenience.

> He always gives 100 percent, that is, when his own best interests demand it.

2. To enclose nonrestrictive modifiers or appositives. A modifier or appositive is *restrictive* when it is essential to the meaning of the sentence. The modifying elements in italics in these sentences are restrictive and are thus not set off:

> The woman *who is walking toward us* is my boss.

> The statistical package *that runs on our mainframe system* still has some bugs in it.

If you are merely adding parenthetical information, however, you do set the modifier off with commas. The modifiers in italics in these sentences are *nonrestrictive:*

> My boss, *who is walking toward us,* is fairly capable.

> The SASS statistical package, *which runs on our mainframe system,* still has some bugs in it.

Do not use a comma:

1. To separate the subject of the sentence from the verb:

> *Error:* The development of an organizational focus on areas of strategic business importance, marks a turning point in a corporation's profile.

2. To separate a compound verb:

> *Error:* Ben and Jerry's "Butter pecan brickle fudge ripple" ice cream whets the appetite, and enchants the mind.

The Semicolon

The semicolon indicates a stronger separation among sentence elements than the comma. Use a semicolon:

1. To separate two closely related independent clauses not joined by a coordinating conjunction:

> The first half was played in constant rain; the second half was played in constant sunshine.

> In the beginning of the summer, she spent her time sailing and swimming; by summer's end, she was devoted to the sailboard, which she rode from dawn to dusk, tacking back and forth across the pond, carving a sleek and silent path across the water.

A *comma fault* or *comma splice* (the terms denote the same error) results if a comma is used between two independent clauses unconnected by a conjunction:

> *Comma fault:* The athletic director thought he was a good writer, he always elected himself spokesperson for the faculty.

2. To separate independent clauses joined by such conjunctive adverbs as *however, nonetheless,* and *consequently* and phrases like "on the other hand":

> She studied hard every day and did all the homework; nonetheless, she failed the final exam and thus failed the course.

3. To separate items in a list when the items themselves are also punctuated:

> He arrived at the campsite with an axe (purchased at EMS for $25); an outfit including shorts, hiking boots, shirt, and hat, all of the latest fashion and obviously recently purchased at L. L. Bean; and a fear of the wilderness that no amount of reading and conversation could abate.

The Colon

The colon builds anticipation while it marks (more strongly than a comma or a semicolon) a division in sentence elements. Use a colon:

1. To precede examples, equations, explanations, illustrations, lists, quotations, and the like after an expressed enumerator term:

> The planning phase is divided into three steps:
> 1. Worry.
> 2. Brainstorm options.
> 3. Prioritize options.

> She scheduled division meetings for four dates: October 10, October 16, November 3, and November 18.

Do not separate a verb and its objects with a colon.

> *Error:* The three most common errors are: faulty diction, faulty spelling, and faulty punctuation. [To correct, simply delete the colon.]

2. To separate two clauses when the second expands on or amplifies the first:

> All this concern for readability can be summed up in one statement: The document works.

[Note: The first letter of the word following the colon is usually capitalized only if the second clause is a complete sentence, but usage varies. Consult the style guide of the organization you work for. Be consistent in any one document.]

3. To mark the end of the greeting in a formal letter:

> Dear Professor Frawley:

The colon is a formal mark; an informal greeting usually ends in a comma:

Dear Bill,

[*Never* use a semicolon after a letter greeting.]

The Dash

The dash is a fairly informal mark that sometimes replaces a semicolon, a colon, or parentheses. A dash can be brisk and effective, just what you need, but use it with caution:

There is no more valuable lesson for the student than observing the research process firsthand and—even more important—participating in it.

Parentheses

Always used as a pair, parentheses subordinate material within a sentence and serve some conventional functions in documentation. Note that the period is placed outside the final parenthesis if the parenthetical expression is part of another sentence; inside, if the parenthetical expression is a sentence in itself. Here are some examples of the use of parentheses:

The Early Avalanche Warning Program (EAWP) . . .
The three criteria are (1) . . . , (2) . . . , (3) . . .
Our profit picture remains bright (Figure 1). [But "Figure 1 shows a bright profit picture."]
Our profit picture remains bright. (Figure 1 shows a chart of profitability over the last five years.)

The Acton (Maine) Landfill permit . . .
Manual of Professional Practice (New York: Macmillan, 1985).

Never place a comma immediately before either the opening or closing parenthesis. The parentheses alone properly enclose the sentence element:

Error: Such an approach, (each person trying to usurp control of the meeting) was typically American, or so they thought.

Brackets

Brackets surround interpolations or comments that an author inserts within quoted material or parenthetical statements inserted within text already in parentheses. Some documentation systems also require the use of brackets:

(See the complete explanation of fund accounting [Reference 5] for a more detailed discussion.)

"With his dynamic and graceful play, Diego [Maradona] carried the day for Argentina."

The Period

A period marks the end of a sentence. Other uses are less fixed, but in general:

1. Use a period with nontechnical abbreviations:

   Mr., Fig., Dr., Vol.

2. Use a period when an abbreviation also spells a word:

   in., no., sect.

The Exclamation Point

The exclamation point puts an emotional finish to a sentence. It tells the reader that the author is (or wants to appear to be) excited or surprised, and that the reader should respond similarly. Exclamation points are common in sales messages:

   You may already have won!
   You'll never see an offer like this again!
   Productivity is up to a record level in the third quarter!

The exclamation point, however, is generally considered too colloquial and too pushy for reports and other, more routine and sober, business documents.

Quotation Marks

Quotation marks enclose directly quoted material:

   "The players were tight," noted Loren Kline, the soccer coach. "They kept trying for the perfect play rather than relaxing and making the easy play."

By American convention, periods and commas belong *inside* the final quotation mark, even though they are not part of the original material; question marks, exclamation marks, semicolons, and colons belong *outside* quotation marks, unless they are part of the quoted material:

   He had what his supervisor termed "an intuitive grasp of finance"; he could sniff out phony balance sheets without doing any arithmetic.

An exception to this usage occurs when quotation marks surround a command in computer documentation. In that case, *all* other punctuation occurs *outside* the quotation marks to avoid a misreading that the comma, for example, is part of the command. Quotation marks may also be used to enclose certain elements in a reference citation (see Chapter 5):

> D. P. Richardson, "Duel Career Marriages: An Exercise in the Fine Art of Fencing," *The Journal of Personality* 1 (1987), 64–82.

The Apostrophe

The apostrophe indicates possession. It can make a real difference in the meaning of a word or phrase. For example, this headline appeared in *The New York Times:*

> Queens Grandmother Wins Lottery

As it stands, the headline means that a grandmother in Queens, a borough of New York City, won. With an apostrophe, however *(Queen's),* the lottery would have gone to the mother of the queen. Make sure you use the apostrophe where necessary:

1. Use the apostrophe plus *s* to form the possessive of nouns, abbreviations, and acronyms:

> the college's campus; the book's cover; the company's image; RCA's approach; DCA's style

Usage varies with words ending in *s;* when in doubt, add another *s:*

> Professor Andrews's textbook

[Note: The possessive of *it* is *its,* with no apostrophe. *It's* is a contraction for *it is.*]

2. Use the apostrophe *after* the *s* of plural nouns:

> the nations' joint approach; the companies' joint action

3. To show joint possession, use an apostrophe and an *s* added to the last member of the group; indicate separate possession by an *s* added to each member:

> Frawley and Bowen's article was widely cited.
> Frawley's and Bowen's priorities differ markedly.

The apostrophe is not used to form normal plurals, nor with plurals of a date or an all-capital abbreviation:

> Books; companies; the 1980s; IRAs; 5s; As.

The Hyphen

Where such other marks of punctuation as commas, semicolons, and periods *separate* items, the hyphen *connects*. It connects two or more words that form a compound noun and two or more words that form a compound adjective before a noun.

1. Hyphenate compound nouns. Such forms are often transitional ones as two separate words grow together. No general rules apply; just be consistent in any one document and adhere to the conventions of your organization. Here are a few examples:

> know-how
> a merry-go-round of mergers
> an up-date
> a Mercedes-Benz

2. Hyphenate compound numbers from 21 through 99 when they are spelled out:

> fifty-five
> twenty-nine

3. Hyphenate compound adjectives that express a unified idea and precede the noun:

> a high-tech future
> full-page advertisements
> 135-year-old sewing-machine business
> seven-inch-thick file
> private-sector financing
> deficit-cutting move
> small-business owners
> Indiana-based program
> truth-in-lending laws

The hyphen is not used if the compound is easily read without it or is a proper noun:

> government-licensed [hyphen needed for clarity] venture capital
>   [no hyphen] companies
> New York-based broker [no hyphen between "New" and "York"]

The hyphen is also not used if the first word is an adverb ending in *ly* or a comparative form:

> a recently developed plan
> more convincing approach

4. Hyphenate words divided at the end of a line and carried to the next line. Divide only between syllables (check a dictionary for correct syllabication).

Underlining and Boldface

Underlining and boldface are both methods of highlighting certain words and phrases in a text. Computer text processing makes such usage easy. Traditionally, an underlined passage in manuscript is printed in italics in the published document, but that distinction is fading as computer text processing allows the writer to create *both* underlining and italics for final printing from a terminal. Consult standard sources like the second edition of the *MLA Handbook*, published by the Modern Language Association, or *A Manual of Style*, published by the University of Chicago Press, for advice about the use of underlining in footnotes and bibliographies. In addition, use underlining:

1. To set off a word being defined or being discussed as a word:

   In this report, we use the word organization to refer to a company of more than five hundred employees.

2. To designate words from a foreign language:

   His middle years were punctuated with a Weltschmertz that his den full of trophies could not alleviate.

3. To highlight important information:

   If he had not responded to the request that very minute, he would never have joined the firm.

Don't overdo underlining. An overly underlined text screams at the reader and may deafen her or him.

Use boldface:

1. To set off certain headings in a text, usually chapter titles and first-order heads (underlining may also be used for headings at other levels; see Chapter 6):

   CHAPTER ONE: DAWN

2. To highlight material in a text as an alternative to underlining. Again, be cautious, and don't overdo.

Abbreviation, Capitalization, and Number Use

Abbreviation

One quick sign of business writing, particularly the writing of bureaucracies, is an abundance of abbreviations. Such abbreviations may make a text unintelligible to outsiders. Use abbreviations, of course, but be consistent in their use. And if you have reason to think that *any* of the readers of your report may not understand a particular abbreviation, write out the word or phrase. Here are some general guidelines:

1. Use commonly accepted abbreviations for the names of groups or organizations. No periods are used, and the letters are typed with no spaces between them. In internal communication, the abbreviation alone is probably enough. For external communication, give the full title at the first mention:

> *For an insider:*
> MEMO
>
>> Re: PPD update
>
> *For an outsider:*
> The Packaged Products Division (PPD) rolled up a record year in 1989.

2. Use an abbreviation for a long word or phrase to be repeated frequently in a report as long as you explain the full phrase at the first mention:

> Our profitability picture was enhanced this year by our new Pride in Excellence (PIE) program and our highly visible PIE charts.

3. Use standard abbreviations after numbers denoting a definite quantity. In general, the abbreviation is used in the singular only, and without periods (exceptions: *figs., vols., nos.*):

> 256 k RAM; 2000 rpm; a 10-k race

4. Form the plural of an uppercase abbreviation by adding a lowercase *s* (no apostrophe):

> CRTs; FTEs

Capitalization

Be sparing, conventional, and consistent in your use of capital letters. Capitalize:

1. The first word of a sentence.

2. The first word of a direct quotation when the quoted material begins a sentence:

> The coach said, "Relax, boys. This is a piece of cake."

An indirect quotation is not capitalized:

> The coach told the team to relax because the game was to be a "piece of cake."

3. The first letter of certain words in report titles and section headings (be consistent).

4. Proper nouns, including titles, names of languages, companies, peoples, races, political parties, religions, historical periods, states, cities, countries, and geographic regions. Sometimes *the* is part of a company or university name and is also capitalized:

> The Ohio State University

5. Registered trademarks, whether used as nouns or adjectives:

> a Xerox® copier

6. Common nouns when used in certain specialized senses. For example, some companies refer to themselves throughout a text as *The Company*. In some reports, the terms *Figure* and *Table* are capitalized. Again, consult the style guide for your organization and be consistent.

Numbers

Much business information is expressed in numbers, often in tabular form. Here are some general guidelines for using numbers in the text itself. Again, styles of presentation differ markedly from company to company. Conform to whatever standards are set, and be consistent:

1. Don't start a sentence with a number; rephrase the sentence or write the number out.

2. Use arabic numerals to express all quantities (unless a company style guide advises differently):

> He bought 9 PCs for his division.

3. Write out approximations or indefinite measurements:

> About one hundred people attended the picnic.

4. Use arabic numbers for figures and tables:

> Figure 10; Table 4

5. Present all sums of money in arabic numbers. Repeat the abbreviation for the currency in a series. For figures over one million, indicate the multiplier in numerals and the zeros in a word (*thousand, million,* and so on):

> £250
> $40
> He collected the following amounts: $1200 (from Accounting); $1500 (from Logistics); and $4500 (from Maintenance).
> $60 million

6. Use numerals for the days but not the months in dates:

> May 10, 1985 [*Not* 5/10/85; the use of numerals is informal and potentially confusing in an international context, as European countries, for example, reverse the order of day and month: May 10, 1987 would be 10/5/87.]

Frequently Misused Words and Phrases

Words and phrases in the documents of organizational life must be *precise*. The misuse of words may confuse or mislead the reader. Here are some commonly misused terms; add to this list any that you know you abuse.

Adapt/Adopt/Adept
Adapt means to modify:

> Adapt these planning methods to fit your own composing style.

Adopt means to take over:

> We adopted the PERT planning technique in our department.

Adept, an adjective, means skillful:

> He is adept at planning large projects.

Advice/Advise
Advice, a noun, means an opinion given on how to handle some situation:

> She profited from her broker's advice.

Advise, a verb, means to give such an opinion, to suggest something:

> Her broker advises her on market trends every week.

Affect/Effect
Affect is most frequently used as a verb meaning to influence:

> The inflation rate affects unemployment.

Effect is most frequently used as a noun meaning a result or a consequence:

> The effect of spiraling inflation was an increase in unemployment.

Affect can also be used as a noun meaning the feeling accompanying an idea; *effect* can be used as a verb meaning to bring about or cause to occur:

> She effected a compromise between union and management on the right-to-work issue.

Among/Between

Among is used for more than two items; *between* is used only for two.

Assure/Ensure/Insure

All of these words mean *to make certain*, but with different connotations. *Assure* is used in the sense of making a person sure of something:

> Let me *assure* you that I'll look over your letter today.

Ensure and *insure* suggest a guarantee against harm or failure:

> An adequate budget is needed to *ensure* the success of the project.

Insure is used in the technical sense of guaranteeing property or life:

> Have you *insured* your bike against loss or theft?

Case

This term is frequently overused in business documents. Save it for specific reference to, for example, a case study or a legal or medical case. The expression in brackets can often be substituted for the phrase on the left; sentences thus gain in brevity and precision:

> In case [if]
> In many cases [often]
> In this case [here]
> In all cases [all; always]

Continuous/Continual

Continuous means without interruption; *continual* means steady but with brief interruptions.

Criterion/Criteria

Criterion is singular, meaning a rule or test; *criteria* is plural, meaning a number of such rules.

Data

Data refers to observations and facts gathered in an investigation and usually used in a raw state, as opposed to *information*, which refers to interpreted data. The term *data* is technically plural (the singular, in

Latin, is *datum*), but it is now beginning to be thought of as a collective that takes a singular verb. Abide by the usage set by your organization.

Discreet/Discrete

People can be discreet, that is, careful about what they say or do; *things* and *information* can be divided into *discrete*—that is, separate—components:

> Managers must be discreet in their attentions to employees.
> We performed three discrete tasks.

Due to the Fact That

Avoid this phrase in formal reports because it is long and roundabout. Instead, substitute *because.*

Etc.

Avoid. Instead, begin a representative rather than inclusive list with a phrase like "such as" or "for example."

Fewer/Less

Fewer refers to numbers, *less* to degree:

> This yogurt has fewer calories than Brand Y.
> This yogurt is less fattening than Brand Y.

Imply/Infer

A writer *implies;* the reader *infers.* An *implication* is thus something given; an *inference* is something taken:

> By his snickers and giggles, he implied that this training program was not to be taken seriously.

> From the chatter and snickers of the participants, we drew the inference that they didn't take this training program seriously.

It's/Its

It's is a contraction meaning *it is; its* is the possessive form of *it:*

> It's clear that this accounting system has outlived its usefulness.

-ize Words

One sign of jargon is the creation of verbs from nouns with the ending *-ize: prioritize, accessorize,* and the like. Although such usage is often accepted in conversation, refrain from it in writing.

Oral/Verbal

Oral refers to something spoken; *verbal* refers to something expressed in words, either in writing or in speech. When you say, then, "She has a *verbal* agreement with the vendor," all you are saying is that she has exchanged words with the vendor, either in writing or in speaking. If you mean that she has only *spoken* with the vendor and has no contract in writing, then say, "She has an *oral* agreement with the vendor."

Percent/Percentage

Percent, meaning "hundredths of," should be used only after a figure; *percentage* is used to express a given part or amount of every hundred and is not used with a figure:

> His car has an efficiency rating of 80 percent.
> Only a small percentage of the fuel's energy is wasted.

Person/People; Personnel/Personal

Person refers to a single human being. *People* is a collective noun referring to a group of persons. *Personnel* are the persons working for a given organization at a given time. *Personal* means private:

> Three persons [not *people*] attended.
> For some reason, the American people still prefer to play football with their hands rather than their feet.
> He deals effectively with personnel issues [issues regarding employees].
> His personal life [his *private* life] is a mess.

Precede/Proceed/Procedure

Precede means to go before; *proceed* means to take action. The noun form of the verb *proceed* is *procedure*:

> Theoretical understanding often precedes practical application.
> He gave him the green light to proceed with the case study.

Respectfully/Respectively

Respectfully means with respect or deference, as in the complimentary close of a letter, "Respectfully yours." *Respectively* means in the order designated:

> Hughes Aircraft and Boeing Vertol contributed $5000 and $7000, respectively.

Respectively can become confusing, however, and forces the reader to return to the beginning of the sentence. Prefer this sentence form:

> Hughes Aircraft contributed $5000; Boeing Vertol, $7000.

Use/Using/Utilize

These words appear too frequently in business writing when other, more precise words should activate the sentence. Eliminate as many instances as you can in revision.

Your/You're

Your indicates possession; *you're* is a contraction for *you are:*

You're sure your father will give you the money?

Suggested Readings

The Context for Business Communication

Drucker, Peter. *Managing in Turbulent Times*. New York: Harper & Row, 1980.

McGregor, Douglas. *The Human Side of Enterprise*. New York: McGraw-Hill, 1960.

Mintzberg, Henry. *The Nature of Managerial Work*. New York: Harper & Row, 1973.

Naisbitt, John. *Megatrends: Ten New Directions Transforming Our Lives*. New York: Warner, 1982.

Ouchi, William. *Theory Z—How American Business Can Meet the Japanese Challenge*. Reading, Mass.: Addison-Wesley, 1981.

Peters, Thomas J., and Robert H. Waterman, Jr. *In Search of Excellence: Lessons from America's Best-Run Companies*. New York: Harper & Row, 1982.

Writing in the Organization: General Guides

Barzun, Jacques. *Simple and Direct: A Rhetoric for Writers*. New York: Harper & Row, 1976.

Colby, John, and Joseph A. Rice. "The Documentation Pyramid: A Better Paper Clip." *Technical Communication* (First Quarter 1978), 4–6.

Corbett, Edward P. J. *Classical Rhetoric for the Modern Student* (2nd ed.). New York: Oxford, 1971.

Fielden, John S. "What Do You Mean I Can't Write?" *Harvard Business Review* (May–June 1964), 144–154.

————. "What Do You Mean You Don't Like My Style?" *Harvard Business Review* (May–June 1982), 128–138.

Flower, Linda. *Problem-Solving Strategies for Writing* (2nd ed.). San Diego: Harcourt Brace Jovanovich, 1985.

Gibson, Walker. *Tough, Sweet and Stuffy: An Essay on Modern American Prose Styles*. Bloomington: Indiana University Press, 1966.

Halliday, M. A. K., and Ruqaiya Hasan. *Cohesion in English*. London: Longman, 1976.

Hayakawa, S. I. *Language in Thought and Action* (3rd ed.). New York: Harcourt Brace Jovanovich, 1972.

Klare, G. K. *The Measurement of Readability*. Ames: Iowa State University Press, 1963.

————. "A Second Look at Readability Formulas," *Journal of Reading Behavior* 8 (1976), 129–152.

Lanham, Richard. *Revising Business Prose*. New York: Scribner's, 1980.

Martin, Harold C., Richard M. Ohmann, and James H. Wheatley. *The Logic and Rhetoric of Exposition* (3rd ed.). New York: Holt, Rinehart & Winston, 1969.

Mathes, J. C., and Dwight Stevenson. *Designing Technical Reports*. Indianapolis: Bobbs, Merrill, 1976.

Menzel, Donald H., Howard Mumford Jones, and Lyle G. Boyd. *Writing a Technical Paper*. New York: McGraw-Hill, 1961.

Munter, Mary. *Guide to Managerial Communication*. Englewood Cliffs, N.J.: Prentice-Hall, 1982.

Olson, Gary A., James De George, and Richard Ray. *Style and Readability in Business Writing*. New York: Random House, 1985.

Pearsall, Thomas. *Audience Analysis for Technical Writing*. Beverly Hills, Calif.: Glencoe, 1969.

Robbins, Larry M. *The Business of Writing and Speaking*. New York: McGraw-Hill, 1985.

Strunk, William, and E. B. White. *The Elements of Style* (3rd ed.). New York: Macmillan, 1979.

Williams, Joseph M. *Style: Ten Lessons in Clarity and Grace*. Glenview, Ill.: Scott, Foresman, 1981.

Graphics

Huff, Darrell. *How to Lie with Statistics*. New York: Norton, 1954.

Matkowski, Betty S. *Steps to Effective Business Graphics*. San Diego: Hewlett-Packard, 1983.

MacGregor, A. J. *Graphics Simplified: How to Plan and Prepare Effective Charts,*

Graphs, Illustrations, and Other Visual Aids. Toronto: University of Toronto Press, 1979.

Computers and Writing

Bridwell, Lillian. "Computers and Composing: Implications for Instruction from Studying Experienced Writers." *Conference on College Composition and Communication,* 1983.

Cherry, Linda. "Computer Aids for Writers." *Proceedings of the ACM SIGPLAN* 16 (June 1981), 61–67.

————. "Writing Tools." *IEEE Transactions on Communication* Com-30:1 (January 1982), 100–105.

Coke, E. "Computer Aids for Writing Text," in D. Jonassen, ed., *The Technology of Text: Principles for Structuring, Designing, and Displaying Text.* Englewood Cliffs, N.J.: Educational Technology Publications, 1982.

Collier, R. "The Word Processor and Revision Strategies," *College Composition and Communication* 34 (May 1983), 149–155.

Daiute, Collette. "The Computer as Stylus and Audience," *College Composition and Communication* 34 (May 1983), 134–145.

Fluegelman, Andrew, and Jeremy Hewes. *Writing in the Computer Age: Word Processing Skills and Style for Every Writer.* New York: Anchor Press/Doubleday, 1983.

Glatzer, Hal. *Introduction to Word Processing.* Berkeley, Calif.: Sybex, 1981.

Howard, J. "Advances in Computer Technology: What Will the Impact Be for the Professional Communicator?" *Proceedings of the 29th International Technical Communications Conference.* Washington, D.C.: Society for Technical Communication, 1982, T-28-30.

Macdonald, N., L. Frase, P. Gingrich, and S. Keenan. "The Writer's Workbench: Computer Aids for Text Analysis," *IEEE Transactions on Communication* Com-30:1 (January 1982), 105–110.

McWilliams, P. *The Word Processing Book.* Los Angeles: Prelude, 1983.

Nancarrow, P., D. Ross, and L. Bridwell. *Word Processors and the Writing Process: An Annotated Bibliography.* Westport, Conn.: Greenwood, 1984.

Rothman, M. "The Writer's Craft Transformed: Wordprocessing," *Oncomputing* 2 (Winter 1980), 60–62.

Schwartz, Helen. "Monsters and Mentors: Computer Applications for Humanistic Education," *College English* 44 (February 1982), 483–490.

Zinsser, William. *Writing with a Word Processor.* New York: Harper & Row, 1983.

Speaking and Listening in Presentations and Meetings

Frank, Francine, and Frank Anshen. *Language and the Sexes.* Albany: State University of New York Press, 1983.

Glatthorn, Allan A., and Herbert R. Adams. *Listening Your Way to Management Success.* Glenview, Ill.: Scott, Foresman, 1983.

Lakoff, Robin. *Language and Women's Place.* New York: Harper & Row, 1975.

Pearce, W. Barnett, and Vernon E. Cronen. *Communication, Action, and Meaning.* New York: Praeger, 1980.

Robert, Henry M. *Robert's Rules of Order: Newly Revised.* Glenview, Ill.: Scott, Foresman, 1981.

Taliaferro, Brook. *Communication Skills for Managers.* American Management Associations Extension Institute, 1976. (Particularly Chapter 6, "Effective Use of Meetings and Presentations"; Chapter 7, "Overcoming Barriers to Communication"; Chapter 8, "Conducting an Interview"; and Chapter 9, "Organizing the Lines of Communication.")

Index

615